CERTIFIED PROFESSIONAL SECRETARY®
CERTIFIED ADMINISTRATIVE PROFESSIONAL®
EXAMINATION REVIEW SERIES

OFFICE SYSTEMS AND TECHNOLOGY

FIFTH EDITION

Diane Routhier Graf CPS, Ed.D.
Northern Illinois University

Betty L. Schroeder, Ph.D.
Northern Illinois University

Carol Mull
Series Editor

A joint publication of
International Association of Administrative Professionals®

International Association of
Administrative Professionals®

and

Upper Saddle River, New Jersey 07458

Library of Congress Cataloging-in-Publication Data

Routhier Graf, Diane, 1943-
   CPS exam review office systems & technology / Diane Routhier Graf, Betty L. Schroeder.—
5th ed.
         p. cm.
   Rev. ed. of: Office systems & administration. c2001, with Betty L. Schroeder as first
author. The edition was split into present volume and: CPS exam review office administration, c2005.
   Includes bibliographical references and index.
   ISBN 0-13-114549-5
   1. Office practice—Automation. 2. Office management. I. Schroeder, Betty L. Office
systems & administration. II. Schroeder, Betty L. CPS exam review office administration.
III. Schroeder, Betty L. IV. Title.
   HF5547.5.R69 2005
   651.3'076—dc22

                                                                    2004003988

Executive Editor: Elizabeth Sugg
Director of Production & Manufacturing: Bruce Johnson
Editorial Assistant: Cyrenne Bolt de Freitas
Marketing Manager: Leigh Ann Sims
Development Editor: Deborah Hoffman
Managing Editor—Production: Mary Carnis
Manufacturing Buyer: Ilene Sanford
Production Liaison: Denise Brown
Production Editor: Lori Dalberg, Carlisle Publishers Services
Composition: Carlisle Communications, Ltd.
Design Director: Cheryl Asherman
Senior Design Coordinator/Cover Design: Christopher Weigand
Cover Printer: Phoenix Color
Printer/Binder: Banta/Harrisonburg

Pearson Prentice Hall™ is a trademark of Pearson Education, Inc.
Pearson® is a registered trademark of Pearson plc
Prentice Hall® is a registered trademark of Pearson Education, Inc.

Pearson Education Ltd.
Pearson Education Singapore, Pte. Ltd.
Pearson Education Canada, Ltd.
Pearson Education—Japan
Pearson Education Australia PTY, Limited
Pearson Education North Asia Ltd.
Pearson Educacíon de Mexico, S.A. de C.V.
Pearson Education Malaysia, Pte. Ltd.

10 9 8 7 6 5 4 3 2 1
ISBN 0-13-114549-5

Contents

Preface

The Certified Professional Secretary (CPS) and Certified Administrative Professional (CAP) Examination Review Series, a four-volume set of review manuals that consists of one review manual for the first three parts of the CPS and CAP Examinations and one for Part 4 of the CAP Examination, is a joint publication of Prentice Hall and the International Association of Administrative Professionals (IAAP). The content of each review manual is based on the current Certification Review Guide published by the IAAP.

CPS and CAP Examinations

The rewards for achieving the Certified Professional Secretary (CPS) and Certified Administrative Professional (CAP) certifications are numerous, as attested to by the more than 65,000 CPS and CAP holders. These rewards include pride in accomplishment, increased self-esteem, greater respect from employers and peers, and confidence to assume greater responsibilities as well as possible college credit toward a degree, pay increases, bonuses, and opportunities for advancement. In today's workplace, having the CPS or CAP credentials can enhance assurance of employability and career advancement.

The CPS Examination is a one-day, three-part examination which includes

Part 1: Office Systems and Technology
Part 2: Office Administration
Part 3: Management

The CAP Examination is a 1½ day, four-part examination which includes

Parts 1, 2, and 3 above
Part 4: Advanced Organizational Management

To apply for the CPS or CAP Examination, the candidate must meet certain educational and professional experience requirements. Visit the IAAP Web site at *www.iaap-hq.org/* to obtain detailed information concerning testing centers, testing dates, application packets, and other information relative to applying for certification candidacy.

CPS and CAP Examination Review Series

The CPS and CAP Examination Review Series provides valuable assistance to the administrative professional preparing for the CPS and CAP Examinations, whether this series is used for group review sessions or self-study. The series provides an excellent learning tool that is focused on key topics necessary for passing the examinations.

The format used in Parts 1, 2, and 3 (Office Systems and Technology, 5E; Office Administration, 5E; and Management, 5E) of the CPS and CAP Examination Review Series is an outline format with multiple-choice review questions. The format used in Part 4, Advanced Organizational Management for the CAP Examination Review, is slightly different based on the scenario-oriented nature of Part 4 of the CAP Examination. The CPS and CAP Examination Review Series provides relevant information to help the candidate prepare for both the CPS and CAP Examinations. However, this does not imply that all information presented in this series will be included on the examinations. Further review is encouraged for the candidate by studying selected titles from the bibliography supplied by IAAP.

Each review manual in the CPS and CAP Examination Review Series includes:

- An overview introducing the reader to the chapter contents.
- Key terms that reinforce essential vocabulary.
- Text in outline form, with examples highlighted in italics, to enhance the explanation given in the text.
- Key examples emphasized.
- Difficult concepts illustrated.
- Check Point sections within each chapter that offer reviews of key concepts.
- For Your Review section at the end of each chapter with practice questions similar to those found on the CPS and CAP Examinations.
- A glossary at the end of each book that provides accessible reference.
- A comprehensive practice exam that simulates the testing environment and provides even more practice.
- Solutions to all check points and review questions, including references to the chapter outline where the answers are explained.
  For example:

      Answer   Reference

      1. *(B)*   *[A-2]* (Section of Chapter)

- An index with page references provided in the Office Systems and Technology, 5E, and the Office Administration, 5E, review manuals.

NEW Online eLearning Format for CPS and CAP Examination Review

The NEW online eLearning format includes all material found in Parts 1–3 of the CPS and CAP Examination Review series plus assessment feedback. You can purchase each title separately or receive a quantity discount when all three titles are purchased.

- Office Systems and Technology, 5E, eLearning version
- Office Administration, 5E, eLearning version
- Management, 5E, eLearning version
- CPS Examination Review Series, eLearning version (includes all three titles)

CPS and CAP Examination Review Guide

The Certification Examination Review Guide should be used to direct any course of study. This guide includes the examination outline, sample questions, bibliography of recommended study materials, and suggestions for examination review. The Certification Examination Review Guide is available free of charge on the IAAP Web site: http://www.iaap-hq.org, then Professional Certification, Forms.

Acknowledgments

The fifth edition of the *Certified Professional Secretary*® *and Certified Administrative Professional*® *Examination Review for Office Systems and Technology* complements the current revised study outline developed for the Certified Professional Secretary® and Certified Administrative Professional® Examinations. Like the other reviews available in the series, *Office Systems and Technology* will be a successful review tool because of the contributions, critiques, and dedicated efforts of a number of individuals who are interested and involved in the certification of secretaries and administrative professionals.

The International Association of Administrative Professionals (IAAP), through the Institute for Certification, has not only provided the incentive for the development of the fifth edition of this review but also valuable input during the review process. We are sincerely grateful for the continued support and endorsement of IAAP and the Institute in the development and revision of the series.

Specifically, we acknowledge the contributions of Dr. Dolores Kelly, Neumann College; Evelyn Mattison, Ergon Corporation; Carol Mull, Greenville Technical College; and Pam Silvers, Asheville-Buncombe Technical Community College, for their helpful reviews and critiques of the manuscript. In addition, the continued support of Kathy L. Schoneboom CPS/CAP, Certification Manager, IAAP, is much appreciated.

The Illinois Division of IAAP and, in particular, those members of the Kishwaukee Chapter, DeKalb, Illinois, who are pursuing or have received their professional certification deserve a special acknowledgment. These groups continue to be extremely supportive and positive about the need for secretaries and administrative professionals to become certified and to participate in professional organizations. Their friendship and encouragement is very much appreciated.

Lastly, we appreciate the leadership demonstrated by Elizabeth Sugg, Prentice Hall, and the many contributions of Deborah Hoffman, Project Manager, and Carol Mull, the Series Editor, in coordinating the reviews and critiques of the manuscript. With their help, we were able to identify and interpret the kinds of information needed by secretaries and administrative professionals to appropriately prepare for the CPS and CAP Examinations.

We hope that all the input provided by professionals and incorporated in the manuscript content for this review will help candidates everywhere in their preparation for the CPS and CAP Examinations.

Diane Routhier Graf CPS, Ed.D.

Betty L. Schroeder, Ph.D.

Chapter 1

Terminology and Basic Concepts of Information Processing

OVERVIEW

Today's business organization functions are impacted by computer-based information systems that are capable of integrating a variety of computer technologies and software applications. Such a system may utilize a mainframe computer, a mid-range computer, or diverse varieties of microcomputers at various locations around the organization. The computer has literally revolutionized business in such a way that many decision-making strategies are feasible only if a computer is used. The computer revolution has changed business operations from data processing to an information processing operation: data still represent raw input with a concentration on meaningful and useful information output.

In this chapter, computer-based information systems are reviewed from the basic technical operation to the new role of information systems for today's digital organization. The information processing cycle is outlined so that administrative professionals can review the basics of an information system. Basic processing operations are part of all computing environments (e.g., capturing data to appropriate data output). The administrative professional should be knowledgeable about these basic operations as well as operation modes and concepts.

As computers revolutionize business organizations, administrative professionals need to be cognizant of the relationship between the information technology infrastructure and the information architecture of the organization. This chapter includes a review of these interrelated concepts.

KEY TERMS

A. The Information Processing Cycle

The major function of processing is to take unorganized facts (**data**) and produce meaningful business information. **Information** is processed data that is timely, meaningful, and useful to the recipient. In a computer-based system, processing data into usable information requires computer hardware, software, and communication channels/networks. Electronic files are established for retention of raw data and information for future use. Processing involves manipulation of raw data through mathematical or logical operations. The basic information processing cycle consists of input, process, and output. The complete cycle includes six steps that involve data origination, data input, processing, storage, output, and distribution (see Figure 1–1).

1. *Data Origination:* Data origination readies data for input. During this step of the cycle, original (raw) data are organized for processing.

   a. *Online processing:* Most networked computer-based information systems are designed for online acceptance of data input. In **online processing** the user enters transactions through an input device that is directly connected to the computer system. If the user receives immediate results, the user considers the processing to be in real time.

FIGURE 1–1   The Information Processing Cycle

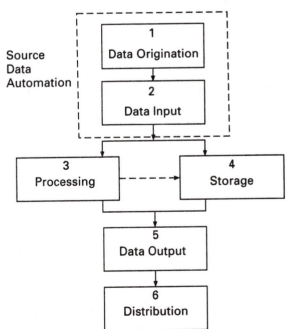

EXAMPLE: *If the processing of a bank withdrawal or deposit is done online, the user will receive a real-time, updated account balance with the bank transaction receipt.*

b. *Batch processing:* Some business transactions are still processed as a group at a future time when it is more efficient for processing. Processing transactions as a group at a future date is referred to as **batch processing.**

EXAMPLE: *In batch processing, such as payroll or inventory control, output is accurate up through the last processing of a specified batch of data. If one batch of data has not been processed, output reports do not reflect the unprocessed batch of data.*

c. *Source documents:* Some processing situations require that an original record, called a **source document,** be prepared. At this point, the business transaction is recorded for the first time. Source documents should contain the type, nature, and origin of the transaction.

EXAMPLE: *ABC Company wishes to purchase a new Model 10586 computer from AJAX Corporation. At the time of the sale, a source document (the sales order form/purchase order) is used to obtain all pertinent data.*

Type of source document: The source document is the sales order form that includes a sequential job (sale) number on it—17478.

Nature of source document: The source document shows that the ABC Company wants to purchase a Model 10586 computer.

Origin of source document: When AJAX's sales representative met with ABC Company, the representative completed a multicopy sales order form that had a sales number preprinted on the form. The sales representative presented the form to the sales department. The multicopies were used to activate inventory control, manufacturing, shipping, and billing. Data input to the computer system was obtained from the sales order form (source document).

2. **Data Input:** Data input can be entered in a batch or online as each transaction originates. With **source data automation,** data can be entered into the computer system at the time the transaction originates.

a. *Batch input:* For batch input, initial data are collected in some convenient format—a source document. Data recorded on a source document (and any other required data collected) are entered at a later time through a keyboard or input device connected to a computer. This method requires data to be recorded twice.

When data are entered into the computer for batch processing, the data are stored in a *transaction file.* At a future time all data are processed in sequence at the same time (in a batch). The transaction file for the specified time period is used to update the *master file.*

b. *Online input:* As each transaction occurs, the data are entered into a computer system. For online input, the input device needs to be connected (online) to the computer system. Direct-access storage devices are required, and data are stored and retrieved from a random location assigned by the operating system. The transaction data are usually processed immediately with the data updated to a *master file* providing real-time results for the user.

Source data automation eliminates the need for manually recording data on a source document and keying data input. Traditional data entry methods are replaced with online terminals and input devices. As data are entered directly into a computer system, machine-readable codes are electronically stored at the time the transaction originates.

EXAMPLE: *ABC Company wishes to purchase a new Model 10586 computer from AJAX Corporation. With source data automation, the sales representative uses a notebook PC (microcomputer) and wand to read the computer number codes in the catalog. Customer data are obtained from the customer database stored on the notebook hard disk, and variable sales data (quantities, where shipped) are entered using the keyboard. All the data (catalog codes, customer information, and variable data) are included on a sales form that is stored in a "New Sales" folder on the notebook PC's secondary storage (hard disk). Data from the sales form are read into AJAX Corporation's main office computer system where product descriptions, prices, and previously stored data are merged with the new sales data to complete the process of the sale.*

3. *Processing:* Input data are changed and/or combined with other data to produce information. Data are processed either in a batch or in real time through online processing. Information is data that has been processed into a meaningful and usable format.

   a. *Processing time:* The length of time required for processing will depend on the amount of data being processed, the type of information to be obtained as a result, the processing mode (batch or online), and the processor unit.

   In both batch and online processing, **turnaround time** (the time it takes between submission of data and receipt of output) is important to the user who is the recipient of the results.

   b. *Central processing unit (CPU):* The **central processing unit (CPU)** is the heart of all computer-based information systems. The CPU processes and manipulates the raw data, moves information around, and performs any required arithmetic or logic operations.

   The processing step may involve a sequence of basic operations: classifying, sorting, calculating, recording, and summarizing data.

4. *Storage:* Storage is important to both the input and the processing steps. **Storage** is where data and information are electronically held for future use. Storage takes place in secondary storage (e.g., optical discs or magnetic disks). Each character (number, alphabetic character, and symbol, including a blank space), is represented by a *byte*. Storage capacity is measured in bytes:

Kilobytes (KB):	1 thousand bytes
Megabytes (MB):	1 million bytes
Gigabytes (GB):	1 billion bytes
Terabytes (TB):	1 trillion bytes
Petabyte (PB):	1 quadrillion bytes

   When organization data are processed in batch (i.e., payroll), the input data are stored in a *transaction file* until the data are processed. The results of the organization's processed data (both batch and online) are stored for future use in the *master file*.

5. *Data Output:* When all business data have been processed (computations made and any other manipulations completed), the information must be communicated to oth-

FIGURE 1–2 Electronic Processing

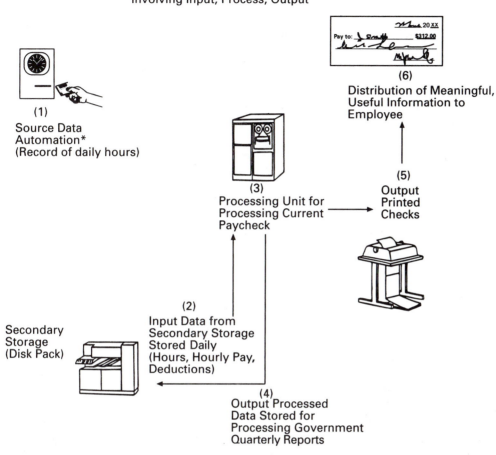

Batch Processing of Employee Paycheck
Involving Input, Process, Output

(1)
Source Data
Automation*
(Record of daily hours)

(3)
Processing Unit for
Processing Current
Paycheck

(6)
Distribution of Meaningful,
Useful Information to
Employee

(5)
Output
Printed
Checks

Secondary
Storage
(Disk Pack)

(2)
Input Data from
Secondary Storage
Stored Daily
(Hours, Hourly Pay,
Deductions)

(4)
Output Processed
Data Stored for
Processing Government
Quarterly Reports

*With source data automation, the need for a source document (time cards) and keyed
data input by an entry operator have been eliminated.

ers. Information may be presented to users by printing reports and distributing these
to interested individuals. Also, business professionals can access reports on their microcomputers. The printed report is called **hard copy.** The electronic output viewed
on a computer screen is called **soft copy.** Both hard copy and soft copy output can be
produced. The form of the output information depends on how it will be used by individuals who are either internal or external to the organization. Figure 1–2 illustrates
printed output for internal distribution.

6. ***Distribution:*** Information in the form of reports can be distributed to users either electronically (soft copy) or in printed form (hard copy). Both hard-copy and soft-copy
documents are distributed to internal office personnel and external business partners
and clients. *Hard-copy* output is typically referred to as a document (e.g., report, letter, memorandum, business form).

Check Point—Section A

Directions: For each question, circle the correct answer.

A–1. The major function of information processing is

    A) storing data/information for future use

    B) facilitation of source data automation

    C) changing unorganized data into business information

    D) preparing source documents

A–2. XYZ Office Supplies, Inc. receives an order for 12 dozen ink-jet printer cartridges from the B&Y law firm. Which one of the following is considered the source document for the transaction?

    A) The check issued by B&Y law firm for payment of the invoice

    B) The inventory record of XYZ Office Supplies, Inc. showing the quantity of ink-jet cartridges available for sale

    C) The invoice issued by XYZ Office Supplies, Inc.

    D) The purchase order received from B&Y law firm

A–3. Source data automation requires the use of a/an

    A) laser disc

    B) online input device

    C) transaction file

    D) original document

B. Information Processing Operations, Modes, and Concepts

In processing data into information, the computer system can do only what it is instructed to do. These instructions come from software program instructions or people using a very high-level programming language called 4GLs (Fourth Generation Languages). Examples of 4GLs are word processing, Internet browsers, and query languages. Administrative professionals may also encounter **natural language processing (NLP),** particularly as a front-end interface to databases. *NLP* is communicating with a computer in English or the natural language of the user. Efficient and effective use of a computer-based information system requires trained people to locate or develop specific business applications for information processing that are compatible with the basic operations and operating modes available in the information system. It is very important for office personnel to know what information needs to be processed, how it will be processed, and the rationale for using the computer.

1. ***Basic Operations:*** Business processing requires specific operations to take place so that specific data can be processed.

    a. *Recording:* Source data are captured (recorded) for processing. Data can be manually recorded in a source document or captured at the source through source data automation.

        EXAMPLE — Source Document: *Payroll data for hourly employees can be manually recorded on a time card. At the end of the week, the time card becomes the source document for inputting the weekly hours.*

        EXAMPLE — Source Data Automation: *In an online input system, the time clock (online input device) is connected to a secondary storage device for storage of the in or out time. When an employee slides the magnetized strip of an identification badge (magnetic card) through the clock, the employee's ID number is recorded from the magnetized strip, and the input time (or output time) is obtained from the clock. The data are recorded in a transaction file on a secondary storage medium (laser disc or magnetic disk) for processing at a later time (in batch).*

b. *Duplicating:* When it is necessary to create more than one record of a transaction, duplication can be accomplished by using multiple-copy forms. Data can also be electronically stored in more than one location.

EXAMPLE: *Although database software reduces data duplication, there are times when database design for information systems requires data to be stored in more than one location.*

c. *Verifying:* Checking the accuracy of data is known as *verification* of data. Sometimes keyboarding or transposition errors are made while entering data into the computer. Source data automation improves data accuracy by eliminating the need for input keying of data.

d. *Classifying:* Data must be identified according to at least one characteristic that is useful in making management decisions. *Classification* may be by type, source, importance, or type of response required.

EXAMPLE: *Sales orders may be classified according to sales districts, amount of sales, sales representative, date (year, month, day), and merchandise sold.*

e. *Sorting:* The physical process of arranging data in specific classifications is known as *sorting.*

EXAMPLE: *O'Riley is a part-time sales clerk who works three hours per week. Each week she fills out her time card and turns it in on Friday morning to her department supervisor. The time cards are sorted into two groups: full-time employees and part-time employees.*

f. *Merging:* Often, two sets of data need to be *merged* (brought together) so that a single report may be developed.

EXAMPLE: *The information from O'Riley's time card (total number of hours worked during the week) will need to be merged with number of exemptions, insurance premiums, hourly wage, and social security percentage in order to compute O'Riley's net pay.*

g. *Calculating:* Perhaps the most important part of the process is the manipulation phase, where any mathematical and logical computations are performed.

EXAMPLE: *O'Riley's take-home pay will be calculated so that the net pay will appear on the appropriate reports as well as her paycheck.*

h. *Storing and retrieving:* As long as the results from processing the data (input) are needed for future business operations, the processed results must be retained *(stored)* in some usable form (e.g., magnetic disk). *Retrieval* is the process of searching for and gaining access to the stored electronic information.

EXAMPLE: *Processed payroll data for a time period are stored in a master file and accumulated so future quarterly and annual reports can be prepared.*

i. *Summarizing:* Often large quantities of data are reduced, or *summarized,* into a more usable form. Details can be accumulated to obtain totals or compute averages.

EXAMPLE: *The total sales for the month can be accumulated for all districts or regions within the company, with totals computed for daily, weekly, and monthly sales. This information can be combined with data from previous months to arrive at accumulated sales for the year to date or for calculating increases or decreases in sales (e.g., weekly or monthly).*

j.   *Report writing:* Facts obtained through the processing of data need to be analyzed and communicated in some type of report form to persons or groups with the responsibility and authority to use the information for decision-making purposes. Facts become information only when they are received when needed, accepted as meaningful, and used by decision makers.

EXAMPLE: *A report of total sales to date, which includes sales districts; amount of sales per marketing representative; and daily, weekly, and monthly totals, may be combined with a report of the goods that have been sold to make decisions on what products need to receive more advertising and promotion dollars during the coming month.*

2.   ***Advantages of Using Computers:*** Both small and large organizations use computer-based information systems to process daily business transactions. The vital role of computer-based information systems in today's organization is based on the speed, accuracy, consistency, and reliability of the computer.

a.   *Speed:* Today's microcomputers process data faster than the mainframe computer of the 1950s. Speeds of computers are measured in:

Microseconds:	one millionth (micro)
Nanoseconds:	one billionth (nano)
Picoseconds:	one trillionth (pico)

Powerful computers operate in nanoseconds and picoseconds. The capacity to store data, images, audio, video, or any digitized data with instant recall has increased the importance of the computer-based information system in business.

b.   *Accuracy:* A computer system does exactly what the software instructions direct it to do. Inaccuracies are human errors. Errors are typically attributed to inaccurate data input, errors in program logic, or a procedural error.

c.   *Consistency:* Computers always do what the software instructions direct the computer to do—over and over again. With consistent, accurate results, businesses confidently address mission-critical issues.

d.   *Reliability:* When it comes to repetitive tasks, computer systems are the most reliable source a business can utilize—day and night. As long as the information system staff maintains the computer-based information system, there should be minimal **downtime** (time when the computer is not in operation).

3.   ***Operation Modes:*** A computer-based information system can be designed with various methods of operation to facilitate specific business needs. Following is a brief review of some of these operation modes.

a.   *Input and output operations:* The way in which data are entered into the computer system affects how the data can be processed. There are two ways of data input and processing: batch input for batch processing and online input for either batch processing or online processing. Data input for batch processing must be stored in sequence; all batch processing is sequential. Data input for online processing is stored randomly on a direct-access storage device.

b. *Remote access:* Sometimes input/output devices located at a remote office (home office of a telecommuter) need to be connected to the firm's information system to enter data as well as receive up-to-date information. A **telecommuter** is an employee who works at home and is connected to the office data through a communications channel (telephone line, cable, satellite).

c. *Multiprocessing:* When two or more application software programs need to be executed simultaneously (at the same time) in a single computer system, **multiprocessing** takes place. This requires the computer system to have two or more central processing units (CPUs). In a multiprocessing environment, the instructions being executed could be from one user or from multiple users. The operating system software needs to support multiprocessing.

d. *Multiprogramming:* To decrease the amount of time a computer is "idle," **multiprogramming** makes possible the concurrent execution of two or more programs. In other words, there is more than one processing job that is being executed at the same time by switching back and forth between the multiple programs until all processing is complete. This means there can be multiple users or one user with several programs. Multiprogramming operating system software directs the CPU to switch back and forth between multiple programs (requests).

e. *Multitasking:* **Multitasking** is multiprogramming on a single user operating system (e.g., Windows 2000 or Windows XP). A single user computer could be a home microcomputer or a notebook.

f. *Online operations:* When data entry devices are connected online to the computer, data can be entered directly into the computer. The computer controls the operations involved.

g. *Interactive operations:* When there is frequent interchange between the user at the data entry terminal and the processor unit during execution of a program, an **interactive mode** is in effect. The user receives prompts from the computer, responds to them, and receives further information or additional prompts from the computer. The result is a flow of information in both directions.

h. *Time-sharing:* In organizations, users may share the computer system resources at the same time; each user acts independently of any other user on the system. **Time-sharing** operating system software differs from multiprogramming in that the operating system provides a fixed amount of time to a user for processing. Since each user uses his or her own computer and communicates with the organization computer on an individual basis, it would seem that he or she is the only person using that system at that time, even though in reality many users are sharing the organization computer time.

i. *Networking:* In the *networking* operation mode, computers at various locations are linked together by communication lines (channels). Data can then be transmitted directly from one computer to another. Networking provides a link between departments and the types of data created in each. Today, organizations recognize the importance of integrating business operations and work in some type of networking environment.

Check Point—Section B

Directions: For each question, circle the correct answer.

B–1. The computer operation that separates sales orders into cash, credit, and layaway groups is known as

  A) classifying
  B) merging
  C) sorting
  D) verifying

B–2. Through system maintenance, downtime is minimized; this increases system

  A) accuracy
  B) consistency

  C) reliability
  D) speed

B–3. Multiprogramming decreases the amount of time a computer is idle by switching back and forth between multiple programs until all processing is complete. Multiprogramming is directed by the

  A) central processing unit
  B) interactive operations
  C) network
  D) operating system software

C. Information System Types, Architecture, and Technology Infrastructure

Meeting the business and technical challenges of the digital organization requires designing/redesigning an information architecture and the information technology infrastructure. In a contemporary computer-based information system, there is interdependence between the firm's business strategy and procedures and the firm's information system.

1. *System Types:* Six types of systems serve the five organizational levels:

System Type	*Organizational Level*
Transaction processing systems (TPS)	Operational
Knowledge work systems (KWS)	Knowledge
Office systems (OS)	Office
Management information systems (MIS) and	
Decision support systems (DSS)	Management
Executive support systems (ESS)	Strategic

  a. *Transaction processing systems (TPS):* **Transaction processing systems** are basic to business operations and are used for capturing the records of daily transactions necessary in conducting business. Typical processing includes sorting, listing, merging, and updating. These processes are predefined and highly structured. Output includes detailed reports, lists, and summaries that are automatically produced on a daily, weekly, monthly, or quarterly basis. The main users of the TPS are supervisors and operations personnel of the functional areas of business: accounting, manufacturing, sales and marketing, finance, and human resources.

  EXAMPLE:

Accounting TPS:	*Accounts Receivable*
Manufacturing TPS:	*Inventory Management*
Sales/Marketing TPS:	*Orders*

Finance TPS:	Cash Management
Human Resources TPS:	Benefits

b. *Knowledge work systems (KWS):* Knowledge workers use **knowledge work systems** to create new information and knowledge. **Knowledge workers** are professionals with advanced degrees (e.g., engineers, information technicians, doctors, scientists). Typical processing includes simulations and models that produce graphical output or models.

c. *Office systems (OS):* Office professionals and data workers are trained personnel who manipulate and disseminate information using electronic office systems. **Office systems** are information technology applications designed to increase productivity by supporting the coordination and communication activities of the typical office. Because of the importance of communication and integration within the organization, office systems are used at all organizational levels.

EXAMPLE:

Word processing and digital filing:	document management
Electronic calendars:	scheduling
e-Mail and voice mail:	communication
Spreadsheets:	numeric manipulation
Presentation graphics:	electronic slide show

d. *Management information systems (MIS):* Managers receive reports and online access to the firm's current and historical records through **management information systems.** MIS use internal data from the TPS to produce structured summary and exception reports addressing management functions of planning, controlling, and making decisions. These reports address routine questions that can be answered through predefined business procedures and are available to the manager on demand (when needed).

EXAMPLE: *The Director of Marketing for Bottles, Inc. compares the sales quota to actual sales before every corporate meeting. The Director has online access to the corporate sales TPS databases and is able to generate a summary report to compare data and to calculate percentage achieved.*

Product	Sales Region	Actual Sales	Sales Quota	Sales Percentage
G256	East	450,632	500,000	90.126
	South	275,450	250,000	110.18
	Midwest	804,338	875,000	91.924
	TOTAL	1,530,420	1,625,000	94.179
B256	East	350,250	325,000	107.769
	South	285,459	275,000	103.803
	Midwest	567,905	650,000	87.37
	TOTAL	1,203,614	1,250,000	96.289

e. *Decision support systems (DSS):* Managers also make decisions that are unique and rapidly changing to meet today's changing global economy. **Decision support systems** use sophisticated analytical models to support semi-structured decisions of a digital organization. DSS use both internal TPS and MIS data as well as external sources and provide an interactive environment where the user can change assumptions, ask new questions, and change the variables in the DSS model.

    f. *Executive support systems (ESS):* **Executive support systems** are for senior management queries on external and internal data. Projections about the future are provided for strategic decisions.

Although a type of information system is designed for specific business processes and user needs, each of the different systems has components that are used by organizational levels and groups other than the intended user. An administrative professional may find information on an MIS, or a manager may need to extract data from a TPS.

2. *Information Architecture:* The conceptual design of how an organization achieves business processes (applications) and goals is the **information architecture.** In order for the design to serve the functional specialty, business users at all levels need to ensure that their current and future information requirements are understood and met.

In preparing the information architecture, the information systems analyst meets with business users to understand their information needs. The systems analyst discusses how computer-based information systems can make business processes more efficient and effective.

It is also important that the systems analyst and information systems designer integrate computer-based information systems within an organization to enhance the organization's collaborative efforts.

Figure 1–3 illustrates how the information architecture includes all functional areas (accounting, manufacturing, sales and marketing, finance, and human resources) and business processes for multiple organizational levels, both internally and externally to the firm. External processes include suppliers, business partners, and customers.

3. *Information Technology (IT) Infrastructure:* The **IT infrastructure** includes all the technical resources shared within the organization. These resources are computer hardware, software, storage, data management, and networks. Figure 1–3 illustrates how the IT infrastructure supports the organization's information architecture.

    a. *Computer hardware:* Computer hardware consists of all physical equipment used for input, process, output, and storage functions in an information system. Hardware includes the central processing unit; input, output, and storage devices; and physical media required for linking these devices together. Computer hardware is covered in Chapter 2.

    b. *Software:* Computer software includes software for operating the system (system software) and software for handling specific business applications (application software). Software is covered in Section III—Chapters 8 and 9.

    c. *Storage:* Physical storage media (magnetic, optical, or tape storage) determine how data can be electronically stored and accessed for processing. Storage is covered in Chapter 2.

    d. *Data management:* How data are organized and stored on the physical media affects the type of information available to the organization's users and external constituents. Data management is covered in Chapters 8 and 9.

FIGURE 1–3 Organization's Information Architecture and Information Technology Infrastructure

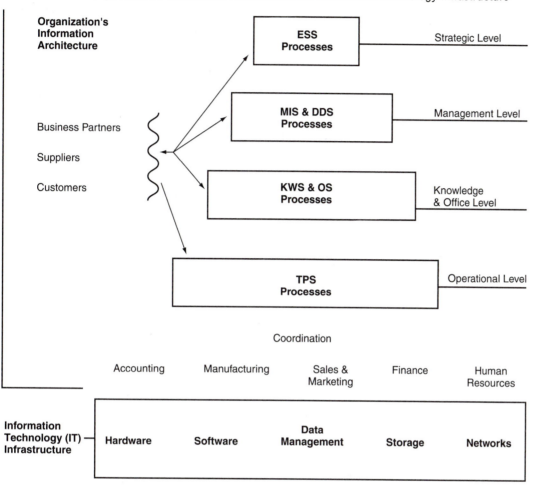

e. *Networks:* A *network* links two or more computers to shared data and physical resources. Networking requires physical communication devices and communications software. Communications technology and networks are covered in Chapter 3.

Business personnel must work closely with information system professionals so that coordination of the information technology infrastructure meets the needs of the organization's information architecture. Such an integrated undertaking requires business professionals to be knowledgeable about information technology and capable of articulating their information requirements.

Check Point—Section C

Directions: For each question, circle the correct answer.

C–1. A highly structured information system basic to business operations that captures daily records is the

    A) knowledge work system

B) management information system

C) office system

D) transaction processing system

C–2. Information architecture is the

A) conceptualized processes for all functional areas

B) hardware, software, and storage devices for a computer-based information system

C) internal and external data management requirements

D) input, process, and output operations of a management information system

C–3. All technical resources shared within an organization are called the

A) computer-based information system

B) decision support system

C) information architecture

D) information infrastructure

D. History of Computing

Computer technology has drastically changed the world over the last decade. Today computers are an important tool in the business office as well as homes around the world. Although most of us have lived through the major computing evolution, history shows that computing was conceived in the mid-1800s with major innovations developed in the 1940s. The intent of this brief history of computing is to place the evolution of computing into perspective for administrative professionals.

1. *Father of Computers:* "The Father of Computers," Charles Babbage, conceived an analytical engine in 1833. After his death in 1871, Babbage's son constructed the analytical engine.

2. *Early Computers:* There were four major computing events in the 1940s, the Mark I, the Antanasoff-Berry-Computer (ABC), the ENIAC, and the stored program concept (EDVAC and EDSAC computers).

   a. *Mark I:* In 1944, the Mark I was produced as a joint effort by Harvard University, International Business Machines (IBM), and the U.S. Department of War. The automatic calculations in the Mark I were based on Babbage's analytical engine.

   b. *Antanasoff-Berry-Computer (ABC):* John Antanasoff and an assistant, Clifford Berry, produced an electronic device called the Antanasoff-Berry-Computer (ABC); it was completed in 1942. In 1974, a Federal court declared Antanasoff the true inventor of the first electronic computer. This court decision was necessary because many considered J. Presper Eckert and John W. Mauchly (University of Pennsylvania) to be the inventors of the first electronic computer.

   c. *ENIAC:* J. Presper Eckert and John W. Mauchly invented the ENIAC (Electronic Numerical Integrator and Calculator). It was completed in 1946 and is recognized as the first large-scale electronic digital computer. The ENIAC had no internal memory.

   d. *Stored program concept:* In the late 1940s, Jon Von Neumann's principle of encoding spurred the development of a stored program computer, the EDVAC (Electronic Discrete Variable Automatic Computer). The *stored program concept* meant a software program could be stored in primary storage with the central processing unit (CPU) accessing the software instructions in sequence and performing required processing. However, the EDSAC (Electronic Delay Storage Automatic Computer) created at Cambridge University, England, was completed several months earlier and is now recognized as the first stored program computer. The computers were used primarily for scientific applications.

3. ***The First Business Computer:*** In 1951, the U.S. Census Bureau purchased a UNIVAC 1 from Remington Rand dedicated to data processing rather than military use. In 1954, General Electric Company became the first private firm to use the UNIVAC 1 for commercial business data processing. Characteristics of the first business computers (1951–1958) are:

   a. The main logic element consisted of vacuum tubes.

   b. Vacuum tubes caused computers to be large and to generate a lot of heat.

   c. Internal storage consisted of a magnetic drum.

   d. Punched cards were used for input.

   e. There was very little system software so application programs were loaded and monitored by computer operators.

   f. Applications were mainly for payroll, billing, and accounting and processed in batch.

4. ***A New Generation:*** With businesses joining the scientific field for using computers, changes started to happen. Computers became faster, memory capacities were larger, and new programming languages were developed making business applications easier to process. Characteristics of these computers (1959–1964) included:

   a. The main logic element consisted of transistors.

   b. Transistors caused computers to become faster, smaller, more reliable, and increased internal storage capacity.

   c. Internal storage consisted of a magnetic core that allowed faster access speeds.

   d. Internal storage was supplemented with secondary storage through the use of magnetic tape and later the introduction of magnetic disks. Using either punched cards or magnetic tape for input, all data were processed in batch.

   e. An operating system was incorporated into the system software; however, computer operators continued to monitor computing activities.

   f. High-level languages (COBOL and FORTRAN) allowed application programs to be problem oriented instead of machine oriented.

5. ***The First Integrated Circuit:*** In 1958, Jack S. Kilby of Texas Instruments invented the first *integrated circuit* that consisted of hundreds of electronic components etched into a silicon chip. Today the integrated circuit is at the heart of all electronic equipment.

6. ***The First Minicomputer:*** In 1965, Digital Equipment Corporation (DEC) introduced the first minicomputer, a scaled-down version of the large mainframe computers.

7. ***Another Computing Era:*** The integrated circuit and the minicomputer made computing affordable for smaller organizations. Characteristics of these computers (1965–1970) included:

   a. The main logic element consisted of integrated circuits (ICs) usually referred to as the chip.

   b. The integrated circuit allowed primary memory to store up to several million units of information at one time.

   c. Internal storage began moving toward metal-oxide semiconductor memory (MOS).

d.   Secondary storage began moving toward magnetic disks allowing for more flexible input and output.

e.   Advances in the operating system made a major impact on processing operations. There was little need for full-time computer operators.

f.   Advances in disk storage and operating systems made online access, interactive processing, and real-time processing possible for business applications.

g.   High-level languages were being standardized, which made application programming easier.

8.   ***The Microprocessor:*** Ted Hoff of Intel Corporation introduced the microprocessor in 1971. The *microprocessor* was the control unit and arithmetic/logic unit on a single chip. Today, a microprocessor is a single chip on which circuitry of the control unit, arithmetic/logic unit, and primary memory are etched. A microprocessor plus chips for input and output operations form a microcomputer.

9.   ***Microcomputer Evolution:*** The microcomputer evolution began in the mid-1970s and has changed the computing environment ever since. Three significant innovations include:

a.   *The first microcomputer:* In 1975, the first microcomputer (MITS Altair), based on the Intel 8080 microprocessor with 256 bytes of RAM, could be purchased as a kit for $500 or assembled for $2,500. It did not include a monitor or keyboard.

b.   *The Apple microcomputer:* In 1976, Steve Jobs and Steve Wozniak developed the Apple I microcomputer in their basement. Although it was a flop, its successor, Apple II, became the first popular home computer in 1977. The Apple II had an MOS 6502 microprocessor, 16K RAM, 16K ROM, as well as a monitor and keyboard. Floppy disk drives were added in 1978. The Apple Macintosh was introduced in 1984; its unique feature was the graphical user interface (GUI) that Xerox introduced in 1981. The Apple Macintosh was stiff competition to both Microsoft's disk operating system (MS-DOS) (1980) and the IBM PC (1981). Today the GUI has changed application software so non-technical office professionals can easily use the microcomputer as a productivity tool.

c.   *The IBM PC, clones, and MS-DOS:* Based on the Intel 8088 microprocessor, the IBM PC was introduced in 1981. MS-DOS, licensed by Bill Gates, was issued with the microcomputer. In just one year, slightly more than 830,000 had been sold. Today the IBM PC and its clones are a powerful standard for the microcomputer industry.

10. ***ARPANET:*** In 1969 a U.S. Department of Defense's Advanced Research Project Agency (ARPA) sponsored a project to electronically link scientists from two different locations (UCLA and Stanford University). By 1971, the project, named ARPANET, included more than 20 sites and by 1981 ARPANET had 200 sites. In 1990 ARPANET evolved into the Internet.

11. ***The World Wide Web (WWW):*** In 1989, a team of scientists led by Tim Berners-Lee, a Swiss physicist, developed an Internet language (hypertext markup language [HTML]), established Internet addresses (universal resource locator [URL]), and had the first server that supported this World Wide Web format. By 1993, traffic on the

Internet grew over 350,000 percent! Today the WWW is the foundation (language standard and Internet address format) for Internet communications and services.

12. **Computing in the 21st Century:** Changes in computing occur daily. Characteristics of computers in the first decade of the 21st century includes:

   a. The internal components now consist of *very large-scale integrated circuits* (VLSICs). *VLSICs* are chips with millions of small microsized transistors placed on silicon chips. VLSICs allow computers to be smaller (notebooks), faster (Pentium IV), more reliable, and less expensive.

   b. Internal storage is mainly semiconductor, where memory is etched onto a small silicon chip.

   c. Secondary storage utilizes magnetic disks, optical discs, and portable USB flash drives that store vast amounts of data in a relatively small physical space.

   d. Systems software expanded to include database management, network management, and sophisticated security monitors to manage both internal and external communications with the computer-based information system.

   e. The Internet and World Wide Web technologies have propelled society and businesses into a cyber e-world where communication with one another around the world can be anytime, anywhere, any place, 24/7 (24 hours a day, 7 days a week).

Check Point—Section D

Directions: For each question, circle the correct answer.

D–1. In 1974, a Federal court declared the true inventor of the first electronic computer to be

   A) John Antanasoff
   B) Charles Babbage
   C) Clifford Berry
   D) John W. Mauchly

D–2. The graphical user interface (GUI) was

   A) conceived by Ted Hoff of Intel Corporation
   B) introduced in 1981 by Xerox
   C) invented by Steve Jobs and Steve Wozniak in 1984 for the Apple Macintosh
   D) licensed by Bill Gates and issued with the IBM PC in 1981

D–3. In 1969 the U.S. Department of Defense sponsored a project that eventually evolved into the

   A) first microcomputer in 1975
   B) Internet in 1990
   C) microprocessor in 1971
   D) World Wide Web (WWW) in 1989

For Your Review

Directions: For each question, circle the correct answer.

1. Output from a computer-based information system that is timely, meaningful, and useful to the recipient is called
   A) data
   B) information
   C) online processing
   D) soft copy

2. Norton uses the bank automatic teller machine to withdraw $200 from her checking account and deposit $450 into her savings account. This is an example of
   A) batch processing
   B) group processing
   C) online processing
   D) real-time processing

3. Every two weeks corporate processes the payroll for all hourly employees at the Glory Day offices. The sequential processing of the hourly payroll is known as
   A) batch processing
   B) multiprocessing
   C) online processing
   D) time-sharing

4. Input data for batch processing are electronically stored in a
   A) database
   B) master file
   C) transaction file
   D) source document

5. During processing raw data are manipulated and changed into information by
   A) multitasking
   B) natural language processing (NLP)
   C) source data automation
   D) the central processing unit (CPU)

6. Healy Corporation encourages all personnel to access reports on their microcomputer. The electronic output viewed on the monitor is called (a)
   A) hard copy
   B) soft copy
   C) source data automation
   D) source document

7. For some business processing, a basic operation is to capture input data on a document (e.g., time card). This basic operation is called
   A) classifying
   B) duplicating
   C) merging
   D) recording

8. Data input accuracy can be improved through the use of
   A) batch processing
   B) interactive operations
   C) multitasking
   D) source data automation

9. A weekly sales report is generated showing the total sales for all districts with a comparison to the same week last year. A basic computing operation in the example is
   A) classifying
   B) sorting
   C) summarizing
   D) verifying

10. Processing speeds for today's micro-computer are measured in

    A) gigabytes
    B) kiloseconds
    C) megabytes
    D) microseconds

11. When all input data must be sequentially stored before processing, this is a requirement for which type of processing?

    A) Batch processing
    B) Multiprocessing
    C) Online processing
    D) Time-sharing

12. Ingham's spouse was transferred to another state. Ingham did not want to quit her position so she arranged to work from her new location via communications connections and to attend the monthly meeting at the office. This is an example of

    A) multitasking
    B) natural language processing (NLP)
    C) telecommuting
    D) time-sharing

13. Multiprogramming on a notebook computer is called

    A) interactive operations
    B) multiprocessing
    C) multitasking
    D) networking

14. Using the automatic teller machine (ATM), Martensen responds to the screen prompts to process her transaction. This is an example of

    A) decision support systems
    B) interactive operations
    C) multiprocessing
    D) networking

15. The information system basic to business operations for capturing the daily records necessary in conducting business is the

    A) decision support system (DSS)
    B) knowledge work system (KWS)
    C) office system (OS)
    D) transaction processing system (TPS)

16. Engineers and other professionals who use simulations and models to create new information and concepts are

    A) information technicians
    B) knowledge workers
    C) managers
    D) telecommuters

17. Electronic scheduling and communication are examples of the

    A) decision support system (DSS)
    B) executive support system (ESS)
    C) knowledge work system (KWS)
    D) office system (OS)

18. Business professionals receive reports and online access to the organization's current and historical records through the

    A) executive support system (ESS)
    B) knowledge work system (KWS)
    C) management information system (MIS)
    D) office system (OS)

19. An information system that uses internal data from the transaction processing system to produce structured summary and exception reports is the

    A) decision support system (DSS)
    B) knowledge work system (KWS)
    C) management information system (MIS)
    D) office system (OS)

20. Blackman uses a sophisticated analytical model that captures data from daily business transactions and external sources to produce scenarios supporting semi-structured situations. Blackman is using a

    A) decision support system (DSS)
    B) knowledge work system (KWS)
    C) management information system (MIS)
    D) transaction processing system (TPS)

21. The conceptual design of how an organization achieves business processes and goals is the

    A) executive support system (ESS)
    B) information architecture
    C) operation mode
    D) stored program concept

22. An information systems analyst meets with business users to understand the organization's information needs. The information analyst and business user are developing the
    A) decision support system (DSS)
    B) information architecture
    C) master file
    D) technology infrastructure

23. The organization's information infrastructure for computer-based information systems consists of
    A) business partners, suppliers, and customers
    B) hardware, software, data management, storage, and networks

    C) operational, management, and strategic processes
    D) transaction processing systems and management information systems

24. The microcomputer evolution began after the invention of the
    A) integrated circuit
    B) microprocessor
    C) stored program concept
    D) transistor

25. In 1969 a U.S. Department of Defense project called ARPANET evolved into the
    A) first microcomputer
    B) Internet
    C) stored program concept
    D) World Wide Web (WWW)

Solutions

Solutions to Check Point—Section A

Answer	Refer to:
A–1. (C)	[A]
A–2. (D)	[A-1-c]
A–3. (B)	[A-2-b]

Solutions to Check Point—Section B

Answer	Refer to:
B–1. (C)	[B-1-e]
B–2. (C)	[B-2-d]
B–3. (D)	[B-3-d]

Solutions to Check Point—Section C

Answer	Refer to:
C–1. (D)	[C-1-a]
C–2. (A)	[C-2]
C–3. (D)	[C-3]

Solutions to Check Point—Section D

Answer	*Refer to:*
D–1. (A)	[D-2-b]
D–2. (B)	[D-9-b]
D–3. (B)	[D-10]

Solutions to For Your Review

Answer	*Refer to:*
1. (B)	[A]
2. (C)	[A-1-a]
3. (A)	[A-1-b]
4. (C)	[A-2-a and A-4]
5. (D)	[A-3-b]
6. (B)	[A-5]
7. (D)	[B-1-a]
8. (D)	[B-1-c]
9. (C)	[B-1-i]
10. (D)	[B-2-a]
11. (A)	[B-3-a]
12. (C)	[B-3-b]
13. (C)	[B-3-e]
14. (B)	[B-3-g]
15. (D)	[C-1-a]
16. (B)	[C-1-b]
17. (D)	[C-1-c]
18. (C)	[C-1-d]
19. (C)	[C-1-d]

20. (A)   [C-1-e]

21. (B)   [C-2]

22. (B)   [C-2]

23. (B)   [C-3]

24. (B)   [D-8]

25. (B)   [D-10]

Chapter 2

Hardware for Computer Operations

OVERVIEW

Although administrative professionals do not need to be computer technology experts, a basic understanding of hardware in the organization's information technology (IT) infrastructure is important in utilizing and promoting organizational performance and productivity.

This chapter highlights the major capabilities of computer hardware starting with the overview of all electronic computer systems.

Often confusing to business professionals are the differences among supercomputers, main-frames, mid-range computers, and microcomputers. These configurations are outlined along with addressing the multifaceted nature of microcomputers in the networked infrastructure.

Computer peripherals—input devices, output devices, and storage devices—are outlined providing administrative personnel with the basic technology used in the field.

KEY TERMS

A. The Computer-Based Information System

The equipment used in processing data is called *hardware*. In addition to the computer itself, other required equipment includes input, output, and storage devices.

The *digital computer* is used to organize numbers and alphabetic data. Data are represented by strings of numbers that are expressed by on or off electrical impulses in a computer system. A numeric 0 represents the off electrical impulse and the numeric 1 represents the on electrical impulse. This two-state (binary) condition is referred to as a **bit.** Either a number one digit (1) for on or a zero digit (0) for off represents this two-state condition. *Bit* is the acronym for *b*inary (b) dig*it* (it). A string of bits (0s and 1s) representing a number or a character (alphanumeric character or symbol [including a blank space]) is called a **byte;** eight bits equals one byte.

EXAMPLE: *The byte for a capital letter "A": 10100001. Each 0 and each 1 is a bit.*

This is known as the American Standard Code for Information Interchange (ASCII). ASCII is used for microcomputers and data transmission.

Another code representation is the Extended Binary Coded Decimal Interchange Code (EBCDIC). EBCDIC was developed by IBM in the 1950s and is the primary mainframe IBM code.

The digital computer is most often used for processing business data. The other computer classification is the *analog computer,* which is used as a measuring device. The functional elements that make up the digital computer system are the input devices, processor unit, output devices, and secondary storage (see Figure 2–1).

1. ***Input Devices:*** A computer system requires devices that can introduce (enter) raw data into the system. Typical *input devices* for human input include keyboards, mouse, trackball, other pointing devices, and touch screens. Source data automation provides input with minimal human involvement. These devices use interactive touch screens, magnetic card readers, optical recognition, and voice recognition.

   The data may be stored for batch processing or processed immediately with real-time results as well as storing the data and results for future use.

2. ***Processor Unit:*** The *processor unit* consists of primary storage (main memory/ internal storage) and the **central processing unit (CPU). Primary storage** consists of read only memory (ROM), random access memory (RAM), and cache memory. The *CPU* is the heart of a computer system and consists of the control unit and the arithmetic/logic unit. Figure 2–1 illustrates the three components of the processor unit: primary storage RAM, the control unit, and the arithmetic/logic unit. The CPU processes data transferred to main memory by an input device and, in turn, transfers the results from main memory to secondary storage and an output device (printers or CRT screen). The CPU operates according to both operating system software and application software instructions.

Chapter 2

Hardware for Computer Operations

OVERVIEW

Although administrative professionals do not need to be computer technology experts, a basic understanding of hardware in the organization's information technology (IT) infrastructure is important in utilizing and promoting organizational performance and productivity.

This chapter highlights the major capabilities of computer hardware starting with the overview of all electronic computer systems.

Often confusing to business professionals are the differences among supercomputers, mainframes, mid-range computers, and microcomputers. These configurations are outlined along with addressing the multifaceted nature of microcomputers in the networked infrastructure.

Computer peripherals—input devices, output devices, and storage devices—are outlined providing administrative personnel with the basic technology used in the field.

KEY TERMS

Bit, 26
Byte, 26
Central processing unit
    (CPU), 26
Channel, 41
Compact disc (CD), 42
Graphical user interface
    (GUI), 34
Hard disk, 42
Interface, 36
Magnetic disk, 42

Mainframe computer, 30
Microcomputer, 31
Microprocessor, 28
Mid-range computer, 30
Monitor, 38
Optical disc, 42
Pattern recognition
    system, 36
Personal digital assistant
    (PDA), 32

Point-and-click devices, 34
Port, 41
Primary storage, 26
Printer, 39
Random access memory
    (RAM), 27
Read only memory
    (ROM), 27
Reduced instruction set
    computing (RISC), 31

A. The Computer-Based Information System

The equipment used in processing data is called *hardware*. In addition to the computer itself, other required equipment includes input, output, and storage devices.

The *digital computer* is used to organize numbers and alphabetic data. Data are represented by strings of numbers that are expressed by on or off electrical impulses in a computer system. A numeric 0 represents the off electrical impulse and the numeric 1 represents the on electrical impulse. This two-state (binary) condition is referred to as a **bit.** Either a number one digit (1) for on or a zero digit (0) for off represents this two-state condition. *Bit* is the acronym for *bi*nary (b) dig*it* (it). A string of bits (0s and 1s) representing a number or a character (alphanumeric character or symbol [including a blank space]) is called a **byte;** eight bits equals one byte.

EXAMPLE: *The byte for a capital letter "A": 10100001. Each 0 and each 1 is a bit.*

This is known as the American Standard Code for Information Interchange (ASCII). ASCII is used for microcomputers and data transmission.

Another code representation is the Extended Binary Coded Decimal Interchange Code (EBCDIC). EBCDIC was developed by IBM in the 1950s and is the primary mainframe IBM code.

The digital computer is most often used for processing business data. The other computer classification is the *analog computer,* which is used as a measuring device. The functional elements that make up the digital computer system are the input devices, processor unit, output devices, and secondary storage (see Figure 2–1).

1. ***Input Devices:*** A computer system requires devices that can introduce (enter) raw data into the system. Typical *input devices* for human input include keyboards, mouse, trackball, other pointing devices, and touch screens. Source data automation provides input with minimal human involvement. These devices use interactive touch screens, magnetic card readers, optical recognition, and voice recognition.

   The data may be stored for batch processing or processed immediately with real-time results as well as storing the data and results for future use.

2. ***Processor Unit:*** The *processor unit* consists of primary storage (main memory/ internal storage) and the **central processing unit (CPU). Primary storage** consists of read only memory (ROM), random access memory (RAM), and cache memory. The *CPU* is the heart of a computer system and consists of the control unit and the arithmetic/logic unit. Figure 2–1 illustrates the three components of the processor unit: primary storage RAM, the control unit, and the arithmetic/logic unit. The CPU processes data transferred to main memory by an input device and, in turn, transfers the results from main memory to secondary storage and an output device (printers or CRT screen). The CPU operates according to both operating system software and application software instructions.

FIGURE 2–1   The Digital Computer System

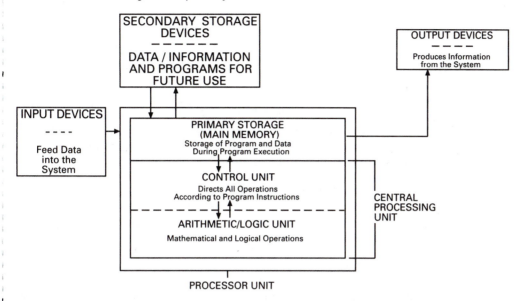

a. *Primary storage:* Primary storage (memory) consists of semiconductor memory chips; a silicon chip consists of integrated circuits made of millions of tiny transistors (i.e., VLSIC—very large-scale integrated circuits). Primary storage is divided into ROM, RAM, and cache memory.

(1) *Read only memory (ROM):* **Read only memory (ROM)** is nonvolatile memory where critical system instructions for starting the computer are permanently stored by the computer manufacturer; this is sometimes called *firmware.* The instructions are available only to the CPU and cannot be changed by business users. The instructions are not lost when the computer system is turned off *(nonvolatile storage).*

Variations of ROM are *programmable read only memory (PROM)* and *erasable PROM (EPROM)* chips. After the hardware is manufactured, PROM chips are programmed, but PROM chips cannot be changed once programmed. The user can load and read instructions from PROM. EPROM chips can be removed from the computer, erased, and reprogrammed with new instructions for the CPU. EPROM chips are common in robotic systems.

(2) *Random access memory (RAM):* **Random access memory (RAM)** is temporarily available for processing business data according to software instructions (system and application). Other terms used when referring to primary storage (RAM) are *main memory* or *internal storage.* Data are transferred from the input devices directly to main memory and must be in main memory to be sent to the output device or to any peripheral equipment (e.g., secondary storage devices). RAM stores the following:

- Input data
- Program instructions (both system and application)
- Intermediate processing results
- Processed data (information) ready for output

RAM is volatile memory; the data are lost when the electrical power to the computer is turned off.

(3) *Cache memory: Cache memory* (pronounced cash) is placed close to the CPU and, thus, is very fast memory. Cache memory complements RAM by temporarily storing blocks of software instructions and data for quick access during processing.

b. *Control unit:* Instruction registers and control circuits are included in the control unit. Under stored-program control (system software), the control unit selects one program statement at a time from main memory. This is referred to as *fetching*. The *control unit* performs the following operations:

- Instruction registers within the control unit are used to select program instructions in the proper sequence.
- The control unit interprets (decodes) each program instruction as it is selected.
- Control circuits are activated to carry out required operations.
- Results are stored.

Unlike computers of the 1950s, today's computers use the *stored program concept* of storing necessary software programs (system and application) in primary storage and accessing the software instructions in sequence by the CPU. The control unit along with main memory makes possible the stored program concept of computer operations.

c. *Arithmetic/logic unit:* The *arithmetic/logic unit* performs all mathematical computations and logical comparisons. The arithmetic circuitry adds, subtracts, multiplies, divides, sets algebraic signs, rounds off, and so on. Logical operations are comparisons for greater than, less than, equal to, and not equal to. Arithmetic operations can be performed only on numeric characters. Logical operations can be performed on numeric, alphabetic, and special characters. Data are transferred as needed from main memory to the arithmetic/logic unit for manipulation and returned to main memory until needed for additional processing or output.

d. *Microprocessor:* A **microprocessor** includes the control unit and the arithmetic logic unit mounted on a single silicon chip. Computers containing more than one microprocessor (CPU) enable the computer to execute more than one instruction, or to process more than one program, at a time; this is referred to as a multiprocessing operation mode.

The microprocessor determines a computer's performance. Administrative professionals should be knowledgeable of the features of the microprocessor that affect performance. These features include clock speed, word length, and bus width.

(1) *Clock speed:* Microprocessors run at a *clock speed* of megahertz or gigahertz. One *megahertz* (1 MHz) equals one million clock cycles per second; one *gigahertz* (GHz) equals one billion cycles per second.

Microprocessors have clock speeds from 1,000 to 2,000 MHz with some measured in gigahertz. (e.g., Intel Pentium 4 clock speed can reach 2 GHz).

(2) *Word length: Word length* is the number of bits (digital 0s and 1s) that the CPU can process at one time. Typical word lengths are 32 or 64; the larger the word length, the faster the chip (e.g., Intel Pentium 4 chip has a 64-bit word length).

EXAMPLE: *A 32-bit CPU can process 32 bits of data in one machine operation (cycle). This is equivalent to four characters (i.e., number, letter, or special character). Note: A blank space is a special character represented by eight bits.*

(3) *Bus width:* The *bus width* is the size of the internal physical path *(data bus)* that data and instructions travel as electrical impulses (bits) between the CPU and the primary storage. The more data that can be moved on the data bus (physical path) at one time, the faster the processing (e.g., Intel Pentium 4 chip has a 64-bit bus width).

3. ***Output Devices:*** *Output,* data that have been processed, may be in a form acceptable for another machine (secondary storage for future reference) or in a form usable and understandable by people (information). Typical output devices for information are printers, monitors, and speakers. When information is printed, it is called *hard copy.* When information can be viewed on a monitor or heard over a recorder, it is called *soft copy.* Soft information can be stored in secondary storage and a hard copy obtained at a future time.

EXAMPLE: *Electronic impulses are used to activate and operate a printer so a printout (hard copy) can be obtained that is readable in our language, not in machine language (bits/bytes).*

4. ***Secondary Storage Devices:*** **Secondary storage** is also called *auxiliary storage.* Data that are to be saved for future processing are stored in a file in secondary storage. According to the application program instructions in RAM (stored program concept), the CPU fetches (retrieves) data from secondary storage when needed for processing. Processed data (information) and applications programs are also saved in secondary storage using unique file names to identify the information or program. Common secondary storage media are magnetic disk, optical disc, DVD disc, USB flash drive, and magnetic tape. Note the difference in spelling between magnetic type disks and optical type discs.

Check Point—Section A

Directions: For each question, circle the correct answer.

A–1. During processing operations, data and software instructions must reside in

A) cache memory
B) random access memory (RAM)
C) read only memory (ROM)
D) secondary storage

A–2. Fetching program instructions, interpreting the instructions, carrying out the operations, and storing results are performed by

A) an arithmetic/logic unit
B) cache memory
C) main memory
D) the control unit

A–3. A 32-bit processor is very common in microcomputers. This is referencing the computer

A) clock speed
B) data code
C) read only memory (ROM)
D) word length

B. Types of Computers

Three categories of computers have emerged for use in business: mainframe computers, mid-range computers, and microcomputers. The supercomputer is used by government agencies and large organizations involved in research-and-development activities. Although the microcomputer is the one most familiar to administrative professionals, it is important to be familiar with the basic characteristics of all types of computers. As business personnel discuss their information needs with information systems professionals, computer options are typically discussed.

1. *Mainframe Computers:* Large organizations and government agencies continue to use the mainframe computer to provide processing services for extensive computing applications that are accessed by thousands of users. With processing speeds greater than 1 trillion instructions per second *(picoseconds)* and primary storage ranging from hundreds of megabytes (one million bytes) to gigabytes (one billion bytes), a **mainframe computer** can support several thousands of online computers throughout the organization. Mainframe computers are also used as superservers for very large client/server networks. Many different types of input, output, and storage devices can be used to interface with a mainframe system.

   Information systems personnel who are trained to interface with a mainframe system are available within a large organization to assist various departments in determining how the computer can best be used for each department's work. Many organizations that moved away from mainframes are moving back because of centralized administration, high reliability and flexibility essential in today's electronic marketplace, and other mission-critical applications. The only traditional mainframe system today is IBM's eServer zSeries. See Chapter 4-C for a discussion on electronic commerce (e-commerce).

   EXAMPLE: *Mainframe applications include:*

   - *Corporate payroll*
   - *Airline reservation systems*
   - *University grade reporting*
   - *e-Commerce with millions of transactions*

2. *Mid-Range Computers:* **Mid-range computers** are less powerful than a mainframe but support computing requirements for small to medium-size organizations as well as e-commerce and networking environments. There are two types of mid-range computers: minicomputers and servers.

   a. *Minicomputer:* A *minicomputer* tends to use the full range of input/output devices available for mainframe computers, but the minicomputer processing capabilities are less than the mainframe computer. These computers support computing needs for small to medium-size organizations. Within larger organizations, a minicomputer can be located to provide on-site processing for users located away from the central computer location. This has led to the concept of distributed processing. A minicomputer may also be used as a front-end processor to a large mainframe system. A *front-end processor* is a special-purpose computer to manage communications traffic between the CPU of the main computer *(host computer)* and peripheral devices in a telecommunications system. These front-end input and output operations include data packet formatting, editing, routing, transmission error control, and speed conversion. Having a front-end processor allows the host computer to concentrate on the main processing of all applications.

EXAMPLE: *The relationship of a front-end processor to the host computer is similar to an administrative professional to an executive. They operate as a team so the executive can concentrate on the strategic operations for the organization.*

b. *Server:* A *server* is a smaller mid-range computer that typically supports computer networks or e-commerce activities. Network servers allow business users to share files, software, and peripheral devices. As hardware for e-commerce, servers deliver Web pages and process purchase and sales transactions. Organizations with heavier e-commerce requirements run their Web and e-commerce applications on multiple servers called server farms. **Server farms** are large groups of servers maintained by the organization or a commercial vendor selling the services to an organization.

EXAMPLE: *Through its mainframe computer, a large university provides computer services to individual departments, faculty, and students throughout the university as long as the user has a terminal and an accurate security clearance to use the computer. Within the College of Business (one of the six colleges in the university), there are specific instructional needs not being addressed through the mainframe computer. The College of Business has installed several separate networks, each with its own server. These networks address specific instructional needs—accounting, sales, information systems, and finance. A separate server is used to maintain the College of Business Web site.*

3. *Microcomputers:* The microprocessor is the main technology of microcomputers. Sometimes the microprocessor is referred to as "the CPU on a chip." A more specific definition of a **microcomputer** is a digital computer that uses a microprocessor, an internal storage chip, an input/output chip, and any additional chips required by the system. Some microcomputers are called *personal computers* or *PCs*. The basic additional components of the microcomputer system include the following:

- Visual display screen; monitor
- Mouse and keyboard
- Modem
- Magnetic disk drives
- CD drives
- Speakers
- Printer (unless networked)
- Microphone (required for voice input)
- Camera (required for teleconferencing)

There are five classifications of microcomputers based on size: workstation, desktop, network computers (NC), notebooks, and personal digital assistants (PDA).

a. *Workstations:* Knowledge workers use workstations to create new information and knowledge. *Workstations* provide high levels of mathematic and graphic capabilities for scientific, engineering, and financial applications. Typically workstations have **reduced instruction set computing (RISC).** RISC enhances the speed of microprocessors by embedding the most frequently used instructions on a chip.

EXAMPLE: *Workstation applications include:*

- *Product design with CAD (computer-aided design)*
- *3-D animation and graphics*

- *Video editing*
- *Investment and portfolio analysis*

b. *Desktop computer:* The *desktop PC* is a powerful microcomputer with graphics, document management, and communications capabilities that can integrate information from diverse perspectives and sources both internal and external to the firm. The desktop PC is the predominant microcomputer in the business environment. A desktop computer system requires primary storage (512 megabytes is typical), a hard disk (secondary storage internal to the system; 20 to 120 gigabytes is typical although storage capacity can be as great as 250 gigabytes), CPU, monitor (screen), keyboard, mouse, speakers, and drive for additional secondary storage (magnetic disk drive and/or CD/DVD disc drive/burner).

These powerful desktop tools are changing the digital office environment. The desktop PC is quite versatile in handling specific business operations in accounting, word processing, statistical analysis, what-if analysis, and other applications. In most companies the desktop PC and application software are used to generate information requested by today's business personnel. The information is designed to better meet the user's needs and can be produced in a relatively short period of time.

c. *Network computer: Network computers (NC)* do not have the full functionality of a desktop PC. NCs are typical in network environments where software, data, and storage are on the network server thus eliminating the need for secondary storage devices at the user's computer. With NCs, user processing power is minimal. The user (referred to as a *thin client*) downloads software and data over the corporate intranet or off the Internet. Because an NC is less complex, it is less expensive to operate and maintain. However, business users resist the lower computing capability and it can be costly to upgrade and maintain servers to meet the business user information needs.

d. *Notebook computer:* Portable computing became popular with the creation of laptop computers. Laptop computers were heavier and bulkier than today's lightweight notebook computer. *Notebook computers* are powerful microcomputers that are small enough to fit into a briefcase. Weighing less than four pounds, a notebook computer offers the same processing power and storage capabilities as a desktop PC and can be used while away from the office. When in the office, the small keyboard and lower monitor resolution of the laptop or notebook computer can be overcome by using a *docking station* to connect the laptop to the desktop keyboard and monitor.

e. *Personal digital assistant (PDA):* As microprocessor chips have gotten smaller and faster, business personnel have come to rely on such mobile devices as handheld computers—the **personal digital assistant (PDA).** PDAs are one of the most popular mobile devices in the handheld category. The touch screen of the PDA and pen-based handwriting recognition allow employees to send and receive e-mail; access the Web; and exchange information such as appointments, sales contracts, to-do lists, and client address books with their desktop PC or Web servers.

Other mobile devices for personal information management include:

- Smart phones: phones with added PDA capabilities
- Pen tablets: used for data gathering
- Pen notebooks: used for data gathering

4. *Supercomputers:* The **supercomputer** is the largest, fastest, most powerful, and most expensive computer. Supercomputers are used by the government agencies such as military and large organizations involved in research-and-development activities that are mathematically intensive, such as those found in the aerospace industry, chemical industries, and weather forecasting.

Check Point—Section B

Directions: For each question, circle the correct answer.

B–1. FORMS, Inc. is a multinational organization with extensive business applications accessed by thousands of users requiring processing speeds in picoseconds. The organization's computer system should be a

A) mainframe system
B) network computer
C) server
D) supercomputer

B–2. A knowledge worker uses a

A) desktop PC
B) notebook computer
C) mid-range computer
D) workstation

B–3. A powerful computer with the versatility of handling word processing, statistical analysis, and what-if analysis is the

A) desktop PC
B) network computer
C) pen notebook
D) personal digital assistant (PDA)

C. Input Devices and Interfaces

Human beings must be able to communicate with the computer; they do this by means of input devices. For processing, the computer needs both program statements and data that are entered into a computer system with an input device. The objective of *source data automation* is to input data with minimal human involvement. Data are gathered and input at the source of the transaction, which speeds up data collection and reduces errors.

To make data input easy, an interface between the user and the computer system is necessary. Being familiar with interface features can be helpful in selecting software and working with information systems professionals when designing custom in-house systems or reengineering purchased systems.

1. *Input Devices for Human Input:* The most common input devices for human input include the keyboard and mouse. The trackball, stylus, and microphone are other input devices used for human input.

a. *Keyboard:* A computer *keyboard* is designed like a typewriter with additional function keys and cursor-control keys. *Function keys* have specialized software instructions coded for the key function; the function is executed when the user depresses the function key. *Cursor-control keys* are arrows for up and down and left and right movement of the cursor; movement is one character or one line at a time.

The keyboard is the most common input device; therefore, proper hand and wrist position is very important. Computer manufacturers have addressed carpel tunnel syndrome, the result of improper hand and wrist position, with ergonomic keyboards to assist users with proper hand placement.

b. *Mouse:* Today, most operating systems software and application software use a **graphical user interface (GUI)** that lets the user point and click or point and drag on icons, buttons, or files on the computer monitor to activate software functions. It is easier to move the cursor to the GUI icon with a pointing device. The *mouse* is the most common pointing device used to move the cursor on the screen (point) and select (click) the option. The **point-and-click device** requires the user to physically move the entire mouse on the mouse pad or desktop, thus moving the cursor on the screen.

c. *Trackball:* Another pointing device for moving the cursor is a trackball. The *trackball* is a round ball that the user rotates to move the cursor. Unlike the mouse, the trackball device itself is not moved. Most portable microcomputers come with a trackball and/or *touchpad* for moving the cursor. A touchpad, also called a *glidepad* or *trackpad,* is a small rectangular touch-sensitive surface usually found at the bottom center of the keyboard. The screen cursor moves in the direction the user's finger moves on the touchpad. Portable microcomputers (notebook and laptop) also have input ports available for plugging in a conventional mouse.

d. *Stylus:* The *stylus* is a rubberized pen device common with handheld mobile computers (PDAs). The stylus allows the user to touch desired menu options or to write on a touch-sensitive screen. The computer responds to the pressure of the stylus. A variation of the stylus is the *digitized tablet and pen* used by engineering and drafting knowledge workers for drawing and creating objects.

e. *Microphone:* Voice-recognition input is improving and is a critical input method for individuals with physical challenges. The *microphone* with a strong clear signal allows people to dictate into the computer. Voice recognition is dependent on appropriate software. A vocabulary database of 30,000 words is typical for general dictation. Technical, legal, and medical voice recognition systems have databases of 300,000 words or more. Since input needs to match the vocabulary database, users must be careful with their diction. Some voice-recognition systems have the user work with the software to "train" it to recognize their voice fingerprints.

2. ***Input Devices for Source Data Automation:*** Source data automation improves the speed and accuracy of data input by capturing the data at the time of the transaction. Common input devices include magnetic recognition, touch-sensitive screens, and optical recognition. Voice-recognition input has become popular for field input and client input calling to the organization's telephone system programmed with voice-recognition software. Pattern recognition (visual) input is now being used for highly structured applications.

a. *Magnetic recognition:* Although *magnetic-ink character recognition (MICR)* has been used by the banking industry since the 1950s, today the use of magnetic recognition has expanded to recognizing stripes on cards and smart cards.

(1) *Magnetic-ink character recognition (MICR):* Used primarily in the banking industry, magnetic-ink characters are formed with magnetized particles of iron oxide on the bottom of the check. Although humans can read the magnetic-ink characters, MICR readers can read between 700 and 1,500 checks per minute; no special data conversion step is needed.

(2) *Magnetic cards:* A credit card or identification badge with a magnetic strip on one side is a *magnetic card* which can be read when swiped through the magnetic reader.

EXAMPLE: *Because humans cannot read the magnetic strips, the strips can contain confidential information. An employee badge can contain an employee identification number and pass code for restricted areas in the organization.*

Smart cards are enhanced with a microprocessor chip embedded in the card. The chip provides significant storage space for digitized data. Smart cards are prevalent in Europe and are gaining acceptance in the United States, particularly in the medical field or for monetary transactions.

EXAMPLE: *Many private health maintenance organizations issue smart health cards that contain the individual's complete health history, emergency data, and insurance policy data.*

b. *Touch-sensitive screen:* A *touch-sensitive screen* allows the person to simply point with his or her finger and touch a specific section (button or square) of the monitor (screen) to activate a particular operation. Sensors in the screen make the computer monitor an interactive input device.

EXAMPLES:

Automatic-teller machines (ATM) allow customers to make bank transactions from remote locations by pointing to the appropriate bank transactions.

Information kiosks to assist clients with product/service information or directions are becoming common in shopping centers, airports, educational campuses, zoos, and other public locations.

c. *Optical recognition:* Optical recognition technology scans the data for input. The three types of scanning systems are optical mark recognition (OMR), the bar code, and optical character recognition (OCR).

(1) *Optical mark recognition (OMR):* The simplest scanning technology is *optical mark recognition (OMR)*, or mark sensing. With OMR, a pencil mark is made in a predetermined grid.

EXAMPLE: *Many business forms today use OMR requiring the user to code the correct response by darkening the space with a pencil. An OMR reader reads the completed document eliminating the need to key in the user's response. OMR is popular in testing environments or for marketing surveys.*

Gender:	❏ *Male*	❏ *Female*
Age:	❏ *21–35*	❏ *36–45*

(2) *Bar code:* Another type of optical recognition is the *bar code* where a laser scanner reads special line codes. Data are represented in a code by the widths of the bars and the distance between the bars.

EXAMPLE: *The most familiar bar code is the universal product code (UPC) on products. Retail establishments have* point-of-sale terminals *that read coded data on merchandise tags.*

(3) *Optical character recognition (OCR):* The third scanning system is *optical character recognition (OCR).* OCR recognizes letters, numbers, and special characters. The major difference between OCR and OMR is that the shape of the character represents the data for OCR, whereas the data for OMR are represented by the position of the mark.

EXAMPLE: *The United States post office relies on both bar codes and OCR to sort and route mail. Laser scanners read and interpret the ZIP Code and POSTNET bar codes to sort millions of pieces of mail to distribution bins.*

d. *Voice input:* Now the human voice can be converted from analog to digital electronic impulses so the computer can process the data. Most voice input applications are highly structured. They are effective in speech-enabled telephone input, quality control, computer-aided design, and laboratory settings. Clear enunciation by the user is important so the input can be matched with the voice-application database. Some software programs can be trained to accept the user's speech patterns and pronunciation.

EXAMPLE: *Voice input can be used for a customer order or request for input using a telephone and for field input by sales personnel, or lab technicians.*

e. *Visual input:* **Pattern recognition systems** *(visual systems)* require a camera to be the computer's eyes. First, a visual database needs to be created. When new data are captured, the image is compared with the digitized visual database. Visual systems are highly structured.

EXAMPLES:

Visual systems are effective for manufacturing inspection processes.

A security system using biometric identification (image of the iris) is a very effective application of visual input.

3. *Interface:* A user **interface** is a combination of hardware and software that makes data input easier. A user interface allows a user to respond to messages presented by the computer, control the computer, and request information from the computer. User interfaces include function keys, screen prompts, menus, and icons.

a. *Function keys:* Located on the keyboard, *function keys* are programmed to carry out specific operations. The software directing the function key simplifies a specific operation for the user.

b. *Screen prompts:* Messages displayed on the screen to help the user while using an application are *screen prompts*.

c. *Menu:* Menus are special screen prompts providing lists of processing options. The user selects from the menu by pressing a number or letter that corresponds to the option desired. A pull-down menu is one displayed across the top of the screen with submenus pulled down from the top as needed.

d. *Icon:* Icons are pictures that represent text. The icons are displayed on the screen to show the program options available to the user.

EXAMPLE: *The graphical user interface (GUI) uses icons and pull-down menus to graphically represent system options. The user points and clicks or points and drags using a mouse, trackball, or touchpad.*

Users should be aware of features that interfaces should include. Being familiar with these features can be helpful in selecting software and in working with information systems personnel when designing custom in-house systems or reengineering purchased systems.

• All system responses should be meaningful to the user. System responses are the messages displayed and the actions the computer takes when a user enters data.

Without system responses, the user does not know if the computer accepted the input or what the computer is doing.

- The simpler the response from the user, the better the interface. Eliminating keystrokes results in faster input and greater accuracy.

- The screen design should be simple, uncluttered, and easily understood. All prompts, menus, and icons within an application should follow a consistent format. Clear screen designs have a significant impact on the usability of the interface.

- When the user makes an error, it should be clear how to correct the error. When an error is made, the user should be notified, the error should be clearly identified, and it should be clear to the user how to correct the error.

Check Point—Section C

Directions: For each question, circle the correct answer.

C–1. With a graphical user interface, a common input device for point-and-click and point-and-drag operations is the
   A) keyboard
   B) mouse
   C) stylus
   D) touch-sensitive screen

C–2. Embedded microprocessor chips allow monetary transactions through the use of
   A) bar codes
   B) magnetic cards

   C) optical recognition
   D) smart cards

C–3. Input data are understood by the central processing unit (CPU) only if it matches the input database. This is a characteristic of
   A) automatic teller machines (ATM)
   B) optical mark recognition (OMR)
   C) point-of-sale terminals (POS)
   D) voice recognition systems

D. Information Output

People must be able to use the output from computerized systems. Output media are the means by which information (processed data) is made available for human use. Output devices are the hardware for producing the information.

1. *Output Media:* Common output media include paper, display, and voice.

   a. *Paper:* A common output medium is paper. Hard copies of documents are created so people can readily use the information. Although the paperless office was predicted for the 20th century, many situations and individuals still require hard-copy output.

   b. *Display:* Another way to make output available for human use is through visual display of the information on a screen. Computer-based information systems have made output to the computer monitor a common means for viewing information. Microform information (microfilm or microfiche) can be displayed on a screen using microform readers. Display of output on a screen is referred to as *soft copy;* the screen image may not be a permanent record of what is shown. To become a permanent record, the soft copy must be saved on a secondary storage device or printed. Many business applications utilize the convenience and cost savings of soft copy through visual display and secondary storage, making hard copy (printed output) optional.

  c. *Voice response:* Voice responses are prevalent in computer business applications. Sometimes the audio response is only a beep; other applications convert digitized data into verbal responses for the user. A common voice response system has mass-produced sound chips embedded in the hardware (e.g., alarm clocks, automobiles, appliances, automatic teller machines). A more advanced voice response system uses speech synthesizers to convert raw data into recognized speech.

   EXAMPLE: *When calling for telephone information, a speech synthesizer converts the stored digital data into an analog response understood by the user. This data becomes useful information for the user.*

 2. ***Output Devices:*** After data are processed by the computer-based information system, output devices make information available to users. Output devices include monitors, printers, plotters, and speakers.

  a. *Monitor:* Soft copy has made the computer **monitor** a common output device in the business office. The monitor has been referred to as a CRT—cathode-ray tube. The CRT uses cathode ray tube technology that shoots beams of electrons to the computer monitor. Liquid crystal display (LCD) technology or plasma technology is used to produce *flat-panel monitors*. It is projected that flat-panel monitors will replace the CRT in the near future. Features of a monitor include viewable size and resolution.

   (1) *Viewable size:* The viewable size of the monitor is the measurement of the actual viewing screen diagonally from corner to corner. Most business personnel select a monitor that is 17 inches or 19 inches; heavy graphic users consider a larger viewable screen (20 + inches). Administrative professionals need to be sure that measurements are for the viewable size and not the actual size of the monitor.

   (2) *Resolution: Resolution* is the number of pixels (dots) that make up the image on the screen and the dot pitch of the monitor.

    (a) *Pixels: Pixel* is short for picture element. The more horizontal and vertical pixels used, the clearer and crisper the image. The passive matrix LCD monitor has a lower resolution than the CRT monitor. The active matrix LCD monitor has a clear, crisp image but is slightly more expensive than the CRT monitor. The plasma monitor has a clear, crisp image with little trailing edge blur (no gray scale), but it is very expensive.

     Pixels come in monochrome (shades of gray) or color. Red, green, and blue are mixed to achieve color; thus, the name *RGB monitor*.

    (b) *Dot pitch: Dot pitch* is the distance between the centers of adjacent pixels. The lower the dot pitch, the greater number of pixels in the display and the higher the resolution.

   (3) *Flat-panel monitors:* Both LCD technology and plasma technology are used for flat-panel monitors. LCD technology uses tiny transistors to reflect light through the liquid crystal to produce high-resolution output. The thinness of the LCD monitor makes it ideal for notebook computers. LCD monitors are also very good for long-term installations. Today many business professionals select the LCD monitor for their desktop PC.

Plasma technology uses tiny light bulbs to ignite the phosphor to produce high-resolution output with little trailing edge blur (no gray scale). Although plasma monitors need to be replaced more often because of the burn-in factor that distorts output quality, plasma technology is often used for large flat-panel monitors (40 inches or larger).

b. *Printers:* Another common output device is the **printer.** The appropriateness of a printer depends on the print quality desired, the production speed, and cost. The output document produced on paper is called *hard copy.* Most printers allow a user to key in text for one document while another document is printing. This process is called *background printing.* Printers are of two types: impact and nonimpact.

(1) *Impact printers: Impact printers* have a printing device that strikes the paper through the ribbon and leaves an impression of the characters. These printers are quite noisy, typically have low-resolution output (print quality), have very limited graphic capability, and are relatively slow. Higher resolution means slower speed. Today, the impact printer is needed when multipart forms, sensitized paper (carbonless paper), or continuous paper (rolls of paper with perforations between forms) are printed. The most common impact printer today is the dot-matrix printer.

(2) *Nonimpact printers:* Several types of *nonimpact printers* are appropriate for information processing output. Because a nonimpact printer does not have a printing device, this printer is quieter and can easily be located anywhere in the office. Images are created on the page through either ink-jet or laser imaging processes.

(a) *Ink-jet printers:* The *ink-jet printer* utilizes a fast-drying electronically charged ink to spray ink droplets through an electronic field to form the character images. These printers are quiet, have high-resolution output for both text and graphics, and are relatively fast (between 4 to 20 pages per minute). The cost of ink-jet printers is relatively low; however, ink cartridges can be costly. Ink-jet printers can print up to four colors of ink at one time on cut-sheet paper. The printer features along with cost make the ink-jet printer popular in office environments.

(b) *Laser printers:* The *laser printer* utilizes an intense low-power light beam capable of simultaneously carrying millions of characters. These printers are also quiet, have very high-resolution output for both text and graphics, and are very fast (desktop laser printers print between 4 to 32 pages per minute and floor model laser printers print between 36 to 300 pages per minute). Laser printers are also referred to as page printers since an entire page of information can be printed at one time. The laser beam merges with a process that uses light to shape character images; toner is used to transfer the image to paper. Laser printers can *duplex* (print on both sides of the paper) and can be used with a variety of cut-sheet paper sizes and styles. The printer features make them desirable output hardware for the office environment; the cost of color laser printers continues to decrease, which makes the desktop model very desirable for individual offices.

c. *Plotter:* A *plotter* is needed for large drawings (e.g., blueprints, maps, architectural drawings). Drum plotters and table plotters move the paper past a stylus (pen) bi-directionally. While the paper moves up and down, the pen moves left and right allowing diagonal as well as vertical and horizontal output.

Large-format ink-jet plotters use ink-jet technology to print on roll-feed paper up to 4 feet wide and 50 feet long. Plotters are used in engineering, drafting, graphic arts, and designing of styled products (e.g., automobiles and dresses).

d. *Speakers:* Any equipment with a voice-response system needs a speaker. Speakers range from tiny devices almost hidden to a dual set of high-quality speakers used for messages as well as music output. For the desktop PC, speakers are an added peripheral; laptop and notebook computers have speakers built into the system.

Check Point—Section D

Directions: For each question, circle the correct answer.

D–1. As the executive assistant for the marketing department, Benson uses her desktop PC to generate and save in secondary storage sales reports showing daily sales by district. These reports include multicolored graphs and are accessed by the marketing manager through the organization's network. Benson's output device should be a/an

A) monitor
B) impact printer
C) microfiche
D) table plotter

D–2. Common monitors on notebook computers use the standard matrix liquid crystal display technology in order to have a

A) color monitor
B) flat-panel monitor
C) high-resolution monitor
D) 17-inch monitor

D–3. The Director of Finance asked her administrative assistant to recommend a very fast, high-resolution printer capable of printing graphics. The administrative assistant should recommend a/an

A) dot-matrix printer
B) ink-jet plotter
C) page printer
D) table plotter

E. Long-Term Storage for the Computer-Based Information System

As organizations become more digital, long-term storage has become a strategic technology. Long-term storage of data and information from the computer-based information system must be in a secure area and readily available. Using the stored program concept, primary storage (RAM) is necessary for processing data. Secondary storage, however, is very important for the long-term storage of the organization's data and information. Because secondary storage is accomplished through the use of peripheral (add-on) storage devices, it is also referred to as *auxiliary storage.* Secondary storage includes magnetic disk and tape, optical disc, and storage area networks. Note the spelling of magnetic disk versus optical disc. In addition to storage types, office professionals should be aware of the secondary storage features: channel, type of access, transfer rate, access time, and secondary storage capacity.

1. ***Characteristics of Secondary Storage:*** Secondary storage units must be attached (online) to the CPU through channels in order for data to be transmitted from the secondary storage device into primary storage. In addition to channels, the type of access, the transfer rate, the access time, and the capacity of the secondary storage device are very important characteristics of secondary storage devices.

a. *Channel:* A **channel** is the necessary communication link that controls the flow of data between the primary storage in the processor unit and the storage device. Data from secondary storage internal to the computer system (hard disk) flow into and out of the processor unit on a *data bus*. Data from secondary storage external to the computer system flow into and out of the computer system through communication lines connected to a port. A **port** is the connection point on the computer where the peripheral communication line is connected.

b. *Type of access:* Files may be accessed sequentially or by direct access.

    (1) *Sequential access: Sequential access* is a method of retrieving records from a file where each record is read, one after another in sequence, beginning with the first record. Magnetic tape can be accessed only sequentially. Batch processing processes data sequentially.

    (2) *Direct access: Direct access* relates to the ability to go directly to the record needed without having to read previous records in the same file. Magnetic disks and optical discs access data both sequentially and directly. When data are processed in real time (with immediate results), direct access is required and the storage device needs to be online.

c. *Transfer rate:* The speed with which data can be transferred from secondary storage to main memory or from main memory to secondary storage is the *transfer rate*. The transfer rate is usually measured in bytes per second (Bps).

d. *Access time:* When processing data with direct access, a major concern is the amount of time required to locate the data needed from the particular storage location in secondary storage and transfer the data to internal storage. *Access time* is the measurement of the time required to find the data location and the time required to transfer the data. Access times range widely. The range of access times is measured in milliseconds (thousandths of a second).

e. *Storage capacity:* The capacity of a secondary storage device is usually stated in terms of number of bytes stored. The modular design of storage devices today allows for a large range of capacity for secondary storage, even on microcomputer systems. Storage capacity is measured in bytes:

- Kilobytes (KB):   1 thousand bytes
- Megabytes (MB):   1 million bytes
- Gigabyes (GB):   1 billion bytes
- Terabytes (TB):   1 trillion bytes
- Petabyte (PB):   1 quadrillion bytes

2. ***Secondary Storage:*** Although the data and software (system and application) needs to be in the processor unit primary storage (RAM) during processing, primary storage is only temporary and would be costly for long-term storage. *Secondary storage* is nonvolatile and thus important in the computer-based information system for long-term storage. The data are not lost when the power is turned off because the bits of data are stored as magnetic spots on magnetic disks and tape or laser microscopic pits on optical discs. Secondary storage is auxiliary to primary storage and is outside the processor unit. Material stored includes raw data, system programs, application programs, and information for future use.

The most common media used for secondary storage are magnetic disk, magnetic tape, and optical disc. In the microcomputer environment, the magnetic disk and optical disc are the most common types of storage. In the mainframe environment, RAID (redundant array of independent disks) is replacing the disk pack. Digital organizations need to address e-commerce needs with new storage technologies such as storage area networks.

a. *Hard disk:* A **hard disk** is sometimes referred to as a fixed disk as it is a nonremovable magnetic disk typical within microcomputers, but outside the processor unit. Hard disks may use one or more magnetic disks for secondary storage. Hard disk storage capacity ranges between 20 GB to 250 GB. An administrative professional involved with digital video may want to consider a 250 GB hard disk.

b. *Magnetic disk:* **Magnetic disks** are a common secondary storage peripheral for microcomputers. The disk is removable from the disk drive, and the data can be transported with the user to other computing environments. A disk is 3 1/2-inch, double-sided storage, with high-density storage technology. The amount of information that can be stored on a disk varies with disk density and quality. The storage capacity of a disk ranges from 320 kilobytes (320 K) (320,000 bytes) to approximately 2.8 megabytes (MB) (2,800,000 bytes) for extra-high-density disks. Although the 3 1/2-inch disk has a hard jacket, care should be taken to protect disks so the disk is not damaged. Once a disk has a bad sector (section), it cannot be used again.

A **USB flash drive** *(flash memory)* has replaced Zip disks and Jaz cartridges. *USB* is an external *u*niversal *s*erial *b*us standard that supports data transfer rates of 12 Mbps (million bits per second). A USB flash drive is an external, portable storage drive that can be carried in a pocket. The flash drive plugs into a USB port on the microcomputer; it is a convenient, easy means for mobile data storage. The removable drive holds 250 MB of data—equivalent to 210 3 1/2-inch disks.

c. *Optical discs:* **Optical disc** technology uses a laser beam of light to store and read data instead of magnetic processes. Laser technology burns microscopic pits onto optical disc tracks as the data are stored. The shelf life of an optical disc is 30 years. Compact discs (CD) use optical disc technology and include compact disc random access memory (CD-ROM), compact disc recordable (CD-R), compact disc rewritable (CD-RW), and digital video discs (DVD). Compact disc storage capacity exceeds magnetic disks; however, transfer rates and access time are slower.

(1) *CD-ROM:* Data saved on a *compact disc read only memory (CD-ROM)* can only be read; it cannot be changed. The storage capacity of a CD-ROM is approximately 650 megabytes (equivalent to over 400 1.44 megabyte magnetic disks), making this type of disc desirable for large quantities of mass-produced data.

EXAMPLES — CD-ROM Data: *Mass-produced directories, catalogs, instruction manuals, encyclopedias, and data bases of financial and economic activity.*

(2) *CD-R:* CD burners now provide individuals with the means to record on compact discs. The *compact disc recordable (CD-R)* allows business users to store (write once) data and information according to the user's needs; storage capacity is equivalent to the CD-ROM disc. Like CD-ROM discs, data saved on a CD-R can only be read; it cannot be changed. At one time this technology was referred to as WORM (write once—read many).

(3) *CD-RW:* CD rewritable (CD-RW) discs now allow users to store, access, and reuse discs in the same way as magnetic disks. CD-RW technology uses laser technology to store the data and magnetic principles to rewrite to the disc (magneto-optical discs). The storage capacity of CD-RW disks is approxi-

mately 2 gigabytes and can be written to nearly a million times without a decline in accuracy.

(4) *DVD:* A *digital video disc (DVD)* provides high resolution, true color, and no flicker output. The DVD is excellent for graphics, sound, and multimedia with upward of 17 GB of storage capacity. Like the CD, there is DVD-ROM, DVD-R, and DVD-RW (DVD-RW is also referred to as DVD-RAM). DVD players are backward compatible; the player can read all types of compact discs (CDs). Some companies refer to DVDs as digital versatile discs. Because of the DVD storage capacity and access speed (nine times faster than a CD because DVD data are more densely packed), organizations are using the DVD-RW for backup and archival storage of large databases and multimedia files.

d. *RAID:* Disk arrays of interconnected microcomputer hard disk drives are replacing the mainframe disk pack for secondary storage. **RAID (redundant arrays of independent disks)** combine 10 to more than 100 small hard disk drives into a single unit. The RAID unit provides large storage capacities and high access speeds; data can be accessed in parallel (at the same time) over multiple channels from many disks. A specialized microcontroller coordinates the hard drives' microprocessors so it appears as a single logical drive to the computer system. RAID units provide a fault-tolerant environment since the redundant design offers multiple copies of data on several disks.

e. *Magnetic tapes:* The first form of secondary storage to be widely used was magnetic tape; magnetic tape cartridges replaced tape reels. *Tape* cartridges provide only sequential access, have a storage capacity over 200 MB, have a transfer rate of 50,000 to 400,000 bytes per second, and are nonvolatile. R-DAT tape technology can store more than 14 GB on a single 90-meter tape. The tape drive reads either one data record or a group of data records at a time. When records are grouped (blocked), the start/stop tape drives stop at the gaps between the blocks. Because of speed, storage capability, and cost, tape continues to be a popular backup medium. For batch processing (sequential access), however, direct-access devices (disks) that provide both sequential and direct access to the data are replacing magnetic tapes.

f. *Storage area network (SAN):* With multimedia, Web activities, and e-commerce escalating in organizations, the amount of data to be stored increases by 100 percent a year! **Storage area networks (SAN)** provide one solution for companies that share information across applications and computing platforms. A *SAN* is a high-speed fiber channel local area network dedicated to storage that interconnects different storage devices (e.g., database servers, RAID, and tape libraries). Although a SAN is expensive and can be difficult to manage, this enterprise-wide infrastructure for data storage provides rapid sharing and access to the organization's stored data. All authorized users can access data from any server in the organization.

Data storage is strategic to the networked operations of an organization. Some organizations elect to seek professional services to assist with storage assessment, design, management, and operations. A **storage service provider (SSP)** offers these services along with online data storage and backup either on-site or off-site. Although SSP services are available 24/7, there is an associated security risk with moving an organization's data off-site. Security and troubleshooting are important issues that administrative professionals need to be able to discuss within their division as well as with information systems personnel. Security and troubleshooting are covered in Chapter 5.

Check Point—Section E

Directions: For each question, circle the correct answer.

E–1. For long-term storage, a computer-based information system must have

A) cache memory
B) random access memory (RAM)
C) read only memory (ROM)
D) secondary storage

E–2. The payroll at Emerson-Fields is batch processed twice a month. The access method for this type of processing must be

A) direct
B) online
C) random
D) sequential

E–3. Laser technology uses a beam of light to burn microscopic pits onto

A) hard disks
B) magnetic disks
C) optical discs
D) redundant arrays of independent disks (RAID)

For Your Review

Directions: For each question, circle the correct answer.

1. The number one digit (1) for on or a number zero digit (0) for off represents the two-state condition called a/an

    A) analog computer
    B) bit
    C) byte
    D) liquid crystal display (LCD) monitor

2. The main memory of the computer where data and program instructions are transferred to and from input devices is called

    A) auxiliary storage
    B) cache memory
    C) primary storage
    D) read only memory (ROM)

3. Raw data in main memory is manipulated and changed by the

    A) central processing unit (CPU)
    B) front-end processor
    C) network computer (NC)
    D) smart card

4. Critical system instructions for starting the computer are permanently stored by the computer manufacturer in

    A) cache memory
    B) magnetic core memory
    C) random access memory (RAM)
    D) read only memory (ROM)

5. Today computers require program instructions, raw data, and processed data to be main memory during the processing cycle. This is called

    A) fetching

    B) multiprogramming
    C) stored program concept
    D) time-sharing

6. Selecting program instructions in sequence, decoding the instruction, and directing the activities for completing instructions are under the direction of the

    A) control unit
    B) host computer
    C) management information system (MIS)
    D) stored program concept

7. Processing comparisons for greater than, less than, equal to, and not equal to are performed by the

    A) arithmetic/logic unit
    B) control unit
    C) firmware circuitry
    D) system software instructions

8. A computer-based information system with more than one microprocessor enables the computer to operate in the

    A) interactive mode
    B) multiprocessing mode
    C) multiprogramming mode
    D) multitasking mode

9. A microprocessor clock speed can run at one billion cycles per second. This clock speed is one

    A) gigahertz (GHz)
    B) megahertz (MHz)
    C) petabyte (PB)
    D) terabyte (TB)

10. The number of bits the central processing unit (CPU) can process at one time is determined by the
    A) access time
    B) bus width
    C) clock speed
    D) word length

11. Farrell needs to use a spreadsheet program to create a new accounting application. To begin her task, Farrell needs to locate and open the spreadsheet program. She will find the program in
    A) cache memory
    B) primary storage
    C) programmable read only memory (PROM)
    D) secondary storage

12. As a systems programmer, Muchow is very excited about her new position where the organization's computer-based information system has processing speeds greater than one trillion instructions per second and supports several thousand online end users. This type of computer-based information system fits the
    A) mainframe computer category
    B) minicomputer category
    C) network computer category
    D) server category

13. A mid-range computer that allows business users to share files, software, and peripheral devices is a
    A) front-end processor
    B) host computer
    C) server
    D) workstation

14. A microcomputer that provides high levels of mathematical and graphic capabilities for scientific, engineering, and financial applications typically has reduced instruction set computing (RISC). RISC
    A) complements random access memory (RAM) by storing blocks of program instructions and data for quick access during processing

    B) enhances computing speed by embedding the most frequently used instructions on a chip
    C) manages communications traffic for the CPU
    D) performs mathematical computations and logical comparisons

15. Oksnevad needs a new microcomputer for his office with a 19-inch screen and an ergonomically designed keyboard and mouse. His responsibilities include Internet communications, word processing, data management, statistical analysis, and developing electronic slide presentations. Oksnevad should get a
    A) desktop PC
    B) network computer (NC)
    C) notebook computer
    D) workstation

16. Field technicians at Hammond International are away from the office 70 percent of the time. Their computing needs include e-mail and Web access, checking appointments and to-do lists, and accessing client information. The best computer for the field technicians while away from the office is a
    A) network computer (NC)
    B) notebook computer
    C) personal digital assistant (PDA)
    D) server

17. For point-and-click operations, notebook computers use a device that rotates to move the cursor. This device is a
    A) glidepad
    B) mouse
    C) touchpad
    D) trackball

18. Many organizations now use employee identification badges that can be read by machines to provide access to restricted areas. These organizations are using
    A) docking stations
    B) magnetic cards
    C) magnetic-ink character recognition (MICR)
    D) smart cards

19. As a new MBA student, Kling used the campus information kiosk to locate her classroom. By pointing with her finger on specific buttons, she was able to maneuver through the kiosk. The information kiosk input device was a

A) function key
B) stylus
C) touch-sensitive screen
D) touchpad

20. When the user makes an input error, the interface should

A) display a different input format and have the user re-enter the data
B) display a system response on the monitor that identifies the error and how to correct the error
C) return to the input screen so the user can re-enter the data
D) return to the beginning of the input operation

21. Organizations that try to achieve the paperless office need to be sure administrative professionals have a/an

A) 17- to 19-inch monitor with high resolution
B) docking station
C) plasma monitor
D) plotter

22. High-resolution monitors have a

A) high number of pixels and high number dot pitch

B) high number of pixels and low number dot pitch
C) low number of pixels and high number dot pitch
D) low number of pixels and low number dot pitch

23. The connection point on the computer where the peripheral communication line is connected is the

A) channel
B) data bus
C) interface
D) port

24. M&A Technologies mass-produce instruction manuals that are shipped with every piece of equipment. What is the best storage media for this application?

A) Compact disc read only memory (CD-ROM)
B) Compact disc recordable (CD-R)
C) Compact disc rewritable (CD-RW)
D) Digital video disc (DVD)

25. Data and information sharing is escalating in today's digital organization. One solution for rapid sharing and access to the data on any of the organization's servers is a

A) storage area network (SAN)
B) storage service provider (SSP)
C) USB flash drive
D) wide area network (WAN)

Solutions

Solutions to Check Point—Section A

Answer	Refer to:
A–1. (B)	[A-2-a (2)]
A–2. (D)	[A-2-b]
A–3. (D)	[A-2-d (2)]

Solutions to Check Point—Section B

Answer	Refer to:
B–1. (A)	[B-1]
B–2. (D)	[B-3-a]
B–3. (A)	[B-3-b]

Solutions to Check Point—Section C

Answer	Refer to:
C–1. (B)	[C-1-b]
C–2. (D)	[C-2-a (2)]
C–3. (D)	[C-2-d]

Solutions to Check Point—Section D

Answer	*Refer to:*
D–1. (A)	[D-1-b and D-2-a]
D–2. (B)	[D-2-a]
D–3. (C)	[D-2-b (2) (b)]

Solutions to Check Point—Section E

Answer	*Refer to:*
E–1. (D)	[E and E-2]
E–2. (D)	[E-1-b (1)]
E–3. (C)	[E-2-c]

Solutions to For Your Review

Answer	*Refer to:*
1. (B)	[A]
2. (C)	[A-2 and A-2-a (2)]
3. (A)	[A-2]
4. (D)	[A-2-a (1)]
5. (C)	[A-2-b and Chapter 1 D-2-d]
6. (A)	[A-2-b]
7. (A)	[A-2-c]
8. (B)	[A-2-d and Chapter 1 B-3-c]
9. (A)	[A-2-d (1)]
10. (D)	[A-2-d (2)]
11. (D)	[A-4]
12. (A)	[B-1]
13. (C)	[B-2-b]
14. (B)	[B-3-a]

15.   (A)   [B-3-b]

16.   (C)   [B-3-e]

17.   (D)   [C-1-c]

18.   (B)   [C-2-a (2)]

19.   (C)   [C-2-b]

20.   (B)   [C-3]

21.   (A)   [D-1-b, D-2-a (1), and D-2-a (2)]

22.   (B)   [D-2-a (2) (a) and D-2-a (2) (b)]

23.   (D)   [E-1-a]

24.   (A)   [E-2-c (1)]

25.   (A)   [E-2-f]

Chapter 3

Telecommunications and Network Technologies

OVERVIEW

In today's dynamic business environment, greater emphasis has been placed on communications processes and the roles that telecommunications technologies play in enhancing office productivity. Communications is the exchange of internal and external messages (both written and verbal) that forms the basis for all office interaction. **Telecommunications** is the exchange of voice, data, text, graphics, or audio and video information over computer-based networks.

Telecommunications technologies affecting internal (interoffice) communication and external (intraoffice) communication includes the integration of telephone services, the computer, and networks to provide verbal and data communications to expedite business operations. Today's competitive business environment would be greatly diminished without telecommunications and computer network enhancements to the communication process.

KEY TERMS

Audio conference, 58
Bridge, 53
Camera phone, 58
Central exchange system
    (CENTREX), 61
Centralized computing, 64
Client/server computing, 64
Collaborative computing, 65
Computerized branch
    exchange (CBX), 61

Digital subscriber line
    (DSL), 54
Digitizing, 64
Enterprise network, 66
Foreign exchange, 59
Front-end processor, 53
Gateway, 53
Global network, 66
International direct-distance
    dialing (IDDD), 59

Inward wide area telephone
    service (INWATS), 59
Local area network
    (LAN), 65
Metropolitan area network
    (MAN), 66
Modem, 52
Multiplexer, 53
Network interface card
    (NIC), 53

A. Telecommunications Components and Functions

Today computer-based information systems require networks and telecommunications technologies. Communication between computing technologies has become as important as the computer itself; some speak of a network like it is the computer. With the deregulation of communication services and improvements in telecommunications hardware and software components, fast, global communication is now available to businesses.

1. ***Telecommunications Industry:*** In 1984 the United States telecommunications industry was deregulated when the Justice Department allowed competition in the selling of telecommunications services and equipment. In 1996 the Telecommunications Deregulation and Reform Act widened deregulation by freeing telephone companies, broadcasters, and cable companies to enter each other's markets. Other countries are starting to change their government-regulated telecommunications services to an open, competitive market. This new market has greatly enhanced the services and equipment for telecommunications.

2. ***Telecommunications Software and Hardware:*** A telecommunications system is a collection of software and hardware for transmitting information between diverse locations. Telecommunications software controls the entire transmission process including the following:

   - Establishing an interface between sender and receiver
   - Routing messages along the most efficient path
   - Ensuring that the right message is sent to the correct receiver
   - Performing editorial data checks for transmission errors
   - Converting message speeds and formats

   Basic telecommunications hardware that supports the data transmission and reception functions includes several types of processors and a network interface card (NIC).

   a. *Processors: Telecommunications processors* are devices necessary for the communications function. Administrative professionals should have an understanding of five of the telecommunications processors: modem, front-end processor, multiplexer, bridge, and gateway.

      (1) *Modem:* The United States telephone system (POTS for Plain Old Telephone Service) is an analog network designed for voice signals. The transmission of digital data over telephone lines is accomplished through a **modem,** a device that converts digital data codes into analog signals and vice versa. Figure 3–1 illustrates this concept.

      Two modems are always required for computers to communicate over telephone lines, one at the sending location and one at the receiving location. The modem at the sending location *MO*dulates the digital data (discrete binary bits) into a continuous stream (analog/voice pitch). When the data reaches the receiving location, it must be *DEM*odulated into discrete binary bits by the receiving location modem for the computer system.

FIGURE 3–1 Communications Links

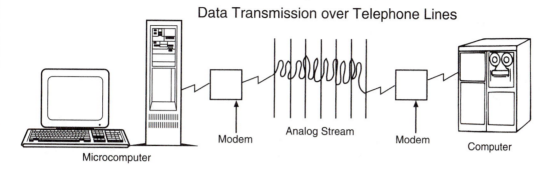

Data Transmission over Telephone Lines

(2) *Front-end processor:* Most organizations' mid-range and mainframe computers communicate with many computers at the same time. Routine telecommunications tasks (getting the message ready for transmission, editing for transmission errors, routing messages) degrade the performance of the firm's main computer system. A **front-end processor** is a small, specialized computer that communicates with the main computer system and manages all the routine telecommunications tasks.

(3) *Multiplexer:* A **multiplexer** allows one communication channel to carry data from multiple sources at the same time. Communication costs are less when multiple users share one high-speed communication channel to send and receive data between computer systems. Like a modem, a multiplexer is needed at both the receiving and sending locations.

(4) *Bridge:* A **bridge** is a communication processor that provides a connection between two similar networks.

(5) *Gateway:* A **gateway** is a communication processor needed to connect two dissimilar networks; the gateway translates the differences between the two systems so the computers can communicate with one another.

b. *Network interface card (NIC):* A **network interface card (NIC)** is an expansion card that connects the microcomputer to a network enabling the exchange of data between computers. The cables or wireless transceivers of the microcomputer must be connected to a NIC card.

3. *Telecommunications Channels:* Analog transmission signals (voice transmission) or digital transmission signals (data transmission) travel through a wide variety of channels. The three types of line channels are twisted wire, coaxial cable, and fiber optics. Wireless transmission includes microwave, satellite, and radio technologies.

Figure 3–2 provides a summary of tethered and wireless telecommunications channels.

a. *Line channels:* The three line channels are **tethered lines** that are continuous; the line needs to be strung and maintained for reliable data transmission.

(1) *Twisted wire:* The conventional telephone line (plain old telephone service [POTS]) consisting of insulated copper wires twisted into pairs was designed for analog (voice) communication. Using a modem, digital data can be sent on the POTS line. Although *twisted wire* is relatively slow and can have transmission interference (data distortion from other electrical sources and wire tapping), it is widely used in networks throughout the world.

FIGURE 3–2 Summary of Telecommunications Channels

Channel	Advantage	Disadvantage
Twisted Wire	• Inexpensive • Easy to install	• Slow; low bandwidth • Subject to data transmission interference/errors • Low security; very easy to tap
Coaxial Cable	<u>Compared to twisted wire:</u> • Higher bandwidth • Less susceptible to interference	• Somewhat difficult to install; inflexible • Medium security; easy to tap
Fiber Optic Cable	• Very high bandwidth • High transmission accuracy • Very good security; difficult to tap	• Difficult to install
Microwave	• High bandwidth • Lower cost than tethered cable	• Need unobstructed line of transmission • Susceptible to interference from environment
Satellite	• High bandwidth • Serves large area	• Need unobstructed line of transmission • Encryption required for security • Transmission time-delay
Wireless Networks	• Easy to install	• Short-distance transmission • Transmission interference • Low security; very easy to tap
Cellular Radio and Mobile Computing	• Convenience	• Service range • Medium security; easy to tap

Telephone service providers also offer a **digital subscriber line (DSL)** that provides high-capacity digital transmission over existing twisted copper lines from the office or home to the telephone switching station. DSL, however, is not used between telephone switching stations.

Some long-distance telephone connections link business telephones in two locations. Companies pay a fixed monthly charge for the use of a leased line. These private lines are also called **tie lines.**

(a) *T-1 line:* A *T-1 line* is a dedicated line that consists of 24 individual channels, each supporting 64K bits per second (bps). Each 64K bit channel can be configured to carry analog (voice) or digital (data) traffic. Businesses and Internet service providers (ISPs) lease or purchase T-1 lines from telephone companies for dedicated communication service and for connecting to the Internet. T-1 lines are sometimes referred to as DS1 lines (*dedicated service lines*).

(b) *T-3 line:* A *T-3 line* is a *dedicated service line* that consists of 672 individual channels, each supporting 64K bits per second (bps) and configured to carry voice or data traffic. T-3 lines are mainly used by ISPs connecting to the Internet backbone. The Internet backbone consists of T-3 connections. T-3 lines are sometimes referred to as DS3 lines.

(2) *Coaxial cable: Coaxial cable* is a thickly insulated copper wire for fast data transmission; the insulation minimizes electrical interference and wire tapping. Coaxial cable offers both baseband and broadband.

(a) *Baseband: Baseband cable* is for analog transmission, and each wire carries only one signal at a time.

(b) *Broadband: Broadband cable* is for digital transmission. Each wire can carry multiple signals at the same time (simultaneously). Broadband cable is used for cable television as well as computer data channels.

Coaxial cable is somewhat inflexible and much more expensive than twisted wire. The speed and reliability of broadband coaxial cable, however, makes it a popular channel for important links in a computer network.

(3) *Fiber optic cable: Fiber optic cable* consists of thousands of fine glass fibers used to transmit light beams (laser technology) that are faster and more durable than copper wire media. Fiber optic cable transmission rates are approximately 640 times greater than coaxial cable and 32,000 times greater than twisted wire. Also, fiber optic cable has a low data transmission error rate (interference) and provides greater security from tapping.

EXAMPLE: *The office network uses both coaxial cable and twisted wire for connecting desktop PCs to the firm's network backbone. Coaxial cable is used on desktop PCs that require fast data transmission. For security as well as greater transmission rates, fiber optic cable is used for the firm's network backbone (the major network channel that handles all the data transmission traffic).*

b. *Wireless channels:* **Wireless channels** rely on low-power radio frequencies or infrared technologies to transmit digital communications between communication devices. Wireless channels include terrestrial microwave, celestial satellites, wireless networks, Bluetooth, and cellular (telephones and mobile devices). Each technology utilizes specific frequency ranges specified by national regulatory agencies to minimize interference and ensure efficient telecommunications.

(1) *Microwave:* Terrestrial *microwave* is an earthbound system that transmits high-speed radio signals between microwave transmission stations. The transmission is point to point in a straight line from one point to the next. Transmission stations are microwave antennas on the top of towers, high buildings, or mountain peaks. Microwave signals cannot bend to the earth's curvature; therefore, the transmission stations need to be spaced approximately 30 miles apart. The broad bandwidth of the microwave channel makes it popular for high-volume data transmission for metropolitan area networks (MAN) and long-distance transmission.

(2) *Satellite:* Celestial *satellite* communication systems are placed in orbit to accept (uplink) and retransmit (downlink) transmission signals from earth microwave transmission stations. Because the satellite rotates with the earth, the earth transmission station remains fixed on the satellite. Although satellite transmission is not suitable for interactive or real-time processing because of transmission time-delays, satellite communication is cost effective for very large quantities of data over very long distances where cable media or terrestrial microwave are difficult to install or not cost effective.

(3) *Wireless local-area networks:* Wiring an office or building for a local area network (LAN) is often costly, and in older buildings it is often difficult to pull the wires or cables. One solution for short-distance connections is installing a wireless LAN using either a low-frequency radio technology or an infrared technology. *Infrared technology* uses infrared light beams to establish the communication links among computers in the network and between computers and network peripherals. Although easy to install, wireless networks are susceptible to transmission interference and tapping by anyone with similar equipment and the same transmission frequency.

Many notebooks have infrared ports for the communication link between the notebook and peripherals eliminating the cable connection.

(4) *Bluetooth:* Using radio technology, *Bluetooth* can transmit data around corners and through objects; it is not a line-of-sight channel like all other wireless technologies. Security, transmission speed, and costs are disadvantages of Bluetooth channels.

(5) *Cellular:* *Cellular* devices are equipped with radio technology for the transmission of voice and data. The Federal Communications Commission established geographic cellular service areas throughout the United States; these service areas fit together like a web to form the backbone of the cellular radio system. *Cellular telephones* are used to transmit voice and data. Although many cellular telephones are analog, digital cellular telephones are becoming more prevalent, particularly in metropolitan areas. Digital transmission means greater bandwidth, greater clarity, less susceptibility to interference, and fewer data transmission errors.

Internet-enabled cellular telephones are also very popular. A special network adapter card can enhance notebooks and personal digital assistants (PDAs) with wireless mobility. Users have access to the Internet as long as the user is in their service area. Although convenient, tapping by anyone with similar equipment and the same transmission frequency is very easy.

Check Point—Section A

Directions: For each question, circle the correct answer.

A–1. A special communications processor for connecting dissimilar networks is a

A) bridge

B) gateway

C) multiplexer

D) network interface card (NIC)

A–2. Smyth & Brothers are installing a new local area network. Fast transmission rates and security are important concerns for the network backbone. The best channel for the network backbone is

A) Bluetooth
B) coaxial cable
C) fiber optic cable
D) twisted wire

A–3. A radio technology established by the Federal Communications Commission that fits together like a web for voice and data transmission is

A) broadband cable
B) celestial satellite
C) cellular system
D) digital subscriber line (DSL)

B. Telephone Communications

Since its invention, the telephone has played an important role in American life and in American business. In recent years, the computer has greatly influenced the types of telephone services available to the customer, switching systems for telephone equipment, and features available on telephone equipment.

1. *Telephone Services:* Both basic and special telephone services are available.

   a. *Basic services:* Business organizations pay a flat rate for telephone service plus a charge for telephone extensions in use throughout the organization. In addition, charges for long-distance calls result from calls made to locations outside the local area. In metropolitan areas, calls between distant points within the local area may be measured in message units. Charges for these calls will depend on how many message units were used.

      (1) *Local call:* A *local call* is one that is placed within a local calling area.

      (2) *Direct-distance dialing (DDD):* *Direct-distance dialing* is a procedure used to place a long-distance call to another telephone number without the intervention of an operator. A long-distance access (1), plus an area code, plus the number of the party with whom you wish to speak needs to be dialed.

      (3) *Person-to-person call:* An operator-assisted call charged to the caller is a *person-to-person call.* The charge is made only if the person being called is able to come to the phone.

      (4) *Collect call:* An operator-assisted call that will be paid by the person or company receiving the call is known as a *collect call.*

      (5) *Card call:* A long-distance call that allows the caller to charge the service to a specific account is either a *credit card call* or a *calling card call.* The card company assigns personal identification numbers (PINs) so the account can be verified before the card call is completed. Credit card calls charge the account and bill the customer at the end of the charge period. Calling card calls are prepaid; the minutes used are deducted from the calling card account balance.

      (6) *Message unit calls:* Calls between widely separated locations within the same metropolitan area are measured in *message units,* a standard base rate used to determine the cost of the call.

   b. *Special services:* Many businesses are finding the special services provided by telephone companies especially helpful in conducting their business both nationally and internationally. Directory assistance, conference calls, emergency calls, text telephones, cellular calls, marine calls, international calls, wide area telephone service (WATS), and foreign exchange are some of the special types of telephone services available to business today.

(1) *Directory assistance:* When administrative professionals need *directory assistance* in locating local or national telephone numbers, either 411 or 555-1212 can be dialed from the telephone or the Internet can be utilized. The Internet has both Yellow Pages and White Pages for locating information. There may be a telephone charge for directory assistance service calls (411 and 555-1212). For toll-free number directory assistance, the administrative professional would dial the long-distance access (1), plus the toll-free area code (800, 855, 866, 877, or 888), plus 555-1212.

(2) *Audio conference:* A telephone call for three or more people to talk with one another is called an **audio conference.** The *conference call* was the first form of audio conference. Three-way calling features allow the caller to set up the audio conference call by pressing and releasing the telephone switchhook.

An *audio conference* for a larger group requires assistance to make all the conference connections. Each participant is provided a log-on code and time for calling the toll-free conference telephone number. With private, high-quality audio communications circuits between conference sites, the audio conference is electronically established and monitored by the business providing the conference call services.

(3) *Emergency 911 calls:* In addition to providing emergency service when individuals call 911, enhanced features allow 911 operators to pinpoint the location of the call without the caller providing this information to the operator.

(4) *Text telephones:* Individuals with disabilities (deaf, hard-of-hearing, or speech impaired) can obtain **text telephones (TT)** designed to accommodate the disability. Organizations that have employees with disabilities need to contact the state telecommunications service to obtain specific information on services available. Often these services are provided free of charge.

(5) *Cellular call: Cellular telephones,* commonly called cell phones, enable callers to make or receive calls anytime/anywhere. Cell phones have made business operations and society more mobile. As a mobile communication device, cell phone batteries need to be recharged by plugging the telephone charger into an electrical outlet or the electrical system of a vehicle. Using the cell phone should not interfere with the privacy of others.

(6) *Camera phone:* **Camera phones** are cell phones enhanced to capture photographic images. The pictures can be immediately sent to other camera phone users along with a message, downloaded to computers, and posted on the Internet. Camera phones are very popular in Asia and Europe. Although fairly new in the United States, privacy, propriety, and industrial espionage issues are already being discussed with regards to the use of camera phones. Effective use of camera phones includes instant communication enhanced with photographs between consultants and suppliers, field representatives and the home office, construction workers and building commissions, and rescue workers and medical facilities.

(7) *Marine call:* A *marine call* may be made to or from a ship at sea by contacting the marine operator.

(8) *International calls:* A call may be placed overseas either with **international direct-distance dialing (IDDD)** or through operator assistance. If direct dialing is used, the international access code, the code for the country called, the city or area code, and the local telephone number are required.

Many individuals take advantage of international calling cards or the Internet phone. Using an international calling card is the same as using a long-distance calling card. Using the computer *(Internet phone)* for calling requires specialized audio software and speakers; the wide use of the Internet has made this service attractive to many individuals.

(9) *Wide area telephone service (WATS):* A firm may want to subscribe to a **wide area telephone service (WATS)** if numerous telephone calls are made to a national, regional, or state area. The cost of WATS service depends on the time the service is in operation, not on the number of calls made. A fixed monthly fee is paid for the WATS hours. If the company uses more than the allotted hours, an additional charge is made to the company. The firm can have a full business-day package or a measured-time package.

- *Full business-day package:* This WATS service provides a fixed number of calling hours per month.

- *Measured-time package:* This WATS service provides a smaller number of fixed hours per month allotted to the company.

EXAMPLE: *The XYZ Corporation has a regional office serving the state of Wisconsin. The regional office makes most of its customer contacts and follow-ups over the telephone. Therefore, full business-day intrastate WATS was purchased. During the month of June, the total number of hours charged for long-distance calls for the XYZ Corporation's Wisconsin Regional Office was less than the fixed monthly fee for the month of June. Therefore, no additional charge was required.*

(10) *Inward wide area telephone service (INWATS):* A firm may want to subscribe to an **inward wide area telephone service (INWATS)** if numerous telephone calls are expected from customers and the firm wishes to pay for these calls. (For the customer, the call is a toll-free call. This means that the firm, not the customer, pays for the call.) This service has increased over the past decade, increasing the INWATS numbers from an 800 area code to also include 888, 877, 866, and 855.

EXAMPLE: *Rodriguez wants to order a blouse from the CB Store. By calling the toll-free number (1-800-755-3300), she can order the merchandise by phone, and the company will pay for the long-distance call.*

(11) *Foreign exchange:* A special service called **foreign exchange** provides customers a local number when calling a business located in another city. The toll charge for the call is billed to the listed number.

EXAMPLE: *The ABC Company, located in Rockford, Illinois, services equipment installed in a number of offices in Bloomington, Illinois (about 95 miles away). ABC subscribes to a special service that lists a Bloomington number in the Bloomington telephone directory, a local call for Bloomington residents. ABC will be charged for the toll charges on all calls received in the Rockford office on this line.*

2. ***Answering Services:*** You may wish to make a special arrangement for your business or home telephone to be answered in your absence by the following:

- An independent answering service whereby an operator actually answers calls and records messages. Messages can be picked up or e-mailed to the recipient.

- An answering machine with a recording device that is activated when the telephone is not answered. A prerecorded message informs the caller that a message can be recorded; a "tone" lets the caller know when to begin speaking. Options may be available for special delivery instructions.

- A voice-mail service, available through the local telephone company or the Internet, as an extra feature for a monthly charge.

3. ***Special Telephone Features:*** Telephone companies continually add special features to telephones to make telephone communication easier and more efficient. Subscribers may pay a separate cost for the feature, which is added to the monthly cost for telephone service. Some of the more commonly used features include call waiting, call forwarding, speed calling, caller ID, repeat dialing, call trace, and taped announcements.

   a. *Call waiting: Call waiting* alerts a person already on the telephone that another call is incoming; the alert is a soft beep. The first caller can be placed on hold while the second call is being answered.

   b. *Call forwarding:* When a business professional knows that he or she will be at a different phone location, *call forwarding* routes incoming calls to another phone number entered into the telephone system. Any incoming calls are forwarded to the new phone location.

   c. *Speed calling:* The telephone can be programmed with a special number code assigned to frequently dialed numbers. Instead of dialing the entire telephone number, *speed calling* allows the caller to use the programmed telephone numbers with the touch of the special number code.

   d. *Caller ID:* A telephone system equipped with the *caller ID* feature displays the name and/or number of the person calling before the receiver is picked up. The person being called can decide whether to answer the telephone or to have a voice message recorded. Callers can block the system from displaying their telephone number on someone else's telephone. The telephone service provider can provide the procedure to block the system.

   e. *Repeat dialing:* Many telephones have a special button for *redialing* the previous number called or redialing a busy number. This service is also available on a pay-per-use basis through the telephone service provider. The telephone provider will call the number once it is no longer busy and call back when there is a connection.

   f. *Call trace:* By accessing *call trace* for the local area (i.e., *57 or *69), the phone number of the last incoming call can be obtained. This is useful after receiving harassing or prank calls. This feature is available on a pay-per-use basis or a monthly charge for heavy tracing use.

   g. *Taped announcements:* Recorded information can be automatically played over the telephone when incoming calls are received.

      EXAMPLE: *Movie schedules at a local theater, the time and temperature from a local bank, and daily prayers from a local church are examples of taped announcements.*

4. ***Telephone Systems:*** Telephone calls are routed to and from the public lines of the telephone company to the private lines within a business organization by means of switching and access systems. The organization installs a telephone system to provide the internal and external communication service desired. Some options include private branch exchanges (PBX), computerized branch exchanges (CBX), and central exchange systems (CENTREX).

   a. *Private branch exchange (PBX):* A **private branch exchange (PBX)** is a special purpose computer originally designed for handling business calls for an organization. Today the digital PBX switching system accepts and transmits voice and data using regular telephone lines; no special wiring is required. However, this lower bandwidth prevents the transmission of interactive video or high-resolution photos.

   A PBX is often used in small organizations or regional divisions where the system serves automated telephone switching and data network requirements. Office personnel can utilize telephone, interphone (calling extension numbers), facsimile, computers, word processors, printers, copiers, and other specialized devices all through the same network. Additional telephone features include repeat dialing, voice mail, speed calling, call waiting, call forwarding, automatic callback, directory services, and records management.

   The PBX interface connects internal communication to the external public or private carrier for external communication. Commercial vendors support PBXs eliminating the need for internal specialists to handle maintenance and system management.

   EXAMPLE: *Transformation Dynamics is a start-up business requiring several telephone extensions and a computer network with shared peripherals (printer, copier). By installing a PBX, telephone calls are automatically directed to the individual's extension, inward dialing is automatic by extension number, and each extension has an automatic outside line. When field representatives are in the office, it is easy to connect their notebooks to the network by plugging in anywhere an existing telephone connection exists. When representatives are out of the office, the call forwarding feature can be activated to have calls directed to their cell phones. The office administrator particularly likes the ability to send a letter to the printer and also dial the copy machine for multiple copies of the letter.*

   b. *Computerized branch exchange (CBX):* The **computerized branch exchange (CBX)** is a computer-based telephone communication system for automated telephone switching and management. A CBX only serves telephone requirements; data network needs are not addressed. The automated telephone features are similar to a PBX: repeat dialing, voice mail, speed calling, call waiting, call forwarding, automatic callback, directory services, and records management.

   EXAMPLE: *Using the systems charge back feature (records management), records are kept of all calls made from a telephone extension. Costs incurred for telephone usage are charged back to the department.*

   c. *Central exchange system (CENTREX):* A **central exchange system (CENTREX)** is leased from the regional telephone company, eliminating the need for large capital expenditures for a telephone system. In a CENTREX system, each extension is assigned a seven-digit number for outside access. The last four digits of the number represent the extension number for internal calls. Also, a seven-digit number is assigned as a general company number if the caller does not know which extension to call. Direct inward dialing and direct outward dialing are available at each extension phone.

EXAMPLE:

Telephone number for company:	*765-2000*
Extension #1:	*765-2001*
Internal Calls:	*2001*
Extension #65:	*765-2065*
Internal Calls:	*2065*

Additional automated telephone features similar to those on PBX and CBX systems enhance the CENTREX system.

5. ***Telephone Equipment:*** Office professionals need to take advantage of the telephone system's special features. Standard telephone equipment in most offices includes many special features. Some of the more commonly used telephones include the key (or button) telephone, the touch-tone telephone, and the speakerphone. Additional peripherals include a call director, pager, paging system, and headsets.

   a. *Key (or button) telephone:* Connected to several telephone lines, each line is represented by a button on the phone. The button illuminates as the line is used for a call.

   b. *Touch-tone telephone:* A *touch-tone telephone* is a telephone with a 12-button keyboard (10 buttons for numbers 0 to 9 plus two buttons for special purposes). Touch-tone telephones are required for computerized systems (PBX, CBX, and CENTREX).

   c. *Speakerphone:* The *speakerphone* is equipped with a microphone and a speaker chip that can be activated for ease in projecting the conversation. The speakerphone frees the user's hands in order to work with resource information necessary for the conversation. When there are two or three individuals in one office, a speakerphone allows all to participate in the discussion.

   A separate speakerphone can be attached to a telephone. The separate speakerphone provides high-quality reception and is typically used with large groups. If the service is desired at both locations of the conversation, two speakerphones will be required, one at each end.

   d. *Call director:* The *call director* is a desktop unit that can handle as many as 100 lines at one location and can be connected to a switchboard or an intercom system.

   e. *Pager:* A *pager* can be carried so that an individual can be signaled by use of a tone or buzz that a call to the home office needs to be returned. The number to be called is projected on the pager.

   f. *Paging system:* An in-house communication system (*paging system*) signals people who are away from their desks that they need to contact their office. The paging system can be a tone or an announcement of the individual's name over a loudspeaker.

   EXAMPLE: *Telcom expects their office personnel to conduct business with a "manage by walking around" philosophy. This collaborative environment has in-*

dividuals in and out of their offices all day. Key executives are contacted on the paging system by a tone.

Black	*— One short beep*
Carlton	*— Two short beeps*
Morrison	*— Three short beeps*
Ryerson	*— One long beep*
Zimmerman	*— Two long beeps*

When paged, these executives are to immediately contact their administrative assistant.

Although the paging system is infrequently used for other personnel, if needed, their name would be announced:

"Martha Anderson—please call 4789."

g. *Headset:* When office personnel need to place (or answer) a large volume of calls, a headset equipped with listening and speaking components provides a more ergonomically designed setting for the user. The user wears the headset, keeping hands free and not requiring the use of the telephone hand piece, which many times produces "telephone ear" after extended use.

The headset is a common peripheral to cellular telephones. The mobile user conducts a safer environment when using a headset while driving a vehicle. The mobile user provides greater privacy by using a headset in public spaces.

In today's dynamic business environment, internal and external communication is affected by the telecommunications technologies utilized. Business operations rely on the accurate and efficient exchange of voice, data, text, graphics, and audio and video information. Telecommunications and communication networks enhance the organization's communication processes.

Check Point—Section B

Directions: For each question, circle the correct answer.

B–1. A long-distance call that allows the caller to charge the call to a specific account number is a/an

A) collect call
B) calling card call
C) message unit call
D) person-to-person call

B–2. As a paramedic for the St. Theresa Hospital Emergency LifeLine, Maki has the technical capability of instantly transmitting critical images to the hospital so physicians are prepared to handle the emergency upon arrival. Maki is equipped with a/an

A) 911 service
B) camera phone
C) inward wide area telephone service (INWATS)
D) speed calling feature

B–3. An in-house communications system that signals people according to their assigned code is a

A) call director
B) central exchange system (CENTREX)
C) paging system
D) speakerphone

C. Communication Networks

Designed on the human communication process, communication in a computer environment transmits documents, graphics, images, or files. There is a sender of information, receiver of information, and a communication channel for delivering the message. In a computer environment, however, data need to be converted into digital information, called bits; this is called **digitizing.** Also, transmission requires adequate bandwidth.

With telecommunications technology addressing computer communication, various computing models evolved: centralized computing, distributed computing, and collaborative computing. Today all three computing models utilize one or more network designs.

1. *Computing Models:* Since the Information Age (1950s), people and businesses have used computers to process and transmit data and information. Today there are three computing models: centralized computing, distributed computing, and collaborative computing.

    a. *Centralized computing:* **Centralized computing** in the 1970s was not a true network because there was no sharing of information and resources. Data were processed in large centralized computers with users entering data from local input devices. Today many organizations utilize centralized computing along with one of the other computing models (distributed or collaborative).

    b. *Distributed computing:* The microcomputer opened the door for users to take control over their computing needs. Organizations took advantage of using smaller computers for specialized processes, allowing office personnel to work on subsets of operations on separate (distributed) computers. *Distributed computing* required networks so information and services could be easily shared between these distributed environments. The network linked the distributed environments as well as provided a communication channel to a centralized operation for organizations continuing with the centralized model. Two widely used distributing computing models are peer-to-peer computing and client/server computing.

        (1) *Peer-to-peer computing:* **Peer-to-peer computing** puts all processing power on the user's desktop PC. All computers on the network can access all organizational data, application software, public files, and peripherals connected to the network. For security and integrity purposes, each computer is assigned through the operating system; Windows 2000, Windows XP, AppleShare, and Novel Netware operating systems are capable of peer-to-peer computing. Computers work together without any central controlling authority. With desktop PCs using less than 25 percent of the processing power, through transparent access peer-to-peer computing can utilize the unused disk space and processing power for large computing tasks.

        (2) *Client/server computing:* One widely used form of distributed computing is client/server computing. **Client/server computing** uses a microcomputer, mid-range computer, or a mainframe as a server to its clients (end user with a desktop PC, notebook, or workstation). Data storage and management, processing logic, and an interface are shared between the server and client. Clients interface with the server over the enterprise network. The server may handle all functions with the client having only an interface to the server (Model 1 in Figure 3–3). Such a client is referred to as a *thin client.* A thin client typically has a network computer (NC) with minimal or no processing logic or storage capacity; all software and data are downloaded over the or-

FIGURE 3–3   Client-Server Computing Models

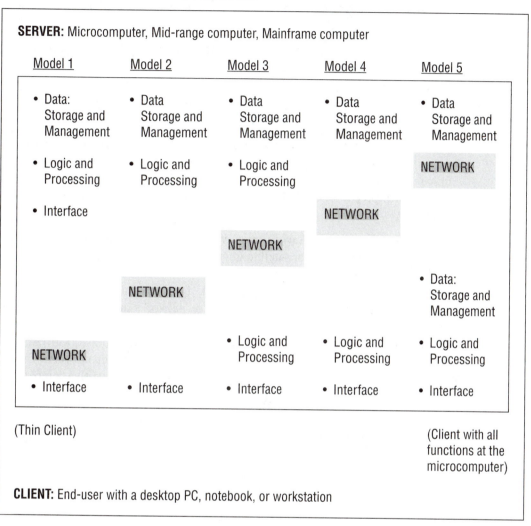

SERVER: Microcomputer, Mid-range computer, Mainframe computer

Model 1	Model 2	Model 3	Model 4	Model 5
• Data: Storage and Management	• Data Storage and Management	• Data Storage and Management	• Data Storage and Management	• Data Storage and Management
• Logic and Processing	• Logic and Processing	• Logic and Processing		NETWORK
• Interface			NETWORK	
		NETWORK		
	NETWORK			• Data: Storage and Management
NETWORK		• Logic and Processing	• Logic and Processing	• Logic and Processing
• Interface	• Interface	• Interface	• Interface	• Interface

(Thin Client)

(Client with all functions at the microcomputer)

CLIENT: End-user with a desktop PC, notebook, or workstation

ganization's network. Within an organization, several client/server computing models will exist. Each end user's computing model depends on his or her
responsibilities and needs. Figure 3–3 illustrates the five models of client-
server computing. The client-server computing model is designed for specific
client applications and is the computing model for Internet processing.

c. *Collaborative computing:* In the 1990s the **collaborative computing** model
emerged. Now networks are networked to accomplish integrated operations and
link common processing tasks. The network infrastructure along with collaborative software tools support data, information, and process sharing.

2. ***Network Categories:*** The need to share data and resources within the organization, the
importance of collaborative activities both internally and externally, and the efficiencies of business-to-business (B2B) and business-to-consumer (B2C) commerce make
the computer network essential to the digital organization. There are two network
sizes: local area networks and wide area networks.

a. *Local area networks:* A **local area network (LAN)** is a private network that supports communications within an office, building, or firm. Electronic equipment
that is even a few miles away can be connected to a LAN. The LAN links electronic

devices so that data can be shared easily and at greater speeds than otherwise provided. Also, the sharing of hardware and software on the network can lower computer costs for a company.

EXAMPLE: *Employees in each of the three departments at Signature Signs (accounting, marketing, and production) have their own microcomputer (a desktop PC, notebook, or workstation) and an ink-jet printer. For high-speed, multiple copies, each microcomputer is networked to a centralized copier as well as a page printer in the production department.*

As operations have become more integrated, sharing of information is important. Information stored on a central hard disk server to which each department's microcomputers are networked provides greater data integrity; there is less duplication of data. Data can be accessed easily and quickly from any location within the network.

b. *Wide area network (WAN):* A *wide area network (WAN)* is a combination of public or private lines, microwave, or satellite transmission for long-distance communications between two or more LANs. Common carriers licensed by the Federal Communications Commission provide a network for both interorganizational and intraorganizational communication. These large networks are necessary for conducting the day-to-day activities of businesses and governments. There are five categories of WANs: an enterprise network, a metropolitan area network (MAN), a global network, a virtual private network (VPN), and a value-added network (VAN). Wide area networks are shrinking distances and enhancing collaborative computing.

(1) *Enterprise network:* An **enterprise network** connects distributed networks of a single organization into one single network. Differing technologies among the organization's networks are addressed in the enterprise network design.

EXAMPLE: *Harrison Engineering has computing in their Chicago (mainframe), Boston (LAN), Seattle (two LANs), and Anchorage (LAN) offices. The enterprise network connects these distributed networks into a single network for the organization.*

(2) *Metropolitan area network (MAN):* A **metropolitan area network (MAN)** is limited to a small geographic area. Typically, MANs connect LANs with fiber optic cable to provide an organization with high-speed data transmission.

(3) *Global network:* A **global network** includes the networks of several organizations internationally. The Internet is the world's largest computer network.

(4) *Virtual private network (VPN):* A **virtual private network (VPN)** is used by many organizations for intranet and extranet security. A VPN uses network firewalls and other measures to establish a secure network when the Internet is the network backbone.

(5) *Value-added network (VAN):* A **value-added network (VAN)** is a private multimedia, multipath, third-party managed, medium-speed WAN. A VAN is an economical alternative because it is shared by multiple organizations. Customers pay a subscription fee plus a fee for the amount of data transmitted. VANs communicate with other VANs to provide communication between firms that are members of different VANs. Services provided by a VAN include network management, e-mail, electronic data interchange, and security. Infonet, Telenet, and Tymnet are three widely used international VANs.

FIGURE 3–4   Types of Network Topologies

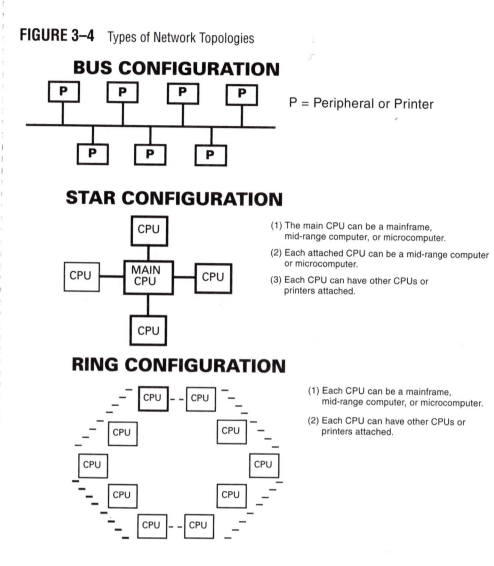

BUS CONFIGURATION

P = Peripheral or Printer

STAR CONFIGURATION

(1) The main CPU can be a mainframe, mid-range computer, or microcomputer.

(2) Each attached CPU can be a mid-range computer or microcomputer.

(3) Each CPU can have other CPUs or printers attached.

RING CONFIGURATION

(1) Each CPU can be a mainframe, mid-range computer, or microcomputer.

(2) Each CPU can have other CPUs or printers attached.

3. *Network Topologies:* Three basic network structures are used in local area and wide area telecommunications networks: a bus configuration, a star configuration, and a ring configuration. A configuration is called **network topology.** All three topologies are common structures for local area networks. The star and ring topologies are common structures for wide area networks. For a schematic of these network topologies, see Figure 3–4.

   a. *Bus topology:* In a *bus network,* a communications channel attaches all peripheral devices. Each device has a communications interface unit that manages the flow of data to and from each device. The bus is a single circuit (twisted wire, coaxial cable, or fiber optic cable) of limited length where devices can be attached at any point. Signals are broadcast in both directions with software to identify which device receives the message. Performance degrades during high-volume network traffic. When two computers transmit messages at the same time, a "collision" occurs, and the messages must be re-sent. Network software controls all network traffic (see Figure 3–4).

   b. *Star topology:* A central computer is required in a *star network.* The central computer is called a central node, central control, switch, or hub. All transactions are processed through the central CPU before being routed to the appropriate network device. This provides a central decision point. However, if the central CPU is down, all shared processing stops (see Figure 3–4).

c. *Ring topology:* To eliminate reliance on a central decision point for WANs, a *ring network* may be implemented. A unidirectional transmission line (one direction) forming a closed path links the CPUs at the remote locations. If a CPU or peripheral is down, a "bypass relay" serves as a partial solution to the issue of network reliability (see Figure 3–4).

No matter what network topology is applied, local area networks are either a client/server or a peer-to-peer computing model.

The impact of information systems and telecommunications technologies on today's dynamic business environment is enormous. Communication is the backbone to all successful relationships and partnerships. Fast and reliable telecommunications technology will continue to be necessary to manage the vast amount of data and information created and utilized in business organizations. Understanding these technologies and effectively utilizing the collaborative opportunities available to administrative professionals enhances the organization's strategic position in today's competitive global business environment.

Check Point—Section C

Directions: For each question, circle the correct answer.

C–1. A distributed model used for Internet processing is

A) client/server computing
B) enterprise network
C) peer-to-peer computing
D) value-added network (VAN)

C–2. A private network that supports communications between electronic equipment within an office, building, or firm even up to a few miles away is a/an

A) enterprise network
B) local area network (LAN)

C) virtual private network (VPN)
D) wide area network (WAN)

C–3. To eliminate reliance on a central decision point for wide area networks, the best topology to implement is the

A) bus
B) global
C) star
D) ring

For Your Review

Directions: For each question, circle the correct answer.

1. A telecommunications processor that converts digital data into analog signals for transmission over an analog communication channel is a/an
   A) bridge
   B) front-end processor
   C) modem
   D) multiplexer

2. A communication processor for connecting two similar networks is a
   A) bridge
   B) gateway
   C) multiplexer
   D) network interface card (NIC)

3. To connect the microcomputer to a network enabling the exchange of data between computers requires the microcomputer cables or wireless transceivers to be connected to a
   A) modem
   B) multiplexer
   C) network interface card (NIC)
   D) tethered line

4. Telecommuters often require high-capacity digital transmission from the home office to the telephone switching station. Telephone companies provide that service with existing twisted copper lines through a
   A) dedicated service line
   B) digital subscriber line (DSL)
   C) T-3 line
   D) tie line

5. A thickly insulated copper wire for fast digital transmission where electrical interference and wire tapping are minimized due to the insulation is
   A) baseband cable
   B) broadband cable
   C) conventional telephone line (POTS)
   D) fiber optic cable

6. A tethered channel with very high bandwidth, high transmission accuracy, and very good security (difficult to tap) is
   A) Bluetooth
   B) coaxial cable
   C) fiber optic cable
   D) satellite

7. Terrestrial microwave, celestial satellite, Bluetooth, and cellular are all
   A) dedicated service channels
   B) digital subscriber lines (DSL)
   C) infrared technologies
   D) wireless channels

8. Every time Kolowsky places a long-distance call to Montano he talks with her assistant. Kolowsky decided he only wants to pay for the call if Montano is available to come to the telephone. Kolowsky needs to place a
   A) credit card call
   B) collect call
   C) direct-distance dialed call (DDD)
   D) person-to-person call

9. What service allows the caller to dial a local number to call a business in another city and the business pays for the call?
   A) Calling card call
   B) Collect call

C) Foreign exchange call

D) Message unit call

10. The advisory committee members are located throughout the United States. For their regular monthly meetings, a toll-free telephone number is called and they join the meeting by providing a log-on code. This is a/an

A) audio conference

B) foreign exchange call

C) inward wide area telephone service (INWATS) call

D) wide area telephone service (WATS) call

11. Mobile communication devices enable callers to make and receive calls anytime/anywhere. This calling service requires a

A) caller ID

B) cellular telephone

C) text telephone (TT)

D) wide area telephone service (WATS)

12. The telephone number for Hickman Suppliers is 1-866-Hickman. This telephone number option is for

A) call tracing

B) foreign exchanges

C) independent message answering services

D) inward wide area telephone service (INWATS)

13. Many businesses allow customers to contact them over an inward wide area telephone service (INWATS). This means the

A) business pays for the call

B) business has a private branch exchange (PBX)

C) communications channels are T-3 lines

D) customer can call 24/7 and receive service

14. To provide quality customer service, Maki selects one day each week to visit clients. To maintain contact with any-one calling the office on the day she is out, she keys her cell phone number into her office phone so all incoming calls are routed to her cell phone. This telephone feature is called

A) call forwarding

B) cellular calling

C) repeat dialing

D) speed calling

15. Instead of dialing the entire telephone number, administrative professionals can program frequently dialed telephone numbers to special locations (codes). The administrative professional touches the special location code when a call needs to be placed. This telephone feature is

A) call waiting

B) caller ID

C) repeat dialing

D) speed calling

16. A telephone system that provides direct dialing from all telephone extensions and can be leased from the regional telephone company is a

A) central exchange system (CENTREX)

B) computerized branch exchange (CBX)

C) private branch exchange (PBX)

D) wide area telephone service (WATS)

17. Wooster is holding a meeting in his office with three colleagues. Wooster places a telephone call to their distributor to obtain her input on the last agenda item. So Wooster and his colleagues can all participate in the conversation, Wooster's telephone equipment needs to be a

A) call director

B) private branch exchange (PBX)

C) speakerphone

D) telephone headset

18. When an administrative professional is away from her office, an in-house communications system can signal her ac-

cording to an assigned code. This is an example of a

A) bridge
B) computerized branch exchange (CBX)
C) paging system
D) speakerphone

19. Converting data into binary bits is called

A) digitizing
B) fetching
C) modulating
D) multitasking

20. Typically less than 25 percent of the desktop PC's processing power and disk space are used. The organization can capture the unused disk space and processing power through

A) centralized computing
B) client/server computing
C) collaborative computing
D) peer-to-peer computing

21. Many of the end users at Cobb & Associates have network computers (NC). They download all application software over the organization's network and save all application files to the network server. The computing model for these end users is

A) centralized computing
B) client/server computing
C) collaborative computing
D) peer-to-peer computing

22. ComCor has computing in their Chicago (mainframe), Philadelphia (LAN), and Los Angeles (two LANs) offices. In order to connect these distributed networks into a single network so employees can access ComCor data from all locations, the organization needs a

A) bus network
B) global network
C) metropolitan area network (MAN)
D) wide area network (WAN)

23. Fridh Architectural Design uses the Internet as the backbone for their extranet. The company wants network firewalls and several security measures. Fridh Architectural Design needs a/an

A) enterprise network
B) value-added network (VAN)
C) virtual private network (VPN)
D) wide area network (WAN)

24. A network topology for local area networks (LANs) where all peripheral devices have a communication interface that manages the flow of data to and from each device is the

A) bus topology
B) global topology
C) ring topology
D) star topology

25. No matter what network topology is applied, the computing model for a local area network (LAN) is either

A) client/server or collaborative
B) client/server or peer-to-peer
C) distributed or collaborative
D) peer-to-peer or centralized

Solutions

Solutions to Check Point—Section A

Answer	Refer to:
A–1. (B)	[A-2-a (5)]
A–2. (C)	[A-3-a (3)]
A–3. (C)	[A-3-b (5)]

Solutions to Check Point—Section B

Answer	Refer to:
B–1. (B)	[B-1-a (5)]
B–2. (B)	[B-1-b (6)]
B–3. (C)	[B-5-f]

Solutions to Check Point—Section C

Answer	Refer to:
C–1. (A)	[C-1-b (2)]
C–2. (B)	[C-2-a]
C–3. (D)	[C-3-c]

Solutions to For Your Review

	Answer	*Refer to:*
1.	(C)	[A-2-a (1)]
2.	(A)	[A-2-a (4)]
3.	(C)	[A-2-b]
4.	(B)	[A-3-a (1)]
5.	(B)	[A-3-a (2) (b)]
6.	(C)	[A-3-a (3)]
7.	(D)	[A-3-b]
8.	(D)	[B-1-a (3)]
9.	(C)	[B-1-b (11)]
10.	(A)	[B-1-b (2)]
11.	(B)	[B-1-b (5)]
12.	(D)	[B-1-b (10)]
13.	(A)	[B-1-b (10)]
14.	(A)	[B-3-b]
15.	(D)	[B-3-c]
16.	(A)	[B-4-c]
17.	(C)	[B-5-c]
18.	(C)	[B-5-f]
19.	(A)	[C]
20.	(D)	[C-1-b (1)]
21.	(B)	[C-1-b (2)]
22.	(D)	[C-2-b]
23.	(C)	[C-2-b (4)]
24.	(A)	[C-3-a]
25.	(B)	[C-3]

Chapter 4

The Networked Enterprise

OVERVIEW

Using new information technologies, firms are creating an information technology (IT) infrastructure that provides a broad platform for electronic business (e-business), electronic commerce (e-commerce), and support for the digital organization. Today's IT infrastructure is based on powerful networks and Internet technology.

Information technologies for the networked enterprise (e-business, e-commerce) is a mix of hardware supplied by different vendors; software interfaces for ease of use; large, complex databases stored in multiple locations; and an integration of internal and external operations via multiple network designs. The IT infrastructure for the networked enterprise supports an electronic platform for internal business operations (e-business) as well as external partnerships with suppliers, distributors, financial institutions, government agencies, and customers (e-commerce). This infrastructure provides accurate, efficient electronic applications supporting the new digital organization of tomorrow. The more prevalent e-business and e-commerce collaboration tools are reviewed in this chapter.

Internet technology and the World Wide Web (WWW) are the heart of the e-business and e-commerce proliferation. Therefore, administrative professionals need to also have a basic understanding of these two important technologies.

KEY TERMS

Collaborative commerce, 89
Computer conference, 78
Data conference, 78
Domain name, 82
e-Business, 87
e-Commerce, 88

Electronic data interchange (EDI), 89
Enterprise system, 88
Extranet, 89
File transfer protocol (FTP), 83

Groupware, 76
Hypertext markup language (HTML), 84
Instant messaging, 82
Internet, 81

A. Collaboration Tools

The Internet has changed people's lives both at home and at work. Today computer users expect immediate access to data and information and support for collaboration with others. Particularly in the work environment, collaborative teams for sharing ideas and resources and creating new ideas must be supported. Administrative professionals need effective communication alternatives, efficient means for coordinating work efforts, and methods for managing tasks and projects.

Groupware includes all software for information sharing, electronic meetings, electronic scheduling, and team writing and projects as professionals work in an anytime-anywhere networked environment. Leading commercial groupware products include Lotus Notes, Opentext Livelink, and Groove, as well as Microsoft Internet Explorer and Netscape Communicator Web browser functions. The IT infrastructure, the Internet, and the WWW support these collaboration tools (communication tools, conference tools, and coordination tools) for both e-business and e-commerce.

1. *Communication Tools:* Electronic communication allows business professionals at all levels to send text, voice, or multimedia messages, documents, and files over telephone and computer networks (intranet, the internal network; extranet, networks for business partners; and Internet, the international network).

   a. *Electronic mail (e-mail): e-Mail* is widely used to send and receive text messages both internal and external to the organization. Attachments to the message make it easy to send documents and files; if the documents are large, they should be zipped. Zipping a document compresses the data for faster transmission as well as ensures formatting consistencies during transmission. Files, once received, need to be unzipped (decompressed).

      Electronic mailboxes are similar to the standard file cabinet where the user has an in-file, out-file, save file, trash file, and composition file. A user can add additional file folders (boxes) if needed. Like all records management environments, users must manage their electronic mail placing messages in appropriate files (boxes).

   b. *Voice mail:* Unanswered telephone messages are digitized and saved until the receiver accesses the voice messaging system for playback and deletes or saves the message for some future action. The mobile employee can easily access voice messages anytime, anywhere. The system date and time stamp provide accurate message documentation for the receiver. Like all communication management, the voice mailbox should be frequently checked and appropriate action taken on all messages.

   c. *Facsimile transmission (Fax):* A facsimile unit is like a copier. A picture or duplicate of the original document (handwritten, graphics, or typewritten information) can be transmitted electronically between two points over telephone or computer networks using a fax machine. The speed of transmission varies from six minutes to less than three seconds, depending on the system.

Today many computer systems are enhanced with fax transmission features or fax mailboxes that provide a central location for receipt of fax transmissions. The recipient can access the mailbox from another fax location and have the documents rerouted. With the wide range of technical capabilities for global communications, facsimile transmission is a stable part of the communications network.

d. *Web publishing:* Internet and intranet (internal) Web servers provide an efficient and convenient way to share information with others. **Web publishing** consists of hyperlinked documents that display text, animation, multimedia, and interactive environments for individual and team activities.

EXAMPLE: *A company intranet is a convenient place to post all human resource forms. The user accesses the appropriate form when needed, completes the variable information, and electronically submits the form to the appropriate division for processing. When forms are updated, users access the latest documents off the intranet.*

2. *Conference Tools:* Electronic conferencing allows users worldwide to meet and work collaboratively. Telephone and computer networks create an environment for working together no matter where (and sometimes when) the conference is held. The ability to meet with a group of people electronically using telephone or computer networks is a *teleconference.* Electronic conferences range from the audio conference format to the more sophisticated electronic meeting room, a full-motion video conference.

a. *Audio conference:* An *audio conference* is the audio (sound) linkage of three or more people at two or more separate locations by means of telephone access or networked computers. A telephone conference call for two or more participants at one location requires telephone speakerphones. A computer network conference call requires the computers to have Internet phone software. When a meeting does not require face-to-face interaction or visual contact between the participants, audio conferencing is very effective and efficient. The main advantage of audio conferencing is its cost; it is the least expensive of the conferencing tools.

(1) *Audio conference guidelines:* Guidelines that enhance the success of an audio conference include the following.

(a) *Distribute conference agenda:* Fax or e-mail a copy of the conference agenda to each participant at least one day prior to the conference.

(b) *Conference moderator:* A moderator makes sure all individuals participate and that the conference objectives are accomplished. Whoever organized the conference typically serves as moderator.

(c) *Conference participation:* To keep the conference manageable, no more than eight persons should participate in an audio conference. With audio conference monitoring equipment, it is possible for more persons to participate.

(d) *Speaker identification:* Before speaking, identify yourself so others know who is making the comments.

(e) *Conference notes:* Meetings requiring documentation can be taped or someone can be appointed to record and distribute important notes. Participants need to be notified at the start of a conference that the conference is being taped.

(2) *Audio conference enhancements:* An audio conference can be enhanced with graphics, documents, and still images. Some organizations bypass the cost of real-time enhancement and still benefit from visual images by sending the visuals in advance to all participants. Means for transmitting visuals include:

- e-Mail
- Facsimile transmission (fax)
- Electronic whiteboard
- Slow-scan video

b. *Computer conference:* Participants in a **computer conference** transmit information to others either simultaneously or on a delayed basis; participation can be anytime, anywhere. The computer conference allows persons to exchange information on a special-topic bulletin board available only to the participants designated to be part of the discussion. Participants access the topic bulletin board, read the new information, and add their input for others to view and offer comments. The posted messages are referred to as *threads.* The discussion comments and documents are stored for future reference and documentation. The computer conference is also referred to as a *discussion forum.* This conference format is popular with busy professionals as well as national and international work groups where time zones affect participation.

EXAMPLE: *The new product research team consists of representation from New York, Seattle, and Tokyo. Twice a day, the researchers activate the new product bulletin board (early in the morning and just before leaving at the end of the day). Through this interchange, they are able to collaborate on product research at their convenience.*

c. *Chat session:* A chat room allows two or more participants to have a simultaneous text conversation; participants must be present at the time of the chat. The rate of conversation is limited to one's keyboarding skills. **Internet Relay Chat (IRC)** is a general chat program for the Internet. Multimedia microcomputers now have a microphone, speakers, and software for audio conversations over the Internet [See: Internet phone, B-1-b (8)].

d. *Data conference:* Users on a computer network with data conferencing software can view, revise, and save changes to text, graphics, drawings, images, and other material displayed on a shared whiteboard. A **data conference** is simultaneous, in real time.

e. *Video conference:* Where participants' actions as well as audio contact are important for collaborative efforts, video conferencing is an alternative to consider. A **video conference** can be either one-way, or two-way full-motion. Video conferences are typically in a conference room equipped with appropriate electronic media.

(1) *One-way video conferencing:* This teleconference allows information transmission of the participant(s) from one location to another but not vice versa. This form of video conference is used for educational lectures, training, and product promotion where seeing the presenter is important. The video communication is one-way with two-way audio communication. However, the audio communication may also be one way.

(2) *Full-motion video conferencing:* Two-way conferencing where all participants can hear as well as see one another in motion is video conferencing at its optimum. The full-motion video conference is called a *two-way video con-*

ference or an *interactive teleconference.* The *electronic meeting room* is where a two-way video conference would be held. The electronic meeting room (teleconference center) must be fully equipped with cameras, overhead microphones, and acoustically treated rooms so audio and video transmission is of the highest quality. Participants sit at a conference table as they would at a face-to-face meeting and confer with the other participants as they are viewed on video screens. This is the most complex and the most expensive form of teleconferencing.

EXAMPLE: *Hotels specializing in conferences and conventions have conference theaters as electronic meeting rooms so full-motion video presentations can be part of the program. These theaters include the latest in teleconferencing technology to allow a presentation from a distant site to have all the visual and audio interaction one would have if the presenter was physically at the hotel.*

The electronic meeting room affects the success of a full-motion teleconference. Three important factors to consider are room location, acoustics, and design.

(a) *Location:* A teleconference room needs to be a quiet, interior room convenient to all potential users.

EXAMPLE: *As the administrative assistant to the vice president of operations, McCae was given the responsibility of securing the room location for the new teleconferencing center. In talking with Bradford, the vice president, she found that four of the five top executives had indicated expanding the executive office area to add an electronic meeting room with directional microphones and speakers. However, McCae's research indicated that the main users would be from the marketing department for product promotion. One of her recommendations was to establish the teleconference room (electronic meeting room) in a more central location close to the marketing department.*

(b) *Acoustics:* Good conference performance depends on acoustical properties providing low reverberation. Echoes in the room can be determined by sharply clapping the hands. If a pronounced echo is heard, the room will require acoustical treatment. Reverberation in a room is referred to as the *rain-barrel effect,* which characterizes the sound picked up by a microphone.

Other acoustical factors include room size; room shape; inside room without exterior windows or walls; ceiling height; wall, ceiling, floor, and furniture coverings; furniture arrangement; mechanical equipment; and participant movement. Some of these acoustical factors require technical assistance. Here are some factors an administrative assistant can monitor:

- Make sure the microphone(s) is close to the speaker(s).
- Do not allow internal motors to run (air conditioning, fans, and heaters).
- Do not allow interruptions from noise created by telephones ringing (including cell phones carried by participants), late arrivals, early departures, pagers, copiers, typewriters, or computers.

(c) *Room design:* Several design factors can facilitate the success of the teleconference:

- Arrange chairs at an appropriate distance from the microphone.

- If the teleconference will be held in an electronic room around a conference table, seating should be arranged so all participants are near microphones, if needed, and have good intraroom eye contact.

- Of the four table arrangements (rectangular, crescent, octagonal, and trapezoidal), the octagonal table offers the best compromise for intraroom conversation. Such a seating arrangement offers good intraroom eye contact and positions participants in good viewing range of the monitors.

3. ***Coordination Tools:*** Coordination tools help professionals manage their joint work efforts. Task and project management tools have been used by office personnel for several decades; today's electronic management tools along with calendars and task lists on the microcomputer desktop make the management function more manageable and effective.

   a. *Electronic calendar: Electronic calendars (e-calendar)* support scheduling appointments, appointment reminders, and tickler files. e-Calendars can be installed with joint management rights (read and write privileges) for the user and his or her assistant. e-Calendars can also have read privileges for other co-workers/team members for determining possible meeting times. Many executives use their PDAs for keeping track of appointments while away from the office. On a regular basis (typically daily), the PDA data are cross-checked with the office e-calendar for changes made either by the PDA user or the administrative professional in the office.

   b. *Project management:* Many projects require tracking to ensure that individual team members are completing their responsibilities. Electronic scheduling, tracking, and charting the completion status of tasks within a project make it easier for team members to adhere to the project timeline.

Utilizing groupware products for effective collaboration has improved communication, conferencing, and project coordination within the organization (e-business) and with business partners (e-commerce). Organization networks (intranet and extranet) along with the Internet continually change how we communicate with one another in this digital world for more effective and efficient business operations.

Check Point—Section A

Directions: For each question, circle the correct answer.

A–1. As office professionals work in an anytime, anywhere networked environment, all software for information sharing, electronic meetings, electronic scheduling, and team projects is called

   A) communication tools
   B) discussion forum
   C) groupware
   D) Web publishing tools

A–2. When conference participants have difficulty meeting because of time zones, a conference arrangement that allows participants to communicate on a specific topic at their convenience is the

   A) computer conference
   B) data conference
   C) interactive teleconference
   D) Internet Relay Chat (IRC)

A–3. Seating arrangements are important in an electronic meeting room. Of the four conference table arrangements, which one offers the best intraroom eye contact and viewing of monitors?

A) Crescent
B) Octagonal
C) Rectangular
D) Trapezoidal

B. The Internet and World Wide Web (WWW)

Linking thousands of individual networks world wide, the Internet is the most well-known and largest implementation of networking. Based on the client/server computing model, Internet technology provides the primary infrastructure for electronic business (e-business) and electronic commerce (e-commerce). Many refer to the Internet as the Net.

The **World Wide Web (WWW)** is a system of universally accepted standards for storing, retrieving, formatting, and displaying information in the cyber (virtual) world (Net). Through global acceptance of these standards, business on the WWW has mushroomed.

Whether at home or in the office, the Internet and WWW are part of our daily lives. Basic principles of the Internet and WWW are important to office professionals.

1. *Internet:* In 1969 the U.S. Department of Defense sponsored a special project, ARPANET, to electronically link scientists and university professors around the world. In 1990 ARPANET evolved into the **Internet.** The Internet is an entity that no one owns; there is no formal management structure. Today with appropriate hardware, software, and access, anyone can use the Internet. Access to the Net provides users with communication tools anytime, anywhere.

   a. *Internet access:* With a computer, modem, standard communications software, and a Web browser (software), access to the Internet can be either through the organization's LAN server or an Internet Service Provider (ISP).

      (1) *LAN server:* Connection to the organization's LAN with a network interface card (NIC) and authorization for Internet access is common in many organizations. The cost of the Internet connection is spread over multiple LAN users. Sometimes costs are charged back to the department or division. *Telecommuters* (employees working at home) who need access to the Internet or the organization's intranet would connect through a serial line Internet protocol/point-to-point protocol (SLIP/PPP) server.

      (2) *Internet Service Provider (ISP):* An **Internet service provider (ISP)** is a commercial organization with permanent connection to the Internet selling temporary connections to subscribers (individuals, educational institutions, businesses, and governmental agencies). There are more than 13,000 ISPs worldwide.

   b. *Communication tools:* Connecting people worldwide, e-mail is an important tool on the Internet. Additional services include instant messaging, newsgroups, listservs, chat, file transfer, information retrieval, and Internet phone.

      (1) *Electronic mail (e-mail):* The simplest and most widely used tool on the Internet is e-mail. *e-Mail* is used to facilitate communication between employees, offices, customers, and business partners.

FIGURE 4–1 Internet e-Mail Address

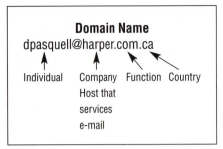

e-Mail requires an address that includes the individual or organization name, the @ symbol, and the domain name. The **domain name** identifies the host or network that services the e-mail and contains subdomains separated by a period. The subdomain farthest to the right is the *top-level domain* and is either a reference to a country with the function at the immediate left, or the top-level is a function (see Figure 4–1). Here are six of the original *domain functions*:

com	Commercial organization
	Operated by Verisign Global Registry Services
edu	Educational institution
gov	Government organization
	(excluding the military)
mil	Military organization
net	Networking organizations
	Operated by Verisign Global Registry Services
org	General organization
	Operated by Public Interest Registry

(2) *Instant messaging:* **Instant messaging** lets business professionals know when a colleague is online so e-mail messages can be communicated back and forth in real time. Instant messaging requires client software. Using the instant messaging software, a contact list is then created. Several instant messaging services support audio conversations as well as video images; see Internet phone [B-1-b (8)].

(3) *Newsgroups:* From the thousands of independent **newsgroups** (forums) available, individuals can join the discussion of their choice to share information and ideas; newsgroups are organized by topic. Discussions take place on electronic bulletin boards where anyone can post messages to read. The posted messages are referred to as *threads*. The required newsreader client software is available on most Internet browsers. Since the user needs to "seek" out the information, this is referred to as **pull technology.**

EXAMPLE: *Travis and Benson are doing market research for their firm. As Benson collects the data in the field, she enters it into a spreadsheet model, providing direction for continued data collection. At the end of each day, Benson uses her notebook computer and e-mails Travis a message with the spreadsheet attached. The next morning, Travis opens his e-mail and is able to open the spreadsheet document for research analysis at the home office. Both Benson and Travis use the same spreadsheet software.*

(4) *Listserv:* Electronic mail lists are another type of public forum for receiving information on selected topics. Individuals register (subscribe) with predefined topics (group). Using e-mail list servers **(listserv),** information submitted by a subscriber to the predefined group is broadcast to all other group members via e-mail. The information is automatically sent to all subscribers on the listserv; thus, this Internet forum is referred to as **push technology.** There are thousands of listserv groups to access. If one subscribes to several listservs, information management is best handled by establishing a specific Internet e-mail address (i.e., Yahoo or Hotmail) for listserv mail. One can unsubscribe from a listserv group at any time.

(5) *Internet Relay Chat (IRC):* Text chatting allows two or more people to have an interactive, real-time conversation. Yahoo Chat offers voice chat capabilities. America Online's Instant Messenger allows people to create their private chat channels with notification when someone from their chat list is online so a chat session can be initiated.

(6) *File transfer:* **File transfer protocol (FTP)** is used to download and upload files. Public FTP sites allow anyone to download books, maps, games, and other free applications over the Internet. Authorized users with passwords can access protected FTP sites. *Archie* is an Internet tool that enables users to search FTP sites for contents.

> EXAMPLE: *Martin's ISP offers Web space for posting pictures for family and friends. As a photographer, Martin uploads new pictures every month. To FTP the pictures, Martin has a log-on ID as well as password to access the Web space with his service provider.*

Most files and digital information accessible through FTP are also available through gophers. A *gopher* is a tool that allows users to locate information stored on Internet gopher servers. *Veronica (Very Easy Rodent-Oriented Netwide Index to Computer Archives)* is a tool for searching text on gopher menus.

(7) *Information retrieval:* With hundreds of library catalogs online, users are able to search databases open to the public by corporations, governments, and nonprofit organizations.

(8) *Internet phone:* Multimedia microcomputers now have a microphone, speakers, and software for audio conversations over the Internet. **Internet phone** calls interface with traditional telephones and other Internet phones. Add a video camera, and one can project his or her image or focus the camera on objects being discussed. Hardware and software is required at both the sending and receiving locations for audio plus visual communication.

    (a) *Sound quality:* Poor sound quality results from latency, jitter, and echo. Words are often missed due to these conditions.

- *Latency* is the delay during the transmission process.
- *Jitter* occurs when large amounts of data clog networks.
- The system microphone and speakers can produce an *echo*. A headset and faster Internet connection can reduce or eliminate the echo.

    (b) *Telephony:* **Telephony** is the technology of translating sound into digital signals, transmitting the signals, and converting the signals back to sound at the receiving end. Telephony is often used to refer to computer hardware and software that performs these functions traditionally performed by telephone equipment.

Organizations are taking advantage of the Internet phone for long-distance domestic and international calls; there is no added cost over the basic Internet connection fees.

With thousands of networks sending large quantities of data over the Internet, the intended sharing of research efforts has been affected. In 1996 U.S. research universities began working on *Internet2,* a private alternative to the now public Internet. Today over 180 universities work with private businesses and government agencies on the Internet2 design. Internet2 has a very high transmission speed (wide band-width), new protocols, and improved security. The advanced technologies of Internet2 are designed to support advanced Internet research efforts and applications.

2. ***World Wide Web (WWW):*** Developed in 1989 by a team of scientists, the *World Wide Web (WWW)* (typically referred to as the *Web*), is a system of universally accepted standards for storing, retrieving, formatting, and displaying information on the Internet. The Web is based on a standard **hypertext markup language (HTML)** that formats documents and utilizes hypertext links to other documents stored on computers in a network (LAN or WAN). Today most businesses exchange HTML documents and images over the global network, the Internet. The Internet is the channel for transmitting Web applications. The universal standards for Web formatting significantly increased Internet use. The term *information superhighway* is often used to refer to the Internet and the electronic links that have networked the world.

a. *Web browser:* Users navigate (move through) the Web with a **Web browser,** a program coded in HTML. The Web browser translates the HTML document into a Web page. Using the browser, users can visit Web sites as well as retrieve, view, and print Internet-posted information. Two popular Web browsers are Netscape Communicator and Microsoft Internet Explorer.

b. *Web site:* A **Web site** consists of all the Web pages maintained by one organization or individual. A typical business Web site consists of text and colorful graphic HTML pages that can be viewed through push-button interactivity. Audio and video animation may be included in the visual presentation.

A Web site consisting of more than one page sets up a home page. A *home page* is the first page of the Web site and typically consists of an introduction to information contained on the site with interactive buttons for Web site navigation.

c. *Web addresses:* To place a Web page on the Internet, a unique address called a **uniform resource locator (URL)** is required. The URL requires a unique name, which must be registered in a *domain function.* Six of the original domain functions are com, edu, gov, mil, net, and org [see Electronic mail [B-1-b (1)].

Unique names are derived from the domain name system (DNS). In 1998 the United States Government assigned management of the Web's address system to the private sector. Eighty-two companies, called registrars, are accredited to register domain names from the Internet Corporation for Assigned Names and Numbers (ICANN) (*www.internic.net*).

With the proliferation of registered names (over 300,000), the top-level specification has been expanded by the following seven domain functions with five others under consideration.

aero	Air-transportation industry
	Sponsored by Societe Internationale de Telecommunications Aeronautiques SC (SITA)
	Restricted to certain members of the global aviation community
biz	Restricted to businesses
	Operated by NeuLevel
coop	Restricted to cooperatives
	Sponsored by Dot Cooperation LLC
info	Information service providers
	Operated by Afilias Limited
museum	Restricted to museums and related persons
	Sponsored by the Museum Domain Management Association (MuseDoma)
name	Personal Web sites; restricted to individuals
	Operated by Verisign Global Registry Services
pro	Restricted to licensed professionals: Accountants, lawyers, physicians
	Operated by RegistryPro

Domain functions under consideration:

arts	Cultural and entertainment organizations
firm	Businesses and firms
rec	Recreational organizations
store	Businesses offering goods for purchase
web	Organizations related to World Wide Web activities

To reach a Web site, the URL is keyed into the address (location) box on the Web browser and consists of www (designating World Wide Web server), registered name, and domain function, each separated by a period. Sometimes, http:// needs to be keyed before the World Wide Web reference or is used if no WWW reference exists. Http:// means hypertext transport protocol, the communication standard used to transfer pages on the Web.

EXAMPLE:

www.niu.edu is the URL for Northern Illinois University

Keying www.niu.edu/admissions directs the user to the Admissions Web page at Northern Illinois University. Any information keyed after a slash navigates to a subdirectory on the Northern Illinois University Web site. A URL can contain more than one subdirectory.

d. *Web search:* In addition to visiting business Web sites, there are databases as well as several billion Web pages dedicated to providing information. With no specific directory for locating this information, one must search for the information using a Web browser or a search engine.

(1) *Searching with the Web browser:* One can search with the Web browser by pointing and clicking on the search icon.

EXAMPLES:

Netscape Communicator's browser is set up by topics: Arts, Games, Kids & Teens, Reference, Shopping, Travel, Business, Health, News, Regional, Society, Computers, Home, Recreation, Science, and Sports.

Microsoft Internet Explorer's browser asks you to choose a category: Web page search, person's address, business, map, look-up a word, and find a picture.

(2) *Search engine:* **Search engines** are tools to help users find the information or services on Web pages. Key words are entered into a search text box; the user must then point and click the start (go/search) button. Most search engines offer "advanced" search features. Searching for information on the Web is *pull technology*; the user is pulling information he or she wants off the Web.

There are hundreds of search engines, some specialized to specific types of information. The databases of search engines are structured differently; therefore, one may have to use several search engines before locating the information. The following guidelines are helpful in conducting a search:

- Read the search engine process for conducting a search.
- Choose the search words carefully; the key words or phrases used are critical to the success of the search.
- Verify the authenticity of the author.
- Verify the information by going to listed sites or checking references.

EXAMPLES — Popular Search Tools:

AltaVista	*(www.altavista.com)*
Ask Jeeves	*(www.askjeeves.com)*
Dogpile	*(www.dogpile.com)*
Excite	*(www.excite.com)*
Google	*(www.google.com)*
Infoseek	*(www.infoseek.com)*
Metacrawler	*(www.metacrawler.com)*
Search	*(www.search.com)*
Yahoo!	*(www.yahoo.com)*

The Internet and WWW technologies are beneficial tools for all business personnel. The technologies change daily; thus, this is an area where administrative professionals need to read professional journals and attend meetings that address the impact computers make on their daily lives—at home and in the office.

Check Point—Section B

Directions: For each question, circle the correct answer.

B–1. A system of universally accepted standards for storing, retrieving, formatting, and displaying information in a virtual world is the

A) domain name system (DNS)
B) Internet
C) uniform resource locator (URL)
D) World Wide Web (WWW)

B–2. The simplest and most widely used tool on the Internet is

A) e-mail
B) information retrieval
C) instant messaging
D) Internet Relay Chat (IRC)

B–3. To compete in today's electronic market, Wong decided to establish a Web site for his business. He has been distributing agricultural products to the Midwest region for five years with long-range expansion to the east and west coasts. He should register his Web site name under which one of the following domain functions?

A) aero
B) com
C) coop
D) net

C. The Digital Organization: Integration and Collaboration

Networking and Internet technology have created a digital world where ways of doing business have changed. The Internet's universal technology platform and the World Wide Web standards for document display and hypertext links are at the heart of the networked enterprise. Internal and external networks are now common with most organizations world wide. Integrating information across the enterprise, within the industry, and globally, is now seamless. The intranet, extranet, electronic data interchange, and networking networks are all components of the digital organization for today and the future. Internet technology is the key enabling technology for the digital integration now expected in business.

1. *Electronic Business (e-Business):* **e-Business** is the internal integration within an organization to enhance and support communication and business operations electronically. Internal networks and the intranet are technologies that support e-business operations.

    a. *Internal networks:* For several decades, local area networks have supported the coordination and management of business processes. Most local area networks support distributed computing within the organization.

    b. *Intranet:* The intranet creates a richer, more responsive collaborative environment for e-business. Based on Internet technology, the **intranet** is a closed, private version of the Internet available only to approved employees. Employees use their Web browser to access company news, forms, updates, corporate policies, databases, or any other information the organization determines important to business operations and employee communication.

EXAMPLE:

Sales & Marketing	*posts sales contacts*
Human Resources	*posts corporate policies and upcoming company events*
Production	*posts order tracking*
Accounting	*posts budgets*

    c. *Enterprise Systems:* An **enterprise system** is an organization-wide information system that integrates key business processes so information flows freely between different divisions (manufacturing, accounting, finance, sales and marketing, and human resources). Enterprise systems provide precise and timely information with a broad organizational view; thus, managers should be more effective in co-ordinating business operations. Figure 4–2 illustrates the independence and integration of typical departments.

  2. ***Electronic Commerce (e-Commerce):*** **e-Commerce** is conducting business online primarily over the Internet. e-Commerce can be the only method for conducting busi-

FIGURE 4–2   Department Integration

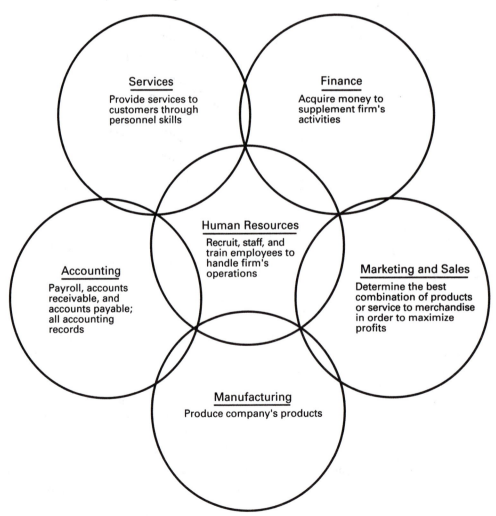

ness, or it can be an enhancement to the traditional brick-and-mortar business operation. Internet business models include business-to-consumer (B2C), business-to-business (B2B), consumer-to-consumer (C2C), or mobile-commerce (m-commerce).

a. *Business-to-consumer (B2C): Business-to-consumer* commerce is the electronic selling of products and services directly to the consumer. Direct sales over the Web occurs directly between the manufacturer and the consumer thereby eliminating intermediary organizations or processes. The elimination of processes responsible for intermediary steps is called *disintermediation.*

b. *Business-to-business (B2B): Business-to-business* commerce is the electronic selling of goods and services among businesses.

c. *Consumer-to-consumer (C2C): Consumer-to-consumer* commerce is the electronic selling of goods and services among consumers.

   EXAMPLE: *e-Bay is a Web auction site providing an electronic platform for people to auction their merchandise to the highest bidder.*

d. *Mobile-commerce (m-commerce):* m-Commerce makes the Web accessible from almost anywhere as individuals use wireless telephones, personal digital assistants, interactive television, and other wireless devices to link to the Internet. m-Commerce means that business can use mobile devices to deliver up-to-date services directly to the customer. This will require, however, that Web sites be designed for wireless devices and services, faster wireless networks be installed, and security on the wireless platform be improved.

3. ***Collaborative Commerce:*** With an atmosphere of trust, businesses are now connecting their operations electronically through **collaborative commerce.** Shared digital systems allow businesses to collaborate with suppliers, engineers, manufacturers, and sales representatives to improve planning, production, and distribution of goods and services.

a. *Private industrial networks:* Internet technology provides a platform where systems from different companies can seamlessly exchange information. Most private industrial networks are designed to coordinate the activities of an organization and their business partners. Some networks serve an entire industry, however.

b. *Electronic data interchange (EDI):* **Electronic data interchange (EDI)** provides computer-to-computer exchange of standard documents (purchase orders, invoices, payments) between two businesses (B2B). Business transactions are structured documents automatically transmitted from one information system to another through a telecommunications network. The elimination of printing and mailing of documents and data input at the receiving site lowers transaction costs. Most organizations participating in EDI use private networks *(value added network [VAN])* or the Internet *(virtual private network [VPN])* for transmission.

c. *Extranet:* Limited access to private intranets extended to authorized users outside the company is an **extranet.** Companies use extranets to coordinate and communicate with business partners and customers. Firewalls are used to ensure that only authorized personnel have access to the intranet. *Firewalls* consist of software and hardware placed between the organization's internal network(s) and an external network (Internet) allowing only authorized access.

   EXAMPLE: *Rockford Tool & Die is a machine tool firm within the automotive industry. Their product catalog is one of the documents on the intranet so any employee can handle customer contacts, e-mail, or telephone. Rockford Tool & Die created an extranet allowing industry customers access to only the product catalog information.*

Using new information technologies, e-business, e-commerce, m-commerce, and the digital organization should be better capable of competing in a global economy.

Check Point—Section C

Directions: For each question, circle the correct answer.

C–1. A rich collaborative environment for e-business throughout the enterprise is created by the

A) extranet
B) intranet
C) Internet
D) local area network (LAN)

C–2. e-Bay is a Web auction site providing an electronic platform to auction merchandise to the highest bidder; this is an example of

A) business-to-business commerce (B2B)
B) business-to-consumer commerce (B2C)
C) consumer-to-consumer commerce (C2C)
D) mobile commerce (m-commerce)

C–3. Hardware and software allowing only authorized access from an external network to the organization's internal network(s) is a/an

A) extranet
B) firewall
C) gateway
D) virtual private network (VPN)

For Your Review

Directions: For each question, circle the correct answer.

1. For the networked enterprise, collaboration tools have become very important. A groupware product that supports many of the collaboration activities is

   A) e-mail
   B) file transfer protocol (FTP)
   C) Lotus Notes
   D) Metacrawler

2. When attaching a lengthy document to an e-mail, the document data should be compressed for faster transmission. Compressing the document is called

   A) encryption
   B) merging
   C) shrinking
   D) zipping

3. Like a copier, a duplicate of an original handwritten document can be transmitted electronically between two points using the

   A) desktop PC
   B) e-mail system
   C) facsimile (FAX) machine
   D) local area network (LAN)

4. Using telephone or computer networks to electronically conduct business with several individuals at the same time is a/an

   A) enterprise system
   B) listserv
   C) telecommuter
   D) teleconference

5. The least expensive real-time electronic conferencing tool is the

   A) audio conference
   B) computer conference
   C) data conference
   D) discussion forum

6. A special-topic bulletin board was set up for 12 conference participants to discuss their collaborative research project. All participants had to check the bulletin board daily and add to the discussion. This type of conference is called a/an

   A) chat session
   B) computer conference
   C) data conference
   D) interactive teleconference

7. Three administrative professionals representing the organization's three regions had a special project that required them to revise several electronic documents (two word processing, one spreadsheet, and an electronic slide presentation). Using the conference white board they were able to meet every day for one hour and finalize the project in record time. The administrative professionals participated in a/an

   A) computer conference
   B) data conference
   C) interactive teleconference
   D) one-way video conference

8. An electronic meeting room is required for a/an

   A) chat session
   B) data conference
   C) one-way video conference
   D) two-way interactive teleconference

9. While working at the office, most administrative professionals access the

Internet from their desktop PC. What is the best way for these administrative professionals to connect to the Internet?

A) Digital subscriber line (DSL)
B) Internet service provider (ISP)
C) Organization's LAN server
D) Serial line Internet protocol/point-to-point protocol (SLIP/PPP)

10. The e-mail address for Marple is *marples@pepper.com.uk* The domain name for Marple's e-mail address is

A) com.uk
B) marples
C) pepper.com.uk
D) uk

11. With appropriate software installed on Sullivan's desktop PC, the system notifies her when a colleague is online. Sullivan and her colleague then participate in a simultaneous (real time) e-mail communication. The communication tool that alerted Sullivan is called

A) fetching
B) instant messaging
C) Internet Relay Chat (IRC)
D) telephony

12. Newsgroups allow anyone to participate in discussions held on electronic bulletin boards. The messages placed on the electronic bulletin board by participants are called

A) notices
B) postings
C) quips
D) threads

13. Using e-mail, information on a specific topic is sent to all registered subscribers. This public forum is called

A) gopher
B) listserv
C) newsgroup
D) paging

14. With all the free information available at public FTP sites, Sanders decided to search for information that could be useful in their department. What

Internet tool would Sanders use to search the FTP sites?

A) Archie
B) Excite
C) Infoseek
D) Veronica

15. A system of universally accepted standards for storing, retrieving, formatting, and displaying information in cyberspace is the

A) Internet
B) Internet2
C) Verisign Global Registry Services
D) World Wide Web (WWW)

16. The information superhighway is often used to refer to the Internet and the electronic links that have networked the world. What universal format creates these electronic links?

A) American Standard Code for Information Interchange (ASCII)
B) Hypertext markup language (HTML)
C) Information architecture
D) Information technology (IT) infrastructure

17. An organization may have hundreds of pages linked together for posting information on the information superhighway. These pages, maintained by the organization, are the

A) home page
B) intranet
C) Web site
D) World Wide Web (WWW)

18. Com, edu, gov, mil, net, and org are the original

A) domain functions
B) domain names
C) global network references
D) uniform resource locators (URLs)

19. What is the communication standard for posting and linking pages on the Web?

A) File transfer protocol (FTP)
B) Hypertext transport protocol (http://)

C) Internet

D) Uniform resource locator (URL)

20. Often administrative professionals search for information on the Web. This method of obtaining information uses

A) file transfer protocol (FTP)

B) pull technology

C) push technology

D) telephony

21. Intranet technology supports integration and collaboration for

A) e-business

B) e-commerce

C) e-market

D) m-commerce

22. Linking to the Web with her PDA, Wells checks the stock market and contacts her broker with buy and sell orders. This is an example of

A) e-business

B) business-to-business commerce (B2B)

C) consumer-to-consumer commerce (C2C)

D) m-commerce

23. Issues being addressed for the future include designing Web sites for wireless devices, installing faster wireless networks, and improving security on the wireless platform. All these are important because of

A) e-business

B) business-to-consumer commerce (B2C)

C) consumer-to-consumer commerce (C2C)

D) m-commerce

24. Many businesses establish partnerships and exchange standard business documents (orders, invoices) over private networks that connect the organizations' computers. This collaborative transaction process is called

A) digital integration

B) e-business

C) electronic data interchange (EDI)

D) m-commerce

25. JB Distributors decided that information on their internal network should be made available to their business partners throughout the United States. JB Distributors installed firewalls allowing authorized clients access to their internal network information. JB Distributors created a/an

A) extranet

B) home page

C) intranet

D) metropolitan area network (MAN)

Solutions

Solutions to Check Point—Section A

Answer	Refer to:
A–1. (C)	[A]
A–2. (A)	[A-2-b]
A–3. (B)	[A-2-e (2) (c)]

Solutions to Check Point—Section B

Answer	Refer to:
B–1. (D)	[B]
B–2. (A)	[B-1-b (1)]
B–3. (B)	[B-1-b (1) and B-2-c]

Solutions to Check Point—Section C

Answer	Refer to:
C–1. (B)	[C-1-b]
C–2. (C)	[C-2-c]
C–3. (B)	[C-3-c]

Solutions to For Your Review

	Answer	Refer to:
1.	(C)	[A]
2.	(D)	[A-1-a]
3.	(C)	[A-1-c]
4.	(D)	[A-2]
5.	(A)	[A-2-a]
6.	(B)	[A-2-b]
7.	(B)	[A-2-d]
8.	(D)	[A-2-e (2)]
9.	(C)	[B-1-a (1)]
10.	(C)	[B-1-b (1)]
11.	(B)	[B-1-b (2)]
12.	(D)	[B-1-b (3)]
13.	(B)	[B-1-b (4)]
14.	(A)	[B-1-b (6)]
15.	(D)	[B-2]
16.	(B)	[B-2]
17.	(C)	[B-2-b]
18.	(A)	[B-1-b (1) and B-2-c]
19.	(B)	[B-2-c]
20.	(B)	[B-2-d (2)]
21.	(A)	[C-1]
22.	(D)	[C-2-d and Chapter 2 B-3-e]
23.	(D)	[C-2-d]
24.	(C)	[C-3-b]
25.	(A)	[C-3-c]

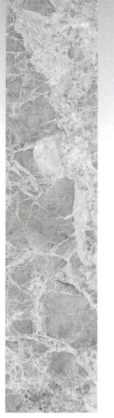

Chapter 5

System Security

OVERVIEW

Security of the information technology infrastructure is a collaborative effort among information systems personnel and the organization's end users. As organizations become internetworked enterprises, the security issue magnifies. Electronic data produces a more responsive business environment while making this key resource more vulnerable to errors, destruction, misuse, and fraud.

When computer-based information systems are down, organizations suffer great losses, both monetarily as well as losing the public's confidence. All business professionals must recognize computer problems as well as assist in creating a secure environment. As administrative professionals understand the dynamics of the systems life cycle, they are better able to communicate and troubleshoot with information technology professionals from analyzing information systems requirements to the ongoing maintenance phase of the internetworked enterprise.

KEY TERMS

A. Systems Personnel and Users

Today information systems are vital to business operations around the world. An organization's information technology infrastructure—hardware, software, data, storage, and the enterprise network—must be protected to ensure accurate and timely processing as well as prevent threats from unintentional and intentional misuse. Information systems personnel, along with end users knowledgeable about their information technology requirements, need to work together to design, build, and maintain a secure technology infrastructure for the organization. A trusting, collaborative effort between these two groups is key to ensuring an infrastructure that meets the daily needs of the organization.

1. ***Information Systems Personnel:*** Information systems personnel are responsible for maintaining the hardware, software, data storage, and networks. In addition to managers and operations personnel, programmers, systems analysts, database administrators, telecommunications/network engineers, and Web/e-commerce specialists are responsible for the technical requirements of the information infrastructure. Administrative professionals need to be able to effectively communicate with these specialists.

    a. *Programmers:* **Programmers** are technical specialists who write and maintain software instructions (code) for the computer. With the proliferation of vendor services for software programs, programmers also need to be able to monitor and maintain these products and services in a secure information systems environment. *Systems programmers* specialize in system software leaving application software issues to other programmers. In small organizations, office personnel explain their software requirements and problems directly to programmers. Many programmers are trained for programmer/analyst positions.

    b. *Systems analysts:* **Systems analysts** translate business requirements and problems into information technology requirements. Because systems analysts are the liaison between the information technicians and business users, their educational background is a combination of information systems and business with very good communication skills. Good systems analysts become effective change agents within the organization.

    c. *Database administrator:* A **database administrator** is responsible for the logical database design, development of the data dictionary, security of the data, and monitoring how others (both users and technical personnel) use data. Data are a key organization resource; therefore, a data/information policy should be established for everyone in the organization to follow. Typically the Chief Information Officer or executive officer of the information systems division is responsible for formulating an information policy. Input from personnel throughout the organization should be sought when developing an information policy.

    d. *Telecommunications/network engineer:* Electronic communication requires constant attention to the information technology infrastructure—hardware, software, data storage, and networks. Installing and maintaining a secure information infrastructure is a very technical operation that is typically staffed by electrical engineers with a specialization in networks. In the information technology industry these individuals are called **network engineers.** Because of the constant changes in the telecommunications field, these employees require seminars and continuing education programs to update skills and knowledge. Often network certification is achieved through specialized seminars and education programs.

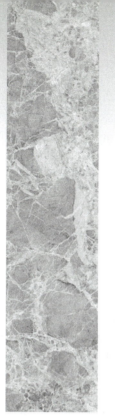

Chapter 5
System Security

OVERVIEW

Security of the information technology infrastructure is a collaborative effort among information systems personnel and the organization's end users. As organizations become internetworked enterprises, the security issue magnifies. Electronic data produces a more responsive business environment while making this key resource more vulnerable to errors, destruction, misuse, and fraud.

When computer-based information systems are down, organizations suffer great losses, both monetarily as well as losing the public's confidence. All business professionals must recognize computer problems as well as assist in creating a secure environment. As administrative professionals understand the dynamics of the systems life cycle, they are better able to communicate and troubleshoot with information technology professionals from analyzing information systems requirements to the ongoing maintenance phase of the internetworked enterprise.

KEY TERMS

Acceptance test, 105
Antivirus program, 108
Biometric control, 105
Conversion, 106
Cracker, 103
Data tampering, 104
Database administrator, 98
Denial of service, 103
Digital certificate, 109
Digital signature, 109
Digital wallet, 109

Encryption, 109
Fault-tolerant system, 106
Firewall, 108
Hacker, 103
Help desk, 100
Hot site, 107
Information center, 100
Information policy, 100
Network engineer, 98
Programmer, 98
Security protocol, 109

Spam, 103
Steering committee, 101
Systems analyst, 98
Systems audit, 111
Systems life cycle, 110
Technology support
    group, 100
Trojan horse, 103
Virus, 103
Web designer, 99
Webmaster, 99

A. Systems Personnel and Users

Today information systems are vital to business operations around the world. An organization's information technology infrastructure—hardware, software, data, storage, and the enterprise network—must be protected to ensure accurate and timely processing as well as prevent threats from unintentional and intentional misuse. Information systems personnel, along with end users knowledgeable about their information technology requirements, need to work together to design, build, and maintain a secure technology infrastructure for the organization. A trusting, collaborative effort between these two groups is key to ensuring an infrastructure that meets the daily needs of the organization.

1. *Information Systems Personnel:* Information systems personnel are responsible for maintaining the hardware, software, data storage, and networks. In addition to managers and operations personnel, programmers, systems analysts, database administrators, telecommunications/network engineers, and Web/e-commerce specialists are responsible for the technical requirements of the information infrastructure. Administrative professionals need to be able to effectively communicate with these specialists.

    a. *Programmers:* **Programmers** are technical specialists who write and maintain software instructions (code) for the computer. With the proliferation of vendor services for software programs, programmers also need to be able to monitor and maintain these products and services in a secure information systems environment. *Systems programmers* specialize in system software leaving application software issues to other programmers. In small organizations, office personnel explain their software requirements and problems directly to programmers. Many programmers are trained for programmer/analyst positions.

    b. *Systems analysts:* **Systems analysts** translate business requirements and problems into information technology requirements. Because systems analysts are the liaison between the information technicians and business users, their educational background is a combination of information systems and business with very good communication skills. Good systems analysts become effective change agents within the organization.

    c. *Database administrator:* A **database administrator** is responsible for the logical database design, development of the data dictionary, security of the data, and monitoring how others (both users and technical personnel) use data. Data are a key organization resource; therefore, a data/information policy should be established for everyone in the organization to follow. Typically the Chief Information Officer or executive officer of the information systems division is responsible for formulating an information policy. Input from personnel throughout the organization should be sought when developing an information policy.

    d. *Telecommunications/network engineer:* Electronic communication requires constant attention to the information technology infrastructure—hardware, software, data storage, and networks. Installing and maintaining a secure information infrastructure is a very technical operation that is typically staffed by electrical engineers with a specialization in networks. In the information technology industry these individuals are called **network engineers.** Because of the constant changes in the telecommunications field, these employees require seminars and continuing education programs to update skills and knowledge. Often network certification is achieved through specialized seminars and education programs.

e. *Web/e-commerce specialists:* Whether the digital organization uses a Web site for informational purposes or for e-commerce, personnel skilled in maintaining the Web server and in the technical development and aesthetic design of the Web site are important. **Webmasters** monitor and maintain Web servers. **Web designers** possess the technical and aesthetic skills for developing Web sites. e-Commerce sites require that Web designers have advanced Web programming skills securely linking the site to organization databases and the enterprise network.

2. *Systems Users: End users* are business personnel who use the information system. Since information systems personnel design applications to meet end-user requirements, it is important for the user to be part of the design, development, security, and maintenance of the organization's information system. End users knowledgeable about information systems are often invited to be part of the system design or development team as well as serve on information technology committees.

In addition to understanding and utilizing the organization's information in a safe and secure manner, end users must protect data stored on their desktop PC. The following guidelines are beneficial in protecting the office microcomputer environment:

a. *Antivirus program:* Make sure the desktop PC, notebook, or workstation is equipped with a virus-scanning program. If the antivirus program does not automatically scan the microcomputer drives, the hard drive should be scanned for viruses at least once a week.

b. *Backup:* Regularly *backup* important documents. Backing up files means storing a duplicate copy of the document or file in another location. USB flash drives provide a convenient backup system for microcomputers. Traveling professionals use USB flash drives as a convenient, easy way to backup documents when away from the office. Many organizations provide disk space on the enterprise or division network for backing up documents and files.

c. *Passwords:* Establish *passwords* to the desktop PC, notebook, workstation, or the organization's network that can be remembered yet not easily figured out by others. Maiden names, birth dates, and other personal information are passwords that others can easily figure out—"guess."

One way to set a password is to create a phrase (i.e., "I really like my work environment"); many times the password needs six characters. Create a mnemonic based on the first letter of each word in the phrase (i.e., "irlmwe"). If the password needs to be changed on a regular basis, use a numbering system to change the mnemonic. Some systems require at least two characters in the password be changed.

EXAMPLE: *System that requires changing at least two characters in the password:*

irlmwe10	*First password*
irlmwe23	*Second password*
irlmwe45	*Third password . . . and so on*

d. *File deletion:* If a file should be permanently deleted from storage, consult the information systems department. Deleted files can still be on the storage medium even though the file name does not appear in the file index. Erase is a software program that permanently deletes the file from the storage medium.

e. *Firewall:* Some desktop PCs, notebooks, or workstations need a firewall. Office professionals who travel with their notebook should have firewalls installed to protect unauthorized access to stored data; Windows XP has a firewall built into the operating system software.

3. ***Systems Personnel and End-User Relationships:*** The working relationship among systems personnel and end users is critical. Because of the interdependence between information systems and business operations, managing the information system resources requires collaboration among technical personnel and business personnel. The following identify several approaches that establish a collaborative environment:

   a. *Technical and administrative support:* Although today's end users are more technically adept, there typically is a learning curve as technology is enhanced or new operations are implemented. Support for end users includes training, help desks, technology support groups, and technology updates.

      (1) *Technology specialists:* Many of the information technology personnel are also trained to interface with end users in supporting their learning needs.

      (2) *Training:* Many organizations support in-house technology workshops for business professionals. [See Information Center (A-3-b)]. Also, organizations may provide support for administrative professionals to attend professional conferences and seminars on information technology topics. To make effective use of the computer-based information system, administrative professionals should take advantage of all training opportunities available.

      (3) *Help desk:* A **help desk** is a support station staffed by an information technology specialist. End users can call, e-mail, or drop in to receive both hardware and software assistance from the help desk technician. Sometimes a help desk is outsourced to a support service where technology help is available 24/7 (24 hours a day, 7 days a week). End users either e-mail or call the support service technicians at the outsourced help center.

      (4) *Technology support group:* As end users become proficient with productivity software (e.g., word processing, spreadsheets, Internet browsers, and searching), the organization identifies them as someone to contact for assistance. Sometimes a **technology support group** initiative is established within a department and not organization wide. An organization must be cautious not to allow these individuals to be interrupted to the point where their normal responsibilities are affected.

      (5) *Technology updates:* Technology updates (newsletters or bulletins) sent from the Information Technology Division or posted on the organization's intranet are very helpful in learning new information about the organization's computer-based information system. Often administrative professionals subscribe to publications that specialize in information technology.

   b. *Information center:* Many large organizations establish an **information center** staffed with technology specialists responsible for supporting end users in using technology (hardware and software), maintaining hardware and software, providing technology workshops and seminars, and recommending new purchases for the user's area of specialty.

   c. *Information policy:* The use, distribution, and security of information are dependent on consistent guidelines for the entire organization. The Chief Information Officer usually is responsible, with input from all levels throughout the organization, for formulating an **information policy.** As a working document, the information policy should be posted on the organization's intranet for easy updates, access, and use.

d. *Joint information systems/end-user teams:* Team management is a collaborative process. Including end users in the planning, application development, budgeting, security, and maintenance teams provides an avenue for important input. Collaboration is an honest, open communication process. Team management success requires:

- Representative input from an organizational perspective
- Top-level executives who utilize team input with clear, complete feedback regarding decisions

e. *Steering committee:* An alternative to team management is the steering committee. The Chief Information Officer or an assistant usually chairs the steering committee with member representation from the information technology division and each functional division within the organization. The **steering committee** focuses on policies for the use of the information system, priorities for system development, budgets for information technology, system security, system maintenance, and system issues. Sometimes the steering committee is supplemented with joint information systems/end-user teams when areas need special emphasis or analysis.

The management of the information technology infrastructure must be dynamic and constantly changing. Change reflects progress in achieving organizational goals dealing with technology. The success of technology decisions rests upon both the information systems personnel and the business users of the system.

Check Point—Section A

Directions: For each question, circle the correct answer.

A–1. Individuals who translate business requirements into information technical requirements are

A) database administrators
B) end users
C) telecommunications specialists
D) systems analysts

A–2. Mathews needs to establish a password for her notebook that must be changed every month. The best password would be

A) her birth date plus the letter "a" (next month she will change the "a" to a "b", and so forth)
B) her maiden name plus the date she set the password (i.e., 91xx for September 1, 20xx)

C) a different name each month which she will remember by recoding it on a small slip of paper stored in her wallet
D) a mnemonic based on a phrase plus the number "1" (next month she will change the "1" to a "2", and so forth)

A–3. Many large organizations provide technical support for office professionals through a/an

A) information center
B) information policy
C) joint information system/end-user team
D) steering committee

B. System Vulnerability

Electronically stored data are more available to all users throughout the organization than manually stored data. Electronic data are more easily integrated with enterprise-wide operations making information more timely, useful, and meaningful. Therefore, electronically stored data are more vulnerable to errors, destruction, misuse, and fraud than manually stored data. Advancements in telecommunications, hardware, and software; the openness of the Internet environment; and the expertise and use of computer-based information systems by everyone have magnified these vulnerabilities.

When computer-based information systems are down, organizations suffer great losses. Organizations with Web sites supporting e-commerce can lose millions of dollars each day the system is down. In addition, the public loses confidence in organizations where the computer-based information system is down on a regular basis or shows signs of lack of maintenance. Administrative professionals should recognize computer problems as well as be involved in creating a controlled environment.

1. ***Threats to the Computer-Based Information System:*** There are many internal and external threats to a computer-based information system. Unintentional threats include errors, software bugs and defects, data quality, and environmental hazards. Intentional threats include hackers, crackers, and viruses. Administrative professionals should recognize these threats and immediately report the problem to appropriate personnel.

   a. *Unintentional threats:* Although unintentional, any threat to the computer-based information system must be detected and immediately addressed. Security of the information system is a concern requiring the attention of everyone in the organization.

      (1) *Errors:* Errors in computer-based information systems can occur at any point in the processing cycle: input, program processing, computer operations (systems software), hardware, and output and distribution. Administrative professionals should check output to identify any inconsistencies or inaccuracies in the document before distribution. Also, all incoming information should be checked for accuracy.

      (2) *Software defects and errors:* Program code defects or errors, commonly called *bugs*, are common in most software programs; it is virtually impossible to eliminate all bugs from large programs. Detecting errors in the analysis and design stage is significantly less costly than after implementation. Involvement by the end user in software testing before implementation, whether the software is purchased or developed in-house, can save the organization a large amount of money, programmers a great deal of time, and end users much frustration. Bugs often occur with purchased software and are typically corrected with a patch from the vendor; however, these corrections can take time.

      (3) *Data quality:* Inaccurate data or data inconsistent with other sources is the most common source of information system failure. Poor data quality creates serious operational and financial problems for the organization. Bad data lead to bad decisions, product recalls, and poor customer relations. Administrative professionals must be cognizant of data input processes, data storage, and data use. An information policy supports data consistency throughout the organization and is an important document for all business professionals to follow. Information systems personnel and system users must pay close attention to computer-based operations throughout the systems life cycle.

(4) *Environmental hazards:* Fires (the most common hazard), floods, power outages, earthquakes, hurricanes, and storms can disrupt computer operations and be very costly to the organization. Control measures to minimize these hazards should be part of the information resource plan. Many times administrative professionals who understand the importance of the data and processes to the organization need to insist on appropriate controls.

b. *Intentional threats:* Intentional threats, whether for mischief, profit, or to disable the system, are increasing every year. Intentional threats can be by outsiders who gain unauthorized access or by insiders who misuse their authorized rights to the computer-based system. An intentional threat can become a computer crime.

   (1) *Hackers:* A **hacker** is a person who gains unauthorized access to a computer network for mischief; a **cracker** is a malicious hacker for profit or one who attempts to disable the system. Attacks in the e-commerce environment demonstrate the vulnerability of computer-based information systems. **Denial of service** attacks are where crackers flood a network or Web server with information requests in an attempt to crash the network. Inconsistencies in the operation of the organization's computer-based information system should be immediately brought to the attention of a supervisor or the information technology division.

   (2) *Viruses:* A computer **virus** is a rogue software program that spreads throughout the network disrupting processing and memory operations and possibly destroying data. Thousands of viruses exist with approximately 150 more new viruses created each month. Many viruses spread through the Internet from downloaded files or files attached to e-mail messages. Confer with information technicians regarding suspected viruses, and follow all instructions provided by these specialists. Characteristics of computer viruses are listed in Figure 5–1.

   (3) *Trojan horse:* A **Trojan horse** is a destructive program that masquerades as a benign application. Unlike viruses, Trojan horses do not replicate. The most insidious type of Trojan horse is a program that claims to rid the computer of viruses but instead introduces viruses into the computer system.

   (4) *Spam:* **Spam** is unsolicited junk e-mail. Not only do computer users receive junk e-mail at home, but it now penetrates many organizations' networks. In addition to interfering with one's work, spamming can consume valuable bandwidth on the network thereby slowing down the network to the point where efficient business communication and operations are affected. All

FIGURE 5–1   Computer Virus Characteristics

Worm viruses are attached to e-mail messages spreading from computer to computer that have Microsoft operating systems and software. Internet traffic is diminished as the virus propagates.
Macro viruses are executable functions inside programs such as Microsoft Word or Excel. A macro virus duplicates through e-mail attachments and can delete files.
File infecting viruses erase a computer's hard drive.
Script viruses (written in JavaScript or VBScript) overwrite .jpg and .mp3 files. Script viruses spread to other systems through Microsoft Outlook and Internet Relay Chat.

e-mail should relate to work activities. Also, e-mails sent to groups of individuals should not be forwarded to another group of individuals; bulk e-mails affect the traffic on the network backbone.

5. *Data tampering:* **Data tampering** is entering incorrect or fabricated data or changing or deleting existing data stored in the organization's files and databases. Insiders are the ones most likely to unintentionally or intentionally tamper with the organization's data.

EXAMPLE — Unintentional Data Tampering:

Errors with data input: transposing numbers or the misspelling of a name.

EXAMPLE — Intentional Data Tampering:

Entering false data into the finance system database to produce inaccurate financial reports for auditors and stockholders.

In addition to producing inaccurate data, some employees are capable of changing the computer program logic so inaccuracies continue on a regular basis.

EXAMPLE: *A bank programmer who transfers money on a regular basis into a dummy account through phony debit and credit transactions.*

The diversity of threats to an organization's computer-based information system is phenomenal. Now that data are recognized as a key organization resource, it is imperative that appropriate controls be implemented to counter these threats.

2. ***Creating a Controlled Environment:*** Although setting controls is the responsibility of the information technology division, business professionals must be aware of the strategies and tools available to deter disasters. Often recommendations by end users alert the information technology division of threats so corrective action can be implemented before a disaster takes place.

A combination of general controls and application controls are common in most organizations. The Internet and e-commerce applications have added another layer of security measures that should be considered and implemented where appropriate.

a. *General controls:* General controls cover the security and use of the computer-based information system including hardware, software, implementation, operations, data storage, and data usage.

(1) *Hardware controls:* Computer equipment must be protected against theft, environmental threats, and obsolescence. The serial numbers of all equipment should be recorded and used for annual checks.

(a) *Theft:* Locking all doors to offices and laboratories when not in use can control hardware theft. Lost or stolen hardware can be identified through annual reviews using equipment serial numbers. Areas with extensive equipment can restrict access to only authorized users by using magnetic cards or biometric controls. Security personnel and/or cameras are another measure many organizations utilize to monitor the computing environment.

(b) *Environmental threats:* Environmental threats can damage or disrupt the computing environment resulting in exorbitant costs while computer programs and data files are recreated. Although fire is the most common threat, other threats include earthquakes, floods, tornadoes, power failures, and other such environmental conditions. It is important that businesses have a disaster recovery plan [see B-2-a (4) (b)].

(c) *Obsolescence:* A replacement system should be designed so equipment is maintained and replaced on a rotating basis throughout the organization. Often the administrative professional is responsible for maintaining serial number lists and communicating accurate equipment information to the information technology division.

(2) *Software controls:* Software controls are very important to the overall processing and performance of the computer-based information system. Information technicians monitor the use of software, prevent unauthorized access, and ensure that appropriate software licenses are in place.

(a) *Access: Access control* restricts unauthorized users from using a microcomputer; the computer-based information system; or specific programs, data within the system, or transactions. Unique user identification such as a password, magnetic access card, or biometric control provides access to valid users.

Biometric controls identify an individual based on physiological or behavioral characteristics. Biometric controls include:

- *Iris:* Comparing a scan of the iris to an encoded and stored video image of the iris pattern and color is considered the most reliable biometric control.

- *Fingerprints:* Matching a fingerprint against a prestored template identifies the user.

- *Signature:* Matching a signature against a prestored authentic signature is replacing the photo ID system.

- *Keystroke:* A person's keyboard pressure and speed are matched against prestored keystroke data.

(b) *Software license:* A *license agreement* allows the purchaser to install the software on one computer so it is available to only one user. A *network license* and a *site license* allow the software to be available to multiple users; the number of users is registered with the software vendor when purchased and can be increased or decreased as needs change. A site license includes users not on the organization's network as well as telecommuters who need to have the software installed on their home microcomputer. A *telecommuter* is an employee who primarily works from home.

The *Software Publishers Association (SPA)* enforces software copyright laws and audits companies to ensure that the software is properly licensed and used. SPA stated that unlicensed use of software amounts to a loss of approximately $15 billion annually to software developers.

(3) *Implementation controls:* Audits during system development ensure that the process is properly managed. Formal reviews by end users are critical. Reviews should check for compliance with business processes, adequate testing, conversion method(s), training plan, and documentation.

(a) *Testing:* Thorough testing ascertains whether the system produces correct results. Programs are never error free; testing is a way of locating as many errors as possible. Users need to provide programmers with all the ways a program or the system can fail, including faulty data. The final test is an **acceptance test** where users evaluate the entire system and indicate how well the system meets the standards established at the beginning of the design or purchase of the system.

(b) *Conversion:* **Conversion** is the process of changing from the old system to the new one. Conversion ranges from direct to phased.

- *Direct:* The old system is replaced with the new system on a specific date. For complex systems, this method can be very risky and therefore costly.

- *Parallel:* Both the old system and the new system are used until everyone is assured that the new system functions correctly. Business professionals need to provide feedback on system response and output. Although costly, this is a safe conversion method and used with more mission-critical systems.

- *Pilot:* A selected area (department or division) of the organization uses a test version of the system. As the department uses the system, it is changed until the system works correctly. At that time, the system is installed throughout the organization in stages or all at the same time.

- *Phased:* When a new system has been adopted, sometimes it is beneficial to introduce it to the organization in stages. A phased approach spreads costs and training sessions over a period of time.

EXAMPLE: *A new payroll system can be phased in starting with salaried employees who are paid monthly, then phasing in hourly employees who are paid weekly. Salaried employees can be trained as to the benefits of the new system. In turn, the salaried employees can provide a positive and supportive environment when the hourly employee payroll system is installed.*

(c) *Training:* End-user support is important for effective system usage. Sometimes formal training is required; at other times user support groups adequately provide the assistance needed. Administrative professionals must ensure that business users in their division are prepared and supported in using the system by submitting recommendations to executives who can ensure that adequate training and support are provided.

(4) *Operations controls:* To ensure that procedures are consistent, controls over the setup of the computer-based information system, processing, and system backup and recovery are necessary.

(a) *Fault-tolerant systems:* **Fault-tolerant systems** are designed with duplicate hardware, software, and power supply so the system will continue operating during system failure. Secondary storage RAID units are often used for fault-tolerant systems.

(b) *Disaster recovery plan:* Business personnel and information technology specialists should develop a plan for running the business in the event of a system outage. The following should be included in a disaster recovery plan:

- Identify mission-critical applications and file storage locations. Periodically data from a microcomputer should be backed up on a removable disk/disc and stored in a fireproof location.

- Identify processing alternatives—manual, disaster recovery service, or backup system at another location. At an external **hot site,** a fully configured backup data center can be designed.
- Identify individuals along with their disaster recovery responsibilities.
- Adhere to procedures that are consistent throughout the organization.
- Obtain senior management support to ensure compliance.
- Annually review the disaster recovery plan. Administrative professionals often serve on committees to review these procedures.

(5) *Data storage controls:* Data security must be incorporated into the network system as well as the database system. In addition to ensuring authorized access to data, it is important to ensure that the data or storage mediums are not damaged. Data backup and recovery procedures and equipment maintenance are important precautions to follow.

(6) *Data use controls:* Formalized standards, rules, procedures, and disciplinary actions to ensure that the organization's general and application controls are followed and enforced is critical. Administrative professionals should be familiar with these manuals and promote compliance.

b. *Application controls:* Application controls are specific to each application and must adhere to the functional area specifications and procedures. Application controls pertain to the input, process, and output of both automated and manual processes.

(1) *Input controls:* Data must be checked for accuracy, completeness, and consistency when entered into the system. There are controls to check for input authorization, data editing, and error handling.

EXAMPLES: *Program routines check data input for consistency, format, and reasonableness.*

Entering a password in all capital letters does not match the format with a system where the password must be in lowercase. The user would be denied access, and a "check password" message would be displayed on the computer monitor.

Asking for a $3,000 withdrawal at a bank automatic teller machine (ATM) is not reasonable when the maximum amount for a withdrawal is $300. The customer transaction would be denied.

(2) *Processing controls:* Using computer matching, run control totals, and edit checks, data can be checked for accuracy and completeness during processing.

EXAMPLES:

Processing payroll includes the matching of employee time cards with a payroll master file. A duplicate time card would be flagged and not processed. At the end of the payroll run, processing reports are generated, reporting duplicate time cards and missing time cards.

Run control totals balance the total number of transactions processed with the total number of transaction inputs and outputs.

(3) *Output controls:* To ensure that the processing results are complete and properly distributed, output controls can be implemented.

EXAMPLES:

Administrative professionals should check all documents for accuracy and completeness before distribution. Errors should be corrected or reported to the information technology division if the correction is under their control. By studying the nature of output errors, information technicians can recommend appropriate controls.

Report distribution logs document that authorized recipients obtained their checks, financial reports, or other critical documents.

    c. *Network and Internet security controls:* Transmitting information via intranets and extranets and linking to the Internet require special security measures. Dealing with crackers, computer viruses, and e-commerce security all require additional security measures.

       (1) *Firewall:* Firewalls are used to ensure that only authorized personnel have access to the organization's private, secured network. **Firewalls** consist of software and hardware placed between the organization's internal network(s) and an external unsecured network (Internet) allowing only authorized access. Firewalls are the most cost-effective solution to the problem of hackers and crackers.

           Administrative professionals who travel with their notebook should have firewalls installed to protect unauthorized access to data stored on the hard drive; Windows XP has a firewall built into the operating system software.

       (2) *Antivirus protection:* **Antivirus programs** should be on the organization's network as well as desktop PCs, notebooks, and workstations. Security suites of software that integrate virus protection with firewalls and Web security are being adopted by most organizations.

           Coping with viruses requires users to have all documents automatically scanned or to periodically scan the office microcomputer system. The following guidelines can help minimize virus vulnerability:

- Do not open e-mails from unknown or suspicious sources, especially e-mails with attachments.
- Delete all suspicious e-mails.
- Download only legitimate files to an external disk/disc. Run the antivirus program on the file before opening it and saving it to the microcomputer hard drive.
- Keep the antivirus program current with virus updates from the software provider.
- Immediately report suspicious activities either on the organization's network or the office microcomputer to the information technology division. Follow their recommendations for addressing viruses.

    d. *e-Commerce security:* When electronically transmitting data between buyers and sellers, it is very important for data to be secure. In addition to secure channels [value-added networks (VAN) and virtual private networks (VPN)], encryption, digital signatures, digital certificates, digital wallets, and security protocols are measures used by most e-commerce organizations.

(1) *Encryption:* Encrypted messages are coded to prevent access and reading without authorization. Complex **encryption** codes are assigned to each character (letter, number, or symbol); the code may use as many as 128 characters for only one character. The message is encrypted using an encryption key. The receiver must have an authorized decryption key to decrypt the code and read the message. There are one-key encryption systems, two-key encryption systems, and a hybrid of these two systems.

(2) *Digital signature:* A **digital signature** is a digital code attached to documents to identify the sender and message contents. To be legally binding, someone must verify that the digital signature belongs to the person who sent the data and that the data were not altered.

(3) *Digital certificate:* Using a certificate authority (CA), a trusted third party, a **digital certificate** is an attachment that verifies the sender to be whom he or she claims.

(4) *Digital wallets:* **Digital wallets** are software that stores credit card and owner identification to be used for e-commerce purchases.

(5) *Security protocols: Secure hypertext transport protocol (S-HTTP)* is a **security protocol** used for secure information transfer over the Internet. S-HTTP provides the client-server environment with a way to encrypt and decrypt transactions. *Secure electronic transaction (SET)* is a more secure protocol using digital certificates and digital wallets for encrypting credit card payments over the Internet and other open networks.

The identification and control of threats to an organization's computer-based information system can be expensive to build and complicated to operate and maintain. A cost-benefit analysis will help the information technology division and corporate executives determine which controls provide the most cost-effective measures. By addressing mission-critical data and processes, financial and accounting systems, and secure e-commerce environments, an organization can invest in the security controls that match the risks the firm is willing to assume.

Check Point—Section B

Directions: For each question, circle the correct answer.

B–1. Attacks by crackers who flood a network or Web server with information requests in an attempt to crash the network is (a)

A) computer operation error
B) denial of service
C) spamming
D) virus

B–2. The administrative assistant of the Human Resource Division is responsible for maintaining and annually checking serial numbers of the division's desktop PCs, notebooks, workstations, and printers. This responsibility is part of the organization's

A) hardware control
B) information policy
C) license agreement audit
D) operations control

B–3. Using the organization's intranet, Sing completed a vacation request for four weeks. The form was not accepted by the Human Resource system because the policy limits vacation to a maximum of two weeks at one time. This is an example of a/an

A) access control
B) application control for reasonableness
C) implementation control
D) data use control

C. System Quality Management: Troubleshooting

Computer-based information systems are a combination of technical and social elements. Dynamic organizations are continually changing, and so must the organization's systems. Organizations need to develop an information systems plan that supports the overall business plan. As administrative professionals understand the dynamics of the systems life cycle, they are better able to communicate and troubleshoot with information technology professionals from design through ongoing maintenance of the internetworked enterprise.

Quality system management is a major challenge for the internetworked enterprise. Many organizations are still designing systems to fully connect and utilize the benefits of intranets, extranets, the Web, and the Internet. No matter where an organization is in the process of computer-based information systems development, security should be part of the process. System audits help with troubleshooting throughout the life cycle of the system.

1. *Systems Life Cycle:* No matter the size of the system, from large mainframe environments to desktop PCs, the application should be designed with the goals and objectives of the internetworked enterprise in mind. Integrating functions and operations is important for internal as well as external processes. In today's networked world, integration and collaboration are key to long-term success. The **systems life cycle** is a dynamic process that requires interaction with personnel at all levels within the organization.

   a. *Analysis:* Analysis is the problem-solving process identifying causes and solutions. Troubleshooting is best handled through logical problem-solving techniques (see C-2).

   b. *Design:* Systems design models how a computer-based information system can meet the information requirements identified in the analysis phase. Systems design can be compared to a blueprint of a new home; the builders need the design in order to accurately build the product. As with all design phases, the end user should have input into the design.

   c. *Development:* Development consists of programming, testing, documenting, training, and converting to the new system.

       EXAMPLE: *Manny is responsible for fundraising contributions for the Fine Arts School at Madison University. Over the years, all contacts and contributions have been manually recorded in journals. With the University's new network, Manny is interested in computerizing the process and integrating processes with the University's Foundation Office so that only one contact database needs to be maintained. Authorizations for read and write privileges will be assigned to select individuals.*

       Working with the Information Technology Division, Manny and a representative from the Foundation meet to analyze and design the system. Manny has the responsibility of developing several word processing applications and a spreadsheet application that interface with the University's database.

After she has developed the applications, Manny tests the applications with her original data. After correcting several bugs, Manny tests her applications with the University's database. After several test scenarios to make the system fail and the errors corrected, Manny is able to directly convert to the new system.

Collaborating with the Foundation and Information Technology, Manny takes the leadership to document the application system design and processes. The documentation is on the intranet with authorized access by selected representatives from the Fine Arts School, Foundation Office, and Information Technology Division. Since this was a collaborative effort among the users and technicians, no training was required when Manny converted to the new system.

  d. *Operation and maintenance:* Once a new system is in full operation, information systems technicians and end users need to carefully monitor the output. Crucial time periods are daily, weekly, monthly, quarterly, semi-annual, and annual activities.

   Maintenance, an ongoing process of the life cycle, includes required changes in hardware and software due to depreciation and new technologies, error detection and correction, changes to meet new requirements within the organization, and improvements in system efficiency and effectiveness. Systems audits are important to the ongoing life of the computer-based information system (see C-3)

2. ***Troubleshooting—Systems Analysis:*** Analysis is the problem-solving process identifying causes and solutions. Troubleshooting is an ongoing part of the systems life cycle and is best handled through logical problem-solving techniques. The primary focus is on users' objectives, organization mission and goals, and detailed procedures involved in the application.

  a. *Analyze operations:* An analysis is needed to determine current users' objectives, operations, and information flow.

  b. *Identify existing problems or inefficiencies:* Any problems or inefficiencies that exist within the present system need to be identified.

  c. *Define alternatives for user's new objectives:* Primary objectives and operations need to be identified along with alternatives for meeting the objectives.

  d. *Evaluate alternatives:* In collaboration with appropriate personnel throughout the organization (technology, budget, users, and senior management), determine which alternative best meets the users' objective and the organization mission and goals.

  e. *Implement and follow-up:* Decisions are best made after a series of iterations and evaluations at each stage in the analysis process. The decision maker often loops back through one or more of the stages during the decision process as well as after system implementation for ongoing evaluation.

3. ***Troubleshooting—Systems Audits:*** Organizations should conduct comprehensive audits on the computer-based information system to determine the effectiveness of all the security controls. Such a **systems audit** should have an unbiased auditor who has a thorough understanding of the organization's personnel structure, business applications and processes, and physical information facilities.

  a. *External audit:* For an *external audit* an external auditor examines the input, process, and output of the computer-based information system as well as reviews any internal audits that have been conducted on a regular basis. A comprehensive audit evaluates all potential hazards and controls in the system: operations, applications, data integrity, security and privacy, disaster planning and recovery, vendor management and licenses, system documentation, training, maintenance, productivity, and budgeting and cost control.

b. *Internal audit: Internal audits* should be done on a regular basis by end users, information technicians, and corporate auditors for financial operations. Several types of audits are used by both internal and external auditors:

(1) *Output audits:* Using specific inputs, *output audits* verify process accuracy. Output audits are fast and inexpensive but may be incomplete (i.e., two errors may cancel one another and produce correct output).

(2) *Computer audits:* Using test data, auditors check the input, process, and output logic of applications and security processes. The effectiveness of computer audits hinges on quality test data to identify system problems.

(3) *Computer-assisted audits:* Using test data and audit software and hardware, business applications and security systems are simulated and tested. Skilled hackers sometimes find lucrative positions testing the network security systems of organizations.

c. *Data audits:* As a critical resource, data quality has become an explicit organizational goal, especially for internetworked enterprises. A *data audit* surveys data files for accuracy and completeness. Surveying end users for their perceptions of data quality, surveying all the data files, or surveying samples from data files are three ways to conduct data audits. Correcting errors and inconsistencies in data to improve accuracy and formats for standard organization-wide usage is called *data cleansing.*

System quality management is a collaborative effort between information technicians and business personnel. Insufficient user involvement in the analysis, design, and ongoing maintenance of the computer-based information system is a major cause of system failure. Administrative professionals who understand the dynamics of the system's life cycle are better able to communicate and troubleshoot with information technology professionals regarding the internetworked enterprise.

Check Point—Section C

Directions: For each question, circle the correct answer.

C–1. The systems life cycle pertains to the analysis, design, development, and maintenance of

A) all computer systems except microcomputer systems

B) all computer systems including microcomputer systems

C) mainly large corporate database systems

D) mainly network environments

C–2. The primary focus of systems analysis is

A) determining how a computer-based information system can meet the user's information requirements

B) identifying the organization's mission and goals, user objectives, and detailed application procedures

C) maintaining systems output for accuracy and completeness

D) testing and debugging the new system

C–3. Using test data, auditors can check the input, process, and output logic of applications and security processes. This is an example of a/an

A) computer audit

B) data audit

C) external audit

D) output audit

For Your Review

Directions: For each question, circle the correct answer.

1. Information technology personnel who write and maintain the code for basic computer operations (input/process/output and security) are
   A) application programmers
   B) network engineers
   C) systems analysts
   D) systems programmers

2. Because data are a key organization resource, most organizations now have data/information policies. Information policies are the responsibility of the
   A) chief information officer
   B) database administrator
   C) information center
   D) joint information systems team

3. The information technology division often hires electrical engineers with a specialization in
   A) application software programming
   B) database design
   C) networking
   D) Web design

4. Valley Auto Glass is enhancing their Web site and needs another professional skilled in the technical and aesthetic development of Web sites. Their employment ad should be for a
   A) Webmaster
   B) Web analyst
   C) Web designer
   D) Web programmer

5. A guideline that traveling professionals should follow for protecting their notebook computer and data is

   A) every week take the notebook to the IT Division to be checked for viruses
   B) backup important documents on a 3 1/2-inch disk and then on the department's network once back in the office
   C) install Windows XP for firewall protection
   D) permanently delete old files from the notebook's secondary storage using the system delete function

6. Prisby is working late and encounters a technical problem. To obtain technical support Prisby should
   A) attend the next in-house workshop on technology
   B) e-mail or call the 24/7 help desk
   C) seek assistance from the technology support group
   D) subscribe to an information technology publication for business professionals

7. Quinn has become very proficient with database applications both on her desktop PC and the enterprise system. To assist other end users at the firm with database applications, Quinn should
   A) attend professional conferences to stay current with new database technologies
   B) become a member of the technical support group
   C) participate on the joint information systems/end-user team
   D) subscribe to a database publication for business professionals

8. Large organizations often support in-house technology workshops through the
   A) help desk
   B) information center
   C) joint information systems/end-user team
   D) steering committee

9. As a new employee with Simmons & Sons, Villatoro wants to make sure he follows the expectations of the organization when using the enterprise database. Villatoro should
   A) attend the joint information systems/end-user team meetings
   B) read the information policy posted on the intranet
   C) schedule a meeting with the chief information officer
   D) subscribe to a database publication for business professionals

10. Which type of data is more vulnerable to errors, destruction, misuse, and fraud? Data stored in/on
    A) enterprise networks
    B) microfiche
    C) traditional file cabinets
    D) USB flash drives

11. With the growing number of internal and external threats to computer-based information, security becomes an important issue that
    A) is controlled through the information policy
    B) is the responsibility of the chief information officer
    C) requires the attention of everyone in the organization
    D) requires outsourcing services

12. Errors in computer-based information systems must be detected and immediately addressed. These errors occur with
    A) data input and information output
    B) data input and processing
    C) input/process/output, computer operations, hardware, and distribution
    D) systems software, input, processing, and hardware

13. Bugs in system software and application software are
    A) corrected faster if the software has been purchased from a software vendor
    B) detected and eliminated during unit tests
    C) less costly if detected before implementation
    D) minor glitches in the software that can be ignored

14. The most common source of errors in computer-based information systems is
    A) application software code
    B) inaccurate or inconsistent data
    C) processing
    D) system operations

15. A person who attempts to disable the organization's Web site is called a/an
    A) cracker
    B) Trojan horse
    C) Veronica
    D) Webmaster

16. A virus attached to e-mails and spread through Microsoft system and application software, diminishing Internet traffic, is a/an
    A) script
    B) spam
    C) Trojan horse
    D) worm

17. All sales data are entered daily through the marketing department desktop PC that requires user identification and a password. When entering an order, a quantity of 6 was entered instead of a 9. This is an example of a/an
    A) access vulnerability
    B) bug
    C) transposition problem
    D) unintentional error

18. Data tampering is most likely to be done by
    A) electronic data interchange (EDI) partners
    B) employees
    C) hackers
    D) online customers

19. Hardware must be protected against theft and obsolescence. A control to address both of these issues is to

A) annually check serial numbers and hardware specifications on each microcomputer, printer, and other equipment and submit a report to the information technology division

B) install biometric controls throughout the organization so access is restricted to only authorized personnel

C) make sure the last person leaving the division locks the office door

D) require all employees to use magnetic cards at the organization's employee entrance

20. Controls that pertain to the input, process, and output of both automated and manual processes are

A) application controls
B) general controls
C) implementation controls
D) operations controls

21. Using a special processor with security software between the organization's internal networks and the unsecured Internet to ensure that only authorized personnel have access to the organization's private network means the organization has a/an

A) denial of service
B) fault-tolerant system
C) firewall
D) two-key encryption system

22. e-Commerce organizations can secure information transfer over the Internet by encrypting and decrypting transactions with

A) digital wallets
B) secure electronic transaction (SET)
C) secure hypertext transport protocol (S-HTTP)
D) scripts

23. An architectural blueprint of a new home is analogous to systems

A) analysis diagrams
B) design models
C) development documentation
D) development programming code

24. Determining objectives and required information flows, identifying inefficiencies, defining system alternatives, evaluating alternatives, implementation, and follow up are all important steps to what process?

A) Audits conducted by external auditors
B) Development phase of the systems life cycle
C) Internal systems audits
D) Systems analysis problem-solving cycle

25. A comprehensive audit that evaluates operations, applications, data integrity, security, backup and recovery, license management, documentation, training, maintenance, productivity, and budgeting and cost control is best handled by the

A) chief information officer
B) external auditor
C) joint information systems/end-user team
D) steering committee

Solutions

Solutions to Check Point—Section A

Answer	Refer to:
A–1. (D)	[A-1-b]
A–2. (D)	[A-2-c]
A–3. (A)	[A-3-b]

Solutions to Check Point—Section B

Answer	Refer to:
B–1. (B)	[B-1-b (1)]
B–2. (A)	[B-2-a (1)]
B–3. (B)	[B-2-b (1)]

Solutions to Check Point—Section C

Answer	Refer to:
C–1. (B)	[C-1]
C–2. (B)	[C-2]
C–3. (A)	[C-3-b (2)]

Solutions to For Your Review

	Answer	Refer to:
1.	(D)	[A-1-a]
2.	(A)	[A-1-c and A-3-c]
3.	(C)	[A-1-d]
4.	(C)	[A-1-e]
5.	(C)	[A-2-e]
6.	(B)	[A-3-a (3)]
7.	(B)	[A-3-a (4)]
8.	(B)	[A-3-b]
9.	(B)	[A-1-c, A-3-c, and B-1-a (3)]
10.	(A)	[B]
11.	(C)	[Overview and B-1-a]
12.	(C)	[B-1-a (1)]
13.	(C)	[B-1-a (2)]
14.	(B)	[B-1-a (3)]
15.	(A)	[B-1-b (1)]
16.	(D)	[B-1-b (2) and Figure 5–1]
17.	(D)	[B-1-b (5)]
18.	(B)	[B-1-b (5)]
19.	(A)	[B-2-a (1) (a) and B-2-a (1) (c)]
20.	(A)	[B-2-b]
21.	(C)	[B-2-c (1) and Chapter 4 C-3-c]
22.	(C)	[B-2-d (5)]
23.	(B)	[C-1-b]
24.	(D)	[C-2, C-2-a, C-2-b, C-2-c, C-2-d, and C-2-e]
25.	(B)	[C-3 and C-3-a]

Chapter 6

Document Layout and Design

OVERVIEW

Document layout, design, and reproduction are tasks administrative professionals may perform whenever a new brochure, handout, flyer, newsletter, or other communication piece is created. These documents can be designed and reproduced using a variety of hardware and software technologies. When creating rather complex documents, the administrative professional will work with designers. Often, the quantity needed will require reproduction services from an in-house center, external reproduction service, or a commercial printer. The administrative professional must be knowledgeable about layout and design principles and reproduction options to ensure a quality final product.

Given the widespread use of reproduction technologies, legal aspects of copying and printing must be considered. The United States Copyright Statute, revised in 1976, was again reviewed in 1994 to address fair use and related technology issues. The Conference on Fair Use (CONFU) expanded on the copyright guidelines to include technology trends.

KEY TERMS

Alignment, 128
Ascender, 131
Comprehensive sketches (comps), 121
Contrast, 131
Cropping, 121
Descender, 131
Dropped capital (drop cap), 134
Eight-panel fold, 123
Four-panel fold, 122
Grayscale, 125

Greeking, 121
Gutter, 135
Halftone, 125
Idea folder, 120
Kerning, 134
Leading, 134
Print run, 125
Printer spreads, 126
Proximity, 128
Pull quote, 133
Repetition, 131
Rotating, 121

Sans serif, 132
Serif, 131
Signature, 122
Six-panel fold, 123
Thumbnails, 120
Track spacing, 134
Trapping, 135
Typography, 127
Visual unit, 128
Washout (creep), 123
White space, 128

A. Document Layout

Before planning the document layout and design process, it is important to know the purpose and intended audience of the final document. Starting with the end in mind ensures that document layout and design is focused on the final product. Document layout involves making decisions about the type of project (brochure, flyer), paper size and type, number of folds, graphics, print run, and reproduction.

1. *Type of Project:* An **idea folder** is helpful in determining the best type of design for a flyer, brochure, post card, multi-page document, or other types of business documents. The collection of sample documents in an idea folder becomes a helpful resource for future projects.

    a. *Review samples:* An idea file of creative, effective document designs is very helpful. When a flyer, brochure, graphic image, type arrangement, or design feature catches the administrative professional's eye, the sample should be saved in an idea folder. Notes about how a design feature created a positive first impression should be recorded on the sample document. These samples can kindle creative ideas for new projects.

    b. *Improve the design:* In addition to good designs, poorly designed documents are sometimes received. The administrative professional can make use of these documents by noting on the document ineffective first impressions the design conveyed. These examples should also be filed in the idea folder as a reminder of design foibles to avoid.

    c. *Sketch thumbnails:* With the purpose of the document and the general characteristics of the audience determined, initial rough sketches (**thumbnails**) on paper help establish basic ideas for the document's layout and design. Brainstorming is an important first step to an effective layout and the final design process. Samples from the idea folder are helpful during the brainstorming stage. Also, brainstorming with associates is helpful when creating thumbnails. Based on the thumbnails, comprehensive sketches will be developed.

        (1) *Purpose:* Different purposes require different approaches. The purpose impacts the decision about whether the document will be a brochure, flyer, post card, or in some other format. Often the project is a repeat assignment and the purpose is clear. For new projects, the purpose must be clearly understood first. Also, a new approach for repeat projects is sometimes needed.

        (2) *Audience:* Writing should always be done with the audience in mind. Characteristics of the audience help determine an appropriate document layout and design. An invitation to an organization's board of directors for a reception with senior administration requires a different type of layout and design than an invitation to all employees regarding the company picnic.

        (3) *Thumbnails: Thumbnails* are rough sketches on paper where layout and design options are explored. The idea is to create many rough sketches without detailed textual information. Software should not be used when creating thumbnail sketches because it is too easy to start concentrating on design details instead of brainstorming new ideas. Thumbnails are mockups or prototypes that are analogous to an outline for writing a letter or report.

(4) *Comprehensive sketches (comps):* Using the computer, the hard-copy thumbnails are refined into **comprehensive sketches.** Comprehensive sketches are typically called *comps.* Nonsense type called "greeking" is often used when keying the comprehensive sketch. **Greeking** shows appropriate type size, line spacing, and text placement but does not include the final text. A comprehensive sketch provides:

- Colors to be used
- Number of pages and/or folds
- Trim size of the final document
- Image placement
- Number of columns (if applicable)
- Type specifications

If an image has been selected, only a portion of the image might be needed for the final document. **Cropping** is trimming the unwanted edges of the image. Ideally images should be cropped before being imported into the document. Once the image is in the document, image placement may include rotating. **Rotating** is pivoting an image around the image's center point. Images can rotate 360 degrees at increments of .01 degrees. Some images require a caption. A *caption* is the line(s) of text that identifies the image and/or the source of the image. The caption is usually placed beneath the image or in close proximity. Image cropping and captions need to be considered when developing comps.

2. *Paper:* When working with a desktop printer (ink-jet or laser) or a convenience copier, the administrative professional has paper size, weight, color, and finish to consider. Additional options for paper size and types can be considered when working with a reproduction center or commercial printer.

a. *Size:* The sheet size of the paper on which the document is printed impacts folding options. The most widely used paper sizes are letter size (8 1/2 by 11 inch), legal size (8 1/2 by 14 inch), and tabloid size (11 by 17 inch). Documents can be created with smaller dimensions based on these three standard sheet sizes.

b. *Weight:* Paper is categorized according to weight. *Weight* is how much a ream (500 sheets) of standard size paper weighs. The administrative professional typically works with 17- to 32-pound paper for office printers or copiers. The 17-pound paper is lighter. For proper paper feed, 18- to 20-pound paper is recommended. The weight of card stock ranges from 65 to 100 pounds and is used for business cards or formal invitations.

c. *Color:* Although dull white is common in the office, white comes in many different shades. The differences between a warm, creamy white or a bluish, gray white should be investigated when creating a document. Many offices also have paper in several basic colors—blue, green, gray, or yellow/buff as well as a wide variety of other colors. Colored pictures, graphs, or clip art typically do not display well on colored paper. A glossy, white paper is recommended when a picture, graph, or clip art is included in the document. Reproduction centers and office supply distributors have a wide variety of colors (even iridescent) and specialty papers that can be very striking for some documents.

Note: Pictures include photographs, illustrations, drawings, and other such images included in documents. Some individuals use the term *charts* when discussing graphs; these terms are interchangeable.

    d. *Finish:* The *finish* of paper ranges from rough to smooth texture depending on the paper grade. An antique finish is a rough texture. Eggshell or vellum finishes are smooth, heavy, and translucent papers. Documents printed on textured finishes (tweed or linen) can have a "fuzzy" look depending on the density of the texture. Parchment is a high-quality, 60- to 65-pound paper stock that is silicon coated and feels like heavy tissue paper. It is an expensive paper; usually one sheet of 8 1/2 × 11-inch parchment is at least $1.25. Reproduction centers with high-volume copiers have many finish options and are better equipped to work with textured papers.

       Paper can be coated or uncoated on one or both sides. Coated paper is smooth and ranges from dull to very glossy. Pictures and graphs have a crisp sharp appearance when printed on coated paper because the ink does not absorb into the paper. Uncoated papers are rougher, more porous, and absorb more ink.

       The cotton content of paper can affect the reproduction process. Many business documents are printed on bond paper.

    (1) *Cotton content:* The *rag content* of paper is the percentage of scrap cloth that is mixed with the pulp fibers during the manufacturing process. High rag content is not recommended for copiers because the cloth fibers tend to separate from the paper and become lodged in critical areas of the copier. Today other materials such as *cotton linters* are used instead of cloth rags. Linters are fine silky cotton fibers that improve uniformity and color properties of paper, resulting in a cleaner, bulkier sheet of paper. The higher the cotton content, the higher the quality of the paper.

    (2) *Bond paper: Bond paper* is strong, durable paper that is especially suitable for electronic printing and use in copiers and desktop printers. Letterheads, business forms, and a variety of business documents can be produced on bond paper. The sheet size of bond paper is typically 17 by 22 inches, and the weight ranges from 13 to 24 pounds. The qualities of bond paper that are especially desirable for document printing are its erase ability, good ink absorption, and rigidity. Bond paper is often called reprographic paper, writing paper, and xerographic paper.

3. **Folding:** Folding the paper changes the size of the document pages. Each time a fold is added, more pages are added to the document. Each page is referred to as a *panel*. Three folding options include four-panel fold, six-panel fold, and eight-panel fold. A **signature** consists of a group of panels that are printed on one sheet of paper for a document.

    a. *Types of folds:* The number of folds for a document should be determined before beginning the comprehensive sketch.

    (1) *Four-panel fold:* Folding a piece of paper in half creates four panels (pages) for a document. A document with four pages has a **four-panel fold.** The vertical fold can be applied to either a *landscape orientation* (holding the paper so it is wider than it is tall) or a *portrait orientation* (holding the paper so it is taller than it is wide).

        EXAMPLE: *A four-panel fold creates two signatures. One signature is for pages 4 and 1 and one signature is for pages 2 and 3.*

(2) *Six-panel fold:* Holding the paper in landscape orientation and folding it in thirds creates six panels (pages) for a document. A document with six pages has a **six-panel fold.** An *accordion fold* (also called a *zig-zag fold*) is when the two parallel folds are in opposite directions. A *c fold* (also called a *letter fold,* a *tri-fold,* a *brochure fold,* or a *spiral fold*) is when the two parallel folds are in the same direction, parallel to each other. A c fold is common for tri-fold brochures. To allow the panels to nest inside one another, the fold for the inside panel is usually 1/8 inch narrower than the other panel. The number of signatures for a six-panel fold varies based on the document design.

(3) *Eight-panel fold:* Holding the paper in portrait orientation, folding it horizontally in half, and folding it vertically in half creates an eight-panel (page) fold (must count both sides of the paper for the fold but only four pages are used for printing). An **eight-panel fold** is also called a *French fold.* A French fold is often used for formal invitations.

b. *Folding issues:* To avoid problems, an administrative professional should be familiar with the following folding issues.

- Dark or metallic ink can smudge when the paper is touched. The paper should be coated prior to folding to avoid smudging and marking.

- Folds should be with the grain whenever possible. Folds at a right angle from the first fold should be scored.

- If the fold is against the grain, consider paper stock with a low cotton content.

- **Washout** is a potential folding problem that occurs when printed matter is trimmed off on the inside panels of a signature. Washout is also called *creep.* The heavier the stock and the more pages that are nested into each other, the bigger the problem with washout.

- Heavier stock paper requires more planning and preparation, primarily to avoid rippling and cracking in the folding machine.

4. *Graphics:* Often images are incorporated into documents. Images can include clip art, photographs, illustrations, drawings, graphs, and so forth. Sometimes the word *chart* is used for the term *graph*; these terms are interchangeable.

a. *Clip art:* Clip art consists of illustrations available with the microcomputer productivity software or can be found by searching on the Web. See Section C regarding legal issues related to reproduction.

EXAMPLE — Productivity Software Clip Art:

Clip art source: Microsoft Word 2000

b. *Images:* Photographs, illustrations, drawings, graphs, or other images are available on the Web, can be scanned, or can be taken with a digital camera. Typically images are used in several different software applications. Therefore, the image needs to be saved in a file format suitable for multiple software applications. TIFF (tagged image file format), GIF (graphical interchange format), JPEG (joint photographic experts group), and BMP (bitmap for pictures) are image formats acceptable for all types of applications.

(1) *Picture format:* Each picture needs to be saved. The *TIFF* format *(tagged image file format)* is the recommended image format for reproduction purposes. Most image editing or print shop software can resave pictures and images in TIFF format. TIFF was created for scanning and should be the image format chosen when scanning images for reproduction.

GIF (graphical interchange format), JPEG/JPG (joint photographic experts group), and *BMP (bitmap for pictures)* are formats often found on the Web or camera options for photographs. Although GIF and JPG formats are common for Web publishing, these formats are not recommended for document reproduction. Using image editing or print shop software, the administrative professional can open and save the file in TIFF format for images used in printed documents.

(a) *GIF format:* The GIF format is a compression technique that supports only 256 colors. GIF is best for Web publishing when an image has only a few distinct colors. *Interlaced GIFs* come into focus slowly as an image loads into the Web browser. *Animated GIFs* are several GIFs saved as a single file. If the Web image is a line drawing, the GIF format is recommended.

(b) *JPEG/JPG format:* The JPG format is a compression technique that supports 16 million colors. JPG was designed to compress color and grayscale continuous-tone images and is best suited for photographs and complex graphics on the Web. As the quality of the JPG file increases, so does the file size and file download time. By compressing the JPG file, a balance between the image quality and the file size can be obtained along with improved download time.

(2) *Web images:* Often images found on the Web are free, although some Web sites charge a nominal fee for an image. Including credit in the document for the image is required; see Section C regarding legal issues related to reproduction.

To save an image file from the Web, the administrative professional would right click on the image and save it in its original format (GIF or JPG). GIF and JPG files should be opened and saved in TIFF format for hard-copy document reproduction.

BMP files are mainly used for background wallpapers and are not recommended for document reproduction.

(3) *Scanning:* A scanner allows text and images to be captured and saved as a file. Like a copier, the image is placed on the glass surface of the scanner, and as the light passes over the image, the light is changed. *CCD (charged-coupled device) technology* captures the changes in the light. These changes should be saved as a TIFF file when the image is used in hard-copy reproduction.

(a) *Scanning guidelines:* The following guidelines help capture a clear image.

- Before scanning an image make sure the glass surface is clean.

- Handle the image to be scanned carefully so there are no fingerprints or scratches.
- Use glossy images (e.g., glossy photograph); glossy images have a clear surface that does not change after it is scanned.
- Close the scanner cover; the cover applies uniform pressure on the image keeping all parts of the image in focus.

(b) *Grayscale:* Anything that is to be reproduced in "black-and-white" should be scanned in grayscale. **Grayscale** is an 8-bit mode; this means there are 254 different shades of gray. "Black-and-white" images are actually shades of gray tones. Any line images (e.g., arrows, shapes, or symbols) that need smooth edges should *not* be scanned in grayscale, however.

(4) *Halftone:* A **halftone** is the reproduction of a continuous-tone image (i.e., photograph that has been converted into a black-and-white image) on paper. Halftones are created through a *dithering* process where the dots are either on or off. The density and pattern of dots are varied to simulate different shades of gray. Dithering creates flat bitmap dots for grayscale images where all the dots are the same size; more dots are used for the dark areas versus the lighter areas of the image. Desktop publishing systems can create halftones by simulating the conventional photographic process.

(5) *Digital cameras:* Digital camera photographs can be transferred directly into the computer, viewed on the computer monitor, adjusted electronically, and saved in secondary storage. A professional resolution or a studio resolution digital camera is very expensive. Therefore, consumer resolution digital cameras are commonly used when taking pictures for company newsletters, flyers, and Web pages. If a regular camera is used, a developer can save the pictures to a photo compact disc.

5. ***Print Run:*** Convenience copiers are used for low-volume reproduction. When working with a reproduction center or commercial print shop, the number of finished pieces required is referred to as a **print run.** Commercial print shops are used for high-quality, large-volume jobs.

Costs for a print run need to be compared. Printing several hundred brochures on a color copier at a reproduction center would cost less than at a commercial print shop. Commercial print shops have high setup costs for the press, but printing is more economical for jobs over 1,000 copies. Once a job is set up on a printing press, there is very little difference between printing 1,000 copies or 10,000 copies. The more copies printed, the lower the per-unit cost. The price per copy does not decrease when using digital printing or a copier.

6. ***Reproduction:*** Administrative professionals can print to a desktop printer, use convenience copiers, use the services of a reproduction center where medium- and high-volume copying is available, or go to a commercial printer. These reproduction options produce different qualities of output. The administrative professional must know what reproduction quality is required for the final product.

a. *Printers:* When only a few copies are needed, desktop printers (ink-jet or laser) are a viable reproduction option. These printers have good resolution, particularly when images are printed. *Resolution* is the number of dots per inch (dpi); the more dots per inch, the higher the resolution and the better the print quality. Office printers range from 600 dpi to 1,200 dpi. Standard paper weight (18 to 20 pound) is best for desktop printers. Other print factors to consider are paper size, print area, and speed.

b. *Copiers:* Convenience copiers are for low-volume reproduction (25 copies of short documents). For small jobs or when budgets are tight, convenience copiers are frequently used.

c. *Reproduction centers:* In addition to low-volume copiers, reproduction centers have sophisticated equipment to handle all types and sizes of jobs (newsletters, brochures, catalogs, or business cards). In-house reproduction centers help control budget costs for large-volume jobs. Reproduction centers also provide quicker turnaround time than commercial printers. Turnaround time must be considered when planning a project. *Turnaround time* is the time required by the reproduction center to complete the print run.

d. *Commercial printers:* Companies use commercial printers for high-quality, high-volume reproduction services. Commercial printers use traditional printing methods, digital printing, or large presses for printing. Commercial printers provide professional expertise for special orders as well as a wide variety of binding options. Print runs for thousands of copies of sales brochures, letterhead, stationery, catalogs, or annual reports are typical jobs for commercial printers. Although a more expensive process, commercial printing is superior to photocopying.

(1) *Digital printing: Digital printing* is ideal for short runs of full-color jobs that need to be printed quickly. Using laser technology, digital printers reproduce entire jobs directly from the computer. Some digital printers require plates (masters) for printing.

(2) *Imagesetter:* An *imagesetter* is a high-end laser printer with very high-resolution output. Instead of using toner, the dots are imprinted on a transparent film that creates a very crisp and clean original. Imagesetter dpi ranges from 1,200 to 4,800. The original is used with commercial presses for final reproduction.

Before the layout and design process is started, a commercial printer needs to answer the following questions:

*   What file format does the commercial printer require?
*   Must a specific color matching system be used?
*   What folding and binding options are available?
*   For bound or folded documents, should the pages be formatted as printer spreads? **Printer spreads** require that the pages be arranged in the order the pages are to be printed. For a four-panel fold, one signature consists of page (panel) 4 on the left of the sheet and page 1 on the right of the sheet. A four-panel fold has two signatures.
*   Can the file be delivered on a disk, CD, or sent over the Internet?

The administrative professional makes several document layout decisions before mocking-up a new design. Taking time to understand the purpose of the document and making decisions about paper size and type, number of folds, graphics, print run, and the reproduction process makes the project more manageable.

7. ***Other Layout Considerations:*** When creating specific types of business documents, banners and mastheads are often used in the design of the publication.

a. *Banner for a publication:* A publication *banner* is the title of a periodical on the cover of a magazine or the first page of a newsletter. A banner contains the name of the publication and serial information—date, volume, and issue number. Volume designates the publication year. The issue number designates the series within the year—weekly, biweekly, monthly, bimonthly, or quarterly. Other information may be included in the banner, such as the name of the sponsoring organization, logo, address, and motto. Graphics are often used in a banner to catch the reader's attention.

b. *Banner for a Web site:* A Web site *banner* is a rectangular advertisement placed on the site either above, below, or on the sides of the Web site's main content. The banner is linked to the advertiser's Web site. In the early 1990s Web banners were simply advertisements with text and graphic images. With today's advanced technologies, Web site banners are more complex and can include animated graphics and sound, along with the text and graphic images. Many e-commerce Web sites use banner advertisements.

c. *Masthead for a publication:* The *masthead,* also called a *nameplate* or *flag,* of a periodical or newsletter is the credit box that gives information about the publication. It begins with the publication title and lists editors, sponsors, writers, illustrators, photographers, and other contributors. The masthead includes such information as the publication's business address, subscription and advertising information, copyright notices, volume and issue numbers, and other publication information. The masthead should not be crowded with too much information, however. The masthead is usually placed on an inside page of the publication. The publication banner and masthead should be complementary in terms of design graphics, fonts, and colors.

Check Point—Section A

Directions: For each question, circle the correct answer.

A–1. When creating a document that includes a colored photograph, the best paper color for reproduction is

- A) blue
- B) buff
- C) green
- D) white

A–2. A common fold for a brochure that uses two parallel folds in the same direction is called a/an

- A) accordion fold
- B) c fold
- C) four-panel fold
- D) French fold

A–3. Which file format supports 16 million colors and is suitable for complex graphics and Web publishing?

- A) BMP (bitmap for pictures)
- B) GIF (graphical interchange format)
- C) JPG (joint photographic group)
- D) TIFF (tagged image file format)

B. Document Design

Based on the comprehensive sketches, attention needs to be directed to document design. **Typography** is the overall arrangement and appearance of printed matter on a page. Effective typography establishes a visual hierarchy by providing text and graphic accents that assist the reader in understanding the message and relationships between headings and subordinate blocks of text. Basic *design principles* include proximity, alignment, repetition, and contrast. Adhering to these four design principles along with an effective use of type, the administrative professional can be involved with producing professional brochures and flyers for the organization.

1. *Proximity:* **Proximity** is about grouping related items together. Logically grouping related information creates organization. To effectively achieve proximity, the administrative professional needs to understand the logical connection of the information, what information should be emphasized, and how to use white space.

   a. *Visual units:* Proximity is about relationships: grouping like information into **visual units** and separating visual units with white space. When information is logically grouped into visual units, the following happens:

      • The page becomes organized.

      • The reader knows the beginning and ending of a visual unit.

      • White space is effectively used.

   b. *Emphasis:* Key words or phrases need to be emphasized with bold, underscore, or a different typeface. To be effective, the administrative professional needs to be selective and emphasize only *key* word(s) or phrase(s).

   c. *White space:* **White space** is the area on a page that is blank—there is no text or graphics. Often, the design novice fills all space with text or graphics making sure there is no white space. In contrast, professional designers make effective use of white space.

      EXAMPLE: *Rogers needed to design a one-page flyer for the fall employee OktoberFest potluck. The visual units included a heading, location, date and time, potluck assignments, and RSVP information. Key words and phrases to emphasize included* OktoberFest, What to Bring, *and* RSVP. *Rogers used a different typeface for the* OktoberFest *and* What to Bring *phrases. Using a graphic as well as white space to separate the visual units, Rogers was able to design an accordion-fold flyer that was easy to follow. The heading at the top of the flyer attracts the reader's attention followed by the event specifics—location, date and time, what to bring, and the RSVP in the lower right-hand corner. Figure 6–1 is the OktoberFest flyer.*

      An *accordion fold* is common for one-page documents printed on one side when the heading at the top is used as an attention getter. When the document is removed from the envelope, the heading is immediately visible with no other distractions.

      A *c fold* is common for a document printed on both sides of the paper with three panels on each side. The signature for the outside consists of panels 5, 6, and 1. The signature for the inside consists of panels 2, 3, and 4. The attention getter heading would be printed in the first panel.

2. *Alignment:* Any text or image placed on a page should have a visual connection with everything else on the page. **Alignment** ensures that the visual units on the page are connected. Text placed on a page must be visually connected (aligned) with all other information on the page. *Horizontal alignment* options include left, right, centered, and justified.

FIGURE 6–1   OktoberFest Flyer. Clip art source: Microsoft Word 2000

The dashes indicate where the accordion folds should be made. The dashes are not part of the OktoberFest flyer.

a. *Left and right alignment:* Left- and right-aligned information has a clean, dramatic look. Usually the terms flush left and flush right are used when referring to left and right alignment.

EXAMPLE:

This material
is flush left.

This material
is flush right.

b. *Centered:* Centered alignment is the most common for novice designers; it is easy and comfortable. Formal announcements and invitations are usually centered. Professional designers are more dramatic in adding space effectively and may even mix alignments.

EXAMPLES:

If information is
centered, make sure
centering is obvious.
Centered information
where the lines are
about the same length
is not a good design.

Centered Information
Is
More Formal

c. *Justified:* When information is justified, the left and right margins are both aligned (flush left and right margins). To justify the right margin, extra spaces are inserted between words; often these spaces create large gaps in a line of print. Justified alignment is common in books.

EXAMPLE: *Information that is justified has an even left and right edge. In order for the right edge to be even, extra spaces are inserted. Often, this leaves large gaps in the line of print.*

d. *Vertical alignment:* By placing an imaginary text box around the visual units, text within the visual unit box can be vertically aligned with the top margin of the box, bottom margin of the box, or centered vertically in the box.

EXAMPLES:

Text vertically aligned with the top of the visual unit box.	*Text vertically aligned with the bottom of the visual unit box.*	*Text centered vertically in the visual unit box.*

e. *Mixed:* When mixing alignments, make sure the information is aligned in some way. Remember to "Keep it simple!" and make sure the units of information on the page are visually aligned. Designers use the following alignment guidelines:

*   Visual units placed on the page horizontally should be aligned with the baseline (bottom line).

- Visual units placed on the page vertically should be aligned with either the left edge or the right edge.
- The edge of a graphic should be aligned with the edges of other visual units.
- Order creates a calm feeling. Everything on the page should be aligned; nothing should be arbitrarily placed on a page.

3. *Repetition:* Some aspect of the design should be repeated throughout the document. Repeating a rule (line), a color, a bold or italic heading, a bullet format, a logo, or any other format feature brings consistency to the document. Repeating a design feature ties the visual units together from the beginning of the document to the end. **Repetition** is a major factor in the unity of the visual units on a one-page document and is critical for multiple-page documents.

4. *Contrast:* **Contrast** occurs when two elements are noticeably different. *Conflict* is when two elements are "somewhat" different but not different enough. Minor differences are conflicting. Conflict should be avoided in a document whereas contrast is important to include in a document. The easiest way to add contrast is with bold and italics. The following are other ways to incorporate contrast into a document:

- A thin line with a thick line (rules)
- A warm color with a cool color
- A small graphic with a large graphic
- A horizontal element with a vertical element

Based on the comprehensive sketches, administrative professionals can determine what information is most important; this information becomes the main focus in the design layout. *Contrast* and *proximity* emphasizes the important information. *Alignment* and *repetition* tie together the visual units.

5. *Typeface Characteristics:* Different typefaces and possibly different type fonts in a document are ways administrative professionals can design with type. Typeface may have stress on the oval (vertical or diagonal) or no stress; serifs (slanted or horizontal) or no serifs; and uniform letter strokes or a thick/thin transition in a letter stroke (light to distinct). When discussing typeface, the portion of a lowercase letter that falls below the baseline is called the **descender.** The portion of a lowercase letter that is above the main body of a letter (i.e., above the height of a lowercase x) is called the **ascender.**

EXAMPLE:

In the English alphabet there are five letters with descenders: *g, j; p, q, and y.*

For the letter f, the ascender *is the part of the vertical line above the horizontal line. In the English alphabet there are eight letters with ascenders: b, d, f, h, i, k, l, and t.*

a. *Stress or no stress on the oval:* Some typefaces have either a vertical or diagonal stress on the oval portion of letters (e.g., o, d, and p). These typefaces include old style, modern, and slab serif. Sans serif typeface has no stress on the oval portion of letters; all letters have a uniform stroke.

b. *Serif:* A **serif** is a small decorative stroke that is added to the end of a letter's main strokes. These cross-lines at the end of a stroke are called slab, wedge, or hair. Serif typeface includes old style, modern, and slab serif. Serif typeface is more difficult to read in small scale (less than 8 point) as well as in very large scale.

FIGURE 6–2 Typeface Characteristics

Typeface	Type Font	Characteristics
Old style (serif)	• Garamond • Times	Diagonal stress on oval, slanted serifs Easy to read, good for long documents
Modern (serif)	• **Times Bold** • Walbaum	Vertical stress on oval, horizontal serifs Distinct thick/thin transition in letter stroke; distinctive Better for short documents
Slab serif	• New Century • Memphis	Vertical stress on oval, horizontal serifs Very good on readability; clean, straightforward look Often used in children's books
Sans serif	• Helvetica • **Gothic**	No stress on oval, letter strokes are uniform No serifs Sans means "without" in French
Script	• *Snell Roundhand*	Handwritten, calligraphy appearance Stunning but harder to read, use sparingly Fancy script should never be in long blocks and never in all caps
Decorative	• IRONWOOD • Hobo	Distinctive but should be used selectively Be creative and use in fun ways
Pi	• Dingbat—❖❁■✳☯☻▼ • Symbol—Σψμβολ	Used to insert symbols, ornaments, bullets, or mathematical symbols into text

c. *Sans serif:* Sans means *without* in French. **Sans serif** means no decorative stroke is added to the end of a letter's main stroke. It is recommended that text in smaller than 8-point scale or very large scale use a sans serif typeface. Sans serif typeface is often used for footnotes, endnotes, or headings.

d. *Stroke:* Letter strokes are either uniform or have a thick/thin transition in a letter stroke (light to distinct). Modern typeface has a distinct thick/thin transition in the letter stroke that gives print a distinctive appearance. Sans serif has a uniform letter stroke.

e. *Specialized typefaces:* Other typefaces include script, decorative, and Pi. All three typefaces have unique features that should be used for special purposes. Script has a calligraphy appearance and, although it is stunning, it can be hard to read. Decorative typefaces add creativity to a document, but the administrative professional should be very selective about its use. Pi typeface is used when ornaments, bullets, mathematical symbols, or other symbols are required in a document.

Figure 6–2 summarizes the characteristics of the various typefaces and provides examples of different type fonts.

6. *Designing with Type:* There are multiple ways to design an attractive, effective document. Understanding the relationships between different typefaces and creating contrast within a document are both important in achieving visually appealing and effective designs.

a. *Selecting different typefaces:* Often different typefaces are used in a document. Relationships between different typefaces are concordant, contrasting, or conflicting.

   (1) *Concordant:* Using only one typeface without much variety in size and emphasis (bold, italic) is a *concordant* relationship. A concordant design creates harmony and calm and is important in some documents. However, consistent use of concordant typeface is not very exciting.

   (2) *Contrasting: Contrasting* typefaces are *distinctly* different from one another. Contrasting typefaces create visually appealing and exciting designs. These contrasts can be emphasized with size, bold, italic, color, and other formatting features.

   (3) *Conflicting:* When two or more typefaces are used that are somewhat similar with only slight differences, a *conflicting* relationship exists. When the visual appearance between typefaces is not the same yet not significantly different, the typefaces conflict. Conflicting typefaces (and designs) should be avoided.

b. *Applying different type:* Creating a contrasting relationship can be fun, but guidelines must be followed for the visual impact to effectively enhance communication. When a document is received, the recipient should be able to identify the purpose or main focus of the document through the organization of the material and the flow of the information. Contrasting type assists in making the message more visually appealing. Following are several guidelines for creating contrast:

   (1) *Size:* Large versus small type is an easy way to create contrast. Type size can be as small as 6 points or as large as 96 points. Points are a horizontal measurement of a line. A 72-point character equals 1 inch. The size difference within a document needs to be significant enough to make a difference; otherwise, conflict is created.

   In some publications pull quotes may be used. A **pull quote** is a small amount of text that is enlarged within an article to catch the reader's attention. Rule lines may be used to set off the pull quote from the rest of the text. Marketing pieces use pull quotes as an attention grabber to entice readers to complete the document.

   (2) *Weight: Weight* of typeface is the thickness of the stroke. Most microcomputer software typefaces have a light, regular, or medium-bold typeface. Weight is the most effective way to add visual contrast to a document; however, a typeface with a strong-bold stroke should also be available. The administrative professional may want to add a strong-bold typeface to the microcomputer software typeface options. Additional typeface is available from software vendors, computer supply centers, or online services. The administrative professional should check with the information technology division first for recommendations on adding typeface options to the microcomputer software.

   (3) *Structure:* The typeface structure varies from no discernible weight shift in the character stroke to greater emphasis on the thick/thin transitions in the stroke. See Figure 6–2 for more details on typeface characteristics.

   (4) *Form:* The form of a letter refers to its shape. Two simple form contrasts are regular typeface versus italic and capital letters versus lowercase. Both italics and all capital letters can be difficult to read. Capital letters should be used only when they add to the design of the document. Although letters in script are stunning, the administrative professional must be cognizant of readability factors and use typeface and fonts accordingly.

A **dropped capital (drop cap)** is sometimes used to emphasize the beginning of a section. A drop cap sets the first letter in the section with a larger and sometimes stylized font. The baseline of the uppercase character is dropped one or more lines below the baseline of a paragraph's first line. Although a drop cap is a useful design tool, it is distracting when overused. Drop caps are either inset within the paragraph or offset. An offset drop cap is in the margin to the left of the paragraph.

EXAMPLES:

EXAMPLE of an Inset Drop Cap:

*T*his is an example of a drop cap that is *inset* within the first paragraph of a section. The first character is larger as well as a stylized typeface has been used.

EXAMPLE of an Offset Drop Cap:

 his is an example of a drop cap that is *offset* into the left margin of a section. An additional stylized feature, the box, encloses the first character.

Notice that the left margin remains the same for all paragraphs and the drop cap is in the left margin of the document.

---

(5) *Space:* Designers also pay attention to spacing between lines, words, and characters; spacing between pages and columns; filling in color gaps; and specialized spacing. Several space issues to consider in document design and reproduction follow.

(a) *Leading:* **Leading** is the vertical space between lines in the text. If two different leading values are specified in a line of print, the larger value applies to the entire line.

(b) *Kerning:* **Kerning** is the spacing of words and characters on a line. Most type fonts have a set width so letters do not run together. However, some letter combinations can appear to be too far apart with the default spacing. Kerning intentionally decreases the default spacing to improve the appearance of the letter combinations.

(c) *Track spacing:* **Track spacing** adjusts the number of words on a line by squeezing or expanding text and adding or removing space from character combinations on a line.

(d) *Characters:* Characters are either monospaced or proportional. *Monospaced characters* use the same amount of space for each character. *Proportional characters* use different amounts of space depending on the shape of the character.

EXAMPLES:

```
Character spacing using a Courier New Font is
monospaced; each character has the same amount
of space. This example is in 12 point.
```

iii   111

mmm   www

The spacing for a Times New Roman font is proportional. The i and l characters require less space than the m and w characters. This example is in 12 point.

iii   lll

mmm   www

(e) *Gutters:* Gutters are required in bound documents. The **gutter** is the space between two sides of adjacent pages. For left-bound documents, the space between the left edge of the right-hand page (odd-numbered pages) and the right edge of the left-hand page (even-numbered pages) is the gutter. For top-bound documents printed on both sides of the paper, the gutter is the space between the bottom and top of two adjacent pages. The space between columns in a multiple-column document is the *alley* although sometimes it is also referred to as the gutter.

EXAMPLE: *When opening a top-bound document that is printed on both sides of the paper, page 2 and page 3 are adjacent and both pages are visible. The space between the bottom of page 2 and the top of page 3 is the gutter.*

(f) *Trapping:* When printing, the position of one or more of the colors may cause a gap of uninked paper between adjacent colors. **Trapping** minimizes the gap by expanding adjacent colors so small amounts of ink overlap and print on top of each other.

(g) *Specialized spacing:* Other spacing considerations are em space, em dash, en space, en dash, and thin space.

- An *em space* is equal in width to the point size; an em space in 8-point type is 8 points wide.
- An *em dash* is a dash the width of an em space and is used to set off portions of text within a sentence.
- An *en space* is equal to half the width of an em space.
- An *en dash* is half the width of an em dash and is used for negative numbers, the subtraction symbol, and to replace the word *to* or *through* (e.g., 8–10 A.M. or Thursday–Saturday).
- A *thin space* is a fixed space equal to one-half of an en space; a thin space is equal to a period in most fonts.

(6) *Direction:* Direction refers to placing text in a contrasting position to the horizontal line. Direction can conflict with alignment. Therefore, one should be certain that the contrast is important to the message before placing any text on a slant.

EXAMPLE: *To make sure the flyer about the OktoberFest date change caught the attention of all employees, Rogers sent out an announcement that had "NEW DATE" slanting upward in the upper left-hand corner of the announcement.*

(7) *Color:* Color produces a reaction from readers. Warm colors (red, yellow, and orange) command attention. Cool colors (blue and green) recede. The eye is

attracted to warm colors, so very little color is needed to create contrast. Light, regular, medium, or strong bold typeface changes the grayscale on a black and white page.

(a) *Primary colors of pigment:* The *primary colors of pigment* are red, yellow, and blue. When these primary colors are combined, they create the secondary colors of green, purple, and orange. All colors are either reflected off of visible objects or viewed directly from the light source.

(b) *Primary colors of light:* The *primary colors of light* are red, green, and blue. These colors are often referred to as *RGB*. RGB is an *additive color system*, a color system where color is added to a black background. Black is the absence of light and therefore the absence of color. Combining the primary colors of light (red, green, and blue), the secondary colors are cyan, magenta, and yellow. Equal amounts of these primary colors produce white. RGB is the color system used for displaying color on computer monitors.

(c) *Primary colors of a subtractive color system:* The primary colors of a subtractive system are cyan **(C),** magenta **(M),** and yellow **(Y).** These are the secondary colors of the RGB system and are often referred to as CMYK. The "**K**" stands for blac**k.** The subtractive process is based on light reflecting from an object and passing through pigments of dyes that absorb (subtract) certain colors allowing other colors to be reflected. The *CMYK color system* is the main color system that defines color in print. CMYK is used only for process color work on a commercial press or a specialty printer. Because the press uses these four inks to create all colors, CMYK printing is called *four-color printing*.

7. **Web Publishing:** Publishing electronically produces a document called a Web page that can be viewed over the Internet. The World Wide Web (WWW) is a system of universally accepted standards for storing, retrieving, formatting, and displaying information on the Internet (see Chapter 4–B–2). The layout and design of a Web site adheres to these standards through the use of hypertext markup language (HTML).

The basic principles of document layout and design are much the same for both Web pages and printed documents. Web publishing, however, must be designed so users with different hardware and software can easily access and read the Web pages. Web pages are "built on the fly" each time the page is loaded into a Web browser. Each headline, line of text, type style, and image is recreated through a complex integration of the Web browser, Web server, and the operating system of the user's computer. Outdated browsers, connect speeds, complex images, unusual typefaces, and designs requiring media plug-ins affect the accessibility of Web pages.

a. *Browsers:* There are approximately twenty-five different Web browsers, and most browsers have more than one version. Public Web sites are usually designed so many types of browsers can access and view information on the Web pages. More sophisticated Web sites in terms of layout, animation, multimedia content, and interaction are less likely to be sites that are multi-browser compatible.

b. *Graphics and connect speed:* Although an increasing number of users have access to faster connections through digital subscriber lines (DSL) and cable modems, the standard modem speed is 56 kilobytes per second (KBps) with an actual download rate of approximately 7 KBps. This means that a GIF or JPEG/JPG image of 40 KB could take almost six seconds to load into the user's

Web browser. The actual download rate varies depending on the user's modem, Web server speed, Internet connection, and other factors. However, the more graphics used on a Web page, the longer the user will have to wait to see the page.

(1) *Home page:* One recommendation is to design the home page so it can load quickly and includes navigation buttons. The *navigation buttons* are links that allow the user to quickly select those pages where desired information is posted on the Web site. Distributing images to Web pages the reader selects through the navigation buttons may be sufficient incentive for the user to wait if the connect speed is slow.

(2) *Background images:* Sometimes a *background image* (also called *wallpaper*) is used instead of a background color. Load time is a factor when deciding to use a background image. Background images are saved in BMP (bitmap for picture) formats.

(3) *Portable network group (PNG): Portable network group* (*PNG,* pronounced "ping") is a patent-free file format that is a replacement for GIF. PNG was specifically designed for Web pages. Currently PNG is not widely supported on the major Web browsers. Once supported by Web browsers (predicted for 2005), PNG would become the desired graphic format for Web design. PNG supports true-color images, alpha channel support for transparency, and automatic corrections for monitor displays.

c. *Type font:* Some type fonts are more legible than others on the computer monitor. Georgia and Verdana are type fonts specifically designed for legibility on the computer screen and offer excellent legibility for Web pages. These fonts are very large compared to more traditional type fonts in the same point size. However, the exaggerated size and heavy letter stroke of the Georgia and Verdana fonts look massive and clumsy when printed on paper. Times New Roman is a traditional type font that was adapted for use on computer screens. Times New Roman is a good font for text-heavy Web pages that will probably be printed rather than read on the screen.

d. *Legibility on the computer monitor:* Because monitors display at different resolutions, the type size can vary. For Web page functionality and readability, consideration must also be given to the standard ways of emphasizing text—underline, color, bold, italics, and capital letters.

(1) *Type size:* Type size can be defined in the HTML code, but the carryover from the print medium has little meaning on a computer screen. For example, a 6-point type is legible on a Windows display with a default resolution of 96 ppi, but on a Macintosh with a default resolution of 72 ppi, a 6-point type is illegible. Also, the browser can resize type that is set in points. Most Web designers use pixel units to define type size. Text defined using pixels is the same size regardless of the monitor resolution settings and the browser's default font size.

(2) *Underlining:* Underlining has a special functional meaning in Web documents for hypertext links. Text on Web pages should not be underlined. The underline should only be used for its specific functional purpose—hypertext links.

(3) *Color:* Like underlining, color has a special functional purpose on Web pages. A hypertext link is displayed in certain colors (default colors are blue and violet). When the user points and clicks on the link, the color usually changes. Since colored text is effective for emphasis and may be desired, dark shades of color

that contrast with the page background color should be used. The default Web link colors (blue and violet) should be avoided when selecting colors for text.

(4) *Bold:* Boldface text gives emphasis because of the contrast in color from the body text. Boldface text is readable on the computer screen and can be very effective when used selectively on Web pages.

(5) *Italics:* Italicized text is attractive, and the contrast with other type catches the reader's attention. However, the readability factor of italicized text on screen resolutions is low. Italicized text should be used sparingly.

(6) *Capital letters:* Capitalized text is very difficult to read in both printed documents and on Web pages. When a Web page is displayed on the computer monitor, there is only one space between words unless the HTML code for a blank space has been used. Therefore, text that is capitalized looks as if it runs together making the reading of the text uncomfortable and slow. If capitalized text is used on Web pages, it should be used sparingly and for single words.

EXAMPLE — Times New Roman Type Font—12 Point:

THE WEB SITE DESIGN IS IMPORTANT TO ATTRACTING AND KEEPING USERS. THE LAYOUT AND DESIGN PRINCIPLES FOR PRINTED DOCUMENTS, ALONG WITH WEB PAGE GUIDELINES, ASSIST DESIGNERS IN CREATING EFFECTIVE WEB SITES.

e. *Creating a Web page:* Web pages can be created using a text editor and keying the text along with the required HTML code. Web design software programs are available that insert the appropriate HTML codes as directed by the designer. Web design software allows the designer to work with blank HTML pages or Web page templates. Also, productivity documents (word processing, spreadsheets, database management, and presentation graphics) can be saved as Web pages.

The typical way to set up a Web site is to create a folder in the microcomputer directory. All the files for the Web site would be saved in the folder along with images and other media files. Web pages can be created and tested off-line until the Web site functions correctly. Once the Web site is ready for public viewing, it must be uploaded (copied) to a Web server. The Web site requires a uniform resource locator (URL) that has been registered in a domain function (see Chapter 4–B–2).

The Internet and World Wide Web are the most exciting technologies to emerge in the past decade. The Web site design impacts the benefits received by business as well as home users. The challenge for designers is to create Web pages that are easy to use while capturing the attention of Web users and providing the necessary information that the target audience wants.

8. ***Proofing and Editing the Document:*** No matter which software program is used to produce the document, the administrative professional should use a spelling and grammar check and proofread the file for errors.

A sample copy *(page proofs)* should be printed for review before the document is reproduced. The document should be proofread for additional errors that the spelling and grammar check did not identify. The design and layout should be checked to determine if any final improvements should be made. Design problems may include misaligned visual units, conflict instead of contrast, or ineffective repetition of a symbol. Some desktop publishing programs and Web design software have tools for checking the document design. Design issues are highlighted for the administrative professional's review.

Developing skill in designing attractive and effective documents requires practice. Examples need to be added to the idea folder and applied as needed in new or revised designs. Many thumbnail sketches need to be created when brainstorming new layouts. The comprehensive sketches enable the designer to address layout in more detail. The four design principles need to be applied when designing new documents or Web pages. Experimenting with different typefaces and creating effective contrasting relationships with type are all important steps to an effective layout and design process.

Check Point—Section B

Directions: For each question, circle the correct answer.

B–1. When designing a document, it is important to group like information together into visual units. This design principle is called

    A) alignment
    B) contrast
    C) proximity
    D) repetition

B–2. The best typeface for small-scale (less than 8 point) type is

    A) modern

    B) old style
    C) sans serif
    D) slab serif

B–3. Which type font was specifically designed for legibility on the computer screen and is excellent for reading soft copy text on Web pages?

    A) Corvisa
    B) Georgia
    C) Times Roman
    D) Wingding

C. Legal Issues Relating to Reproduction

Given the widespread development and availability of intellectual property today, administrative professionals should be aware of legal consequences of adapting information from various sources. Some of the documents that are illegal to reproduce include classified government documents, automobile registrations, passports, visas, citizenship papers, and amateur radio operator licenses. The United States Copyright Statute of 1909, revised in 1976 and enhanced by the Conference on Fair Use (CONFU) in 1994, provides stringent guidelines for the reproduction of copyrighted material. The 1994 Conference established a set of guidelines addressing technological trends dealing with multimedia, visual archives, and digital libraries.

1. *Copyrighted Materials: Copyrighted materials* are defined as "original works of authorship fixed in any tangible medium of expression." Such works are considered copyrighted from the moment of creation whether they are published or not. The use of a copyright notice on works published on or after April 1989 is optional. Textual material prepared for an employer is considered copyrighted by that employer unless an agreement exists between the employer and the employee.

2. *The Copyright Law of 1976:* To help institutions in the promotion of reading and advanced study, a fair-use clause was written into the copyright legislation. The *fair-use clause* specified certain circumstances where the reproduction of copyrighted material is appropriate as long as the reproduction is used for the following:

   • Commentary
   • Criticism

- News reporting
- Scholarship or research
- Teaching, including multiple classroom copies for one-time use
- Other circumstances

3. ***The 1994 Conference on Fair Use:*** The 1994 Conference on Fair Use addressed multimedia, visual archives, and digital libraries. The guidelines were strengthened by stating that it is not an infringement of copyright for a library or archive to reproduce a copy or phonorecord of original work or to distribute such copy or phonorecord if:

- The reproduction or distribution is made without any direct or indirect commercial advantage
- The library or archive collections are open to the public
- The reproduction or distribution of the work includes a notice of copyright

The 1976 copyright law defined *phonorecord* to mean sounds (e.g., song) that are perceived, reproduced, or otherwise communicated either directly or with the aid of a machine or device. A phonorecord is an original copy of a recording in cassette, LP, compact disc, or any other medium that is filed with the Library of Congress along with copyright information. The medium is not important; however, to meet the requirements of the definition, the recording must be a "material object" (i.e., sounds that constituted an original composition).

4. ***Reproducing Materials from Copyrighted Sources:*** Permission to reproduce copyrighted material can be obtained by writing to the copyright owner, asking to reproduce the material, and describing the planned use of the material. The reasons for reproduction should be stated in the request. In some cases, a fee will be charged to use the material. Credit must always be given to the original author.

5. ***Copyrighted Materials on the World Wide Web:*** An information source found on a Web site must be checked carefully to see whether the information is copyrighted. The general rule of thumb for material on a Web site is that it is copyrighted. Permission must be obtained before that information can be reproduced, unless the fair-use clause is in effect or there is definite proof of no copyright. When using copyrighted material on a Web site, the phrase "Reprinted with Permission" (along with the name of the copyright holder) should be included next to the copyrighted material. "Reprinted with Permission" indicates that permission from the original author has been granted.

6. ***Photographs:*** The photographer usually holds photograph copyrights. Obtaining permission for text material does not necessarily include permission to use photographs or other images included with the text. Permission may be required from multiple parties. An image caption should include the name of the artist, title of the image, source where the image was obtained, copyright date, the date the image was originally published, and the download or acquired image date.

Legal matters dealing with copyrights, particularly with online material and multimedia, can be quite complex. Administrative professionals should consult with experienced legal counsel before making major decisions dealing with material obtained from such sources.

Check Point—Section C

Directions: For each question, circle the correct answer.

C–1. A copyright notice

 A) does not have to be included on material published after April 1989

 B) is for printed material and does not affect Web publishing

 C) means permission has been granted for others to use the material

 D) must be included on all published works in order to protect the original author

C–2. Since 1976 others can reproduce copyrighted material for comment, criticism, news reporting, scholarship, and other like situations. Making copies for these specific circumstances is covered by the

 A) copyright notice

 B) fair-use clause

 C) library and archive guidelines

 D) United States Copyright Statute

C–3. Original material published on a Web site is

 A) considered public domain and can be used by others without obtaining permission or giving credit to the original author

 B) copyrighted and permission to reproduce the material as well as giving credit to the original author is required

 C) posted for others to use without asking for permission but credit must be given to the original author

 D) protected by copyright laws only if a copyright notice is posted on the Web site

For Your Review

Directions: For each question, circle the correct answer.

1. When brainstorming about a new publication, a useful resource for creative and effective examples is a/an
   A) basic how-to book on layout and design
   B) desktop publishing online tutorial
   C) idea folder
   D) reproduction center

2. An important first step to designing an effective document is creating many rough sketches. These paper-and-pencil sketches are called
   A) comps
   B) grayscale
   C) greeking
   D) thumbnails

3. Taking away unwanted edges of an image is
   A) cropping
   B) greeking
   C) rotating
   D) sizing

4. Hoyle has several photographs to include in a marketing brochure. For a crisp, sharp appearance when the photograph is printed, what type of paper should Hoyle use?
   A) Antique finish
   B) Buff color
   C) Glossy coated
   D) High rag content

5. One vertical fold applied to a landscape orientation is a/an
   A) brochure fold
   B) four-panel fold
   C) French fold
   D) six-panel fold

6. Text that is trimmed off on the inside panels of a signature is called
   A) creep
   B) cropping
   C) grayscale
   D) leading

7. What file format was created for scanning and is the best file format for reproducing graphics on hard copy?
   A) Bitmap for pictures (BMP)
   B) Graphical interchange format (GIF)
   C) Joint photographic experts group (JPEG)
   D) Tagged image file format (TIFF)

8. When glossy images are scanned, the saved image is usually
   A) discolored
   B) fuzzy around the edges of objects
   C) the same as the original
   D) washed out from glare

9. Rotondo needs a moderately priced camera for company newsletters, flyers, and Web page pictures. The best recommendation is a
   A) consumer resolution digital camera
   B) professional resolution digital camera
   C) regular camera
   D) studio resolution digital camera

10. With a limited budget and quick turn-around time, the best way to obtain 1,500 copies of a newsletter is a/an

    A) commercial printer
    B) department convenience copier
    C) imagesetter
    D) in-house reproduction center

11. When designing a document, like information should be grouped together into

    A) banners
    B) panels
    C) thumbnails
    D) visual units

12. A common horizontal alignment for books is

    A) flush left
    B) flush right
    C) justified
    D) mixed

13. The purpose of placing an imaginary text box around a visual unit is to

    A) horizontally align text below the visual unit box
    B) justify text within the visual unit box
    C) make placement of the visual unit easier
    D) vertically align text within the visual unit box

14. A good rule of thumb for alignment is

    A) centered text is easy to read
    B) keep it simple
    C) use the same alignment throughout a document
    D) variety adds spice to the document

15. When designing multiple-page documents, an important principle for creating unity among the visual units is

    A) alignment
    B) contrast
    C) proximity
    D) repetition

16. What two design principles emphasize the important information in a document?

    A) Alignment and contrast
    B) Alignment and repetition
    C) Contrast and proximity
    D) Proximity and repetition

17. Which typeface has a uniform stroke for all letters—no stress on the oval portion of letters (e.g., b, q, and o)?

    A) Modern
    B) Old style
    C) Sans serif
    D) Slab serif

18. In the company newsletter, Zepeda incorporated several customer comments. The comments were enlarged and rule lines were added to draw attention to that section and the related material. This technique is called

    A) inset
    B) kerning
    C) pull quotes
    D) trapping

19. A useful design tool that sets the first character in a section with a larger and sometimes stylized font is called a

    A) drop cap
    B) halftone
    C) printer spread
    D) signature

20. Squeezing or expanding text and adding or removing space from character combinations on a line is

    A) leading
    B) kerning
    C) track spacing
    D) trapping

21. For left-bound documents, the space between the left edge of the right-hand page (odd-numbered pages) and the right edge of the left-hand page (even-numbered pages) is the

    A) alley
    B) gutter
    C) printer spread
    D) white space

22. A straight line that is half the width of the point size and used to replace the word *to* or *through* (e.g., 8–10 A.M. or Thursday–Saturday) is called a/an

   A) em dash
   B) en dash
   C) hyphen
   D) negative symbol

23. What color system defines color for commercial presses?

   A) Additive color system
   B) CMYK
   C) RGB
   D) Primary colors of pigment

24. What is the best way to emphasize text on a Web page while maintaining effective readability on the computer screen?

   A) Boldface the text
   B) Type the text with all capital letters
   C) Type the text in italics
   D) Underline the text

25. The 1994 Conference on Fair Use stipulates when it is permissible for a library or archives to reproduce a phonorecord. What is important to the definition of the term *phonorecord*?

   A) The medium must be a cassette, LP, or compact disc
   B) The recording must be for a commercial endeavor
   C) The recording must be a "material object" (i.e., sounds that constituted an original composition)
   D) The recording must be a song that is reproduced with the aid of a machine

Solutions

Solutions to Check Point—Section A

Answer	Refer to:
A–1. (D)	[A-2-c]
A–2. (B)	[A-3-a (2)]
A–3. (C)	[A-4-b (1) (b)]

Solutions to Check Point—Section B

Answer	Refer to:
B–1. (C)	[B-1-a]
B–2. (C)	[B-5-c]
B–3. (B)	[B-7-c]

Solutions to Check Point—Section C

Answer	Refer to:
C–1. (A)	[C-1]
C–2. (B)	[C-2]
C–3. (B)	[C-5]

Solutions to For Your Review

Answer	Refer to:
1. (C)	[A-1 and A-1-c]
2. (D)	[A-1-c (3)]
3. (A)	[A-1-c (4)]
4. (C)	[A-2-d]
5. (B)	[A-3-a (1)]
6. (A)	[A-3-b]
7. (D)	[A-4-b (1)]
8. (C)	[A-4-b (3) (a)]
9. (A)	[A-4-b (5)]
10. (D)	[A-6-c]
11. (D)	[B-1-a]
12. (C)	[B-2-c]
13. (D)	[B-2-d]
14. (B)	[B-2-e]
15. (D)	[B-3]
16. (C)	[B-4]
17. (C)	[B-5-a]
18. (C)	[B-6-b (1)]
19. (A)	[B-6-b (4)]
20. (C)	[B-6-b (5) (c)]
21. (B)	[B-6-b (5) (e)]
22. (B)	[B-6-b (5) (g)]
23. (B)	[B-6-b (7) (c)]
24. (A)	[B-7-d (4)]
25. (C)	[C-3]

Chapter 7

Document Reproduction

OVERVIEW

As a part of image processing, reproduction technology has been and continues to be in a constant state of change. Much of the technology used in the 20th century has become outdated and obsolete because of the speed and quality characterized by newer reproduction processes for producing copies of documents. The term **reproduction** is defined as the preparation of multiple copies of images.

Copy processes are combined with duplicating, printing, and imaging processes to create multiple copies of original documents. Using a word processing or desktop publishing program, administrative professionals can create professional-looking documents, such as company brochures, informational bulletins, and notices. The document is the *camera-ready copy* to be used as masters or originals for producing multiple copies.

Imaging processes may be xerographic, electrostatic, or laser in nature. Depending on the imaging desired and the quality preferred, these processes help create images that can be reproduced in quantity via a duplicating or printing process.

No product is complete until it has gone through some type of finishing process: collating and stapling, binding, or folding. Laminating in a plastic coating is used to preserve documents.

This chapter briefly covers the major reproduction processes (copying, duplicating, composition, and imaging) that administrative professionals encounter.

KEY TERMS

Binding, 159
Collating, 159
Diazo, 151
Digital duplicating, 153
Direct-image master, 152

Electrostatic imaging, 157
Electrostatic master, 152
Facsimile (Fax), 157
Fiber optic imaging, 158
Job recovery, 150

Laminating, 160
Laser imaging, 158
Metal plates, 152
Offset cylinders, 152
Offset duplicating, 152

A. Copying and Duplicating Technologies

Copying, often referred to as *photocopying,* involves the creation of exact images directly from original copies of text material through xerographic, fiber optic, or laser imaging processes. *Duplicating* is concerned with the creation of multiple copies of originals as required for stockholders, customers, and other large-quantity functions. Copying processes tend to be used to produce limited numbers of copies, whereas duplicating processes are used when hundreds and thousands of copies of the same document are needed.

1. ***The Copying Process:*** *Copying* involves the creation of exact images directly from one or more originals. An original is the actual printed, typeset, or graphic copy from which copies can be prepared. Basically, copiers fall into categories based on volume.

   a. *Copiers classified by output volume:* Office copiers can be classified according to the number of copies produced during a given period of time. The following descriptions are divided into low-volume, medium-volume, and high-volume output.

      (1) *Low-volume copiers:* Copiers used for low-volume output are typically located near the administrative professional and are often called *convenience copiers.* A particular department may have its own copier, or one or two departments may share a copier. Convenience copiers are affordable for the small business or department, easy to operate, and used most profitably when fewer than 25 copies of a relatively short document are needed. Although the per-copy cost tends to be higher than with other copying processes, a copier should be used for multiple copies instead of the desktop ink-jet or laser printer. The desktop printer is intended for printing one or two copies of a document.

         (a) *Volume output:* The number of copies produced each month typically is no more than 20,000 copies. Copies are produced at speeds of up to 30 copies per minute. Toner probably needs to be changed every 2,500 to 3,000 copies, while a drum may yield 30,000 to 50,000 copies before replacement is necessary.

         (b) *Basic features:* Following are some of the basic features of low-volume copiers:

            • Copies may be produced on plain or colored paper (17 to 32 pounds), company letterhead, or business forms.

            • A 10- to 20-bin collator can be attached to collate pages for a relatively short document.

            • Collated pages can be automatically stapled or stitched in the upper left corner of the document.

            • The images on the original copies can be reduced 50 to 99 percent or enlarged from 101 to 400 percent.

            • Manual two-sided *(duplexing)* color copying is possible.

(c) *Office use:* Low-volume copiers can produce any type of copying from printed pages to artwork. Even address labels can be copied in order to make multiple copies of mailing lists. Overhead transparencies can also be prepared by feeding acetate sheets through the copier.

(d) *Skills needed:* No special skills are needed to operate a low-volume copier. Clearing paper jams and replacing toner cartridges are among the operations that administrative professionals need to be able to handle.

(2) *Medium-volume copiers:* Copiers used for medium-volume output are generally operated by a small number of trained administrative professionals. In a large organization, a given department may have its own medium-volume copier, or there may be a more centralized reproduction center offering 24-hour service to all departments. The per-copy cost is less than copies made with a low-volume copier.

(a) *Volume output:* The monthly copy volume for this category is usually in the range of 20,000 to 125,000 copies. Medium-volume copiers produce 30 to 60 copies per minute, and special features can be added easily to the equipment. Heavier stock paper (17 to 110 pounds) can be used with the equipment.

(b) *Basic features:* Following are some of the basic features of medium-volume copiers:

- The images on the original copies can be reduced to 50 percent or enlarged to as much as 400 percent.
- Automatic sizing of page images permits the use of different paper sizes.
- Black-and-white images on plain or colored paper, company letterhead, or business forms are the most common.
- Automatic duplexing (copying on both sides of paper) is a standard operation.

(c) *Office use:* Medium-volume copiers can produce a wide range of copying, from printed documents to those that incorporate illustrations and artwork. Medium-volume copiers have a lower per-copy cost than low-volume copiers and are used for longer documents and reports and larger quantities.

(d) *Skills needed:* Users of medium-volume copiers need to be trained to operate the equipment. If the copier is housed in a department, one or two administrative professionals are often trained to handle all copying. If the copier is housed in a centralized in-house copy service, trained staff makes all copies. Trained administrative professionals or reproduction center personnel handle simple equipment maintenance including toner replacement. Vendor services handle all other maintenance on the copier.

(3) *High-volume copiers:* Only trained personnel would run high-volume copying processes. Jobs would be forwarded to a centralized copy or printing service located within the organization, and finished copies would be delivered within a 24- to 48-hour time period, depending on the schedule and job priorities.

(a) *Volume output:* The monthly copy volume for high-volume copiers ranges from 200,000 to 750,000 copies. Such equipment produces copies at rates from 85 to 120 copies per minute.

(b) *Basic features:* Here are some of the basic features of high-volume copiers:

- Automatic duplexing is a standard feature.
- Stapler-sorters attached to the copier can collate and staple up to 50 pages.
- Reductions from 99 to 64 percent and enlargements to 200 percent are common.
- An automatic feed feature sets the copier to feed in a stack of originals, one at a time.

(c) *Office use:* Copying jobs that entail longer documents needed in quantity are handled very well with high-volume copiers. When an operator is interrupted while making copies, the copier will "remember" the point where the original job has been stopped and continue the process from that point. This feature, called **job recovery**, makes it possible to do a "rush" job for someone and then continue the previous job. Transparencies can also be made on high-volume copiers.

(d) *Skills needed:* High-volume copiers usually require trained technicians who are equipped to handle troubleshooting, maintenance and replacement of parts, and replacement of toner and drums. These technicians also follow directions and establish schedules to complete jobs to meet the deadlines of users in other departments.

b. *Specialized copiers:* Some copiers are specialized for custom work in the office. An enhancement for documents that have been produced as only black-and-white images for many years is color copying. Large and oversized documents can be reduced in size for easier dissemination. Computer technology has revolutionized copying processes to meet a range of office needs.

(1) *Color copiers:* Copiers that reproduce color are essential in the office for preparing illustrations and graphics to complement documents and reports. The cost per copy is higher than black-and-white copying, but the high quality of the colored copies enables the copy to be color copied.

(a) *Colored original:* The original copy may be in color, and it may be necessary to reproduce copies (in black and white as well as in color) from the colored original. More than one color may be used on a particular original. Today most copiers can reproduce both black-and-white and colored copies. Although the cost of producing color reproductions is high, the cost is justified when organizations require colored reproductions.

(b) *Color toner:* Interchangeable color toner cartridges make it possible to have more than one color available when the copier can handle only one color at a time. Some color copiers have the capacity for more than one toner color at a time.

(2) *Digital copier/printer:* In the past all copiers have been analog. Today digital technology allows data to be transferred in a series of bits rather than as a fluctuating (analog) signal. Digital technology provides faster, clearer, and higher-quality output. *Digital copiers* accept originals downloaded from computer-based information systems for printing. These copiers are expensive because of the integration of digital technology and copying and printing operations into one piece of equipment.

(a) *The process:* Microprocessor technology allows the digital copier to accept input from one or more other devices—a computer, an optical character reader, other digital copiers—and provide hard-copy output at local or distant sites. An interface is required in order to submit information from other equipment to the digital copier for printing. If the administrative professional submits information from the desktop PC to be printed at the digital copier/printer the quality of output is about 15 percent better than copies made from a hard copy. Digital copiers are sometimes referred to as *information distributors*.

(b) *Basic features:* The ability to print hard copy from electronic signals makes the digital copier a versatile system for office use. When the digital copier serves as the only printer, the organization is at a disadvantage if there is a breakdown, there is no printer. The following advantages of digital copiers include:

- 120 pages or more can be printed per minute.
- Very high resolution quality is provided—600 plus dots per inch (DPI).
- Excellent quality for copying photographs and drawings.
- Up to 11 multicolor printing is possible.

(c) *Office use:* Some of the major uses for the digital copier/printer are in typesetting, producing microfilm from electronic records stored in memory, and receiving and transmitting information from computer-based information systems. This process is efficient and effective for form design, where the form is printed at the same time as the variable data. Both the form and the variable data are electronically generated. With digital copiers, data can easily be distributed throughout the networked organization.

(3) *Multifunction units:* Office technology has advanced to the point where multifunction units are used in small business offices and in home offices. Such units as a copier-printer, a copier-printer-fax, or a copier-printer-fax-scanner provide a combination of functions for the office that has a limited number of copies and faxes to prepare and send or requires scanning to be performed. One caution is that though the price may be fairly reasonable for this array of technology, repairs may be more complicated because of the integration of technologies into one unit.

(4) *Large-document reproduction:* Some documents are difficult to copy because of size. Documents such as computer printouts, large drawings, and oversize sheets (larger than 8 1/2 by 14 inches) often must be reduced to a size that coincides with the physical storage space available for these documents.

(5) *Diazo:* Copies of engineering and architectural drawings are often made through the **diazo** process; the original document is in a translucent state. Only documents with printing on one side of the page can be reproduced with the diazo process. A diazo copy will accept ink or pencil additions. Deletions or erasures need to be made with special correction devices.

2. ***The Duplicating Process:*** Whereas a copier prepares copies directly from an original document, *duplicating* requires an intermediate step—the preparation of a master to use in reproducing copies. Once the master is prepared, copies may be reproduced directly from the master. Today offset duplicating and digital duplicating are the basic

duplicating processes. After many years of use, the spirit and stencil duplicating processes have been replaced with high-tech, high-volume copying and duplicating processes.

a. *Offset duplicating:* **Offset duplicating** is based on the principle that grease and water do not mix. The image area is receptive to ink (grease), and the non-image area is receptive to water.

(1) *Offset masters:* The material to be duplicated is prepared on an offset paper master, an electrostatic master, or a metal plate.

(a) *Offset paper master:* The **direct-image master**, as this type of master is commonly called, is a smooth paper material that is prepared by keying or writing directly on it. It is necessary to have a printer that is suited to offset duplication or special writing implements (reproducing pens or pencils). One paper master can produce up to 2,500 copies.

(b) *Electrostatic master:* The original material is hard copy printed or drawn (usually with black ink) onto a sheet of bond paper. Then it is copied onto a sensitized offset master by inserting the original along with the master into a copier. The image is transferred from the original to the offset master during this copying process. **Electrostatic masters** can be used to duplicate as many as 5,000 copies.

(c) *Metal plate:* **Metal plates** are especially useful in duplicating forms or other documents that will be rerun from time to time. The plates can be saved and used a number of times before a new plate needs to be made. A camera is used to produce a picture of the original material that is being transferred to the metal plate. This plate is the most expensive of the three types of masters, but it will produce the largest number of copies. Some metal plates can produce as many as 50,000 copies.

(2) *The process:* The offset duplicator may be a tabletop model, a more sophisticated floor model, or a fully automated system with such features as automatic document feeding or master making. There are three **offset cylinders** that work together to produce the duplicated copy.

(a) *Master cylinder:* The master or plate is attached to the *master cylinder* and inked.

(b) *Blanket cylinder:* The ink on the master creates a reverse image of the material on an intermediate *blanket cylinder*.

(c) *Impression cylinder:* This image is offset (duplicated) from the blanket cylinder onto a piece of paper moving through the duplicator that is then forced against it by the *impression cylinder*.

(3) *Office use:* The offset duplicator can quickly produce a large number of copies at an economical cost. The per-copy costs are low, but the initial equipment costs tend to be high and trained operators are essential. Once the first copy is produced (the most expensive copy to produce), subsequent copies are produced at a lower cost. Offset duplicating offers excellent duplicating quality. Depending on the master, between 2,500 and 50,000 copies can be produced from a single master. Color duplicating (of very good quality) is possible as well as printing on both sides of the paper.

b. *Digital duplicating:* **Digital duplicating** combines convenience copying with the economy of offset printing. Medium- to high-volume printing requirements can most often be met with digital duplicating systems. Compatibility with micro-computers allows digital duplicators to function with a computer interface that requires no additional hardware.

(1) *Basic features:* Low copy cost, color printing, and large image sizes are some of the key features of such a digital system.

- All models incorporate microcomputer compatibility.

- Color cylinders are available in standard colors (up to as many as 15) and unlimited custom colors for effective color copying.

- Up to 120 copies per minute may be produced.

- Typically, print modes include photo, text, and both photo and text.

- Zooming capability from 50 to 499 percent provides a range of reduction and enlargement possibilities.

- A built-in touch-screen editing system allows operators to manipulate documents through the various production phases.

(2) *Office use:* An additional computer interface to a digital duplicating system can create a desktop publishing system to handle the preparation of office publications. With the range of color capabilities, documents and reports can be prepared with a very professional look.

Check Point—Section A

Directions: For each question, circle the correct answer.

A–1. Wilhelm needs 10 copies of a three-page document. Which type of equipment should Wilhelm use to complete this task?

A) Convenience copier
B) Information distributor
C) Ink-jet desktop printer
D) Mid-volume copier

A–2. When is a desktop copier-printer-fax-scanner unit recommended for an office?

A) Digitized documents and a low volume of copies and faxes are regularly produced

B) Hard copy output is required at both local and long distance sites
C) The unit can be shared within a department
D) Trained professionals are available to operate the unit

A–3. What reproduction process is based on the principle that grease and water do not mix?

A) Diazo
B) Digital duplicating
C) Information distributor
D) Offset duplicating

B. Typesetting and Composition Processes

Text material for professional publications such as newspapers, magazines, newsletters, company brochures, or pamphlets must be prepared through a *typesetting* process that produces a master copy in the type style and size of type desired. The composition process complements the typesetting process by formatting the text into appropriate page and document layout. Word processing and desktop publishing programs are the most popular software programs that administrative professionals use to create small publications. Administrative professionals can save application documents as Web pages.

1. ***Typesetting and Composition Measurements and Style:*** Type sizes and styles may vary within the same document. The following are some terms used by printers to indicate type size, line length, and type style.

   a. *Points:* Character size is measured in **points**, from 6 points to 96 points. Common point sizes for text are 10 or 12 points. One inch equals 72 points.

   b. *Picas:* **Pica** is the measurement used for the width and length of a line. There are 6 picas to the inch.

   c. *Typefaces:* A **typeface** may be italic or bold (light, regular, medium, and strong); stress on the oval (vertical or diagonal) or no stress; serifs (vertical or horizontal stroke to complete the letter) or no serifs (sans serif); and uniform letter strokes or a thick/thin transition in a letter stroke (light to distinct). See Chapter 6, Figure 6–2 for details about typeface characteristics.

   d. *Type font:* A group of letters, numbers, and symbols with a common typeface is called a **type font.** Font refers to the style of the characters. A font consists of two elements: typeface and point size.

      EXAMPLE: *Times Roman, old style, 10 point*

↑	↑	↑
Font	Type face	Type size

2. ***The Typesetting Process:*** **Typesetting** (sometimes called *cold type*) principles are followed to produce typeset copy by electronically converting keyed words into professional-looking type. Once text has been keyboarded and stored in the typesetter CPU, it will not have to be keyed in again before the camera-ready copy is produced. Usually, typeset pages will contain more copy than an ordinary printed page from a word processing or desktop publishing program. Word processing and desktop publishing documents can also be saved as pages for Web sites.

   a. *Copy input:* Equipment for copy input may be of two types: direct entry or electronic entry.

      (1) *Direct entry:* The operator keys in the characters to be typeset, along with machine instructions and codes, via the typesetting keyboard. The characters appear on a display screen during keyboarding. Proofreading and revision of text may take place before the copy is finally typeset.

      (2) *Electronic entry:* Using a word processing or desktop publishing program, text is keyed and saved on disk/disc. The administrative professional selects printing options for bold, underscore, or different fonts in the software program; the appropriate command codes are inserted into the text.

   b. *Copy output:* The exposed photosensitive material (paper or film) is taken from the typesetter and put into a processing unit. The material, once it is processed, is then ready to become part of the original copy. The *camera-ready copy* (copy that is ready for printing) can then be used to make the plates necessary for printing.

3. ***The Composition Process:*** The types of composition equipment available to use in actually composing articles, columns, or even pages for a publication include photo-composers and computer-assisted composition processes, including word processing and desktop publishing.

   a. *Photocomposition:* Often referred to as *direct entry* composition, **photocomposition** is the process whereby the composer automatically sets the type as the text is being keyed from the keyboard. The typed characters and symbols appear on a display monitor, and the images on the monitor are photographed in order to create the black-and-white text needed for printing. Following are some of the more outstanding features of photocomposition:

      (1) Both paragraph text and headlines can be produced using the photocomposer.

      (2) A complete page of text material can be composed without the need to prepare text in strips or pieces that need to be pasted up for later printing.

   b. *Word processing and desktop publishing:* The electronic office now includes the ability to produce camera-ready copy for printing from the microcomputer. This is possible with either word processing or desktop publishing software. Both software programs provide many different type sizes and styles; the ability to merge graphs, pictures, and illustrations with text; and special border and background effects.

      (1) *Hardware:* Word processing and desktop publishing programs require a microcomputer with graphic capabilities, a high-resolution display monitor, and a laser printer. The graphic capability is required to project graphs, pictures, borders, and different-size letters. The high-resolution monitor allows soft copy to be displayed almost as clearly as the printed copy. WYSIWYG (pronounced whizie-wig) is an acronym for "what you see is what you get." The laser printer produces a high-quality image very quickly. Sometimes a scanner is used to digitize pictures and store the pictures in secondary storage. These stored images (files) are later merged with text (word processing or desktop publishing documents [files]).

      (2) *Software:* The ability to select different type fonts, sizes, and typeface; to merge illustrations with text; and to incorporate special effects is possible through the use of word processing or desktop publishing software. Enhancements to both word processing software and desktop publishing software are overcoming the differences between the two programs. A number of word processing packages now offer desktop publishing features, and word processing features are being added to desktop publishing systems. Word processing and desktop publishing programs are designed to complement rather than to substitute for each other.

   c. *Computer-aided composition:* Original text that has been keyed in with word processing programs can be converted with composition software programs so that master pages for reproduction and publishing can be created. Typesetting and print codes must be inserted into the recorded text with instructions for headings, type styles, spacing, and other format features. The master (original) pages that are created are then used to print the copies of the document, report, or booklet.

      (1) *Illustrations and artwork:* Pictures or original artwork can be scanned or redrawn using graphic arts software. These illustrations can then be imported into the master text at the appropriate locations.

(2) *Master text:* The master pages created for the manuscript must then be proofed and edited by the user (author) to locate any errors in word text, page layout, spacing, or document content.

Whereas word processing and desktop publishing programs are geared toward the preparation of smaller documents, more sophisticated computer-aided composition processes are typically applied to multiple-page manuscripts and books that will be aimed at high-volume reproduction.

d. *Web pages:* Although organization Web pages are typically created by Web designers, administrative professionals can also save their application documents as Web pages. Web pages use the same design principles as other business documents and presentations. The four design principles—proximity, alignment, repetition, and contrast—along with designing with type are presented in Chapter 6, Section B. Word processing, spreadsheet, presentation graphics, and desktop publishing documents can be saved as Web pages or frames.

(1) *Saving documents as Web pages:* Instead of using the standard *"Save"* command, the administrative professional would use the *"Save As"* command. Both the *"Save As Web Page"* command or the *"Save as type"* dialog box allow the administrative professional to select the Web page (.htm, .html) option. When the document is saved, basic hypertext markup language (HTML) code is inserted into the Web page document.

(2) *Creating a Web page:* Administrative professionals can create Web pages using the application software templates, Web page software, or coding HTML into a document using Notepad. *Notepad* is a basic text editor for creating Web pages. Administrative professionals interested in creating Web pages should have training (beginning to advanced courses or workshops). Also, there are hundreds of resources on the Internet for learning how to create Web pages. Administrative professionals can search for "Web page tutor" or "HTML tutor" and select the best tutorial that fits their knowledge level needs.

It is very important that the organization's Web site incorporate a consistent image. The administrative professional must work with others in the organization to support consistency throughout the organization's Web site.

Check Point—Section B

Directions: For each question, circle the correct answer.

B–1. The typesetting measurement for the width and length of a 1 inch line is

A) 6 picas
B) 10 picas
C) 12 points
D) 72 points

B–2. Ruhmor is creating a publication and is trying to decide whether the letters should have serifs and whether he should use bold and/or italic. Ruhmor is making a decision about the

A) point characteristics
B) type font
C) type set
D) typeface

B–3. Brummett has decided to create a brochure using her microcomputer. What software is she likely to use?

A) Notepad
B) Photocomposition
C) Presentation graphics
D) Word processing

C. Imaging Processes

The traditional way to produce a master (original) was to type it using a typewriter. Today computer technology provides the opportunity to key or scan in text or other emerging technologies for original copies of documents, to prepare originals electronically, and to make copies of documents using various imaging processes.

1. *Facsimile Imaging:* **Facsimile (fax)** technology is used in two ways in the electronic office: imaging from one location to another (facsimile transmission) and imaging from an original copy to a duplicating master (electronic scanning).

    a. *Facsimile transmission (Fax):* Many times, documents (text, drawings, charts, maps, and so on) need to be transmitted from one location to another. This can be accomplished through the use of facsimile transmission over telephone lines or microwaves. This type of communication is machine to machine—from the sending unit to the receiving unit. The time lapse can be from three seconds to six minutes for one page, depending on the technology being used.

       EXAMPLE: *Jensen has been directed to send a copy of a five-page document as fast as possible. Her alternatives include facsimile transmission or the U.S. Postal Service. If she decides to send it by fax, it will take approximately 5 minutes (1 minute × 5 pages) to send the entire document. Since the document is short, Jensen decides to fax the document from her desktop PC; the cost is less than express mail and the copies will arrive within a few minutes.*

    b. *Electronic scanning:* Electronic **scanning** processes are used for digitizing text from a printed page and transferring it to a computer disk/disc or to a master for printing. Different electronic scanners are used for each process.

       (1) *Converting text to word processing:* An electronic scanner (a full-page scanner or a partial-page scanner) can be used to convert printed text to word processing.

          EXAMPLE: *With a typical scanner for the business office costing less than $100, scanning costs for a page are minimal. A scanner with high photo resolution can be purchased for approximately $200.*

       (2) *Converting text to master:* Any time a duplicating master can be prepared without having to rekey or redraw the document, valuable time is saved. An original copy of a page can be electronically scanned to produce an electronic master to use in reproducing individual copies on an offset duplicator or printer. This process will produce masters for duplicating processes in approximately 4 to 6 minutes.

       Scanning is an excellent alternative to rekeying text. Proofing the stored text is extremely important to be sure that any scanning errors (i.e., text or word processing format commands) are corrected. Format commands may not be read properly during the scanning process and may need to be reinserted into the text.

2. *Electrostatic Imaging:* An offset master or overhead transparency can be produced from an original that is placed in a copy machine through a process called **electrostatic imaging.**

    a. *Creation of master:* Instead of copy paper, a sensitized master is used; the master is immediately ready for use in the offset duplicating process. Sometimes the electrostatic copier is a modular attachment to the offset duplicator.

b. *Production of overhead transparencies:* For overhead transparencies, the blank transparency is used in place of copy paper. The image from the original is transferred to the transparency sheet. Only transparency sheets designated for use in a copier may be used.

3. ***Imaging Processes in Copier Operation:*** Although copiers appear to be simple and easy to operate, imaging processes can be quite complicated. The most common imaging processes are xerographic, fiber optic, and laser processes.

a. *Xerographic process:* Plain-paper copiers use a xerographic process to produce images. **Xerographic imaging** uses a camera to project an image of the original onto a positively charged drum. When a sheet of plain paper, which is negatively charged, passes over the drum, the image adheres to the paper and is permanently fixed with heat. A powdered or liquid toner is used to develop the image on the exposed paper.

b. *Fiber optic process:* With **fiber optic imaging**, an electrographic process exposes the electrically charged drum to the original document that is being copied. Tiny glass strands replace the lenses and mirrors of the traditional xerographic copier. These tiny strands transmit information in the form of pulsating laser light from the original document to a drum. Each glass fiber carries a small portion of the image. Toner is fused to the paper instead of the drums, providing a copy of the original document. The light source must remain fixed while the paper moves past the light source on a moving platen. Fiber optic copiers have few parts, so the copier tends to be smaller and less expensive than traditional xerographic copiers. Perhaps the only disadvantage of the fiber optics copier is that it is slower than other low-volume, convenience copiers.

c. *Laser process:* Desktop laser printers now interface with microcomputers to produce high-quality, high-speed multiple copies for the administrative professional. The quality of laser print is comparable to typesetting jobs. **Laser imaging** utilizes a beam of light that reflects off a series of mirrors. The final mirror diverts the image to a drum, which transfers the image to paper.

Check Point—Section C

Directions: For each question, circle the correct answer.

C–1. What is the transmission channel for sending a facsimile (fax)?

A) Cellular
B) Internet
C) Local area network (LAN)
D) Telephone lines

C–2. The process for making an overhead transparency from an original on a copy machine is called

A) diazo
B) duplicating

C) electrostatic imaging
D) scanning

C–3. A common imaging process that uses a camera to project an image of the original onto a positively charged drum is called

A) diazo
B) fiber optics
C) laser
D) xerographic

D. Finishing and Binding Processes

After copies are duplicated or printed, finishing processes such as collating, stapling or stitching, binding, and folding help complete the job and give it that "professional look."

1. *Sorting and Collating:* The process of sorting each page into a set of pages is called **collating.** A stand-alone collator may be used that can collate up to eight pages at one time, or a collator may be attached to a copier or a duplicator that can handle up to 50 pages at one time. Online sorters allow copies to move directly from the copier or duplicator to the sorter without any intervention by the administrative professional.

2. *Stapling or Stitching:* Final documents can be stapled in the upper left corner or stapled down the left edge or across the top of the document with two to three staples. Small electric staplers are helpful in fastening relatively small packets in the office. When the document is folded, **saddle-stitch binding** uses two or more staples at the fold of the paper.

   Some electronic collators will staple or stitch the copies in the upper left corner as soon as the collating is complete. Stitching is used when the packet of collated pages exceeds the size of ordinary staples. **Stitching** uses a roll of wire from which staples are automatically cut to the size needed. An assembling unit may be attached to a copier or a duplicator to provide online finishing: receiving the copies, jogging the copies into a stack, stapling, and depositing the set in a tray for pickup.

3. *Binding:* In addition to stapling, other **binding** processes available to the administrative professional include three-ring binding, plastic comb binding, spiral binding, Wir-O binding, Velo binding, and fastback binding. For large documents, the administrative professional would use a professional *bindery* service to do the binding. A bindery can also do sewn-and-glued binding, case binding, and lay-flat binding.

   Except for three-ring binding and plastic comb binding, once binding is placed along the edge of the document, it is difficult to remove or add pages to the document. Typically binding is along the left edge of a document. Legal documents, however, are typically bound across the top of a document. An extra 1/2 inch is added to the left margin for the binding on left-bound documents. For top-bound documents an extra 1/2 to 1 inch is added to the margin next to the page gutter.

   a. *Three-ring binding:* Paper punched with three holes along the left edge is inserted into a three-ring notebook. Although the loose-leaf inserts are easy to add and remove, this process has the least professional appearance.

   b. *Plastic comb binding: Plastic comb binding* inserts a strip of plastic with teeth into rectangular holes along the edge of the paper. Kits allow the administrative professional to punch holes in the paper as well as holding the teeth open when inserting the paper. The typical thickness for plastic comb binding is 2 inches.

   c. *Spiral binding:* Either a metal or plastic spiral coil is inserted through holes along the edge of the paper. Spiral binding uses a single spiral coil.

   d. *Wir-O binding:* For sturdier binding, *Wir-O binding* inserts two wire teeth through the rectangular holes along the edge of the paper.

   e. *Velo binding: Velo binding* uses two plastic strips along the edge (one plastic strip on top of the document and one plastic strip on the bottom of the document). Plastic pins hold the plastic strips together; heat binds the pins and plastic strips.

f. *Fastback binding:* With *fastback binding,* a cloth or paper strip is wrapped around the spine (document edge to be bound) and then glued. Although pages can come unglued if the document is frequently used, fastback binding is the most professional-appearing binding process.

g. *Sewn-and-glued binding:* A bindery sews the pages together and glues the pages to a cover. *Sewn-and-glued binding* is common for softcover books.

h. *Case binding: Case binding* requires a bindery to sew the pages together, glue the pages to a gauze strip, glue on end pages, and attach the document to hard covers. This is the most common binding process for hardcover books.

i. *Lay-flat binding:* For *lay-flat binding,* a bindery first grinds the spine of the document to create a flat edge. The cover is glued to the book at each side of the spine; this allows the pages of the book to lay flat when opened.

4. *Folding:* Often, duplicated material needs to be folded into booklet or pamphlet form. Electronic folding machines can be set to fold single folds, letter folds (6-panel fold; two parallel folds), accordion folds (6-panel fold; two parallel folds in the opposite direction), or French folds (8-panel fold). These are the most common types of folds for business booklets and pamphlets. For a more detailed discussion on folding, see Chapter 6, Section A-3.

Top-of-the-line folders can fold at speeds of up to 30,000 sheets per hour. Attractive folding techniques save paper cost because documents can be produced in reduced sizes, ready for mailing and distribution. Large folding systems fold, insert, seal, and stamp bulk mailings.

5. *Laminating:* The **laminating** process protects and preserves documents and other frequently used items from wear and tear. Laminating uses pressure and heat to permanently bond together the original document to a plastic film covering. The plastic film covers both sides of the original and should be trimmed approximately 1/4 inch beyond the edge of the document to ensure a long-lasting seal and clean appearance. Items the administrative professional might want to laminate include letters, office forms, certificates, tags, menus, photos and images, and electronic presentation slides.

Check Point—Section D

Directions: For each question, circle the correct answer.

D–1. The Valley Community Theater bound a 25-page program booklet by using a roll of wire and cutting staples to fit the size of the booklet. This binding process is called

A) fastback
B) spiral
C) stitching
D) Wir-O

D–2. Which binding process makes it easy to remove or insert pages to the document at a later time?

A) Case
B) Plastic comb

C) Spiral
D) Velo

D–3. The physician's office has a document all patients are required to read before seeing the physician. What is the best way to protect the document from wear and tear?

A) e-Mail the document to the patient prior to the visit
B) Laminate the document
C) Place the document on the intranet
D) Provide each patient with a photocopy of the document

For Your Review

Directions: For each question, circle the correct answer.

1. The marketing department was given budget approval for a new copier that could handle approximately 100,000 copies per month and print at least 50 pages per minute. The best copier for the marketing department is a

    A) color copier
    B) convenience copier
    C) high-volume copier
    D) medium-volume copier

2. One important feature of copiers is duplexing. Duplexing means that

    A) a copy job can be interrupted to do another job and then the first job can be returned to and completed
    B) copies can be enlarged up to 130 percent
    C) the copier can copy on both sides of a sheet of paper with one operation
    D) the copier feeds two originals at a time for faster per-page copying

3. Morgan is sending an announcement to 350 people about the *Document Design Seminar* on April 25. The artwork on the announcement requires printing to be on heavy stock paper. The best reproduction process is

    A) diazo copier
    B) digital copier
    C) low-volume copier
    D) medium-volume copier

4. The typical copier housed in a centralized reproduction center for handling 450,000 copies per month is the

    A) digital copier
    B) high-volume copier

    C) medium-volume copier
    D) multifunctional unit

5. Clark was running a 1,500 copy job and was interrupted to do a "rush" job for the President. Clark was able to continue the original job from the interruption point. This feature is called

    A) duplexing
    B) fetching
    C) job recovery
    D) turnaround time

6. What is the best equipment for making 50 copies of a document that includes clip art with multiple hues?

    A) Color copier
    B) Color printer
    C) Convenience copier
    D) Diazo copier

7. The Fabiano Law Firm's centralized reproduction center processes 425,000 copies each month from originals downloaded through the local area network (LAN). What type of copier meets these requirements?

    A) Digital copier
    B) High-volume copier
    C) Medium-volume copier
    D) Multifunctional unit

8. An engineering drawing is typically reproduced using a/an

    A) diazo copier
    B) high-volume copier
    C) information distributor
    D) multifunctional unit

9. A direct-image master is required for

A) diazo copiers
B) information distributors
C) multifunctional units
D) offset duplicators

10. A common typesetting measurement for a character is

A) 6 picas
B) 10 picas
C) 8 points
D) 12 points

11. Characters with a vertical or horizontal mark to complete the letter have a

A) san-serif
B) serif
C) stress
D) stroke transition

12. Times New Roman in 10 point is an example of a/an

A) pica size
B) type font
C) type style
D) typeface

13. Cold type is

A) composing with word processing
B) formatting text into page and document layout
C) photocomposition
D) producing a master in a specific text style and size

14. In comparison to an ordinary printed page from word processing or desktop publishing programs, the amount of copy on a typeset page is typically

A) less than the ordinary printed page
B) more than the ordinary printed page
C) the same as the ordinary printed page
D) the same as the desktop publishing printed page but more than the word processing printed page

15. In the typesetting process, copy that is ready for making the masters for printing is called

A) camera-ready copy
B) digitized copy

C) direct-image copy
D) electronic copy

16. VandeMerk was asked if she would post her tracking spreadsheet on the organization's intranet. What is the easiest way for VandeMerk to make the tracking spreadsheet into a Web page?

A) Create a document with Web page software and import the spreadsheet data
B) In the computer directory, click on the file name and change the spreadsheet extension to .html
C) With the spreadsheet in an active window, select "Save as Web page"
D) Use Notepad and copy the spreadsheet data into a Web page template

17. The processes for digitizing hard copy text and storing the data on a computer disk/disc is called

A) diazo processing
B) duplication
C) photocomposition
D) scanning

18. An offset master can be produced from an original that is placed in a copy machine through a process called

A) electronic scanning
B) electrostatic imaging
C) facsimile imaging
D) photocomposition

19. What imaging process uses tiny glass strands to replace the lenses and mirrors of the traditional copier?

A) Diazo
B) Fiber optics
C) Laser
D) Xerographic

20. What imaging process is comparable to typeset jobs?

A) Diazo
B) Fiber optics
C) Laser
D) Xerographic

21. How much extra space should be added to the margin of a legal document for binding?
    A) 1 inch on the left margin
    B) 1 3/4 inch on the left margin
    C) 1 inch on the margin next to the gutter
    D) 2 inch on the top margin

22. Case binding is done through a/an
    A) bindery
    B) copier with proper attachments
    C) kit used by the administrative professional
    D) reproduction center

23. What binding process uses pins inserted through strips (one on top of the document and one on the bottom of the document) and fuses the pins and strips together with heat?
    A) Fastback
    B) Lay-flat

    C) Plastic comb
    D) Velo

24. What is a common binding process for soft cover books?
    A) Case
    B) Lay-flat
    C) Sewn-and-glued
    D) Stitching

25. A letter fold is a/an
    A) 6-panel fold; two parallel folds
    B) 6-panel fold; two parallel folds in the opposite direction
    C) 8-panel fold
    D) single fold

Solutions

Solutions to Check Point—Section A

Answer	Refer to:
A–1. (A)	[A-1-a (1)]
A–2. (A)	[A-1-b (3)]
A–3. (D)	[A-2-a]

Solutions to Check Point—Section B

Answer	Refer to:
B–1. (A)	[B-1-b]
B–2. (D)	[B-1-c]
B–3. (D)	[B-3-b]

Solutions to Check Point—Section C

Answer	Refer to:
C–1. (D)	[C-1-a]
C–2. (C)	[C-2-b]
C–3. (D)	[C-3-a]

Solutions to Check Point—Section D

Answer	*Refer to:*
D–1. (C)	[D-2]
D–2. (B)	[D-3]
D–3. (B)	[D-5]

Solutions to For Your Review

Answer	*Refer to:*
1. (D)	[A-1-a (2)]
2. (C)	[A-1-a (1) (b) and A-1-a (2) (b)]
3. (D)	[A-1-a (2)]
4. (B)	[A-1-a (3)]
5. (C)	[A-1-a (3) (c)]
6. (A)	[A-1-b (1)]
7. (A)	[A-1-b (2)]
8. (A)	[A-1-b (5)]
9. (D)	[A-2-a (1) (a)]
10. (D)	[B-1-a]
11. (B)	[B-1-c and Chapter 6 B-5-b]
12. (B)	[B-1-d and Chapter 6 Figure 6-2]
13. (D)	[B-2]
14. (B)	[B-2]
15. (A)	[B-2 and B-2-b]
16. (C)	[B-3-d (1)]
17. (D)	[C-1-b]
18. (B)	[C-2]
19. (B)	[C-3-b]
20. (C)	[C-3-c]

21. (C)   [D-3]

22. (A)   [D-3]

23. (D)   [D-3-e]

24. (C)   [D-3-g]

25. (A)   [D-4 and Chapter 6 A-3-a (2)]

Solutions to Check Point—Section D _____

	Answer	*Refer to:*
D–1.	(C)	[D-2]
D–2.	(B)	[D-3]
D–3.	(B)	[D-5]

Solutions to For Your Review _____

Chapter 8

System Software for Computer Operations and Management

OVERVIEW

Today software comprises a large percentage of the computer-based information system costs. While hardware costs have dramatically decreased, organizations find that software development is a slow and complex process requiring ongoing updates and maintenance; therefore, it is expensive. However, computer-based information systems require software in order to function.

There are two broad types of software: system software and application software. **System software** provides the instructions that control computer operations, network management, database management, and system security. **Application software** provides the instructions for processing general purpose end-user applications as well as applications specific to the organization's functional areas.

Of the two types of software, system and application, system software is of primary importance for the control and management of the computer-based information system. The stored program concept and today's system software make computing environments very effective and user friendly. System software consists of a set of generalized programs that include the operating system, network management, database management, system utilities, and performance and security monitors. As administrative professionals complete tasks using a computer-based information system, these system software management programs are invoked.

System software provides the interface between computer networks and hardware and the application programs of end users. Also, administrative professionals regularly use system software utilities. Understanding how system software controls the computer-based information system makes it easier for administrative professionals to adapt to new functions and capabilities of the system.

System software that supports program development and software engineering are not used by administrative professionals and, therefore, are not covered in this review.

After reviewing the features of system software, the features of end-user application software as well as application software specific to business functions are covered in Chapter 9.

KEY TERMS

A. Operating System

The most important system software is the operating system. The **operating system** manages the operations of the central processing unit (CPU); controls the input, output, and storage resources; and controls computer system tasks. Although it sounds very technical, several operating system basics help put a perspective on the importance of this necessary component of the computer-based information system which administrative professionals regularly use.

1. *Starting the System:* Simply turning on the on/off switch starts the computer system; many individuals say, "**Boot** the system." Turning on the computer system begins the boot process. The system module to boot the computer is stored in ROM (read only memory). This system module performs a system check to ensure that RAM (random access memory), input/output devices, and the system electrical components are operational. All other operating system modules are stored in secondary storage. During the boot process, the operating system programs required for standard processing are loaded into RAM. At this point, the operating system takes control of the computer-based information system.

2. *User Interface:* Interaction with any computer system is controlled by the operating system through a *user interface*. The three main user interfaces are command-driven, menu-driven, and graphical user interface (GUI).

   a. *Command-driven interface:* A **command-driven interface** requires the user to enter brief user commands. The enter key submits the command to the operating system for decoding and execution. MS-DOS is a command-driven operating system. Technical users sometimes prefer a command-driven interface for greater functional control. For most end users, the command-driven interface has been replaced with the graphical user interface (GUI).

   b. *Menu-driven interface:* A **menu-driven interface** presents the user with a menu of options. The user selects the correct option by pointing and clicking with an input device (i.e., mouse or trackball) or touching a touch-sensitive screen. For many of the GUI icons, once the icon has been clicked, the operating system provides menu options. Many automatic-teller machines (ATM) and information kiosks have menu-driven interfaces.

      EXAMPLE: *Olsen arrived early for his 1 p.m. appointment and decided to have lunch. Unfamiliar with the office complex, he went to the information kiosk and touched the menu choice "Restaurants." A schematic of the office complex floors appeared indicating which floor Olsen was on, along with symbols for each of the restaurants on various floors. Olsen touched the symbol for one of the restaurants and a more detailed description of the restaurant type, hours, and special features appeared. Based on the information from the menu-driven kiosk, Olsen was able to have a quick lunch before his appointment.*

c. *Graphical user interface (GUI):* Most microcomputer operating systems provide the easy-to-use **graphical user interface (GUI)** that uses icons, bars, buttons, boxes, and images. The user selects the desired function with a point and click of an input device such as a mouse on the appropriate graphic. A GUI hides system software complexities from the end user.

A social interface is the next evolution of GUIs. A *social interface* uses cartoon characters, animation, and voice to guide the user through required computer functions.

3. ***Interrelated Operations:*** When administrative professionals work with application software, the commands to open and process the application are interpreted through the operating system. In addition to providing the user interface, an operating system performs resource management, process management, and task management. Figure 8–1 illustrates how system software serves as the control mechanism for users, application software, and hardware.

a. *Resource management:* The operating system manages computer, network, and storage resources and input/output peripherals.

EXAMPLE: *The saving of a word processing document to a disk/disc, displaying the text on a monitor, or printing a hard copy is under the control of the operating system.*

(1) *Computer resources:* The operating system allocates primary memory (RAM) for data, application programs, and system programs during processing; this is the *stored program concept.*

FIGURE 8–1 Interrelationship Among System Software, End Users, Application Software, and Hardware

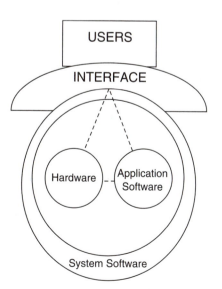

(2) *Virtual memory:* The operating system schedules work in various areas of primary memory so different parts of different jobs can be processed concurrently (multitasking/multiprogramming). **Virtual memory** simulates more internal memory space by dividing an application program into fixed pages. The system places in primary memory only those modules (pages) currently in use and brings other "pages" from secondary storage when needed. Extending primary memory to secondary storage allows users to work with application programs that are more complex (larger) than what primary memory can handle at one time.

b. *Process management:* The operating system controls the processing of all jobs. The simplest processing is loading only one application into main memory and processing (executing) the application. The program uses computer resources until processing is done. *Multitasking* (Windows 2000 and Windows XP) or *multiprogramming* (mid-range and mainframe computers) are two process management models where the execution of two or more programs are processed concurrently; the operating system switches back and forth among the programs until all processing is done.

Multithreading is a form of multitasking. **Multithreading** concurrently executes more than one task of a single application.

c. *Task management:* The operating system keeps track of each computer job, who is using the system, what programs have been executed, and unauthorized attempts at system access. Application software works through system software in order to process any functions of the application.

4. ***Types of Operating Systems:*** There are many different operating systems for the microcomputer, servers, mid-range and mainframe computers, and supercomputers. Mobile devices require operating systems specific to the functions of the device. Administrative professionals with a basic understanding of various operating systems can converse more easily with information technicians as well as technically adept end users.

a. *Microcomputer operating systems:* Windows is the leading series of microcomputer operating systems. Windows 2000 and Windows XP are operating systems with a GUI interface. Windows 2000 is a renamed version of Windows NT 5.0, a powerful multitasking/multiprogramming, multiprocessing operating system used for high-end microcomputers and servers.

Windows 1.0 through Windows 3.1 provided the GUI interface for MS-DOS (a text-based Microsoft disk operating system); Windows 1.0 through Windows 3.1 are not operating systems.

A new Windows operating system featuring natural interfaces (speech recognition and handwriting) is currently referred to as *Blackcomb*.

The operating system for Macintosh computers is Mac OS. Other microcomputer operating systems include Windows 98, Windows ME, Windows NT, UNIX, Linux, and OS/2.

b. *Server operating systems:* Departmental server operating systems are UNIX, Linux, Windows 2000, Windows XP, and Novel NetWare. These operating systems provide the reliability, backup, network management, directory services, and security required for department operations.

Figure 8–2 highlights features of the more common operating systems for microcomputers and servers.

FIGURE 8–2 Common Operating Systems for Microcomputers and Servers

Operating System	Features
Windows XP	32-bit consumer and business version 64-bit business/professional version For powerful microcomputers and network servers Supports Internet, multimedia, security, and client computing (client/server operations)
Windows 2000	Renamed version of Windows NT 5.0 32-bit OS For microcomputers and network servers Supports networking and Internet services
Windows ME	32-bit OS Major updates to Windows 95 For home microcomputers Supports plug-and-play, digital media, home networking, and online activities
UNIX	32-bit OS For powerful microcomputers, servers, mid-range, and mainframe computers Supports powerful applications and is popular for Web and network servers Its portability across computing platforms and support for many different devices is a major advantage
Linux	32-bit OS Open source software available on the Internet; free alternative to UNIX Supported by programmers online; support and documentation can be concerns
Mac OS x	32-bit OS For Macintosh and Apple computers Supports multimedia and has a new suite of Internet tools (iTools)

c. *Mid-range and mainframe operating systems:* Operating systems for enterprise-wide computing generally run mainframe and mid-range computer systems. These operating systems must manage complex operations, access to large databases, online support, and security for multiple concurrent users (thousands). IBM OS/390, VM, VSE, and OS400 are operating systems designed for enterprise computing.

d. *Supercomputer operating systems:* Either the Cray Unicos or IBM's AIX are operating systems designed to manage the multiprocessing (multiple CPU) environment of the supercomputer.

e. *Mobile device operating systems:* Operating systems for handheld computers and mobile telephones include the following.

• Windows CE is a 32-bit operating system with scaled-down versions of Microsoft Word, Excel, PowerPoint, and Internet Explorer.

- Pocket PC is a version of Windows CE for personal digital assistants (PDAs) and handheld computers.

- Palm OS was developed by Palm for the PalmPilot handheld, pen-input PDA.

- Windows Embedded NT 4.0 offers more system capabilities and flexibility than Windows CE.

- Embedded Linux is a compact version of Linux used by both IBM and Motorola for mobile devices.

5. *Navigation in a GUI Environment:* An operating system with a graphical user interface (GUI) is a common microcomputer system software for business. After the system has finished booting the GUI operating system, the monitor displays the operating system desktop. The administrative professional can customize the desktop by placing shortcut links, identified with an icon, for frequently used programs.

A GUI uses keyboard, point-and-clicks, and point-and-draw operations for input. Programs and files are opened from the desktop into a window. The following general overview about navigation can be applied to any program (system and application) working in a GUI environment.

a. *Desktop:* The operating system **desktop** displays a taskbar and program or file icons. Default icons typical on the desktop include computer directory, documents, network places, recycle bin, and network browser. The user easily opens files and applications by pointing and clicking the appropriate icon or button on the desktop.

(1) *Taskbar:* The **taskbar** contains a start button and icons for all programs that are running. The default location of the taskbar can be moved to the sides or top of the desktop, hidden, or customized.

(a) *Start button:* By clicking on the *start button,* a menu for programs, documents, settings, search, help, and shut down appears. Pointing to the menu buttons, submenus appear. If additional information is required to execute the command, an ellipsis follows the menu command or menu subcommand (e.g., Shut Down . . .). When the desired option(s) is located within the subcommand, the administrative professional clicks to activate the selection .

(b) *Program buttons:* For each program the administrative professional opens, a program button appears on the taskbar. The administrative professional clicks on the program buttons to switch between running programs. More than one program window can be on the desktop at one time. When two or more programs are concurrently processing in a single-user microcomputer environment, this is referred to as *multitasking*.

(2) *Computer directory:* The *computer directory* icon provides access to all files on the microcomputer hard disk, disk drive, CD-ROM drive, and mapped network drives. Using the directories, the administrative professional can search for and open files and folders and perform utility functions from the menu bar or toolbar. A microcomputer control panel icon directs the administrative professional to utility functions.

(3) *Documents:* Documents is a default storage location for files, graphics, and other documents, including saved Web pages. A folder icon named Documents can be located through the computer directory or placed on the desktop as a shortcut to saved documents.

(4) *Network places:* The network places icon provides a link to shared resources on the network to which the microcomputer is connected. Shortcuts to computers, Web servers, and FTP (file transfer protocol) servers are automatically connected through network places. If the administrative professional is a member of a workgroup, a link to computers in the same workgroup can be created.

(5) *Recycle bin:* The **recycle bin** stores deleted items until the bin is emptied. If the recycle bin has not been emptied, any deleted item can be retrieved/restored.

b. *Shortcut:* The administrative professional can place an icon on the desktop for any frequently used programs, documents (files or folders), hardware (printer or copier), or Web page. A **shortcut** is a link (displayed on the desktop as an icon) to any item accessible on the microcomputer or on the organization's network. In addition to placing a shortcut on the desktop, these links can be added to the operating system start button menu or in specific folders.

c. *Input operations:* To communicate to the microcomputer what needs to be accomplished, the user points at the icon or button with an input device (mouse, trackball, touchpad, or other input device). The input operation is click, double click, or drag.

(1) *Click or double click:* To process a function (i.e., open a file or a program), the user needs to point at the icon or button and either click or double click; many operations require double click. For right-hand users, the click or double click is with the left side of the mouse or touchpad button. Left-handed users need to use the system utility to change the mouse functionality.

(2) *Click and drag:* To move an item on the screen or copy files between secondary storage windows, the administrative professional would use click and drag. The left button of the mouse or touchpad is clicked and held. Moving (dragging) is accomplished by moving the input device (mouse or finger across the touchpad).

EXAMPLE: *Samuelson wants the desktop taskbar to be at the right side of her screen. She points to the taskbar at the bottom of the screen, clicks and holds the left button on her input device, then drags the taskbar to the right side of the screen.*

(3) *Right click:* Tapping the right button on the mouse or touchpad displays a context-sensitive menu. A **context-sensitive menu** is an on-screen menu that provides a shortcut to functions related to the window or object the pointer is on at the time of the right click.

d. *Window:* When a program is opened (system or application), it opens into a window. A **window** is an overlay on the desktop. An open window for a system or an application program includes a title bar, menu bar, and toolbar.

(1) *Title bar:* The **title bar** displays horizontally across the top of the program's open window. The name of the window appears on the left side of the title bar with minimize, maximize/restore down, and close buttons on the right side. The window name changes to coincide with the window that is currently active.

(a) *Minimize button:* Clicking the *minimize button* moves the program window from the desktop. The program button still displays on the operating system taskbar. The program can be moved back to the desktop by pointing and clicking on the taskbar program button.

(b) *Maximize/restore down button:* Clicking the *maximize button* displays a full screen of the open window. To reduce the size of the program window, restore down needs to be clicked. The *restore down* option makes it easy for the administrative professional to view several program windows (system or application) on the desktop at the same time.

EXAMPLE: *Ling is working on three applications: two word processing documents and a spreadsheet. In order to see all three applications, he has each window open in a restored down state. By pointing to the program window title bar, Ling can click and drag the windows to different locations on the desktop. A click on the program window title bar brings the window to the forefront so he can work on the application while reading soft-copy information in the other applications.*

(c) *Close button:* Clicking the *close button* closes the application/program.

(2) *Menu bar:* Just below the title bar is a menu bar. Typically a GUI **menu bar** includes file, edit, view, insert, format, tools, and help functions. Clicking or pointing on a menu option results in a pull-down menu for various functions specific to the application or operating system utilities.

Many of these function commands are hard coded into the keyboard. Depressing keyboard function keys or depressing the correct combination of keys on the keyboard activates the functions that are hard coded into the keyboard.

(3) *Toolbar:* Just below the menu bar is a toolbar. The **toolbar** displays icons (tools) for frequently used menu options or commands for the program/application in the open window. To execute a command, the administrative professional simply clicks on the appropriate icon. The icon graphic represents the action of the command. Administrative professionals can customize the toolbar to include only those functions that are frequently used.

(4) *Dialog box:* A **dialog box** displays whenever the software (system and application) provides information to the end user or the software needs the end user to enter information or make a selection. The dialog box is where the end user and the computer system submit communication back and forth.

e. *Troubleshooting—Help:* A soft-copy help manual *(help menu)* provides system and application assistance. Help is typically accessed from the system or application menu bar, but it can also be accessed through the Web. The help manual provides an index of topics as well as a search option for seeking answers to questions about working with the operating system or application software. A **help manual** is documentation from the vendor to support the administrative professional in using the software and troubleshooting issues. A separate help manual is available with each application (i.e., operating system, word processing, spreadsheet, database management, presentation graphics). The administrative professional should use the help menu as the first recourse when troubleshooting.

Operating systems on microcomputers provide an easy-to-use computer system environment for administrative professionals by minimizing the amount of intervention required by the user during processing. The operating system provides a common set of instructions for all applications to use. The primary purpose of the operating system is to maximize the productivity of a computer system by efficiently managing the computer-based information system.

Check Point—Section A

Directions: For each question, circle the correct answer.

A–1. The system module to boot the computer is permanently stored in

    A) RAM (random access memory)
    B) ROM (read only memory)
    C) secondary storage
    D) virtual memory

A–2. The user interface for a computer-based information system is controlled by the

    A) application software specific to the function

    B) operating system
    C) process management operation
    D) systems utility

A–3. Valmont is starting a small business. A good operating system for the company's three microcomputers and one department server is the

    A) Novel Netware operating system
    B) OS400 operating system
    C) Windows ME operating system
    D) Windows XP operating system

B. Utilities and Language Translators

System software includes utility programs for routine, repetitive tasks. The administrative professional will use many of the system utilities available on the microcomputer.

    Language translators are special system programs that translate a program's language (i.e., C++ or HTML) into machine language (1s and 0s) so the computer system can process the program statements.

1. *Utility Programs:* **Utility programs** are common to all computer system software. There are many utilities. Some of the more common utilities include creating directories, creating new folders, restoring deleted files, editing, security, disk defragmentation, and formatting disks. Because most administrative professionals work in a graphical user interface (GUI) environment, the description of the following utilities applies to the GUI environment.

    a. *Desktop:* The desktop is what displays on the monitor after the system has finished booting. The desktop taskbar and two desktop icons, computer directory and recycle bin, include utility functions that the administrative professional uses. The open window menu bar and toolbar of system software and application software includes many utilities used on a daily basis.

        (1) *Taskbar start button:* By clicking on the taskbar start button, the menu displays an option for settings. The settings submenu allows the administrative professional to click on the control panel icon. The **control panel** allows the microcomputer user to change the appearance and functionality of the operating system by selecting the appropriate icon. In a networked environment, the administrative professional may be "locked out" from changing the functionality of the microcomputer operating system. In such a situation, the administrative professional would need to seek assistance from an information technology specialist. The following utilities are typically available through the microcomputer control panel:

            • Accessibility options
            • Adding and removing hardware or programs

- Administrative tools: configures the computer settings
- Configure Internet options
- Customize desktop
- Customize keyboard settings
- Customize mouse settings
- Diagnostics: microcomputer troubleshooting
- Folder options: customize file and folder display, change file associations
- Network and dial-up connections
- Password settings and management
- Security management
- Setting date and time
- System information and changing environment settings

(2) *Computer directory:* Another way to open the control panel is to point and click the computer directory icon on the desktop. The control panel is a sub-icon.

(3) *Recycle bin:* The *recycle bin* stores deleted files, folders, graphics, and Web pages until the bin is emptied. If the recycle bin has not been emptied, any deleted items can be retrieved/restored.

b. *Menu bar and toolbar:* The *menu bar* and submenus in system software and application software provide the administrative professional with utility functions for managing files and folders and customizing the desktop and windows. The *toolbar* displays icons for frequently used menu options for the operating system program in the open window (e.g., file and folder search, copy, move, delete, and undo). The following are common utilities used on a regular basis:

(1) *Folder and file utilities:* Folders as well as folder contents (files) can be added, deleted, and renamed. The properties (i.e., location, size, when created, and attributes) of the folder or contents can be displayed.

(2) *Edit utility:* The *edit utility* allows the administrative professional to cut, copy, paste, and move folders, files, Web pages, or any application where the user has editing rights.

   EXAMPLE: *Walworth wants to have a duplicate of a file copied from the hard disk to a backup disk. To do this, Walworth first opens both the hard disk drive window and the backup disk drive window. To copy the file, he clicks on the file icon in the hard disk directory, holds, and drags the file icon from the hard drive window to the backup drive window. The operating system processes the copy utility.*

(3) *Utility tools:* With utility tools, the administrative professional can customize the folder, file, window, and desktop settings.

c. *Disk defragmentation:* When files are updated, the computer saves updates on the largest continuous space on the disk, which is often on a different sector than the other parts of the file. Over time, files become fragmented. When files are fragmented, the computer must search the disk each time the file is opened to find all of the file parts; this slows down response time. Disk **defragmentation** is the process of rewriting parts of a file to contiguous sectors on a disk to increase the speed of access and retrieval.

(1) *Virtual File Allocation Table:* Each disk in a Windows operating system environment has a *Virtual File Allocation Table (VFAT)*. The VFAT records information about clusters of data (in the table). The information stored in the VFAT contains the location of the stored data cluster and how the data can be used. Clusters of data are chained together to store information that is larger than the capacity of a single storage cluster area. Data use includes: open files cannot be reopened and protected files may be read only or only available to authorized users.

EXAMPLE: *The operating system searches the VFAT file to find the beginning location of a data cluster. The operating system checks an entry within the data cluster to determine if the cluster is chained and, if so, the location of the next data cluster. This process continues until the last data cluster for a large file is read and there is no additional chaining entry.*

(2) *Disk/disc directory:* When files (data) are saved to a computer-based information system, each file is assigned a unique file name. The file names appear in a disk/disc directory for easy access (double click on the file name for most operating systems with a GUI). There are many places to access disk directories in the microcomputer environment. The more common locations include computer directory, list of recently used documents (start button/ documents), and desktop shortcut icons (documents folder).

d. *Disk formatting:* Formatting disks removes all the information from the disk and formats the disk tracks and sectors for the specific operating system. A disk cannot be formatted if files from the disk are open, the contents of the disk are displayed, or the disk contains the operating system or boot partition. A quick format removes files from the disk without scanning the disk for bad sectors. Use the quick format option only if the disk has been previously formatted and you are sure the disk is not damaged.

2. ***Language Translators:*** All programs (system and application) consist of a set of instructions written in a programming language (C++, Visual Basic, HTML, COBOL). Using a language translator, the programming language modules are translated into a machine language (binary bits/1s and 0s) that the computer understands. The two ways to translate the programming language are with a compiler or an interpreter.

a. *Compiler:* A *compiler* is a language translator that changes the programming language modules (source code) into machine code (object code). A compiled program links all object code modules to be reused. The source code does not have to be recompiled unless there is a change. C++, Visual Basic, and COBOL are programming languages used in the business environment that need to be compiled before executing the application.

b. *Interpreter:* An *interpreter* is a special compiler that translates and executes each program statement one at a time. Every time the statement is processed, it needs to be interpreted; a machine language program is not saved for reprocessing. Java is a Web programming language that is interpreted. Java applets are interpreted "on-the-fly" as the applet is executed by a client computer.

System utility programs are very important for efficient and secure computing environments. A graphical user interface makes it easy to use system utility programs. Therefore, the administrative professional who is aware of these utility programs has the appropriate tools at his or her fingertips for effective data and system management.

Check Point—Section B

Directions: For each question, circle the correct answer.

B–1. When using a graphical user interface, the start button is located on the

A) application menu bar
B) control panel
C) desktop taskbar
D) system title bar

B–2. The process of rewriting parts of a file to contiguous sections on a hard disk to increase the speed of access and retrieval is

A) disk defragmentation
B) editing

C) multitasking
D) virtual memory enhancement

B–3. Java is a Web programming language that requires the Java applet to be translated "on-the-fly" for fast Web processing. The Java applets are translated by a special purpose program called a/an

A) command-driven interface
B) compiler
C) interpreter
D) system utility

C. System Support Programs

The networked enterprise requires additional system support programs. These special support programs include performance monitors, network management, database management, security monitors, and middleware on the organization's servers.

1. *Performance Monitors:* To keep a computer running efficiently, **performance monitors** watch and adjust the usage and performance of the system. The networked enterprise relies on information technicians to check output from performance monitors so system maintenance is quickly addressed. End users can check the microcomputer system diagnostics (performance) by using the control panel system utilities.

2. *Network Management:* With the heavy reliance on intranets, extranets, LANs, the Internet, and other WANs, a variety of system software for network management is required.

   a. *Network software:* Each network has a network operating system, performance monitors, and telecommunications monitors. Network servers and other computers on the network use the software programs to manage network activities.

   b. *Software functions:* Basic network management software functions include checking input/output activities, assigning priorities to data communication requests, and detecting and correcting transmission errors.

   c. *Network programs:* Common network programs include Windows 2000 (renamed version of Windows NT 5.0), Windows XP, Novell NetWare, and IBM Customer Identification and Control System (CICS). Novell NetWare is widely used for complex interconnected local area networks whereas IBM-CICS is widely used for mainframe-based WANs.

3. *Database Management:* For enterprise-wide data management, a mainframe or mid-range computer system with a **database management system (DBMS)** is required. A DBMS is a very important system software package that controls the development, use, and maintenance of the databases for the organization. Data are a highly valued corporate resource for organizations today.

a. *DBMS software:* Each organizational database system consists of a set of programs for creation of the data structures, transaction processing, and performance and maintenance monitors. An organization typically has several databases created to meet the networked enterprise's information requirements.

b. *Software functions:* The DBMS data structure integrates collections of files and records so different users throughout the organization can easily access the same database. The DBMS simplifies processing transactions (data retrieval) through query displays and reports.

   Application programs (i.e., payroll, inventory) that obtain data from the enterprise database and end users who obtain their data with the DBMS **manipulation language** eliminate the need for another program to obtain required information output. A manipulation language contains commands that permit business professionals to interactively extract data for specific information needs. The most prominent manipulation language is *structured query language (SQL).* Most users refer to the manipulation language as the *query language.*

   EXAMPLE: *The administrative professional in the logistics division can query the manufacturing database for inventory, production, product description, and unit price displays in real time on her desktop PC.*

   Accountants can also query the same database for specific accounting queries. Data integrity is enhanced when corporate databases are shared for important organization information.

c. *Types of databases:* Database management systems can reduce program-data dependence and data redundancy as well as improve data integrity. There are several ways the database can be modeled—hierarchical, network, and relational. Databases can be centralized or distributed using different models. The object-oriented DBMS allows organizations to store images and voice in the database. Online analytical processing (OLAP), data warehouses, and hypermedia databases are new trends in database design.

   (1) *Hierarchical DBMS:* The first database design was the *hierarchical model* where data are organized in a treelike structure (similar to an organization chart). The top of the structure is called the *root* and all related data elements are pieces of records called *segments.* The hierarchical structure depicts one-to-many relationships. The hierarchical model is highly structured and all data access must be specified in advance; there are no ad hoc data queries. Changes in the DBMS require major changes to the application program. Hierarchical DBMSs are still in existence today where high-volume transaction processing is required. These DBMSs are referred to as *legacy systems.*

   (2) *Network DBMS:* As business processing became more prevalent, the *network model* supported the need for a many-to-many data relationship. Although an improvement in data access, the network DBMS, like the hierarchical model, does not support ad hoc queries and is highly structured requiring major

programming changes if there are changes in the DBMS. Both the network and the hierarchical models are not used for new DBMS designs.

(3) *Relational DBMS:* The most popular database model today for both enterprise databases and microcomputers is the *relational model*. Data are organized in simple two-dimensional tables (called *relations*) in a relational DBMS. The relational model is very flexible. Using the manipulation language, data tables are joined for ad hoc queries in real time. New data and records can be added to the database without any programming changes required in existing application programs. For a more detailed discussion on the relational DBMS see Chapter 9, Section B-6.

(4) Centralized and distributed databases: A *centralized database* is common for a client/server network. A *distributed database* stores the organization's data in more than one physical location. Distributed databases can be partitioned or duplicated.

   (a) *Partitioned distributed DBMS:* A *partitioned database* stores only the necessary data at another location. Changes in the database are usually made in batch with the main database during slow times (at night).

   (b) *Duplicated distributed DBMS:* A *duplicated database* replicates the entire central database at all remote locations. This approach is used when the locations need all the data for operations (e.g., airline reservations). Changes made at one location are automatically replicated at all other locations.

   Although distributed databases may reduce the vulnerability of a single, central database, distributed databases are highly dependent on quality telecommunication channels that can be vulnerable.

(5) *Object-oriented databases:* Today there is a need to store images, photographs, voice, and videos for business applications. The conventional models (hierarchical, network, and relational) are not suited for storing data for multimedia applications. The *object-oriented DBMS* stores data and procedures as objects that are retrieved and shared. The objects can contain multimedia data. Object-oriented databases are not efficient when processing many transactions, however.

(6) *Online analytical processing (OLAP):* Business professionals often need to analyze large volumes of data from multiple views (multidimensional). A *multidimensional database* or a relational database multidimensional tool enables the end user to view the same data from different perspectives. Multidimensional data analysis is also called *online analytical processing (OLAP).*

(7) *Data warehouses:* A **data warehouse** integrates current and historical transaction data from the organization's multiple LANs and storage area network (SAN). Using report and query tools, business managers extract data from the data warehouse. The integrated data from the functional areas assist business professionals with analysis and in making better decisions for the organization. Operational TPS data are copied to the data warehouse as often as required—monthly, weekly, daily, or even hourly.

   (a) *Data mart:* A **data mart** is a small data warehouse containing only a portion of the organization's data for a specialized function or work group.

(b) *Datamining:* **Datamining** is the analysis of data stored in a data warehouse to identify patterns and relationships for predicting future trends and consumer behaviors and for making better decisions.

(8) *Hypermedia databases:* Web sites store information as linked pages containing text, sound, video, and graphics in a hypermedia database. A *hypermedia database* organizes data into a network of nodes connected by links that are specified by the user. Searching for information does not require a predetermined scheme. Users search through related information based on hyperlinks.

d.   *DBMS programs:* Common mid-range and mainframe computer programs used for organizational databases include IBM's DB2 and Oracle Corporation's Oracle 9i.

4.   *Security Monitors:* System control is managed with specialized security monitor programs. The computer-based information system and system resources need to be protected from unauthorized use, fraud, and destruction. **Security monitors** control the use of hardware, software, and data resources. The security monitor maintains statistics on system use and unauthorized access. These statistics provide an information technician/manager or microcomputer end user with important security information.

5.   *Middleware for Application Servers:* Applications designed to interact between organizations are complex because of hardware and software differences; this is also true if two different computing platforms exist within an organization. Application servers provide a middleware interface between an operating system and user applications from a different computing platform (i.e., Windows, Unix, OS400). **Middleware** translates the different operating system protocols and manages the exchange of information between the two environments.

With a basic understanding of computer-based information system software, the administrative professional should be able to communicate more easily with information technicians and technically adept end users. Knowledge of system software functions and utilities enables the administrative professional to be more effective and efficient with computing environments. The user-friendly GUI interface between computer networks, hardware, application programs, and end users supports a better understanding and usage of the computer-based information system.

Check Point—Section C

Directions: For each question, circle the correct answer.

C–1.   Checking input/output activities, assigning priorities to data communication requests, and detecting and correcting transmission errors are a function of the

A)   language translator
B)   middleware for application servers
C)   network operating system
D)   system utility program

C–2.   Working from her office, Whitehead queries for organization information on budget line items. Queries are a function of

A)   database management systems
B)   network management systems
C)   performance monitors
D)   operating systems

C–3.   Applications designed to integrate operations between systems with different computing platforms (different hardware and software) can communicate through

A)   an interpreter
B)   context-sensitive menus
C)   middleware
D)   network operating systems

For Your Review

Directions: For each question, circle the correct answer.

1. Which software provides the instructions that control computer operations, network management, database management, and system security?
   A) Application
   B) Management information system
   C) Operating system
   D) System

2. Which software manages the central processing unit (CPU)?
   A) Operating system
   B) System utilities
   C) Transaction processing system
   D) Windows CE

3. "Boot the system" means
   A) checking the hard disk for bad sectors
   B) running a virus check on the computer system
   C) starting the computer system
   D) troubleshooting the operating system

4. An interface that uses cartoon characters, animation, and voice to guide the user through required computer functions is the
   A) application interface
   B) command-driven interface
   C) graphical user interface (GUI)
   D) social interface

5. What resource management operation simulates more RAM by placing only the application program modules (pages) that are currently required in RAM and leaving the remaining modules in secondary storage until needed?
   A) Multiprocessing
   B) Stored program concept
   C) Virtual memory
   D) WYSIWYG

6. An operating system for a department server is
   A) Blackcomb
   B) IBM eServer
   C) IBM OS/390
   D) Windows XP

7. What does it mean when a graphical user interface (GUI) menu displays a function followed by an ellipsis (e.g., Customize . . .)?
   A) A patch is required before the function is operational
   B) Additional information is required to execute the function
   C) The function is infected with a virus
   D) The function was not installed

8. If the administrative professional is a member of a workgroup, where can a link to computers in the same workgroup be created?
   A) Computer directory
   B) Context-sensitive menu
   C) Network places
   D) Toolbar

9. Soft-copy documentation from the vendor to support the administrative

professional in using the software and troubleshooting issues is the

A) context-sensitive menu
B) dialog box
C) help manual
D) open window

10. Creating new folders, renaming files, and disk defragmentation are

A) data management operations
B) desktop icons
C) operating system utility functions
D) toolbar operations

11. Configuring Internet options, customizing keyboard and mouse settings, and microcomputer troubleshooting are all done through the

A) context-sensitive menu
B) control panel system utilities
C) file allocation table (FAT)
D) open window toolbar

12. It is easy for an administrative professional to restore a deleted file if the

A) defragmentation function is activated
B) deleted file has been placed in the recycle bin
C) deleted file was write protected
D) find/replace function is used

13. The location of a data cluster from a file and the linking of the file's data clusters is maintained in the

A) computer directory
B) fault-tolerant system
C) relational table
D) virtual file allocation table (VFAT)

14. A language translator that saves the programming language modules (code) into a machine code program to be reused without retranslation is a

A) bridge
B) command-driven interface
C) compiler
D) system utility

15. The applets of Java, a Web programming language, are translated every

time a client computer executes the applet. This language translator is the

A) gateway
B) interpreter
C) middleware
D) system utility

16. What resource do information technicians use to check the networked enterprise so maintenance is quickly addressed?

A) Manipulation language functions
B) Middleware translations
C) Performance monitor reports
D) Telecommunication monitors

17. A common network operating system for a small local area network (LAN) is

A) IBM-CICS
B) Linux
C) Novell NetWare
D) Windows XP

18. What does the administrative professional need in order to interactively extract specific data from the enterprise database?

A) Hierarchical DBMS
B) Middleware
C) Online analytical processing (OLAP)
D) Structured query language (SQL)

19. An example of a legacy system is a

A) distributed database
B) hierarchical DBMS
C) object-oriented DBMS
D) relational DBMS

20. Which database model is highly structured, requires all data access to be specified in advance, and requires major changes to the application program when changes are made in the DBMS?

A) Hypermedia DBMS
B) Network DBMS
C) Object-oriented DBMS
D) Relational DBMS

21. A database model used for both enterprise data management and on microcomputers is the
    A) hypermedia DBMS
    B) network DBMS
    C) object-oriented DBMS
    D) relational DBMS

22. Where are historical data from the enterprise's multiple LANs integrated and stored so business professionals can manipulate the data for analysis and decision making?
    A) Compiler
    B) Data warehouse
    C) Object-oriented database
    D) Storage area network (SAN)

23. Web sites store information as linked pages containing text, sound, video, and graphics in a/an
    A) data mart
    B) hypermedia database
    C) object-oriented database
    D) relational database

24. What database organizes data into a network of nodes connected by links specified by the client in a client/server environment?
    A) Data warehouse
    B) Hypermedia database
    C) Object-oriented database
    D) Relational database

25. How is the issue of different computing platforms (i.e., desktop PC client and mainframe database) addressed within an organization?
    A) Application servers provide a middleware interface
    B) Data marts are established
    C) Online analytical processing (OLAP) is provided
    D) Performance monitors are used

Solutions

Solutions to Check Point—Section A

Answer	Refer to:
A–1. (B)	[A-1]
A–2. (B)	[A-2]
A–3. (D)	[A-4-a and A-4-b]

Solutions to Check Point—Section B

Answer	Refer to:
B–1. (C)	[B-1-a (1)]
B–2. (A)	[B-1-c]
B–3. (C)	[B-2-b]

Solutions to Check Point—Section C

Answer	Refer to:
C–1. (C)	[C-2-b]
C–2. (A)	[C-3-b]
C–3. (C)	[C-5]

Solutions to For Your Review

	Answer	Refer to:
1.	(D)	[Overview]
2.	(A)	[A]
3.	(C)	[A-1]
4.	(D)	[A-2-c]
5.	(C)	[A-3-a (2)]
6.	(D)	[A-4-b]
7.	(B)	[A-5-a (1) (a)]
8.	(C)	[A-5-a (4)]
9.	(C)	[A-5-e]
10.	(C)	[B-1]
11.	(B)	[B-1-a (1)]
12.	(B)	[A-5-a (5) and B-1-a (3)]
13.	(D)	[B-1-c (1)]
14.	(C)	[B-2-a]
15.	(B)	[B-2-b]
16.	(C)	[C-1]
17.	(D)	[C-2-c]
18.	(D)	[C-3-b]
19.	(B)	[C-3-c (1)]
20.	(B)	[C-3-c (1) and C-3-c (2)]
21.	(D)	[C-3-c (3)]
22.	(B)	[C-3-c (7)]
23.	(B)	[C-3-c (8)]
24.	(B)	[C-3-c (8)]
25.	(A)	[C-5]

Chapter 9

Software for Business Applications

OVERVIEW

Application software provides the instructions for processing applications specific to the organization's functional areas as well as general purpose applications for end users. Although administrative professionals primarily work with general purpose applications for improved productivity in the office, application software specific to the functional areas supports most of the business processes throughout the organization. Whether or not the administrative professional is involved with application specific software, output from these systems permeates the organization.

A review of application specific software provides an overview of traditional business functions. The Internet has changed how businesses view computer-based information systems. Organizations now strive to be networked enterprises as well as internetworking the organization with other business partners. Examples illustrate how these enterprise systems affect the administrative professional's business day.

Administrative professionals use general purpose application software on a daily basis. The general purpose applications software review concentrates on the more common applications in business—word processing, spreadsheets, database management, electronic presentation, and graphs.

Organization costs for application specific and general purpose software are high; administrative professionals need to make effective use of all types of application programs. Also, how the organization configures, implements, and manages computer-based information systems affects the computing environment of the administrative professional. Understanding how computer-based information systems are configured and managed within the organization assists the administrative professional in becoming a valued member of an information technology team for the organization.

KEY TERMS

A. Types of Application Software

Three types of application software exist in most organizations. **Application specific software** is used for daily operations within the organization. In today's networked world, cross-functional working relationships require cross-functional information. *Enterprise systems* address the cross-functional needs of organizations. The microcomputer and *general purpose application software* completely changed the computing environment for businesses and end users. Now end users have hands-on computing power that improves office productivity.

1. *Application Specific Software:* Within a particular business or industry, application specific software is developed for business operations. These applications vary from department to department according to each department's function. Although most application specific programs were custom designed by in-house application programmers, today's programs can also be purchased from vendors or custom developed by software vendors. *Cross-industry application software* (e.g., payroll, accounts receivable, or inventory) is software designed for generic use by many businesses. *Industry-specific application software* (e.g., credit loan programs, legal programs, or insurance programs) is designed for specialized industries.

   EXAMPLE: *In most large corporations where the information technology department is involved with the development of new applications for Web servers, there could be a waiting period of two or three years for new application specific programs. To meet computing needs, many organizations have turned to software vendors for application specific software needs. Also, general purpose application software for the microcomputer addresses many of the information processing requirements within the organization's functional areas.*

   The following application specific software is common in all organizations.

   a. *Accounting applications:* Basic accounting data are important to a business for internal decisions and reports to stakeholders and government agencies. Four basic accounting applications are used in most companies: accounts receivable, accounts payable, payroll, and general accounting.

(1) *Accounts receivable:* Accounts receivable monitors sales accounts for which the customer has a period of time to pay the balance. The functions usually included in the accounts receivable system are the following:

- Recording the sales on account
- Checking the customer's credit
- Invoicing
- Recording cash sales
- Updating accounts as payments are made
- Billing
- Analyzing account balances

EXAMPLE: *The administrative professional in the marketing division receives a monthly sales report. The sales report includes total sales as well as sales for each of the organization's three regions.*

(2) *Accounts payable:* Accounts payable is a system for paying obligations of the company. In addition to the general accounts payable application, networked enterprises may use electronic data interchange (EDI) or private industrial networks to electronically transmit payments.

(3) *Payroll:* Computations in handling the payroll are intricate. With source data automation, the payroll application generates checks that are accurate and timely with minimal human intervention. The application keeps all records for required reports, especially reports required by the government.

EXAMPLE: *Bi-monthly paychecks are received from the payroll system. Often the paycheck envelope includes notices about deduction changes, benefits summary, or changes to the system.*

(4) *General accounting:* Companies must keep track of assets, liabilities, capital, income, and expenses. To do this, every company must establish an accounting system that will produce data for information reports—a balance sheet showing assets, liabilities, and capital and an income statement showing income (revenue) and expenses. Computer systems can perform accounting functions more accurately, faster, and with less expense than manual processes.

EXAMPLES:

Data from the general accounting transaction processing system are used to produce the annual stockholder's report.

The administrative professional in the information technology division manages the division's budget. Through the intranet, she has online, real-time access to the budget lines for the division.

b. *Marketing applications:* The development of products, pricing, and promotion are primary marketing functions. Information systems collect daily marketing data and store the transactions in the marketing transaction processing system. Business personnel, management information systems, and decision support systems use data from the marketing transaction processing system.

EXAMPLE: *The marketing system provides timely, consistent, and accurate information for analysis and decisions about the product line, pricing strategies, and promotional campaigns.*

c. *Financial applications:* Firms must identify sources of funds and acquire enough funds to support marketing, manufacturing, and daily operations. These funds must then be controlled and secured. Information provided by the financial system describes money flow so business personnel can handle financial decision-making responsibilities.

EXAMPLE: *The portfolio analysis function provides an overview of the organization's investments. Authorized users can track investments online in order to determine when changes should be made.*

d. *Operations applications: Computer-aided design (CAD)* and *computer-aided manufacturing (CAM)* are software programs that have automated the product design and manufacturing functions of many manufacturing firms. *Material requirements planning (MRP)* software helps firms anticipate future raw material needs. Production, inventory, quality, and distribution tracking are all manufacturing and logistic operations that can be automated through various information systems.

(1) *Production:* Today most production lines are enhanced with automated features (including robots) to ensure quality products in a minimal amount of time. The machine control function of production systems provides accurate input for precision in the manufacturing process.

EXAMPLE: *The administrative professional in the operations division receives daily reports on operations productivity. These reports help in making decisions about changes in the production process or required meetings.*

(2) *Inventory:* Computerized inventories are perpetual; that is, every addition or deletion from inventory stock is recorded, and the quantity on hand is updated on a regular basis. Online inventory applications that process in real time update each transaction when the transaction is entered. Daily updating is also common.

EXAMPLE: *A computer-based system with computerized inventories becomes an analytical tool. Utilizing essential information from the inventory system, an analysis of the demand for products makes it easy to forecast future inventory needs.*

(3) *Distribution tracking:* Transportation agents using mobile devices can capture pickup, routing, and delivery data. As data are transmitted to the organization's computer-based information system, distribution tracking provides valuable information for both customer service and quality management of distribution procedures.

EXAMPLE: *When the administrative professional receives a call from a customer seeking information about expected delivery, she can query the distribution tracking system for pickup and delivery data and immediately inform the customer with up-to-date, accurate information.*

(4) *Quality control:* Quality control is important to all information systems for operations applications. Quality control is embedded into all operations applications.

e. *Human resource applications:* Today government reports are required on the recruiting, staffing, and training and development of an organization's human resources. These processes can be effectively managed with a human resource information system. Human resource applications help with long-range hiring requirements, managing equitable compensation packages, and career counseling for employees.

EXAMPLE: *Mathews has been with Abbots for three years and feels she is ready for a promotion. She accesses the organization's Career Board on the intranet to see what positions are currently open and what the requirements are for the position.*

Often application specific software is designed for different computing platforms (mainframe, mid-range, or department servers). These independent applications create inefficiencies within the organization when data cannot be easily shared among the systems. Cross-functional work teams and business strategies require computer-based information systems to consider alternatives for enterprise computing.

2. ***Enterprise Integration:*** Today business personnel seek cross-functional information. Timely and accurate organizational data needs to be available throughout the enterprise. Instead of focusing on information process requirements, enterprise integration software focuses on supporting clusters of business processes involved in the daily operations. To achieve enterprise integration, organizations can purchase or lease *enterprise systems* or use *enterprise integration software.*

   a. *Enterprise systems:* Enterprise systems consist of a set of interdependent modules for applications in accounting, marketing and sales, finance, production and distribution, and human resources. Information from an enterprise system is effective by providing cross-functional data combined from different areas of the organization.

   EXAMPLE: *A sales representative in the field uses her notebook to immediately transmit completed orders. When the order enters the enterprise system, the production division is notified, the just-in-time inventory system is activated, and a shipment date is scheduled. The sales representative is able to immediately inform the customer of a shipping date. As the transaction is processed, accounting processes (accounts payable and receivable, product costing, and accounting reports) are automatically updated with accurate and timely data. The accounting process is current through the latest transaction completed.*

   (1) *Enterprise data:* Data from the functional areas are stored in centralized databases common to all organization users. A common user interface allows business applications and personnel to seamlessly share information no matter where the data are located or who needs to use the data.

   (2) *Vendor support:* The enterprise system is a large complex application. Vendors can configure the software to support unique business processes and provide installation, maintenance, and training services. Instead of installing all modules at one time, organizations often choose to phase in the cutover (conversion).

   Some organizations install only one or two enterprise system modules while utilizing the independent application specific programs for certain business applications. Some organizations implement the enterprise system and continue to support independent application specific programs for unique business processes that the enterprise system cannot handle.

   b. *Enterprise integration software:* Many organizations cannot discard all the application specific programs for business functions. The efficiencies of some application specific programs are essential, making it too risky to change. An organization with independent application specific programs that also needs cross-functional information for competitive business decisions can use special software for integration within the organization.

(1) *Middleware:* Middleware creates an interface (bridge) between systems running on different platforms. Middleware provides the connection so independent applications can share data and communicate with each other.

(2) *Enterprise application integration software:* As an alternative to middleware, organizations can now purchase enterprise application integration software to connect independent applications. Internetworking between businesses can also be accomplished with enterprise application integration software.

3. ***General Purpose Application Software:*** Because of the microcomputer and general purpose application software, office productivity has improved. **General purpose application software** performs common business tasks for the user—word processing, spreadsheet, database management, electronic presentation, and graphs. These programs, used directly by the non-technical end user to develop computer applications, are categorized as fourth-generation languages (4GL). The programs are common in the office as well as the home and are purchased individually, as an integrated package, or as a suite. Because of productivity gains in the office, these programs are often referred to as *productivity packages.*

a. *Word processing:* Word processing is a very popular application program used by all levels of personnel throughout the organization. *Word processing* packages have transformed the creation, editing, revision, formatting, and printing of documents by electronically processing text. The data can be enhanced by different formats, graphs (charts), images (clip art and pictures), and symbols (shapes, arrows, and drawings). The administrative professional can also use the standard formats for business letters, memoranda, and other business forms stored in word processing templates.

b. *Spreadsheet:* A *spreadsheet* is an electronic worksheet. Any business application requiring numeric calculation, sorting, or data analysis is suitable for a spreadsheet. Once the data are entered in its appropriate row and column (cells), calculations can be automatic based on the formulas entered. The spreadsheet program is popular with administrative professionals responsible for business processes that require numeric calculations, data analysis, and what-if modeling.

c. *Database management:* Many departments have the responsibility of recording and filing information. Business data can be electronically stored with *database management software.* The data are stored on a secondary storage device and accessed as needed. A popular business situation utilizing data management software is the mailing list. The data can be queried for information and also used for mailings. The administrative professional should make sure department databases do not duplicate organizational database efforts or affect data integrity. A detailed discussion on enterprise-wide data management is in Chapter 8, Section C–3.

d. *Graphics:* Images are sometimes easier to understand than the written word. Horizontal bar charts, vertical bar charts, pie charts, and line charts (also called graphs) are all possible ways to display information when graphics software is utilized. A printer or plotter capable of printing graphs must be used for hard-copy output.

Also, *presentation graphics* programs are used to prepare multimedia presentations that include graphs, pictures, animation, sound, and video enhancements.

The multi-color, multimedia presentation developed with a graphics program provides effective supporting information for a speaker. Electronic presentations are also used in information kiosks, broadcasting the presentation on the Web, and supporting electronic group collaboration activities.

4. *Software Procurement:* To meet the information needs of the organization in a cost-effective manner, the issue of custom-designed software versus off-the-shelf software needs to be addressed. Through the Internet, application service providers (ASPs) are another alternative for acquiring software.

   a. *Custom-designed software:* **Custom-designed software** is developed by an in-house programmer or contracted from a software vendor. Because of software costs, many organizations contract with software vendors. Software from vendors can be purchased or leased. Vendors provide installation, maintenance, and training services. An in-house information technician knowledgeable about application software ensures that someone from the organization can communicate with the software vendor.

   b. *Off-the-shelf software:* **Off-the-shelf software** provides the microcomputer user with easy-to-use general purpose application software. This software is purchased from software vendors with supporting manuals and help services. For the organization, the information technology division usually manages the procurement and license of off-the-shelf software. During installation, an information technician makes sure that the microcomputer and appropriate software are configured for the organization's network.

   c. *Application service provider (ASP):* An **application service provider (ASP)** leases software to organizations through the Internet or a private network. Hardware can also be leased through an ASP. The ASP manages all applications and computing services including updates and maintenance. Another alternative is to lease the software per transaction; the organization pays for each transaction processed through the ASP. Organizations attempt to lower technology costs through ASP services.

In the networked organization the administrative professional interfaces with application specific software and general-purpose software on a regular basis. Organizational costs supporting the computer-based information system should be balanced by the benefits the administrative professional obtains through improved productivity and a user-friendly computing environment. These benefits are best achieved when the administrative professional is knowledgeable about the functionality of both application specific and general purpose application software.

Check Point—Section A

Directions: For each question, circle the correct answer.

A–1. Which one of the following is an example of cross-industry application software?

   A) Accounts receivable
   B) Credit loans
   C) Middleware
   D) Word processing

A–2. Cross-functional integration is best achieved through

   A) database management systems
   B) enterprise systems
   C) general purpose application software
   D) human resource programs

A–3. Programs that can be used directly by non-technical end users to develop business applications are

A) application specific software
B) fourth-generation languages (4GL)
C) industry-specific application software
D) integration software

B. Using General Purpose Application Software

Non-technical business professionals have hands-on use of computing power through advancements in user-friendly software, fourth-generation languages (4GLs), and graphical user interfaces (GUIs). The computer makes the dissemination and analysis of information easier, enhancing decision making with more accurate, timely, and relevant documents. The most common general purpose programs include word processing, spreadsheets, database management, electronic presentations, and graphs. As microcomputer systems are used more and more for end-user applications, attention to the integrity of the organization's data is very important. Coverage of the more common general purpose application software for end users follows.

Note: No particular brand of software is used as a frame of reference for the following descriptions; rather, concentration is on the feature and its function or use.

1. *Software Suites and Integrated Packages:* Both software suites and integrated software packages provide word processing, spreadsheets, database management, and graphic programs. The programs have common functions, and data are easily transferred between the programs.

    a. *Functionality differences:* The difference between a software suite and an integrated package is functionality. A *software suite* has the same functionality as complete versions of the individual software programs. Although an *integrated package* can handle all applications well, it does not have the same power or sophistication as the individual program or software suite. Integrated packages are common for home computing.

    EXAMPLE: *Microsoft Office is an example of a software suite while Microsoft Works is an example of an integrated package. Both provide word processing, spreadsheet, database management, electronic presentations, and graphs. A document prepared in an integrated package typically can be opened in the companion software suite; however, the reverse usually is not true.*

    b. *Common functions:* Functions common throughout a software suite or integrated program include settings of default values, commands (bold, underline, italic), revisions (delete/cut, copy, move, paste, insert), and other utility functions typically on the menu bar and toolbar for GUI users.

2. *Data Integrity:* As the administrative professional uses general purpose software, data accuracy and *data integrity* become an important consideration; this is particularly true with data used in spreadsheet and database management applications. Redundant data storage occurs when different divisions throughout the organization collect the same data for different general purpose applications. If the data are available from the organization's database, the administrative professional should attempt to access and use the organization's data for general purpose applications. This ensures that organizational data updates and corrections are reflected in the general purpose application. The administrative professional must be cognizant of how independent applications can affect data accuracy and integrity.

3. ***Active Window:*** When an application program is opened with a graphical user interface (GUI), it opens into a window. The *active window* is in the foreground and the title bar is highlighted. Several applications can be open at the same time. The administrative professional works with the active window. Movement from one window to another is accomplished by clicking on the window title bar. A menu bar and toolbar are included on each window screen.

   EXAMPLE: *Varzavand is working with both a word processing and a database application. The database application has the data structure restored down so the field names can easily be referenced while she is keying text in the word processing document. The word processing application is in the foreground and the title bar is highlighted; this is the active window.*

   a. *Menu bar:* The GUI *menu bar* is below the title bar and typically includes file, edit, view, insert, format, tools, and help functions along with submenus for each function. If additional information is required to execute a menu subcommand (e.g., Font . . .), an ellipsis follows the command. When the desired option is located within the subcommand, the administrative professional points and clicks to activate the selection.

   b. *Toolbar:* The GUI *toolbar* is just below the menu bar and contains icons, buttons, and boxes for common application tasks. The toolbar functions can be accessed more quickly than by using the menu bar. The administrative professional can add any common functions to the toolbar. The following are typical tasks on a toolbar when the application software is installed:

   - Open an active window for a new document
   - Open a document from secondary storage
   - Save
   - Print
   - Spelling and/or grammar check
   - Edit functions: delete/cut, copy, paste
   - Format functions: bold, italic, underscore
   - Alignment functions: align left, center, align right, justify (not applicable to database applications)
   - Undo and redo functions

   c. *Dialog box:* A *dialog box* displays whenever the application software provides information to the end user or the software needs the end user to enter information or make a selection. The dialog box is where the end user and the computer system conduct an interactive communication.

   d. *Help menu:* Most software suites and integrated packages provide a soft copy *help menu* for asking questions about application functions. The help menu assists with learning about program functionality or troubleshooting an application. Often assistance is provided through a "wizard" (animated image) that guides the administrative professional through the application by answering and asking questions in a dialog box.

4. ***Word Processing:*** Word processing software allows the administrative professional to electronically create, edit, revise, format, save, and print documents. The software program must be compatible with the operating system. Following is a generic

description of features available on most word processing applications software. Different word processing programs (e.g., Microsoft Word and Corel WordPerfect) may require a different set of commands but all offer these generic features.

a. *Default values:* Preset *default values* are used to create a standard format that the administrative professional may choose to use or change. In other words, margins, tabs, spacing, and placement of text are already in effect once the system is ready for use unless the administrative professional decides to change the settings. The following are examples of defaults that may be preset in a word processing program:

- Page size, 8 1/2 by 11 inches, standard
- Top and bottom margins on a page, 1 inch
- Left and right margins, 1.25 inch
- Left justification
- Single spacing
- Page orientation, portrait
- Standard tabs set every half inch
- Type font, Times New Roman

Headers, footers, and page numbers are not a part of the preset default format and need to be set, depending on the document requirements.

b. *Commands:* Typically the software program displays the text on the monitor exactly the way it will print—WYSIWYG (**W**hat **Y**ou **S**ee **I**s **W**hat **Y**ou **G**et). The administrative professional may choose to see commands along with the text on the monitor. To view the keyed text along with codes (commands) for printing the text, the administrative professional needs to switch to the code input mode. *Commands* are codes that instruct the computer to perform certain functions. Commands to the printer for special effects (such as bold, underscoring, or italic) can appear on the monitor or be embedded within the text. Most versions of word processing programs use fewer screen codes and more icons on the top or bottom of the monitor for the administrative professional to point and click for activation.

EXAMPLE: *To activate the bold command when a word processing program in a GUI environment is used:*

> *Click the bold icon:* **on**
> *Type in: Microcomputer Usage*
> *Click the bold icon:* **off**

The toolbar icon clicked on either side of the word string establishes a command interpreted by the operating system for the CPU. The CPU processes the command, sending the information to the printer to print these words in bold. On the screen, the administrative professional sees only the text, **Microcomputer Usage,** *usually in bold within the surrounding text; this lets the user know these words will print in bold.*

If a word has been typed without the bold commands, the bold command can be inserted at a later time by selecting the word* with an input device (such as a mouse), and then point and click on the bold icon. The command is inserted before and after the word(s) selected.

*Note: To select the word(s) with an input device, the administrative professional highlights the word by clicking and dragging the input pointer over the word.

Sometimes a command feature can be a hindrance when viewing soft copy. The *print preview* command allows the administrative professional to view hard-copy output on the monitor before printing.

c. *Word processing features for creating a document:* If a new document is to be created, the administrative professional needs to open the word processing program and make sure that the screen is in document mode. **Document mode** means the program has a screen ready to accept keyed text. With a graphical user interface, the document mode is an active window. Following are the basics for creating a new word processing document.

(1) *Opening a document:* Some word processing programs require that a new document be named before it is opened. In this case, a file name must be assigned to the document, and then the application is in document mode for keying text. Other programs open in document mode so the administrative professional can make format decisions about the document and then begin keying text. A file name must be provided in order to save the document to a disk/disc.

(2) *Keying text:* The word wrap feature is in effect as text is keyed. If a word extends beyond the right margin, it will automatically be placed on the next line; this is **word wrap.** Decisions about hyphenation should be made after the document has been keyed but before it is printed in its final format.

(3) *Paragraph indentations:* Default tab stops usually are every 1/2 inch. The administrative professional can change indentations by using the increase indent or decrease indent on the toolbar or by clicking and dragging the tab marker on the horizontal ruler. For a hanging indent, click and drag the tab marker to the position where the indent should start. The format menu should also provide the administrative professional menu options for the hanging-indent format.

(4) *Alignment:* On the word processing toolbar, text can be aligned left, right, centered, or justified. If text has already been keyed, the alignment can be changed by blocking (highlighting) the text and then selecting the desired alignment icon on the toolbar.

(5) *Automatic features:* Word processing programs have automatic features to complete the keying of words, to make corrections, and to automatically insert formats.

(a) *Automatic completion of words:* For selected words, the automatic function can finish the word that is being keyed. While keying certain words, a dialog box appears with the complete spelling of the word. The administrative professional can continue keying the word or use the enter key to have the remainder of the word automatically inserted.

EXAMPLE: *Once several letters have been keyed for most months in the year, the program displays the complete spelling of the month in the dialog box. Depressing the enter key, the remainder of the word is inserted.*

(b) *Automatic correction of words:* The automatic correction function detects and corrects misspelled words and incorrect capitalization.

EXAMPLES:

*When the administrative professional keys **adn**, the word changes to **and** after the space bar is depressed.*

The automatic correction function capitalizes the first word of a sentence, days of the week, months of the year, first letter of text in a table cell, and so forth.

In addition to the words on the built-in corrections list, the administrative professional can add words to the list through the tools menu.

The automatic correction function also inserts symbols for certain text (e.g., key (c) and © appears). If the symbol is not wanted, the administrative professional can backspace after the symbol appears but before depressing the space bar; the symbol reverts back to the keyed text.

Automatic correction can be turned on or off and changed through the tools menu.

(c) *Automatic format of text:* The automatic format function quickly formats headings, numbered lists, fractions, e-mail addresses; replaces two hyphens (--) with a dash (—); and so forth. The administrative professional can control these changes while keying, or turn off the automatic format function through the tools menu.

(6) *Bullets and numbered lists:* Bullets and numbered lists are part of the automatic format function. After the first entry, succeeding entries appear with a bullet or number until the enter key is depressed twice. Depressing the enter key twice returns to the previous keying mode. Text that has already been keyed can be changed to a bullet or number format by blocking (highlighting) the text and selecting the desired option from the toolbar.

(7) *Inserting images:* In addition to keyed text, the administrative professional can insert clip art, graphs (charts), pictures (from a scanner, digital camera, or off the Web), and symbols (e.g., shapes and arrows) into the document. Insert is a menu bar option.

Clip art, graphs, and pictures can be formatted so the image is to the left or right of the text, in with the text, behind the text, or in front of the text. Right click on the image and follow the context-sensitive menu to format the image layout for the text wrapping style desired.

(8) *Revising text:* After the text has been proofread, changes may need to be made. Common changes include inserting new text, deleting and undeleting text, and replacing text by keying over it.

(a) *Blocking sections of text:* A block of text is a word, a group of words, one or more lines of text, paragraphs, and so forth. Blocked text may be moved, copied, deleted, or appended to another document.

(b) *Edit utilities:* The edit utility allows the administrative professional to delete/cut, copy, and paste text, graphs, or images within the document or among any other documents within the productivity application suite or integrated package. Edit utilities are on the toolbar or can be accessed through the edit menu.

(c) *Undo text:* Sometimes text is erroneously deleted, changed, or formatted and the administrative professional needs to undo the action. The computer system usually stores the last several changes. By pointing and clicking the undo icon on the toolbar, the administrative professional can reverse the action(s).

(d) *Searching for text:* The search feature helps locate a specific character string each time it occurs within text. Most search features can search forward or backward through a document to find the character string. When the string has been located the administrative professional can make a decision about the text. The search feature is usually in the edit menu.

(e) *Replacing text:* Incorrect text can be replaced easily by keying correct text over incorrect text. The system can make the substitution automatically if the search-and-replace feature is activated.

EXAMPLE: *Ongena wants to replace the word 'computer' with the words 'computer system' each time the word appears. He activates the command for the search feature and sees the prompt Search For. Ongena keys 'computer' and enters the appropriate command key. Ongena responds to the query Replace With by keying 'computer system.' The computer may also ask whether Ongena wants to confirm each replacement; in other words, check each replacement. Ongena's response is 'No.' The search/replace function searches and makes all substitutions without any additional input from Ongena.*

(9) *Saving the document:* Saving should take place frequently during the keying of a document. A very short document should be saved immediately after it has been keyed. A longer document should be saved often during the keying process, perhaps after several lines or paragraphs. The administrative professional has two choices in saving a document:

- Save the document, but keep the document open so more text can be keyed.
- Save and close the document, proceeding to a different word processing document, or save and close the document and also close the word processing software.

Word processing documents can be saved onto the hard disk, an external disk/disc, or both.

(10) *Spell check:* Spelling dictionaries and spell checks are an essential part of word processing software. Text can be run through a spell check by word, page, or document to see whether words in the document are accurate. Many spell checks are operational while the administrative professional is keying text. If a word is spelled incorrectly, the spell check alerts the administrative professional so the word can be immediately corrected or checked by running the spell check on the word. Sometimes words are corrected while the user is keying text (automatic correction function).

When the spell check is run to check pages or an entire document, words that do not match the words in the spelling dictionary are highlighted along with a list of possible alternative words. The administrative professional must make a decision as to whether the word is, in fact, correct or needs editing. Spelling words can be added to the electronic dictionary. Once corrections in the spelling of words have been made, the document should be saved again.

Note: Cautious proofreading is still necessary to ensure that all spelling errors have been detected and corrected; some words are spelled correctly but used incorrectly in context (e.g., *their* rather than *there*).

(11) *Grammar check:* A program that checks the grammar in a document will examine subject-verb usage, punctuation, spacing, and sentence structure to identify any grammatical errors in language usage. The text can be corrected as these grammatical errors are detected. If corrections have been made in the text, the document should be saved again.

Some word processing programs have the spell and grammar checks in one function.

(12) *Thesaurus:* Sometimes the same word is used over and over again, and a different word with similar meaning would provide more variety in the writing. As text is keyed, the thesaurus feature can be activated to display words that have the same or similar meaning as the one being keyed. Words need to be selected carefully so the original meaning is not changed. If the text for the document is changed in any way, it should be saved again.

(13) *Hyphenation:* Once a document is keyed and edited, decisions about hyphenation can be made. When the hyphenation feature is activated, the system will do three things.

- Check to see whether the word extends beyond the right margin (the hyphenation zone)
- Check the word with the hyphenation dictionary to see where it might be hyphenated
- Give a prompt (dialog box) to the administrative professional that a decision needs to be made (optional)

The administrative professional needs to decide whether the hyphenation feature follows the hyphenation guidelines adopted by the organization. If the hyphenation feature does not meet organization standards, the administrative professional needs to turn off the hyphenation feature.

d. *Merging documents:* Information that is *constant* can be stored and later merged with *variable* information to be inserted within the text of the document. *Constant data* are information that will not change but will be used on every document produced. *Variable data* changes from document to document; the information is used on only one document. With some word processing software, the constant information would be stored in a *primary file* (main document file), and the variable information would be stored in a *secondary file* (database—a data file or data source).

EXAMPLE: *Using a word processing program, the administrative professional creates a* primary file *(a letter) and a* secondary file *(names, addresses, and other variable information for insertion into the letter). The text-merge function combines the constant information (the letter) with the variable information (name, address, and so on) for each letter that is produced.*

The merge function benefits the administrative professional as well as the organization. While the program is running the merge function, the administrative professional is free to work on another task. For the organization, the initial cost of a large merge operation is with the first letter; each subsequent letter lowers the per-output costs.

e. *Multiple-page documents:* The format for multiple-page documents, such as reports, should include headers, footers, page numbers, table of contents, footnotes or endnotes, and bibliography or works cited. Page breaks and section breaks may also be required.

(1) *Headers:* A **header** is a group of words or a short phrase that appears within the top margin of each page as an identification of the document. The header is especially helpful if one or more pages of the document become separated from the rest. A header can appear on every page, on every odd-numbered page, or on every even-numbered page. A header can be deleted on selected pages if desired (e.g., often the first page of a report or chapter that includes a title does not include a header).

(2) *Footers:* A **footer** is a group of words that appears within the bottom margin of each page, again identifying the document. The footer functions in exactly the same way as the header. A footer can be deleted on selected pages if desired.

(3) *Page numbers:* The type of page numbers desired needs to be selected from the choices available in the word processing program. Typically, Arabic numbers (1, 2, 3) or roman numerals (i, ii, iii) are selected. These page numbers may be placed in as many as 10 standard locations. The page number can be eliminated on any page if desired. Lowercase roman numerals (i, ii, iii) are typically used on pages preceding the report itself (title page, transmittal memorandum or letter, table of contents, and list of figures or tables). Arabic page numbers are placed consecutively on all pages of the report, the bibliography or works cited, and appendices.

10 Standard Locations for Page Numbers
- Top-left corner, every page
- Top-center, every page
- Top-right corner, every page
- Top-left corner, even pages
- Top-right corner, odd pages
- Bottom-left corner, every page
- Bottom-center, every page
- Bottom-right corner, every page
- Bottom-left corner, even pages
- Bottom-right corner, odd pages

(4) *Page breaks:* In long documents the administrative professional may need to end a page prior to the bottom margin.

(a) *Hard page break:* Entering the page break command places the appropriate codes for ending the page before the bottom margin; this is referred to as a *hard page break*. A *soft page break* is the automatic page break inserted by the word processing program at the point where the bottom margin is set. When a hard page break is inserted, the remainder of the page appears blank or sometimes a hard page-break line is drawn horizontally across the soft-copy document.

(b) *Widow/orphan function:* With the **widow/orphan function** on, the word processing program makes automatic decisions about page breaks by eliminating a widow/orphan line on the bottom or top of a page. A widow/orphan line is one line of a paragraph on a page (bottom or top) by itself. The widow/orphan function inserts a page break so two or more lines of a paragraph are on a page.

(5) *Section breaks:* Documents can be divided into sections to vary the layout of the document. Sections can be within a page or between pages. Following are common section breaks utilized in word processing documents:

- *Continuous* inserts a section break and starts the new section on the same page.
- *Next page* inserts a section break and starts the new section on the next page.
- *Odd page* inserts a section break and starts the new section on the next odd-numbered page; the same section break can be applied to *even page*.

The layout of the section can be changed for margins, paper size and orientation, paper source, page borders, headers and footers, page numbering, footnotes and endnotes, and columns.

(6) *Table of contents:* A word processing program can create a table of contents for a document. Several levels of headings can appear within the table of contents. As the text for the document is keyed, the administrative professional marks each heading that will be included in the table of contents. When the text for the document is ready for printing, the administrative professional provides instructions for generating the table of contents, complete with leaders and page numbers.

(7) *Footnotes and endnotes:* Many documents include citations to references in the form of footnotes (at the bottom of each page), endnotes (at the end of a section of the document or chapter), or in-text citations (within the paragraphs). As the text for the document is keyed, footnotes, endnotes, or citations can be keyed. When the document is printed, the pages will include the footnotes, endnotes, or in-text citations, whichever style is selected for references in the document. In case of document revision, footnotes or endnotes are automatically renumbered and placed on the appropriate pages if the text containing the references is moved to another location.

(8) *Bibliography or works cited:* Word processing programs have the features necessary to develop bibliographies to accompany long documents. Most standard word processing programs include the capability of setting an acceptable format for a bibliography or works cited.

f. *Formatting a document:* If the default settings are appropriate for the document, no changes in format will be necessary. The default settings are accepted, and the document is printed.

(1) *Changes in document format:* If the format of the entire document needs to be changed (e.g., margins, printing in landscape or portrait), the administrative professional makes these changes through the menu bar.

Some formats for the entire document require the text to be blocked and the format change made for the blocked text (e.g., font changes).

(2) *Changes in format for part of a document:* Sometimes a paragraph or list in the document needs a different format (e.g., an indented, single-spaced paragraph or a single-spaced numbered list inserted into double-spaced text). For this type of format change, the text must be blocked (highlighted) and the format changed.

g. *Tables:* A *table* can be designed very easily with word processing. The word processing program enables the administrative professional to set tabulations, view the table with or without ruled lines, and easily move to the desired input cell within the table with the tab key. Decisions can be made on the width of each column so that the text will fit within the space desired. If the table includes mathematical computations, the program performs required calculations automatically according to the formula entered. Changes to the table (inserting and deleting rows or columns) are easily accomplished through the table pull-down menu.

h. *Text in columns:* Text can also be placed in *columns* on a page resembling columns in a newspaper. The size of each column can be specified, along with the number of columns. The only restrictions are the space available on a sheet of paper. Usually, text is placed in two or three columns. Illustrations, charts, and pictures can be inserted into the columns along with the text.

i. *Macros:* Tasks that are performed repeatedly can be automated through macros. A macro is a series of word processing commands and instructions that the administrative professional groups together as a single command to automatically accomplish a task. Macros need to be saved under a unique file name. Typical uses for macros include:

- Routine editing and formatting
- Combining multiple commands; for example, inserting a table with a specific number of rows and columns, size, and boarders
- Making a dialog box option more accessible
- Automating a complex series of tasks

For quick access to macros, the administrative professional can add the macro to the toolbar, menu bar, or as a shortcut option on the desktop.

j. *Document protect/unprotect:* Documents can be protected for inserting comments and tracked changes. To let only authorized reviewers insert comments, a password can be assigned to the document. A detailed discussion on tracked changes can be found in *Office Administration*, Chapter 7, Section C-5-c(2).

k. *Page orientation:* The page orientation (layout) can be either portrait or landscape. *Portrait* is the standard setup and prints horizontally across the 8 1/2 inches of a piece of paper. *Landscape* prints across the 11 inches of a standard size sheet of paper. A page, a section, or the entire document can be set up to print in portrait or landscape. Changing the page setup is an option on the file menu.

l. *Printing:* The print icon on the toolbar typically prints one copy of the entire document as formatted. From the file menu, the administrative professional can activate the appropriate print options (current page only, selected pages, or all pages) and identify how many copies. Page setup (margins, paper, and layout) and a print preview are other common menu options.

5. ***Spreadsheet:*** The spreadsheet is an electronic version of a worksheet written manually on paper. A spreadsheet application is applicable to business situations that involve

numbers and calculations or data analysis. Sorting either numeric or text data is also a spreadsheet function. Following is a generic description of typical spreadsheet software features.

a. *Spreadsheet features for creating a worksheet:* If a new document is to be created, the administrative professional needs to open the spreadsheet application and make sure the screen is in document mode. With a graphical user interface, the document mode is an active window. Following are the basics for creating a new spreadsheet document.

(1) *Opening a document:* The document mode is a single spreadsheet, usually called a **worksheet.** Sometimes several worksheets are available through the active window; in this case the document mode is called a **workbook** and the administrative professional would be using one of the *worksheets*. When there are multiple worksheets available in the active window, the administrative professional needs to click on the appropriate worksheet tab to have the correct worksheet in the active window. Throughout this review, the term *worksheet* is used in discussing spreadsheet features.

(2) *Worksheet organization:* The worksheet is organized into rows and columns that make up a grid. The intersection of a row and column is a cell.

(a) *Column:* **Columns** are typically identified by a letter (e.g., A, B, . . . IV) horizontally across the top of the worksheet. Data in columns are read vertically. There are 256 columns in a standard worksheet.

(b) *Row:* **Rows** are typically identified by a number (i.e., 1, 2, . . . 65,536) vertically down the side of the worksheet. Data in rows are read horizontally. There are over 65,000 rows in a standard worksheet.

(c) *Cell:* A **cell** is the intersection of a row and column where the administrative professional enters text, numbers, and formulas. The **active cell** is highlighted (i.e., outlined in dark) and is the cell where data can be entered. Each cell has a unique address that consists of the column letter and row number. This unique address is the **cell reference.**

EXAMPLE: *When a new worksheet is opened, the cell reference is A1 and the cell is highlighted. The administrative professional can enter data in active cell A1. The administrative professional can use the input device to point and click on another cell to make it the active cell or use the cursor-control keys (up/down, left/right arrows) or depress the enter key to move down a row.*

(3) *Entering data:* Data are entered into an active cell and consist of text, numbers, or formulas.

(a) *Text data:* When text data (also called a *label*) are entered, the data are aligned left. Text information is *alphanumeric data* (text, symbols, and numbers not used for calculation [i.e., social security number]) as well as titles in the worksheet (e.g., column headings, row headings, and worksheet headings).

(b) *Numeric data:* When numeric data are entered, the data are aligned right. Typically, the only character entered with numeric data is the decimal when needed. If symbols (e.g., dollar sign for currency or the percent symbol for percentages) are entered with the number, the number may be automatically formatted according to the symbol.

(c) *Formulas:* A formula is an equation that performs arithmetic or logic operations on worksheet data. Using worksheet data or a cell reference, formulas perform calculations and data analysis. Formulas need to be entered according to the spreadsheet program. Some spreadsheet programs use parentheses [()] to indicate a formula while others require that the formula begin with an equal sign (=). To gain knowledge about formula specifications, the administrative professional can receive training, use the spreadsheet manual, or use the soft-copy help utility.

(d) *Formula operators:* Operators for typical business calculations include adding (+), subtracting (-), multiplying (*), and dividing (/).

The numeric values to be calculated (a constant number or cell reference) are separated by the calculation operator. Calculations are performed from the left to right following the mathematical precedence used in algebra:

First:	negative values (-)
Second:	percentages (%)
Third:	exponentiations (^)
Forth:	multiplication (*) and division (/)
Fifth:	addition (+) and subtraction (−)

Parentheses change the order of a calculation.

EXAMPLES: *30+2/2 = 31*
The mathematical precedence divides before adding

30*2/2 = 30
Multiplication and division are in the same mathematical precedence; therefore, starting from the left, 30 is multiplied by 2 before the product (answer) is divided by 2

(30+2)/2 = 16
The parentheses changes the order of the calculation

Logic operators (also called comparison operators) can be performed on alphanumeric data (text, symbols, and numbers). Formulas can also compare worksheet values and join data. Logic operators include:

- Equal to (=)
- Greater than (>)
- Less than(<)
- Greater than or equal to (>=)
- Less than or equal to (<=)
- Not equal to (<>)

EXAMPLE: *The Product Revenue worksheet, Figure 9–1, consists of the product number* (text data) *and net cost* (numeric data). *Three additional columns include* formulas, *one for the selling price, one to copy the total sold from a different worksheet, and a calculation for revenue.* Text information *includes a worksheet heading (PRODUCT REVENUE) and column*

FIGURE 9–1 Product Revenue Worksheet Before Formats

	A	B	C	D	E	F	G	H	I
1					PRODUCT REVENUE				
2									
3	PRODUCT		NET		SELLING		TOTAL		
4	NUMBER		COST		PRICE		SOLD		REVENUE
5									
6	B9743		43219.6		45380.58		14		635328.12
7	K2864		6824.7		7507.17		32		240229.44
8	N3459		14924		15894.06		21		333775.26
9	R4682		3469.6		3816.56		45		171745.2

Formulas:

Selling price is based on percentage increases (data set up in rows 3–6 in column P of the worksheet). The more the administrative professional uses work areas for changing calculations instead of hard numbers in the formula, the more effective the spreadsheet application and the easier to make changes. In this example, all the administrative professional needs to do is change the net cost or the percentage of increase; the selling price will recalculate.

	N	O	P
1	Calculation for Selling Price		
2			%age Increase
3	B9743		0.05
4	K2864		0.1
5	N3459		0.065
6	R4682		0.1

Selling price is a multiplication of net cost times %age Increase which calculates the amount to be added to the net cost.
Selling price formula for cell E6: C6*P3+C6

Total Sold obtains data from the Total Sold worksheet in cell C8.
Total sold formula for cell G6: 'Total Sold'!C8

Revenue is a multiplication of selling price times total sold.
Revenue formula for cell I6: E6*G6

Once the formula is entered into the respective cell (E6, G6, and I6) the formulas can be copied to other cells; all formulas are a **relative reference** copy.

E6–copied to E7–E9
G6–copied to G7–G9
I6–copied to I7–I9

headings. Text data for headings are often called labels. *Figure 9–1 illustrates the worksheet data exactly as entered before any formats; Selling Price, Total Sold, and Revenue columns are the results of formula calculations.*

(e) *Functions: Functions* are predefined formulas that perform calculations by using specific values, called the argument, in a particular order or structure. The argument is placed in parentheses following the function name and typically is a range of cells. Functions can be used to perform simple or complex calculations. The more common business functions include:

- *Sum*—adds all the numbers for a range of cells (argument)
- *Avg*—calculates the arithmetic mean (average) for the argument
- *Median*—calculates the middle number (median) for the argument (i.e., half the numbers have values greater than the median and half the numbers have values less than the median)
- *Min*—calculates the smallest number (minimum) for the argument
- *Max*—calculates the largest number (maximum) for the argument
- *Pmt*—calculates the loan payments for the argument (interest rate, length of the loan, and principal amount of the loan)

(4) *Alignment:* The spreadsheet toolbar allows the administrative professional to point and click to align data left, right, centered, and justified.

(5) *Automatic features:* Spreadsheet programs have automatic features to complete the keying of words, to make corrections, and to automatically insert formats. Using the tools menu, an administrative professional can add words and symbols to the built-in automatic feature list.

- Words can be completed by using the enter key when the dialog box appears with the complete word.
- Misspelled words are corrected and symbols are inserted for certain text (e.g., key TM followed by the space bar and ™ appears).
- Preset worksheet formats can be selected through the format menu.

(6) *Lists:* Lists allow the administrative professional to manage and analyze data. The following are guidelines for entering data in a list.

- Use only one list per worksheet
- Design the list so all rows have similar items in the same column
- Leave at least one blank column and one blank row between the list and other data on the worksheet; however, avoid blank rows and columns within the list
- Place critical data above or below the list; critical data can be hidden and accidentally deleted when placed to the left or right of a list
- Do not have any hidden rows or columns when making changes to the list
- Use formatted column or row headings (labels); headings are used to create reports and find and organize data in the list

(a) *Finding data in lists:* The administrative professional can quickly find data in a list through the lookup function, vertical lookup, and horizontal lookup. The data in a list should first be sorted in either ascending or descending order. *Ascending order* is A–Z or 0 to highest number. *Descending order* is Z–A or highest number to lowest.

- *Lookup function* finds a value in a row or column.
- *Vertical lookup (vlookup)* requires row headings (labels). Using the leftmost column, the administrative professional can look up a value in another column based on the row heading.

- *Horizontal lookup (hlookup)* requires column headings (labels). Using the topmost row, the administrative professional can look up a value in another row based on the column heading.

(b) *Filters:* A **filter** is a quick and easy way to work with a subset of data in a list without having to sort (ascending or descending) the data list first. A filtered list displays only the worksheet rows that meet the criteria (filter) specified for a column. Rows that do not match the filter criteria are hidden. The administrative professional can edit, format, chart, and print data displayed in the filtered rows.

(7) *Inserting images:* Clip art, graphs, pictures (from a scanner, digital camera, or off the Web), and symbols (shapes, lines, and arrows) can be inserted into the worksheet. Images can be formatted to fit with the other data in the worksheet. The insert icon is on the worksheet menu bar.

(8) *Revising data:* Common changes include inserting new data, changing formulas, and replacing data by keying over it. The following functions are common for revising data.

- Using the *edit utilities*, data (a cell or a block [range of cells]) can be moved, copied, deleted, and pasted within the worksheet or among any other documents created in the productivity application suite or integrated package. A block can also be printed or appended to another worksheet.

- The computer system usually stores the last several deletions; using the *undo command*, the administrative professional can undelete.

- The *search* feature helps locate a specific character string. When the string has been located, the administrative professional can make a decision about the data. The *search and replace* function replaces incorrect data with new data.

To copy a formula, the administrative professional needs to determine if the formula to be copied is a relative copy (reference), an absolute copy, or a mixed copy.

(a) *Relative reference:* A **relative reference** changes the cell reference in the formula relative to where it is copied.

EXAMPLE:

The formula in cell N5 is SUM(B5:N5).

The formula is copied to cell N6—down one row but in the same column. The reference in the formula (B5:N5) will change relative to the new cell location (down one row).

After copying, the formula in cell N6 is SUM(B6:N6).

(b) *Absolute reference:* An **absolute reference** holds the cell (row and column) reference in the formula constant (absolute). An absolute reference does not change the row and column reference when it is copied to another cell. A spreadsheet code needs to be inserted into the formula to hold the row and column reference constant. The dollar symbol ($) is often used to code an absolute reference.

EXAMPLE:

Cell P5 contains a function that needs to be replicated in several other worksheet cells whenever the function is changed.

Cell A4 is the first time a formula is entered to replicate the function results in P5. The formula in cell A4 is =$P$5. The dollar symbol holds the column and row reference absolute when it is copied.

The formula in cell A4 is copied to D5 and H9.

After copying,
the formula in cell D5 is =$P$5
the formula in cell H9 is =$P$5

All three cells (A4, D5, and H9) will display the same function calculation as the one in cell P5. Whenever the function results in P5 changes, cells A4, D5, and H9 automatically changes.

(c) *Mixed reference:* A *mixed reference* is when a column reference is absolute and the row reference is relative or the column reference is relative and the row reference is absolute.

EXAMPLE:

The formula in cell R15 is SUM($A1:$M1) The column reference is absolute with the dollar symbol and the row reference is relative.

The formula is copied to T18; over two columns and down three rows. The data to be summed for T18 is in the same columns (A through M) and down three rows (4).

After copying, the formula in T18 is SUM($A4:$M4).

(9) *Saving a worksheet:* The administrative professional should save frequently during the keying of a worksheet.

(10) *Spell check:* Text can be run through a spell check by word or worksheet to correct any misspellings in the worksheet.

b. *Formatting data:* Formatting includes centering or right alignment of headings; bold, italic, underlining, and color; changing fonts; shading; and borders. Format changes can be made to a cell, row(s), column(s), or the entire worksheet. An administrative professional can also change row height and column width, split cells, merge cells, and center headings over several columns. Format changes are easily accomplished by pointing and clicking on the appropriate toolbar icon. Formatting options are also available through the menu bar pull-down menus.

Typically numeric data are formatted for a specific numeric value (number with decimals, currency, percentage, fraction, date, time, or a custom format). Other formats include headers, footers, and page numbers, and freezing rows and columns.

(1) *Numeric formats:* The default numeric format has no specific number format and displays one digit following the decimal when the far right digit is a zero (i.e., 12.10 appears in the cell as 12.1). Numeric data entered with the dollar symbol ($) inserts the dollar sign and commas but not the decimal place for zero cents unless the decimal point is keyed. Using the format menu, numeric data can be formatted (for a cell or a range (block) of cells) as follows:

- *Number*—specifies decimal places and negative value format
- *Currency*—inserts dollar sign, commas, and decimal places as specified
- *Accounting*—inserts dollar sign, commas, and decimal places as specified; the dollar sign and decimal are aligned in the column

- *Percentage*—inserts percent symbol and decimal places as specified
- *Fraction*—specifies type of format

EXAMPLE — Monetary Formats:

Numeric data are entered into a cell with a default, number, currency, or accounting format.

Numeric Data	Cell Format
3829.1	*Default format*
3829.10	*Number format*
$3,829.10	*Currency format*
$3,829.10	*Accounting format*
$ 829.10	*Accounting format*
$3,829	*Default format; entered with $ Format changes to currency*
$3,829.00	*Default format; entered with $ and . Format changes to currency*

Date and time formats are also typical options used in worksheets.

Figure 9–2 illustrates the Product Revenue worksheet after formats have been added to the column headings and numeric data in the Net Cost, Selling Price, and Revenue columns.

2. *Euro convert:* Numeric data can be converted to euros, from euros to a euro member currency, or from one euro member currency to another euro member currency. Currencies available for conversion are from the European

FIGURE 9–2   Product Revenue Worksheet After Formats

	A	B	C	D	E	F	G	H	I
1					PRODUCT REVENUE				
2									
3	PRODUCT		NET		SELLING		TOTAL		
4	NUMBER		COST		PRICE		SOLD		REVENUE
5									
6	B9743		43,219.60		$43,219.60		14		$605,074.40
7	K2864		6,824.70		$6,824.70		32		$218,390.40
8	N3459		14,924.00		$14,924.00		21		$313,404.00
9	R4682		3,469.60		$3,469.60		45		$156,132.00

Formats Include:
1. The five column headings were centered over the columns.
2. Net Cost data were formatted as numeric—commas and additional ciphers were added through formatting.
3. Selling Price and Revenue data were formatted as currency—commas, ciphers, and dollar signs were added through formatting.

Union (EU) members that have adopted the euro. The conversion function uses fixed conversion rates established by the EU.

(3) *Headers:* A header is a group of words or a short phrase that appears within the top margin of each page as an identification of the document.

(4) *Footers:* A footer is a group of words that appears within the bottom margin of each page, again identifying the document.

(5) *Page numbers:* Page numbers appear in the header or footer. A dynamic date and time can also be included in the header or footer. The administrative professional needs to point and click the appropriate icons for inserting and automatically incrementing page numbers, date, or time.

(6) *Page breaks:* For long worksheets, sometimes the page break for hard-copy output is not at a logical place. The administrative professional can change the page break by adjusting the break line. In the print preview mode, the administrative professional can click and drag the break line to the desired location.

(7) *Keeping row and column headings visible:* Typically, the row and column headings are helpful while using the worksheet soft copy. To keep the headings visible, the administrative professional needs to freeze the row and/or column headings. The freezing/unfreezing of the row or column headings is a window menu function.

    (a) *Column headings:* Column headings are the top horizontal row(s) (pane). Select the row below where the split is to appear and "freeze the column headings" above the row by selecting the menu option.

    (b) *Row headings:* Row headings are the left vertical column(s) (pane). Select the column to the right of where the split is to appear and "freeze the row headings" to the left of the column by selecting the menu option.

    (c) *Both column and row headings:* Both column and row headings can be held constant (frozen) by selecting the cell below and to the right of where the split is to appear. "Freeze" the headings (row and column) by selecting the menu option.

    EXAMPLE — Column Headings Held Constant:

    The worksheet loan input data (rows 1, 2, and 3) and the column headings (rows 4 and 5) need to be visible as the user scrolls the worksheet to analyze the Outstanding Balance over the months.

    To freeze these rows, the cell selected (active cell) was A6 (one row below and no columns to the left). The window function to freeze the rows above was selected from the menu bar. In Figure 9–3 the dark horizontal line under row 5 indicates that rows 1–5 with the column headings and input data will remain on the monitor when the administrative professional scrolls vertically down the worksheet.

c. *Macros:* Tasks that are performed repeatedly can be automated through spreadsheet macros. A macro is a series of worksheet commands and instructions that the administrative professional groups together as a single command to automatically accomplish a task. Macros need to be saved under a unique file name.

d. *Document protect/unprotect:* When multiple users share a worksheet, changes (revisions) can be tracked. A password must be assigned to the worksheet to set up the revision tracking function (also called change history). If multiple worksheets are

FIGURE 9–3 Worksheet with Column Headings Held Constant (Frozen)

	A	B	C	D	E	F
1	LOAN	280000.00		TOTAL INT. PAID:	$324,346.76	
2	INTEREST	6.00%				
3	TERM	360				
4					OUTSTANDING	
5	PAYMENT/Month	PAYMENT AMT	PRINCIPAL	INTEREST	BALANCE	
6	1	1678.74147	278.7414704	1400	279721.2585	
7	2	1678.74147	280.1351778	1398.606293	279441.12	
8	3	1678.74147	281.5358704	1397.2056	279159.58	
9	4	1678.74147	282.9435704	1395.7979	278876.64	
10	5	1678.74147	284.3582704	1394.3832	278592.28	
11	6	1678.74147	285.7800704	1392.9614	278306.5	
12	7	1678.74147	287.2089704	1391.5325	278019.29	
13	8	1678.74147	288.6450204	1390.09645	277730.64	
14	9	1678.74147	290.0882704	1388.6532	277440.55	
15	10	1678.74147	291.5387204	1387.20275	277149.01	
16	11	1678.74147	292.9964204	1385.74505	276856.01	
17	12	1678.74147	294.4614204	1384.28005	276561.55	Year One
18	13	1678.74147	295.9337204	1382.80775	276265.62	

available in the active window, the password is assigned to the workbook. Tracking revisions is protected with the password and only authorized users (those who know the password) can make changes. The default time frame for maintaining the revision tracking function (usually one month) can be changed. The protected worksheet can be unprotected by those who know the password. However, removing the password protection also removes the ability to make shared revisions to the worksheet.

e. *Page orientation:* The page orientation can be either portrait or landscape. Portrait is the standard setup for 8 1/2 by 11-inch paper. Landscape prints across the 11 inches of a standard size sheet of paper. Often the landscape page orientation is used for a worksheet in order to accommodate more columns on one hard-copy page.

f. *Printing:* Before a hard copy can be printed, the print area (cell range) needs to be identified. The administrative professional blocks (highlights) the range of cells that contains the worksheet data, and then sets the print area through the appropriate option on the file menu. The print icon on the toolbar typically prints one copy of the print area; the print area must be set before printing. From the file menu, the administrative professional can activate the appropriate print options (selected pages or all pages) and identify how many copies. Page setup (margins, paper, and layout) and a print preview are other common menu options. Worksheet headings that are "frozen" can be set up to repeat on hard-copy pages by inserting the appropriate commands in the page setup menu.

g. *Graphs:* Worksheet data are often used to create graphs—bar, line, pie, and so forth. The visual graph (also called a chart) often makes it easier to understand the worksheet data. See Section B-7-a for more details on creating graphs from worksheet data.

6. ***Database Management:*** The general purpose application software for database management provides the user with a process to create a collection of related records electronically stored for selection, sorting, and merging with other data. A *database* is a collection of related data arranged for easy retrieval and use in preparing documents (e.g., reports and forms) or obtaining answers to queries. A *query* is a question the administrative professional submits to a database system for an answer. General purpose database programs for the microcomputer are usually relational databases.

EXAMPLE: *Databases are created for membership records in professional associations. The International Association of Administrative Professionals (IAAP) has a database of all active members. Every time a mailing needs to be prepared for the members, the database provides the data for the member mailing labels. Choices can be made as to the label arrangement and exactly what information will be placed on the labels. In addition, labels can be sorted in ZIP Code order so the mail meets the U.S. Postal Service bulk-mail standards.*

a. *Features used in creating a database:* The administrative professional needs to open the database program and make sure the screen is in document mode. With a graphical user interface (GUI), the document mode is an active window. The administrative professional should be prompted to open an existing database file or create a new file. Following are the basics for opening a new database file.

(1) *Opening a new database file:* The document mode is a database file. Most database programs require that a new file be named before it is opened. The administrative professional should assign a file name that reflects the contents of the database; then the program opens into document mode.

(2) *Database organization:* A relational database is organized into a collection of related tables. The relational database tables look like a worksheet from a spreadsheet application. *Rows* in the table are called **records** and *columns* in the table are called **fields.** A table structure needs to be created to identify each field in the table.

(a) *Relation:* A **relation** is a two-dimensional table where data about a specific topic in the database (e.g., products, suppliers, or prices) are collected. The relation is more commonly referred to as a *table.* Using a separate table for each topic in the database means that the data are stored with minimal data redundancy.

EXAMPLE: *The International Association of Administrative Professionals (IAAP) membership database consists of many tables. The main table contains member information; this table is named membership. Another table contains officer information; this table is named officers. There are tables for each committee that contain committee membership information; each table is named according to the committee it represents.*

(b) *Record:* Each row in the table is a record. A *record* contains data pertaining to one unit (person, place, or thing).

EXAMPLE: *In the IAAP membership table there are records for each active member. Figure 9–4 illustrates 452 records. Each record in the membership table contains the identification number, name, home address, and home telephone number for one member. When a record is used, all data pertaining to that particular unit (member) are available.*

FIGURE 9–4   Schematic of a Membership Table in a
Database File

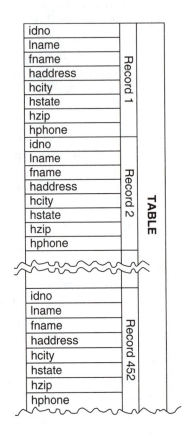

(c) *Field:* A *field* contains descriptive characteristics of a person, place, or thing. A data field is also referred to as a *data element*. Each data field name within the table must be unique (e.g., a different name for each field).

In a relational database, one data field needs to uniquely identify the record; all records in the table must contain unique data in that field. This unique field is a *key field* (usually referred to as the **primary key** or sometimes called the *control field*). The primary key cannot be a name, ZIP Code, or any other personal information as the data may not be unique.

EXAMPLE: *In the IAAP membership table there are eight fields for each record. Figure 9–4 illustrates that the field names are idno, lname, fname, haddress, hcity, hstate, hzip, and hphone. Each member has a unique identification number (idno) that is the primary key for a record in the membership table.*

(d) *Table structure:* The **table structure** describes each field within the table. The following information is required in the table structure design view: field name, type of data for the field (e.g., text, numeric, currency, date/time, and autonumber), and which field is the primary key. The field size is typically set at the maximum length but can be changed by the administrative professional.

An *autonumber* field automatically increments when a new record is entered. If a primary key has not been identified, the database system may establish an autonumber field to function as the primary key.

FIGURE 9–5 Membership Table Structure Design View

Field Name	Data Type	Description
idno	numeric	Primary key—Identification number that uniquely identifies each member
lname	text	Member's last name
fname	text	Member's first name
haddress	text	Home street address (including apartment number)
hcity	text	Home city
hstate	text	Home state or province; must be two state abbreviation in capital letters, no punctuation
hzip	numeric	Home ZIP or postal code; must be 9-digit ZIP Code with no hyphen
hphone	numeric	Home telephone number; must include area code. Only numbers, no hyphens

The table structure is the design of the table. Including a description of the data in the table structure design view provides additional information about the data for end users. Some database environments refer to the table structure design view as the data dictionary. A *data dictionary* is an automated (or manual) tool for storing and organizing information about the data maintained in a database. Data dictionaries for the enterprise database management system provide many advantages to the organization—standardization, user access rights, aliases, data structure consistency, and so forth.

EXAMPLE: *Figure 9–5 is the table structure design view for the IAAP membership table. The table structure provides valuable information on input data requirements.*

(e) *Save the table structure:* The table structure must be saved within the database before data can be entered. A unique table name is required when saving the table structure for the first time.

(3) *Entering data:* With the database open, data are entered into the table fields of a record; a record is added to the table when a new entry is made.

(a) *Open table:* A table from the database must be open in order to enter data. The table displays a *data view* similar to a worksheet in the spreadsheet software. The table field names appear across the top row of the data view. Each row in the table data view is a record.

(b) *Data entry:* Data are entered into the table structure data view. Data must match the field data type identified in the table structure design view. When all data for a record have been entered, the record is usually saved by the database management system.

EXAMPLE: *The table structure design view in Figure 9–5 prevents the administrative professional from entering text data into a numeric type data field. If text data were entered for the identification number, ZIP Code, or telephone number, the data would not be accepted. Also, the table structure can be set so a 9-digit ZIP Code and an area code for the telephone number are required.*

(4) *Revising data:* Common changes include inserting new records, deleting records, or updating a data field by keying over the old data on a record. These changes are made in the table structure data view. The user must have authority (edit privileges) to make changes to the database. The toolbar displays icons for common edit utilities.

- Delete/cut, copy, paste, move
- Undo
- Search and replace

(5) *Saving data:* When all data for a new record have been entered or a data field is changed, the update is usually saved immediately by the database management system. When a record has been deleted, the database management system typically requires a confirmation through a dialog box. If any table structure updates need to be saved, the system dialog box communicates with the administrative professional for required action.

(6) *Spell check:* Data can be run through a spell check by word or table structure data view to check text data in the database for correct spelling. The spell check will also stop at each e-mail field allowing the administrative professional to check the data for accuracy; this feature can be turned off.

b. *Formatting data:* Data formats are set in the table structure design view: currency, date, time, memo, and autonumber. These formats appear on data queries, reports, and forms. The formats can be changed when reports or forms are created. In addition, other formats can be added to reports for hard-copy output.

c. *Query:* A data *query* contains commands that permit administrative professionals to interactively extract data from the database for specific information needs. The administrative professional can bring together data from multiple tables and sort the data in a particular order (ascending or descending). Numeric calculations on groups of records can also be included in a data query. To create a query, the required tables, field names, and criteria must be specified in the query design view. If the data are to be sorted (ascending or descending), this command must be included in the query design. The query "Wizard" is often used when learning how to design queries.

EXAMPLE:

The most common query is to select *data from one or more tables by using the criteria specified in the query. Only the records that meet the criteria will display in the query results.*

With a query of the IAAP membership table for the fname, lname, and hphone for all members in hstate="WI" (criteria), the following results would display on the monitor:

MARLYS	*ADAMS*	*7152429830*
ROBERTA	*WHIMMER*	*7154428733*

Queries are often called "quick and dirty reports" because the query results are accessed on demand (when needed) and do not include formatting. A hard copy can be printed of the query results.

d. *Report:* A report is an effective way to present the output in a more formal business format. The administrative professional has control over the size and appearance of the report. The information in a report comes from the database table(s) as well as numeric calculations (expressions) on groups of records. To create a report, the required tables, field names, and criteria must be specified in the report design view. The report design view includes a report header, page header, detail, and page and report footer.

(1) *Report header:* The report header is where the administrative professional keys the title that is descriptive of the report.

(2) *Page header:* The page header is where column headings for the data fields from the table(s) or numeric calculations appear. The headings appear as field names. The administrative professional should format the headings as complete words and include capitalization where appropriate.

EXAMPLE:

In turning the IAAP memberships query for the fname, lname, and hphone for all members in hstate= "WI" into a formal report, a descriptive title could be:

IAAP Wisconsin Membership

the column headings would appear as:

fname   lname   hphone

The administrative professional should change the column headings to:

First Name   Last Name   Home Telephone

or

Name   Home Telephone

(A column heading can be centered over multiple columns)

(3) *Detail:* The field names or expressions (numeric calculation for totals and subtotals) appear on the report design *detail section*. These names *must not* be changed. The field names and expression references are used to extract the required data from the database tables. Each record extracted appears as detail on the report when displayed as soft copy on the monitor or when a hard copy is printed.

(4) *Page and report footer:* A dynamic date (changes every time the report is displayed or printed) and page numbers often are included in the footer. The report footer is for multiple-page reports. The administrative professional can also add other information to the page and report footer.

(5) *Other report features:* In addition to the lines and borders that are included on reports, the administrative professional can also add images and graphs.

- Clip art and pictures (scanned, digital camera, or off the Web); these images can also be formatted as watermarks.
- Graphs (charts) can be created based on the numeric data included in the report.

A query can be used to create a report. Like queries, reports are produced on demand. The report "Wizard" is often used when learning how to design reports.

e. *Forms:* Forms are used for data entry, to create a custom dialog box, and to open other forms or reports. The form data comes from the database table(s) or a calculation (expression) that is stored with the form design. To create a form, the required tables and field names must be specified in the form design view. The form design view includes a form header, detail, and form footer.

    (1) *Form header:* The form header is where the administrative professional keys a title that is descriptive of the form.

    (2) *Detail:* The field names appear twice in the *detail area* of the form design view. The field name to the left is used as a heading and should be spelled out and capitalized to clearly identify *prompts (headings)* on the form. The field names to the right are used to input or extract the required data from the database tables; these field names *must not* be changed. These fields become *text boxes* to display data from the tables or enter data into the tables. Text boxes can also be used for expressions to calculate totals.

    (3) *Form footer:* The form footer includes a date, page number, or any other information the administrative professional wants to add to the bottom of the form. This information only appears on hard copies of the form.

    (4) *Graphic elements:* In addition to the lines and borders that are included on forms, the administrative professional can also add images (clip art and pictures). These images can be formatted as icons for the form. Once the image has been added, it can be edited.

f. *Revising reports and forms:* Changing the report or form design view automatically changes the output. Common edit utilities displayed on the database management system toolbar include:

- Delete/cut, copy, paste, move
- Undo
- Alignment

g. *Automatic features:* Database management programs have automatic features for changes made to the database and formats.

    (1) *Automatic correction:* Administrative professionals with write access (authority to make changes) can rename tables, fields, queries, reports, forms, text boxes, or other database objects. Changes made to an object are updated in other related objects with the automatic correction feature. The automatic correction feature looks for and notes discrepancies between the corrected object and other related objects. Only users authorized to make changes can save the changes that the automatic correction feature notes. The corrections are based on the date/time stamp for each object.

    EXAMPLE:

    Late in the afternoon on October 6 an administrative professional with write access made changes in three table structures. (The date/time stamp on the table structures was October 6, 4 P.M., 4:15 P.M., and 4:25 P.M., respectively.)

    On October 7, Seaworth used an existing report (last revised in September) that used data from two of the revised table structures. The automatic correction function looked for and fixed the discrepancies between the report and the two table structures. Seaworth does not have write access (au-

thority to make changes), so the automatic corrections could not be saved to the report design view.

Later that day, Caron used the same report. The automatic correction function fixed the discrepancies. Caron has write access and saved the changes to the report design view.

On October 7, Seaworth again used the report. The automatic correction function was not required.

(2) *Automatic format:* In the design view for reports and forms, there are automatic formats that the administrative professional can select. If a report or form is created with the "Wizard," the automatic format options are presented in a dialog box. The administrative professional can customize a format or create and save a format for automatic use at a future time.

h. *Macros:* A macro is a set of one or more actions, each performing a particular operation. A macro can be a single macro composed of a sequence of actions or it can be a macro group. A conditional expression (if-then-else condition) can be used to determine whether an action should be completed when the macro runs. Administrative professionals may consider a macro for common tasks (e.g., printing a report). Macros need to be saved under a unique file name.

i. *Printing:* The administrative professional can obtain a hard copy of the database table structure and records, queries, reports, and forms. The print icon on the toolbar typically prints one copy. From the menu bar, the administrative professional can activate the appropriate print options (selected pages or all pages) and identify how many copies. Page setup (margins, paper, and layout—portrait or landscape) and a print preview are other common menu options.

7. ***Graphics Applications:*** Graphics applications include the creation of graphs or a presentation graphics application. Although there are programs specific to creating graphs (also called charts), the administrative professional often creates graphs with a spreadsheet program and worksheet data. The following discussion of graphs uses a spreadsheet program and worksheet data.

a. *Graphs:* **Graphs** (*charts*) enhance the presentation of factual data. The values in a graph are linked to the worksheet from which the graph is created. The graph is updated when the administrative professional changes the data on the worksheet. Decisions need to be made as to the best type of graph for the data: bar graph, line graph, pie graph, and so on.

(1) *Bar graph:* A *bar graph* shows a comparison from one time period to another, for example, sales for the year 2003 as compared with sales for the year 2004. A bar graph is also called a *column graph.* The bar graph uses bars of equal width to show quantities (values) on one axis and the factor to be measured on the other axis (see Figure 9–6).

(2) *Line graph:* The *line graph* consists of a series of connected lines showing a particular trend in business data for equal time intervals; for example, the sales for each month during a particular year. Multiple factors can be identified on one line graph; a line for each factor is included on the graph. The vertical axis (Y) identifies the factor and quantity being measured, and the horizontal axis (X) identifies the time period under observation. These axes form the grid upon which the data are recorded (see Figure 9–7).

FIGURE 9–6   Example of Bar Graph

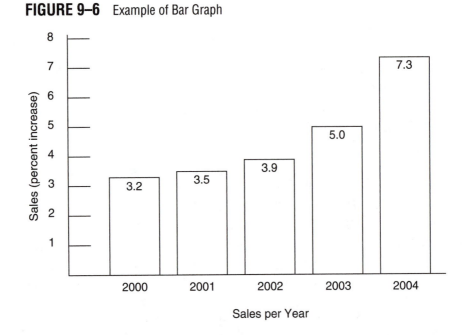

Sales per Year

FIGURE 9–7   Example of Line Graph

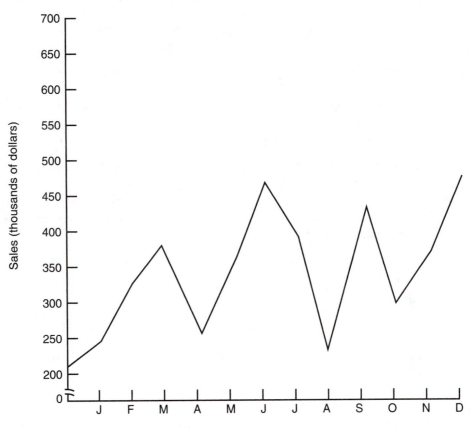

Sales by Month, 20XX

(3) *Pie graph:* The *pie graph* represents the parts that make up a whole. The circle equals 100 percent; the sections represent parts of the whole (smaller percentages of the whole 100 percent). When totaled, the smaller percentages always equal 100 percent.

Similar to the pie graph is the *doughnut graph*. A doughnut graph shows the relationship of parts to a whole for two or more data series. Each ring in the doughnut graph represents a different series of data.

Sometimes parts of the graph need to be emphasized. A section or sections of a pie graph or section(s) in the outer ring of a doughnut graph can be pulled out *(exploded)*. Using click and drag, the section(s) can be pulled out for greater emphasis.

The data from Figure 9–8 (spreadsheet application for a budget) is the input for the pie graph (Figure 9–9) generated with the spreadsheet software graph function.

The icon for creating a graph is on the spreadsheet program toolbar. After the administrative professional has determined the type of graph, the graph toolbar options assist with producing the graph. Most microcomputer spreadsheet programs have a "Wizard" that guides the administrative professional through the steps in creating a graph. Using a printer (ink-jet or laser) or plotter, the administrative professional can print hard copies or transparencies. Graphs can also be exported to other applications in the software suite or integrated package.

b. *Presentation graphics software:* The preparation of visual aids to supplement presentations is a popular business application. Typically, the presentation software is part of a compatible suite of software applications so word processing documents,

FIGURE 9–8   Spreadsheet for Budget and Actual Expenses

MONTHLY BUDGET MARCH 20XX

	Estimated Budget	Actual Budget	Difference
Gross income	$2,000	$2,000	$0
Less 20% tax	400	400	0
Net income	$1,600	$1,600	$0
Expenses:			
Rent	$350	$450	$100
Car payments	150	200	50
Gasoline	30	40	10
Utilities	120	170	50
Entertainment	100	120	20
Food	150	150	0
Clothing	200	180	−20
Total expenses	$1,100	$1,310	−210
Income less expenses	500	290	−210
Less 10% savings	160	160	0
Balance	$340	$130	−$210

FIGURE 9–9   Pie Graph of Actual Budget

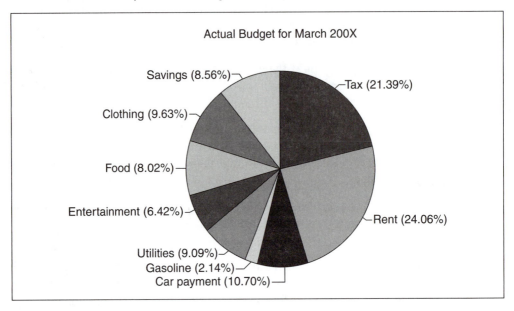

Actual Budget for March 200X

Savings (8.56%)

Tax (21.39%)

Clothing (9.63%)

Food (8.02%)

Entertainment (6.42%)

Rent (24.06%)

Utilities (9.09%)

Gasoline (2.14%)

Car payment (10.70%)

spreadsheet worksheets, and graphs can be used in the presentation program. Clip art, pictures, Web enhancements, animation, and sound can be added to an electronic presentation. The result is a professional set of visuals for an oral presentation as a slide show or transparencies, an information kiosk presentation, a presentation in an electronic collaboration environment, or a Web presentation.

(1) *Document mode:* The administrative professional needs to open the presentation graphics application and make sure the screen is in document mode. With a graphical user interface (GUI), the document mode is an active window.

(2) *Opening presentation graphics:* When the application is open, the administrative professional can choose to use the application default settings or establish different settings. Default settings are often used to create a presentation.

    (a) *Default settings:* The default settings control the placement of objects, color schemes, and transition between slides.

    (b) *Slide orientation:* The default slide orientation (layout) is landscape. *Landscape* creates a slide where the width is greater than the height. The slide orientation can be changed to *portrait*; the slide height is greater than the width. Landscape is the more common layout for slides.

(3) *Presentation graphics organization:* Typically, there are two presentation graphic views for an active window when creating an electronic presentation: normal and slide sorter. When creating the presentation, the slide show view is used to check (test) the presentation features.

    (a) *Normal view:* A *normal view* allows the administrative professional to enter data into a slide pane, speaker notes in a note pane, and view an outline of the presentation in an outline pane.

    (b) *Slide Pane:* The *slide pane* displays a single slide for text, graphs, clip art, animation, audio, and Web links. The slide pane is where an administrative professional creates and edits an electronic presentation. The slide is what the audience sees during a presentation. Miniaturized versions of the slides can be printed as a handout for the audience.

(c) *Notes pane:* The *notes pane* includes details about the key points presented on the slide. Each slide has a corresponding notes pane. During the oral presentation, the audience only sees the slide. The speaker uses the notes to present the necessary background about the key points on the slide.

In addition, the notes pane can be created for an information kiosk or Web presentation. The notes pane is saved with the slide pane so the user can view both. When the kiosk or Web user views the key points on a slide, the notes pane provides the background details for the slide.

Another alternative is to create a self-running slide show for an information kiosk or the Web with voice added for slide narration. Voice narration is also used to assist users in accessing a slide show on the Web.

(d) *Outline pane:* The *outline pane* displays a presentation in outline format showing slide titles and text. This view is helpful when organizing and developing the content of the presentation.

The user (a speaker or a user in an electronic collaboration environment or on the Web) can navigate through the electronic presentation by pointing and clicking on the outline headings.

(e) *Slide sorter view:* The *slide sorter view* displays miniature versions of all slides in the presentation. The administrative professional can easily cut, copy, paste, and move slides to modify the presentation.

(f) *Slide show view:* The *slide show view* displays the slides as an electronic presentation on the computer monitor. This view duplicates how the presentation will handle slide transitions, effects, timings, and animations when presented on the information kiosk, the Web, or during an oral presentation.

(4) *Entering data:* Data are entered into the slide and the notes pane.

(a) *Slide:* A slide is the slide view alone or the slide pane in the normal view. Text, graphs, animation, clip art, audio, Web links, and other presentation data are entered into a slide. Slide default layouts include:

- Title slide
- Bullet list
- Two column
- Table
- Text and clip art or image
- Graph or text and graph

(b) *Notes pane:* The notes pane is where additional information about the slide is added. During an oral presentation the speaker uses the notes when discussing the slide information. The slide should enhance the oral presentation.

(5) *Alignment:* The toolbar allows the administrative professional to point and click to align the information on the slide to the left, right, centered, or justified.

(6) *Automatic features:* When entering text, misspelled words are corrected and symbols are inserted for certain text (e.g., key R followed by the space bar and ® appears). Also, an automatic feature allows words to be completed by using the enter key when the dialog box appears with the complete word. Using the tools menu, an administrative professional can add words and symbols to the built-in automatic feature list.

(7) *Special effects:* Visuals, sound, and animation are common special effects added to electronic presentations. Moderation is important; the special effect should enhance the points on the slides and not distract the audience from the presentation.

    (a) *Transitions:* **Transitions** are special effects that introduce a slide in the presentation. The transition speed between slides can vary throughout an electronic presentation and slides can be introduced from the top or bottom of the screen, left or right, and with or without sound. Changing the transition effect can bring attention to a new section in the presentation or emphasize a key slide.

    (b) *Animation:* **Animations** are special sound or visual effects that can be added to the text. Occasionally including music or sound during a slide transition or animation can keep the audience focused on the presentation. Changing the presentation can hold the audience's attention if the special effect is used with moderation and enhances the presentation. Videos can also be included as part of a presentation. An important guideline to remember is that animation should enhance the presentation and not be overused.

(8) *Revising the slide and notes:* Information on the slide and notes pane can be revised with edit utilities. The toolbar displays icons and buttons for common functions:

- Delete/cut, copy, paste, move
- Undo and redo
- Search and replace

(9) *Formatting the slide and information:* The administrative professional can apply a *slide design* from the presentation graphics design templates. The slide design is applied to all slides in the presentation. The design can be applied at any time or the design can be changed at any time.

Font changes and formatting effects can be made to the design on individual slides. The administrative professional should follow layout and design recommendations provided in Chapter 6 if the slide design is modified. By clicking on the toolbar icons and buttons, text format changes include:

- Font style and size
- Bold, italic, underline, and shadow
- Color

(10) *Spell check:* Text can be run through a spell check by word, slide, or entire presentation to see whether text in the document is spelled correctly.

(11) *Saving data:* Saving should take place frequently when creating or editing an electronic presentation. A short presentation should be saved immediately af-

ter it has been keyed. A longer presentation should be saved often during the keying process, perhaps after each slide has been created.

(12) *Macros:* Tasks that are performed repeatedly can be automated through macros. The presentation graphics macro needs to be saved under a unique file name. The administrative professional may create a macro for routine editing and formatting, combining commands, or automating a complex series of tasks.

(13) *Document protection:* If the electronic presentation is on a whiteboard or a chat room bulletin board to enhance collaboration, the presentation contents should be locked so the group members cannot make changes to the presentation. The presentation outline allows users to easily navigate through the electronic presentation by pointing and clicking on the outline headings.

(14) *Printing:* The administrative professional can obtain a hard copy of the slides, notes, outline, or a miniature view of the slides for handouts. The print icon on the toolbar typically prints one copy of the presentation slides or the normal view. From the menu bar, the administrative professional can activate the appropriate print options (selected slides or all slides and identify how many copies). If a design has been applied to the slides, either the grayscale or pure black and white print options are recommended before printing; many of the designs require too much ink on a hard-copy page. Page setup (size of slides and layout—landscape or portrait) and print preview are other menu options. The default for printing slides is landscape. The default for printing notes, outline, or handouts is typically portrait. Handouts print from two to six slides per page. When three slides are printed on a page, usually a note-taking section is provided on the handout.

For more information on presentation graphics applications, see *Office Administration,* Chapter 5, Section C.

8. ***Software for Other Business Applications:*** The microcomputer is especially versatile for a variety of business applications. Some of the preferred applications are desktop publishing, Web browsers, and groupware.

   a. *Desktop publishing:* The goal of desktop publishing is to combine computer technology with word processing, graphics, and page layout to create high-quality documents that incorporate text, graphics, and other pictures and images.

Text can be created with the desktop publishing program or initially with a compatible word processing program and then converted to desktop publishing. Desktop publishing enables an organization to use in-house services to produce newsletters, manuals, flyers, announcements, brochures, forms, calendars, booklets, and similar types of publications. Major publishers often use desktop publishing software in the creation of books that are printed for mass consumption.

These publications require high print quality; therefore, attention during the production process is on page format, different printing options, artwork, electronic paste-up, and final printing and finishing. Without a desktop publishing program, many administrative professionals use the features of a word processing program for producing documents. Page format, printing options, inserting images, and paste-up are very similar between desktop publishing and word processing software. There are two desktop publishing features, however, an administrative professional should know when communicating with someone using desktop publishing software.

(1) *Page format:* Page format pertains to the number of columns per page, the number of pages in the publication, and any special lines such as banners or headlines. The following format functions are considerations in establishing an attractive page format.

 (a) *Leading:* Leading is the space between the lines.

 (b) *Kerning:* Kerning is the spacing of words and characters on a line to justify copy.

 (c) *Track spacing:* Track spacing is adjusting the number of words per line, squeezing or expanding text, and adding or removing space from character combinations on a line.

(2) *Finishing:* The finishing processes used for documents produced through desktop publishing depend on the particular specifications of the document. A newsletter may need to be folded for mailing or distribution. Single sheets may need to be stapled or bound in a booklet. Printed covers (also produced with desktop publishing) may need to be added to the document before binding. The objective is to make the finished product as attractive as possible, yet cost effective.

Chapter 6 presents other important layout and design information when creating documents with desktop publishing software or word processing software.

b. *Web browser:* Users navigate the Web with a Web browser. Web browser software tools make it easy for the administrative professional to access Web pages and Internet resources. Web browser software uses the point-and-click graphical user interface. This feature is used throughout the Internet to access and display information stored at Web sites. A Web browser is the primary interface for accessing the Internet.

(1) *Applications on the Web:* General purpose applications can be integrated with the Web. It is common for Web pages to use information already saved in word processing documents, spreadsheets, databases, and electronic presentations. Using the general purpose application, hyperlinks can be added to existing documents (files).

 (a) *Word processing:* A word processing document can be saved as a Web page. The "save as" function requires the administrative professional to select *Web page (HTML)* instead of word processing for the type of save format. Basic Web page HTML codes are added to the document.

 (b) *Spreadsheet:* A spreadsheet application can also be saved as a Web page. Basic Web HTML codes are added to the document when the *Save As Web page (HTML)* option is selected. Another way for administrative professionals to display spreadsheet data on the Web is to incorporate the worksheet or the worksheet graph into a word processing document or an electronic presentation.

 (c) *Database:* Viewing records in a database on the organization's intranet or Web site are popular in today's networked world. A data access page needs to be created in the database management application in order to view records on the intranet or Internet. A *data access page* is a special page designed for viewing data, analyzing data, and entering and editing

data. The functionality of the data access page can be restricted to authorized users.

(d) *Presentation graphics:* Presentation applications can be saved as Web pages; each slide becomes a Web page. The presentation outline makes it easy for the intranet/Internet user to navigate through the presentation. The notes page can be included in the Web page to provide details about the key points on the slide.

(2) *Coordination tools:* Electronic coordination tools help professionals manage their time and joint work efforts. Many Web browsers provide electronic management tools that make the management of activities easier and more effective.

(a) *Electronic calendar: Electronic calendars (e-calendars)* support scheduling appointments, appointment reminders, and tickler files. e-Calendars can be installed with joint management rights (read and write privileges) for the user and his or her assistant. e-Calendars can also have read privileges for other co-workers/team members so they can view the calendar to determine possible meeting times. Professionals with PDAs cross-check the PDA data with the office e-calendar for changes and updates on a regular basis.

(b) *Electronic tickler:* An *electronic tickler file (e-tickler)* provides the administrative professional with an electronic to-do list with daily reminders of tasks that need to be accomplished. The tasks in an e-tickler can be prioritized. When the coordination tool is opened at the beginning of the day, reminders of tasks to be completed are provided. These lists should help the administrative professional organize and manage daily activities.

c. *Groupware:* Groupware supports collaboration within and among work groups. Groupware includes software for writing and communicating (word processing and e-mail), information sharing (chat [IRC] and data conference), electronic meetings (computer conference and video conference), scheduling (e-calendars), and electronic project management (timelines and tracking). The network connects the members of a group or different groups who work with compatible software within the organization as well as from widely dispersed locations. Often these teams are referred to as **virtual teams;** teams that work together over the network with little or no face-to-face contact.

Check Point— Section B

Directions: For each question, circle the correct answer.

B–1. Productivity software common for home computing is a/an

A) application specific program
B) cross-functional application
C) integrated package
D) software suite

B–2. Redundant storage of business transactions (e.g., sales, customer information) occurs when different divisions throughout the organization collect the same information for different applications. Redundant storage affects

A) cross-functional integration
B) data integrity
C) industry-specific applications
D) information access

B–3.   What software supports collaboration within and among work clusters?

A)   Cross industry

B)   General purpose
C)   Groupware
D)   Productivity packages

C. Configuration, Implementation, and Management

How the organization configures the internal network affects the configuration for microcomputers connected to the network. Systems analysis identifies the information needs for the organization's employees, customers, and business partners. Thinking about a problem or opportunity holistically is one of the most important aspects during this process. Systems analysis should be an ongoing process as technology committees identify new opportunities, review ongoing computer-based information system designs, and maintain and enhance the computing environment.

Acquiring, testing, and converting to new systems will keep the computer-based information system dynamic. Processes for managing the computer-based information system should be applicable to all employees. The administrative professional knowledgeable about computing environments can play a key role in system configuration, implementation, and management.

1. *Configuration:* Computers used throughout an organization need to be configured for the specific local area network the computer interfaces, the organization's intranet, and the external Internet if this option is available to the computer user. Through an analysis of information needs, the administrative professional's functional requirements become the basis for the desktop computer configuration.

   a. *Information technology division:* Information technology (IT) personnel are responsible for configuring the organization's computers. Administrative professionals need to know their information/computer requirements and be able to communicate these requirements to the appropriate IT personnel or committees. End users who make changes to their computing environment without communicating with IT personnel make managing the organization's computing environment difficult.

   b. *End-user development:* Microcomputers and general purpose application software (a fourth-generation language tool [4GL]) puts computing power in the hands of the end user. Organizational concerns with end-user developed applications include:

      • Quality control over development
      • Inadequate interface with other existing systems—both organizational and departmental
      • Inadequate knowledge for development
      • Lack of documentation
      • Added responsibility for IT division
      • If the end user requires assistance

   c. *Outsourcing:* To control computing costs, many organizations have outsourced the computer operations. *Outsourcing* is contracting with another organization (or individual) for parts or all of the computing operations.

   Administrative professionals need to realize that the configuration of the computing environment is dependent on many operations throughout the organization. The networked enterprise requires some standardization in hardware, software, and network design in order to control computing costs.

2. ***Implementation:*** All computer-based information systems have a life cycle (analysis, design, develop, implement, and maintain). This life cycle is an ongoing process looping back to a phase in the cycle as necessary. Administrative professionals should be involved with the organization's information system life cycle (see Chapter 5, Section C-1). The administrative professional is responsible for managing the life cycle for end-user developed applications.

a. *Implementation for enterprise applications:* Formal reviews by end users are critical. Reviews should check for compliance with business processes, adequate testing, conversion method(s), training plans, and documentation.

(1) *Testing:* Users need to provide application programmers with all the ways a system can fail, including faulty data. Testing consists of:

- *Unit tests:* testing the module
- *System tests:* testing the system (complete application with test data)
- *Acceptance test:* final testing by end users to determine that the system meets functional information requirements

(2) *Conversion:* Conversion is changing from the old system to the new one. The cutover can be direct, parallel, pilot, and phased. See Chapter 5, Section B-2-a (3) (b) for details on these conversion methods.

(3) *Training:* Sometimes formal training is required; at other times user support groups adequately provide required end-user assistance.

(4) *Documentation:* In addition to documentation for the application programmers, documentation for the user is important. Samples of system input screens, forms, and reports generated are helpful user documentation. Today many organizations place user documentation on the organization's intranet for easy access and updates. To make it easy for the end user to find the documentation, it should be linked to the functional application.

b. *Implementation for end-user applications:* End users should test the application, determine a conversion method, document the application, and determine training requirements for other users.

(1) *Testing:* No matter the size of an application, it should first be tested for accuracy before being applied to daily operations.

(2) *Conversion:* Since most end-user applications are small and easy to use, the direct cutover method for implementation is common.

(3) *Training:* If other users in the division use the application, administrative professionals must ensure that these users are properly trained.

(4) *Documentation:* Documentation for end-user applications can be as simple as one sheet explaining how to use the application to small application manuals available to all users. When the administrative professional uses an application on a quarterly or semiannual basis, documentation is beneficial.

Hopefully, the applicability of the end-user application to the organization's mission and goal was determined before the application was developed.

3. ***Management:*** An organization's computing environment must be managed and maintained. This is a dual responsibility between IT personnel and end users.

   a. *System maintenance:* Monitoring, evaluating, and modifying the system is an ongoing process. The administrative professional needs to observe computer operations for system issues, evaluate output for application issues, and observe users to identify areas where training would improve the use and effectiveness of the computer-based information system. This is true of the organization's system as well as end-user developed applications.

     (1) *Trouble log:* The administrative professional should keep a log of hardware and software issues. Repeated malfunctions to the enterprise system, departmental system, or microcomputer system should be reported to appropriate personnel. The reporting date and the date when the issue was corrected should be logged.

     (2) *Output:* An easy way to evaluate the effectiveness of the system is to evaluate its output. Output evaluation for small applications may be sufficient. However, the administrative professional must realize that output evaluation does not always identify all possible errors.

     System and application errors must be corrected. End-user developed applications may be easily modified. Application specific software should be audited annually and may require time for modifications depending on priorities in the IT division. The administrative professional needs to be aware of computing needs throughout the organization and the priority process.

   b. *Organization change:* Dynamic organizations change. Government regulations force organizations to change. New technology brings change to the organization. Changes in the organization's goals, business processes, and competitive strategies impact the effectiveness of the computer-based information system. Often end users resist change. It is incumbent of the administrative professional to be aware of required changes and to support these efforts within the organization.

Check Point—Section C

Directions: For each question, circle the correct answer.

C–1. Control over application development, lack of documentation, and inadequate interfaces with other applications are all concerns with

   A) application service providers (ASPs)
   B) custom-designed software
   C) end-user developed applications
   D) enterprise systems

C–2. When an application programmer asks an administrative professional to provide faulty test data to try and make the application fail, the test data is being used for a/an

   A) acceptance test
   B) conversion test
   C) system test
   D) unit text

C–3. Whose responsibility is it to monitor and evaluate the organization's computing environment?

   A) Chief information officer (CIO)
   B) End users and information technology personnel
   C) Information technicians
   D) System programmers

For Your Review

Directions: For each question, circle the correct answer.

1. Through the intranet, Shodeen has on-line access to the budget lines for the logistics department. What application software provides Shodeen with the budget information?

   A) Application specific
   B) General purpose
   C) Industry specific
   D) Operations

2. What type of business application program consists of a set of interdependent modules for applications in accounting, marketing and sales, finance, production and distribution, and human resources?

   A) Cross-industry application software
   B) Enterprise system
   C) Management information system
   D) Middleware

3. Which option should an organization consider in an attempt to lower business software costs?

   A) Application service provider (ASP)
   B) In-house custom design
   C) Off-the-shelf software
   D) Storage service provider (SSP)

4. When general purpose, end-user software is ready for input from an administrative professional, this is called the

   A) active window
   B) data access page
   C) desktop
   D) workbook

5. When using the spreadsheet program, Nguyn periodically receives information or is asked to provide information or make a selection about the application. This interactive communication with the software is accomplished with the

   A) active cell
   B) dialog box
   C) document mode
   D) open window

6. Skarka often transposes the "o" and "i" when keying the word *professional*. However, the word processing program displays *professional* after he keys *professoinal* and depresses the space bar. The word processing feature that makes this change is the

   A) automatic correct
   B) edit utility
   C) spell check
   D) word wrap

7. When several worksheets are available in the spreadsheet document mode, the administrative professional can switch back and forth among the worksheets by pointing and clicking on the

   A) menu bar
   B) title bar
   C) toolbar
   D) worksheet tab

8. What must be incorporated into a spreadsheet design if the administrative professional wants to sort the spreadsheet data and/or find certain information? A

   A) function
   B) list

C) macro
D) relative reference

9. All numeric data in the worksheet cells B4 through B56 need to be formatted with a dollar symbol, commas, and decimal places (e.g., $1,330.50). The dollar sign and decimal place need to be aligned. How does an administrative professional insert this format into the spreadsheet design?

A) Block the cell range and select the accounting option from the format/cells menu
B) Block the cell range and select the currency option from the format/range menu
C) Block the cell range and select the number option from the format menu
D) In the active cell enter the numeric data with the dollar sign; the dollar sign, comma, and decimal places are inserted

10. Before a hard copy of a worksheet can be printed, the administrative professional must

A) block the range of cells that contains the worksheet data and set the print area
B) freeze the row and column headings
C) save the worksheet
D) select the print preview menu option

11. Microcomputer database management programs are typically

A) hypermedia
B) network
C) object oriented
D) relational

12. A two-dimensional table where data about a specific topic in the database are collected is the

A) field
B) element
C) record
D) relation

13. The human resource employee database table has eight fields: first name, last name, street address, city, state, ZIP Code, telephone, and employee number. Which one must be the primary key?

A) Employee number
B) Last name plus first name
C) Street address
D) ZIP Code

14. Edelman wants to extract the names and telephone numbers for all members in the database with a 312 area code. She would like the output sorted in alphabetical order by last name and presented with headings and page footers. Edelman needs to create a database

A) form
B) list
C) report
D) query

15. When the administrative professional wants to show comparisons from one time period to another, the best type of chart is the

A) bar
B) doughnut
C) line
D) pie

16. The marketing department wants a visual image of the five representatives' sales trends for the current year. The best visual image would be a

A) line graph
B) pie graph
C) worksheet
D) word processing table

17. Marquart Landscaping had an electronic presentation developed for the Web. Users can navigate through the presentation by pointing and clicking on the

A) browser back and forward buttons
B) notes pane
C) outline pane headings
D) slide pane

18. Ollnau has just finished creating an electronic presentation and needs to delete several of the slides and rearrange others. To accomplish this task, Ollnau would select the slide and make the revisions in the

    A) normal view
    B) slide sorter view
    D) slide show view
    E) slide pane

19. Ashcraft's electronic presentation included a different transition and animation for each slide. He asked for your critique. Your comment should be

    A) a different transition between slides and a lot of animation brings attention to the key points on each slide
    B) changing the presentation using different transitions and animation helps hold the audience's attention
    C) moderation is important; transitions and animation should be used only when it enhances the presentation
    D) presentations should have very little animation and only one transition style in an electronic presentation

20. When using a productivity software suite, tasks that are performed repeatedly should be

    A) automated through a macro
    B) common functions within the suite
    C) defaults on the desktop
    D) included on the menu bar

21. Oltmanns is planning to publish a booklet that requires high print quality with extensive artwork. The best program for creating, formatting, and inserting images is a/an

    A) desktop publishing program
    B) graphics program
    C) industry-specific program
    D) integrated package

22. One format function in desktop publishing is to adjust the spacing of words and characters on a line for justified copy. This is called

    A) kerning
    B) leading
    C) left justification
    D) track spacing

23. Electronic reminders that provide a list of prioritized tasks to help the administrative professional organize and manage daily activities is the

    A) e-calendar
    B) e-tickler
    C) filter
    D) information center

24. The best way to provide end users with timely, current documentation about the enterprise system would be to

    A) link the documentation to the enterprise system function and post it on the intranet
    B) offer required training sessions once a month
    C) provide the end user with documentation in a three-ring notebook so updates and changes can be easily inserted
    D) report new system features in an information technology newsletter

25. Varalli keeps a log of hardware and software issues. When there are repeated malfunctions to her desktop PC, she has a log to support a request for troubleshooting service from the information technician. Varalli is helping with the organization's information system

    A) configuration
    B) implementation
    C) management
    D) testing

Solutions

Solutions to Check Point—Section A

Answer	Refer to:
A–1. (A)	[A-1]
A–2. (B)	[A-2]
A–3. (B)	[A-3]

Solutions to Check Point—Section B

Answer	Refer to:
B–1. (C)	[B-1-a]
B–2. (B)	[B-2]
B–3. (C)	[B-8-c]

Solutions to Check Point—Section C

Answer	Refer to:
C–1. (C)	[C-1-b]
C–2. (C)	[B-2-a (3) (a) and C-2-a (1)]
C–3. (B)	[C-3]

Solutions to For Your Review

	Answer	Refer to:
1.	(A)	[A-1-a (4)]
2.	(B)	[A-2-a]
3.	(A)	[A-4-c]
4.	(A)	[B-3]
5.	(B)	[B-3-c]
6.	(A)	[B-4-c (5) (b)]
7.	(D)	[B-5-a (1)]
8.	(B)	[B-5-a (6)]
9.	(A)	[B-5-b (1)]
10.	(A)	[B-5-f]
11.	(D)	[B-6]
12.	(D)	[B-6-a (2) (a)]
13.	(A)	[B-6-a (2) (c)]
14.	(C)	[B-6-d]
15.	(A)	[B-7-a (1)]
16.	(A)	[B-7-a (2)]
17.	(C)	[B-7-b (3) (d)]
18.	(B)	[B-7-b (3) (e)]
19.	(C)	[B-7-b (7)]
20.	(A)	[B-4-i, B-5-c, B-6-h and B-7-b (12)]
21.	(A)	[B-8-a]
22.	(A)	[B-8-a (1) (b) and Chapter 6 B-6-b (5) (b)]
23.	(B)	[B-8-b (2) (b)]
24.	(A)	[C-2-a-(4)]
25.	(C)	[C-3-a (1)]

Chapter 10
Furniture, Equipment, and Supplies

OVERVIEW

The creation of workspace layouts and designs necessitates careful systems analysis that results in more functional environments. The private-office arrangement is the traditional approach to layout with private offices separated from general work areas. The open-office arrangement, including landscaped or modular approaches, offers functional work areas with modular furniture and aisle space to control the flow of communication throughout the division. The open arrangement is typical for telecommuters, business professionals who work from home. To control space costs, organizations are also utilizing hot desking as a space allocation alternative.

More attention is being focused on the design of work areas so business professionals have quicker and easier access to equipment, work in process, and cross-functional operations. Supplies, reference materials, or other accessories should be within reach. Securing new office furniture and equipment requires analytical judgment and participation on the part of administrative professionals to assist in making selections that will improve the environment for the entire organization.

Procurement principles for furniture, equipment, and supplies are important to ensure quality while controlling costs. Quality and lower costs are two important benefits an organization receives when purchasing is properly managed and controlled. Selecting reliable suppliers helps ensure that new technologies and ergonomics standards are incorporated into the work environment. Administrative professionals who are knowledgeable about managing the procurement process help with controlling and maintaining quality workplace furniture, equipment, and supplies.

KEY TERMS

Capital equipment (assets), 249
Cybernetics, 239
Data flow diagram, 239
Euthenics, 240
Full-service supplier, 256
Global procurement, 249
Hot desking, 242
Inventory control, 256

A. Office Layout and Design

The work environment affects administrative professionals psychologically, sociologically, and physically—whether a traditional or modern office design is applied. The *traditional (closed) design* is usually referred to as the *private office*. Business personnel requiring private space have offices separated from general work areas. The *modern design* is usually referred to as the *open office*. Two open-office approaches, *office landscaping* and *modular*, design the work area without permanent walls and with flexible furniture and aisle space to accommodate the communication flows throughout the division. The design of home work areas typically tends to reflect the open-office arrangement since a portion of the living space may be remodeled or rearranged into a comfortable workspace.

1. ***Planning an Office:*** An office environment needs to be planned so business professionals are able to function effectively and productively. These factors should be considered before any long-range decisions about the office environment are made.

   a. *Strategic planning for the business:* The alignment of the physical facilities with the strategic plans for the business over the next few years is essential, resulting in fewer unexpected changes in the direction of the business as well as enhancing the communication flow necessary for office operations.

   b. *Cost of work area design:* Costs refer to equipment, furniture, remodeling, renovation, and replacement. Work areas that are cost effective are more useful to the business over time.

   c. *Job functions:* The job functions of administrative professionals are constantly changing. The dynamics of technology for the networked enterprise require administrative professionals to be aware of design functions to meet today's needs and to be flexible in accommodating future changes. The arrangement of the desktop PC or notebook, with appropriate seating and lighting, is very important for all administrative professionals. Job functions must be analyzed to determine the allocation of physical resources to these functions.

   d. *Computer requirements:* Studies by Louis Harris and Associates indicate that on the average computers are used more than four hours per day. The number of people who use a computer more than five hours a day has increased to more than 50 percent of all business personnel. Additional considerations are the required cabling, space, and employee comfort.

   e. *Employee expectations:* Today administrative professionals are concerned about the work environment and their own health and comfort (ergonomics). Noise control, proper lighting, and display monitor health issues are of prime importance to employees. Ergonomic factors need proper consideration as new office environments are planned.

2. ***Designing Appropriate Office Layouts:*** Often administrative professionals are involved with the design of the office environment. Collaborative teams representing all organizational levels and all divisions often provide recommendations on work area design and remodeling.

   a. *Goals of office layout:* The effective arrangement of furniture, equipment, and other physical components to accommodate work tasks and facilitate efficient workflow within available floor space is very important.

      (1) *Analyzing information and workflow patterns:* Information processed within the organization should flow in a forward direction. The transmission of information, as related to a specific process, through either face-to-face or electronic communication is called **workflow**. **Cybernetics** refers to the information flow resulting from the communications systems being used.

         (a) *Process chart or data flow diagram:* Existing office systems and procedures must be studied, especially when delays or bugs in the process are identified. The speed of each procedure should be examined in relation to the entire process. In addition, overall productivity associated with each step of the process should be ascertained and monitored.

            A process chart (or a data flow diagram) is an illustration of existing office procedures. The **process chart** illustrates distances and delays involved in the entire process or procedure from start to finish. A **data flow diagram** graphically illustrates the computer-based information system's component processes and the flow of data between the processes. For both manual and electronic information flow, administrative professionals often provide input to the analysis of process flows (steps) ensuring that proper business forms, processes, and routing are followed.

            Total quality management advocates that a process step (steps to process a document) should be included only if the individual (step) receiving, reviewing, or sending the document adds value to the final document.

         (b) *Office layout chart:* The movement of a document can be charted using the actual floor plan of the office to develop the resulting workflow pattern. For the networked enterprise, an **office layout chart** is important to identify personnel or departments that frequently work together. When face-to-face sessions are required, the close proximity of personnel and work areas facilitates process efficiency.

      (2) *Allocating space for office functions:* Departments that have frequent contact with each other need to be located physically near each other. Central services, such as an in-house reproduction center, should be located near departments that most frequently require the service. Within specific departments, space should be allocated according to employee needs and job tasks.

         EXAMPLE: *Following are suggested space allocations for business professionals at specific levels:*

Position	*Space Allocation (square feet)*
Administrative personnel	*70–100*
Supervisor	*100–150*
Junior/first-level executive	*150–200*

Middle-level executive   *300–350*
Top-level executive   *350–500*

Office furniture also requires certain space allocations. Following are recommended space requirements:

Furniture	**Space Allocation**
Administrative professional desk (U-shaped)	*60 square feet*
File cabinet (letter-size)	*5–7 square feet*
Primary aisles	*6–8 feet wide*
Secondary aisles	*4–5 feet wide*

(3) *Providing appropriate office environmental needs:* Proper lighting, sound control, and interior decorating are important in meeting comfort and employee satisfaction needs regarding the office environment. **Euthenics** is the science of bettering employee conditions by improving the work environment.

(4) *Eliminating structural barriers:* To provide for handicapped or disabled business professionals, structural barriers must be eliminated. The open-office concept has been very useful in this regard. The Vocational Rehabilitation Act of 1973 requires all new United States Federal buildings and private companies receiving more than $2,500 in Federal funds to provide accessibility to handicapped employees. The Americans with Disabilities Act of 1990 is another Federal legislative act that provides for the accommodation of qualified disabled persons in the workplace. Administrative professionals should use the Americans with Disabilities Web site (*ww.usdoj.gov/crt/ada/ adahom1.htm*) for current information.

b. *Flexibility in workspace layout:* Workspace planners need to be concerned with future expansion, shifting of departmental functions, and increasing or decreasing numbers of employees. Flexible layouts of the work area can result in improved communication networks as well. As space arrangements are changed, telephone and computer networks may also need to be changed. For security and safety reasons, telephone numbers are often assigned to a location and should not be reassigned to new locations. An annual space analysis or review may be helpful in maintaining a flexible plan.

3. ***Types of Office Design:*** There are two basic types of office designs: the *private office* (*traditional*) and the *open office* (*modern*). Depending on the needs of the organization, these two basic designs can be modified to suit specific work needs and preferences. Also, organizations may support the home office for the telecommuter. For the telecommuter, equipment, furniture, and supply requirements need to be addressed by the organization. Surveys conducted by the Society of Human Resource Management indicate that during poor economic conditions and high unemployment, organizations in the United States often decrease family-friendly program opportunities and support (e.g., flex scheduling, job sharing, and telecommuting).

a. *The private office:* The **private-office design** is known as the *traditional (closed) design* or *bull-pen approach*. Business professionals are typically housed in offices separated from general office areas where office support personnel are located. The following are reasons for the private office.

(1) *Nature of the work:* The confidential and private nature of the work can better be accomplished with a closed office environment.

(2) *Level of concentration required:* The work of some administrative professionals requires a high level of concentration. The private office furnishes a quieter environment for working.

(3) *Prestige:* The private office often conveys more prestige and higher status for the business professional.

The private-office design is not considered an efficient arrangement in terms of space utilization. Authorities have calculated that only 50 percent of the space devoted to private offices is used efficiently.

b. *The open office:* Since 1960, the use of the **open-office design** has been prominent, especially in the United States. The open office situates business professionals and functions in relatively open areas to accommodate the workflow and communication required. The open-office design is characterized by these features: large open areas of workspace with only a minimum of permanent walls, use of modular furniture systems, clustering of workspaces, and the use of accent colors to enhance the work area decor. Two popular approaches used for open-office design are office landscaping and the modular office.

(1) *Office landscaping:* The concept of *office landscaping* was first introduced by the Quickboner Team, a group of German consultants commissioned by the University of Hamburg to study offices. The purpose was to develop methods to increase the overall efficiency of office functions through the application of scientific approaches. The team found that face-to-face communication was important for efficient office operations. Today's collaborative team structure benefits from an open-office design.

(a) *Primary focus:* Office landscaping places primary emphasis on analyzing office procedures and controlling workflow.

(b) *Special features of office landscaping:*

- A minimum number of permanent walls
- Work areas located to result in more efficient workflow and enhanced communication
- Utilization of acoustical devices and noise control
- Uniform air conditioning and humidity control
- Use of partitions, modular furniture, and planters to provide privacy and beauty
- Use of well-designed work areas to complement work functions

(2) *The modular office:* In this type of open-office design, office furniture is creatively used in the workspace to meet the specific needs of the employee. The *modular office* is also referred to as the *modern office.*

(a) *Primary focus:* The modular office focuses on planning and arranging the individual workspace to allow for a variety of interchangeable components to meet individual needs and to serve as a basis for expandable office systems. Today many private offices utilize modular furniture and wall units, electrical slots, built-in lighting features, and the use of color and texture to complement the office design.

(b) *Special features of the modular office:*

- Basic units of furniture: desk surfaces, end supports, filing units, shelves, and drawers
- Wall panels or partitions on which furniture units can be attached or suspended
- Electrical outlets for use with electronic equipment and "slots" for electrical cords
- Built-in lighting fixtures for task lighting
- Use of color and texture to complement the office design

(3) *Home work area:* Ergonomics is also important to the telecommuter's home work area. Although the open office is the most typical arrangement, the following factors should be taken into consideration when establishing an office at home.

(a) Work area furniture must minimize employee fatigue and maximize functionality and comfort.

(b) Proper lighting is required for the entire office area as well as for task lighting.

(c) All equipment needs to be functional including sufficient outlet connections and use of safety features such as surge protectors.

(d) Network connections to the office and technology support are important.

(e) Sufficient storage space must be provided. The amount required will depend on secondary storage availability on the microcomputer or the organization's network.

(f) Atmospheric conditions must be a priority consideration.

(g) Acoustics must be considered to provide privacy when needed.

(h) An analysis of work and traffic flow is necessary for efficient task processing as well as access to the workspace by the telecommuter and clients (if necessary).

(i) The finishing touches of the home work area (pictures and personal items) complete the aesthetic appeal of the home office environment.

(4) *Hot desking:* With some offices in use only 10 to 20 percent of the time, workspace designers have recommended that the space be shared by two or more employees. This approach, known as **hot desking**, can reduce office space costs for organizations. Hotelling and motelling are two hot desking alternatives. These space design alternatives are most successful for field representatives, sales personnel, consultants, and contract personnel who are frequently away from the office. Some organizations have become partners in providing "hot desks" for each other's traveling professionals.

(a) *Hotelling: Hotelling* is an open-office design with unassigned desks. A business professional needs to call in advance to pre-book a workspace (or microcomputer and support facilities required) for a specific period of time. A reservationist, often in the human resource division, handles all bookings.

Acts 4:8
Matthew 6: (handwritten)

e pre-
ige for

espe-
ling to

4. **Space L** will be
used. Ac func-
tions wi (writ-
ing, plai ed that
correlat contin-
uous ac ity.

   a. *Fac* he fol-
   low hin the
   org

   •

   •

   •

   •

   •

   •

   • Communication requirements for all work areas

   b. *Steps in planning workspace:* When considering workspace requirements, these basic steps should be kept in mind:

   (1) *Defining goals:* The work to be performed must be identified and appropriate goals must be established.

   (2) *Establishing space requirements:* Information about each work activity must be collected to determine whether the assigned space helps or hinders those functions. Communication and workflow processes are vital considerations. Space requirements for administrative professionals should be determined on the basis of this analysis.

   (3) *Developing new workspace plans:* Alternative work area and individual workspace layouts need to be developed to facilitate different patterns of information flow; administrative professionals and workspace designers need to think "outside the box."

   (4) *Selecting and implementing the best alternative:* Finally, the most feasible work area layout needs to be selected for testing and eventual implementation. Flexibility should be a key in planning workspace that will permit a variety of office activities to be performed.

5. **Computer Software for Workspace Design:** Administrative professionals can utilize workspace design software to assist with workspace layout and design. The features and characteristics of the work area structure, including spatial dimensions, can be manipulated so proposed layouts and designs can be viewed on the microcomputer monitor before a final decision is reached. Physical structures in the work area as well

as microcomputer arrangements can be studied thoroughly before decisions are made about resource allocations needed for such renovation.

Check Point—Section A

Directions: For each question, circle the correct answer.

A–1. A telecommuter's workspace usually is designed according to what office model?

   A) Bull-pen
   B) Open office
   C) Private office
   D) Traditional

A–2. In designing a new electronic sales order form, the path for transmitting information related to processing the order was documented. This path is called the

   A) form design

   B) job analysis
   C) procedures analysis
   D) workflow

A–3. With some offices in use only 20 percent of the time, workspace designers often recommend that two or more employees share the same work area. This approach is known as

   A) hot desking
   B) modular
   C) office partners
   D) open office

B. Work Area Use and Maintenance

The work area needs to be planned and designed to meet the individual needs of each business professional (executive, manager, or administrative professional). As technology is integrated into most office operations, increased attention is being focused on ways to lessen fatigue, boredom, mental exhaustion, and stress. A National Institute of Occupational Safety and Health study indicated that individuals who worked with display monitors on a regular basis tended to experience more stress than other office personnel. Work area design and use depends on organizational needs, task performance needs, and behavioral considerations.

1. *Organizational Needs:* Initially, work areas are designed so the organizational objectives can be met. Work areas and individual workspace must support communication (interpersonal and computer-based), flow of information through the organization, and access to record systems with common information files.

   a. *Face-to-face communication:* Within any organization there is a need for face-to-face interaction with other people for planning and completing work assignments.

   b. *Electronic communication:* In addition to interpersonal communication, provision must be made for electronic communication (use of computers, telephone, fax, and other electronic devices).

   c. *Information flow:* For business transactions and processes to take place, information must flow easily from task to task, from department to department, and externally to other organizations. An enterprise network enhances electronic information flow throughout the organization and externally to business partners.

   d. *Record systems:* People need to be able to access information, whether that information has been filed as hard copy in file cabinets or as soft copy within an electronic system. Records should be accessible when the information is needed and in the form required by the user.

2. **Task Performance Needs:** Workspace must be designed and equipped so specific tasks can be performed efficiently and accurately according to required time schedules.

a. *Arranging the work center:* One of the "rules of thumb" that administrative professionals are often required to follow is that the top of the work surface (desk) and drawers within the work area should be arranged so working from the work area is efficient and productive.

(1) *Placement of office equipment:* Deciding where to place specific office equipment (e.g., microcomputer or telephone) depends on the need for ready access to the equipment.

(a) *Microcomputer system:* The microcomputer should be placed directly in front of the user to allow for working either to the left or right, whichever is a more comfortable arrangement.

- The keyboard and mouse should be easily accessible and ergonomically designed.

- Most workspace furniture should have a microcomputer keyboard shelf, directly in front of the administrative professional, that slides back under the central desktop when not in use.

- The display monitor should meet the ergonomics viewing triangle requirements (see Chapter 11, Figure 11–1). A raised platform for the display monitor is recommended to achieve proper height.

- Any console or conversation module that is part of the furniture system should be appropriately positioned with the work surface so placement will not interfere with routine computer operations. For easy access, consoles often are positioned behind the administrative professional's chair.

- The printer should be located on a separate work surface near the computer. Acoustical sound covers should be used as needed. Shared printers should be placed in close proximity to all microcomputers sharing the equipment.

- Disk drives and other storage devices may be located next to the display monitor for easy access or within the microprocessor tower that is typically on the floor near the microcomputer.

(b) *Telephone:* The telephone should be on the work surface in an easy-to-reach location; notepads and pens should be within arm's reach. Administrative professionals who are on the telephone for extended periods of time should use a headset for speaking and listening instead of using the telephone handset. Besides improving listening comfort, the headset relieves the administrative professional's hands for note taking and computer work required during the conversation.

(c) *Dictation-transcription unit:* For ease of listening and transcribing, this unit should be placed next to the microcomputer. Most organizations that require transcription processing provide for dictation and transcription through the local area network. The earphones and foot pedal that connect to the network are the only additional equipment required by the administrative professional.

(d) *Peripheral equipment:* Other office equipment used occasionally (copier, postage meter, fax, folding machine, and collator) should be placed in an area where the equipment is shared with other office personnel. Sometimes, work areas are available so several departments can use and share the equipment.

(2) *Arranging desk accessories:* In addition to electronic accessories, most administrative professionals have a calendar, in/out trays or baskets, small organizer, pen set, and other desk accessories. These accessories should be arranged neatly within reach on the desktop or on a work surface extension.

(3) *Arranging office supplies:* In addition to locked storage for supplies purchased in large quantities, small office supplies in limited quantities are typically stored systematically in desk drawers: stationery, envelopes, labels, papers, forms, pens/pencils, clips, and disks/discs.

(4) *Arranging reference materials:* General-purpose application software now includes dictionaries, a thesaurus, word finders, and general office procedures manuals. Directories can be set up in electronic address books. All postal information including ZIP Codes can be located online at *www.usps.com*. Intranets provide electronic internal directories and standard operating procedures. In addition to references available through the networked computer-based information system, general office references that the administrative professional may need on, in, or near the desk include the following:

- Unabridged dictionary
- Word finder
- Thesaurus
- Office procedures manual or handbook
- Frequently used directories (local and/or long-distance telephone directory; internal extension directory should be on the intranet)
- Company policies and procedures manuals, unless on the intranet
- Index file of people and companies frequently contacted

Administrative professionals should use online references from the microcomputer and the enterprise network as much as possible. Electronic references remove the clutter from the work surface and provide the most dynamic, accurate information when these electronic sources are properly updated and maintained.

b. *Utilizing devices for personal comfort:* Mental exhaustion, fatigue, boredom, and stress affect the productivity of the person who works with computers and other electronic equipment. Following are ways in which workspace design and the types of equipment selected may alleviate physical discomfort for administrative professionals.

(1) *Chair adjustments:* Office furniture manufacturers have created chairs that are adjustable in terms of changing the chair height, tilting the seat pan, and placing backrests and armrests in the most comfortable positions. The con-

tour of the chair can be matched to the physical requirements of a person's body through a custom design.

(2) *Use of modular design:* Individual employees can arrange their own work areas to suit left- or right-handed preferences. Private workspace can be created through the use of privacy panels. Recent research shows that employees who have the opportunity to help design their own workspace tend to be satisfied with the environment.

(3) *Work surface adjustments:* The height of work surfaces should have the flexibility to be raised or lowered. Some of the latest designs in modular furniture for microcomputer systems have four different work surfaces that can be raised, tilted, or lowered: a center work surface, one to the right of center, one to the left of center, and one to the back of center that can be raised to hold a display monitor.

(4) *Display monitor placement:* Placing the monitor on a small, raised platform brings it to eye level. The monitor can also be tilted for ease of viewing and glare elimination. Screen brightness, color, and contrast can also be adjusted for optimum user accommodation.

(5) *Keyboard platforms:* Movable keyboards that are wireless or attached by cable to the processing unit can be placed directly on the work surface or on a keyboard shelf that pulls out from under the center work surface. Mousepads typically are to the left or right of the keyboard. When not in use, the keyboard shelf can be pushed under the work surface until needed.

c. *Maintaining security of information:* Information needs to be kept secure and, in many cases, private. Only people with security clearances should be permitted access to certain information. A workspace design with locked areas helps control physical access to stored information.

(1) *Placement of partitions and wall panels:* Separate workspace is created through the use of panels and partitions. Panels and partitions help maintain privacy for the person who is working on a particular project. The arrangement of workspace versus conversation areas will keep the information in the area where the administrative professional works concealed when colleagues enter the work area.

(2) *Positioning display monitors for limited access:* Data and text easily viewed over the administrative professional's shoulder can compromise information security. The display monitor should be placed so that people entering the work area can be easily seen and the information on the display screen concealed.

(3) *Screen savers:* A screen saver appears on the display monitor in place of the data or text when the administrative professional ceases to work with the text for a designated number of seconds or minutes. A screen saver can help maintain privacy of information on the display monitor.

(4) *Clustering workspace for work groups:* Planning work areas so access is available only through an intermediary (a receptionist or a locked door) may reduce the tendency of other personnel to unnecessarily gain access to work areas.

3. ***Behavioral Considerations:*** How administrative professionals adapt behaviorally to workspace design is very important. Following are some aspects of workspace design that affect acceptance.

   a. *Need for territoriality:* All business professionals want to feel that a particular space or work boundary is available. The individual workspace provides a sense of the administrative professional's personal space; clustering of several employees' workspace provides a sense of belonging to a work group.

      EXAMPLE: *Nameplates on modular partitions or a display case, with names of department members listed, give employees a sense of belonging to the organization or work group.*

   b. *Personalizing the workspace:* Allowances need to be made for administrative professionals to personalize their individual workspace with items such as family pictures, plants, or artwork.

      Plants that are well maintained and artwork complementary to the office design can add a positive, relaxing texture to the work area.

   c. *Social needs:* Facilities adjacent to or near the work areas—lounges, cafeterias, recreation areas, and fitness or workout rooms—provide for the social needs of office employees.

4. ***Network Requirements:*** Any special requirements necessitated by departmental, enterprise, or global networks need to be considered in the design of individual workspaces. Cabling is an important factor since microcomputers must communicate with other microcomputers as well as with peripheral equipment (such as printers). The objective of such planning is to make the presence of the computer-based information system at the individual workspace an efficient, easy-to-use tool and the presence of any network almost transparent to each user.

Check Point—Section B

Directions: For each question, circle the correct answer.

B–1. A workspace design that supports communication and information flow will include access to a/an

   A) hot desk
   B) integrated organization network
   C) knowledge work system
   D) process chart

B–2. Carlsen's workspace is an open office where his workspace is behind modular panels. One of Carlsen's main responsibilities is customer relations requiring him to be on the telephone 60 percent of the day. For task support and comfort, Carlsen should

   A) have a speakerphone
   B) request that a conversation area be designed for his workspace
   C) use a headset
   D) use the organization's motelling private office telephone

B–3. An easy way to incorporate a behavioral consideration into the administrative professional's workspace is to

   A) allocate a 150 square foot workspace
   B) allow the workspace to be personalized with family pictures, plants, and artwork

C) provide access to electronic reference materials (e.g., thesaurus, intranet directories, Internet search)

D) provide an ergonomically designed chair with adjustable height, backrest, armrests, and seat pan

C. Procurement Procedures

For the organization, three major benefits are derived from focusing on purchasing (procurement) and inventory management: cost, quality, and technology. Selecting the right suppliers impacts quality and cost of any item purchased. New technology innovations and ergonomics standards can be incorporated into office processes through planned purchases of furniture, equipment, and services.

Administrative professionals need to be cognizant of the organization's procurement process. Materials management has been popular since the mid–1960s. Global procurement is changing the way many organizations handle their procurement processes. Purchasing decisions about capital equipment, services, office supplies, and repair and maintenance often require input from administrative professionals. It is important to be familiar with the procurement cycle so that administrative professionals can effectively deal with purchasing decisions.

1. *Materials Management:* In the mid-1960s, materials management became very popular. **Materials management** means that one division manages the combined related functions of purchasing, inventory control, receiving, and storage. The overall objective of materials management is procurement from an overall organizational concept (total system) rather than from individual functions or activities. Planning, managing, and controlling purchases is a major area for potential cost savings to the organization.

2. *Global Procurement:* Over the past several decades, technology and **global procurement** has made significant differences in an organization's purchasing structure. Some of these differences include the following:

   a. *Competition:* Global competitors from the Pacific Rim and Europe provide alternative purchasing options. Many of the global firms emphasize quality at a lower cost in order to capture market share.

   b. *Technology:* The current rate of technology change is unprecedented; the product life cycle is shortening. Technological innovations around the world change every few months instead of every few years.

   c. *Global networks:* The ability to coordinate purchasing activities through worldwide networks (Internet, extranets, and e-commerce) makes global purchasing an option for achieving high quality with lower costs.

3. *Types of Purchasing:* Three major categories of purchasing are capital equipment (furniture, computers, and other office equipment); services; and maintenance, repair, and operating items.

   a. *Capital equipment:* **Capital equipment** is a nonrecurring asset intended for use over a period of years. Capital equipment (assets) includes office furniture, computers, printers, copiers, and other office equipment. Large sums of money are required for capital equipment purchases. A budget line in the long-range financial plan is required for these purchases. Often, the relationship with the supplier lasts through the useful life of the equipment. Therefore, suppliers with reputable service and maintenance qualifications are very important.

b. *Services:* The procurement of services occurs throughout the organization. **Services** include equipment repair (e.g., copy machines and telephones), maintenance not performed by staff, and grounds and facilities upkeep. Often cafeteria services and business operations are contracted through outside sources. These services are typically procured at the organizational level and can be complex to manage. The administrative professional needs to be aware of contractual services and report areas that require attention to the appropriate division within the organization. An effective relationship with service suppliers must be managed to ensure quality service at the best price.

c. *Maintenance, repair, and operating supplies (MRO):* Organizations often have specialized departments responsible for technical maintenance and repairs to the computer network and peripherals (IT Division) as well as general facility maintenance and repair (Maintenance and Service Division). Ordering office supplies is often the responsibility of a procurement division within the organization. For smaller firms, an individual assumes the responsibility for purchasing **maintenance, repair, and operating supplies (MRO).**

(1) *Centralized operations:* When MRO is centralized, as it often is to control costs, the dispersion of these items throughout the organization makes monitoring inventory and supplies difficult. Often, the administrative professional manages department furniture and equipment inventory lists for the organization, with annual reports confirming that the items are in the department and in good working order.

EXAMPLE: *All furniture, microcomputers, printers, and copiers purchased for National's Human Resource Department were delivered with National's identification code affixed to the item. Shelton, Director of Human Resources, has an inventory list for all capital equipment in his department. Every October, Shelton is responsible for ensuring that the furniture and equipment on the Human Resource Department's inventory list is accurate and the equipment in good working order. Shelton's administrative assistant conducts an annual inventory review and files an inventory report with National's audit team.*

(2) *Purchasing office supplies:* Typically, administrative professionals process a purchase requisition to order office supplies. The purchase requisition is sent to the appropriate division within the organization that handles procurement. Some organizations eliminate this middle step and send purchase requisitions directly to a central supplier where orders are processed (see Section D–2-c). Weekly or monthly purchase reports are sent to the organization's procurement division. Often departments have a budget line (usually with a monetary cap) for small purchases that arise during the business day; sometimes a petty cash fund is available for small purchases.

(3) *In-house maintenance and repair:* Often an in-house maintenance and repair form is needed to request maintenance and repair that is required outside the normal daily, weekly, monthly, or quarterly in-house service. The administrative professional should ensure that capital assets are properly maintained, thus extending the life cycle of the item.

EXAMPLE: *At Kolchin's last staff meeting, several of the administrative professionals complained about delayed response on the organization's network during certain times of the day. Kolchin obtained specific information from the staff—details on what happens, length of the delayed response, and time of the day when this happens. After the meeting, Kolchin immediately completed the information technology maintenance form on the intranet reporting the department's network issues.*

4. ***Procurement Cycle:*** The procurement cycle for office furniture, equipment, and supplies includes identification of need, evaluation of supplier, selection of supplier, procurement, and continuous performance measurement and management of suppliers.

   a. *Identification of need:* It is important for administrative professionals to identify furniture, equipment, services, and office supply requirements. High-cost items such as furniture and equipment require long-range planning and budget approval. Office supplies and maintenance and repair services typically require an annual review to adjust budgets for the next fiscal year.

      (1) *Reorder point:* A **reorder point** system is one way to recognize that departmental office supplies need to be ordered. When office supplies reach a given level, the individual responsible for maintaining the supplies inventory would activate the order process. The reorder point is a trigger in a computerized inventory record system for automatically indicating the need to purchase an item.

      (2) *Purchase requisition and purchase order:* The most common way to activate the order process is to complete a purchase requisition and submit it to the division in charge of purchases. **Purchase requisitions** are internal documents often available on the organization's intranet. Once approved, the division in charge of purchases submits a **purchase order** to the supplier. If the organization eliminates the purchase requisition step, the administrative professional would send a purchase order directly to a central supplier. Important data required on both purchase requisitions and purchase orders include:

      - Date submitted
      - Description and quantity of items requested
      - Unit cost
      - Date required
      - Delivery and billing addresses
      - Requisition number (purchase order only)
      - Account to be charged (purchase requisition only)
      - Authorized signature

   b. *Evaluation of suppliers:* Most organizations have existing supplier sources for routine supplies and services. These sources need to be monitored for quality of product and price. For capital purchases (furniture and equipment), potential suppliers should be identified.

      (1) *Potential supplier list:* One way to identify potential suppliers is to develop a **potential supplier list**. The list can be generated from several sources:

      - Marketing representatives
      - Information databases
      - Trade journals

      EXAMPLE: *Mueller works for a mid-sized firm that is planning an expansion. As a member of the Building Committee, Mueller volunteered to gather information on furniture designs and suppliers. Mueller performed several Web searches, requested literature from suppliers, purchased two office and furniture design magazines, and contacted a colleague who works at an organization that had purchased new furniture last year. Mueller is culling through the information to present her findings to the Building Committee next week.*

(2) *Preferred supplier list:* A preferred supplier is one whose past performance demonstrated quality products or services at a fair price. Maintaining a **preferred supplier list** lets the organization deal with suppliers of known performance capabilities.

(3) *Evaluation criteria:* Organizations use a variety of criteria to evaluate potential suppliers. The data gathered are either informally or formally weighted to determine potential suppliers. When purchasing critical capital assets, a cross-functional purchasing team may visit a supplier's facilities. The following criteria are commonly used for evaluation:

- Past performance in product design and quality
- Management capabilities and commitment
- Technical abilities
- Costs
- History of meeting delivery schedules
- Services: product warranties, repairs

c. *Selection of supplier:* Once a final supplier list has been compiled and evaluated, the suppliers are usually categorized (i.e., ranked or grouped [superior, very good, average]). Competitive bidding and negotiation are two common methods for final supplier selection.

(1) *Competitive bidding:* Three to five of the top suppliers on the supplier list is sent a **request for proposal (RFP)**. An RFP asks the suppliers to submit a bid for a prospective purchase. The most qualified bidder should receive the purchase contract. Often bid acceptance is based on price. When technology and/or quality factors are important to the final procurement decision, organizations must be careful not to rely on price alone. It is very important for organizations to carefully design the RFP; this method is effective for items with straightforward specifications. Any ergonomics standards expected with furniture and equipment need to be stipulated in the RFP. If the lowest bidder does not receive the purchase contract, that supplier should be informed as to the reason(s).

(2) *Negotiation:* Face-to-face **negotiation** is best when specifications about the item are vague. This sometimes is the case with technology and the enterprise system. As organizations develop relationships with selected suppliers, the negotiation process should develop into a "win-win" situation. In addition to known specifications, negotiations should cover terms and conditions of the purchase, quality expectations, purchase procedures, delivery schedules, and continuous performance improvement objectives.

The supplier's ability to meet the buying organization's expectations requires a clear understanding of performance requirements. Organizations that make procurement an important function within the organization and ensure proper management of procurement receive quality products, cost-saving benefits, and satisfied employees.

d. *Procurement:* The most common method of initiating a purchase is the purchase order. Information required on the purchase order includes quantities and item description, unit cost, delivery address, billing address, and requisition number. The **requisition number** is a control number from the buying organization that links purchasing approval to an authorized individual. Many times a delivery date is important and should be included on the purchase order. Any ergonomics standards expected with furniture and equipment need to be stipulated. The purchase cycle time can be shortened through electronic data interchange (EDI).

EXAMPLE: *Abbot's purchase order form has two important notices:*

*"**IMPORTANT:** If the product or service cannot be delivered on or before the required date, notify us **immediately**."*

*"**NOTICE:** Equipment and services under this contract must comply with all applicable state and federal safety codes for places of employment, including OSHA."*

e. *Continuous performance measurement and management of suppliers:* Managing the procurement cycle is very important. Once a supplier has been identified, the most common way to manage quality is to track performance over time. A *preferred supplier list* is developed through this process. Also, it is common for MRO suppliers to have extended contracts. Organizations need to monitor the delivery and services provided by MRO suppliers to ensure quality throughout the contract timeline. Continuous measurement is necessary to identify areas requiring attention and to track supplier performance improvement over time. Without a performance measurement system, the buying organization lacks the quantitative data necessary to support future purchase decisions.

EXAMPLE: *Based on Mueller's thorough investigation into furniture designs and suppliers, the Building Committee was able to recommend RFPs be sent to four suppliers. One year later, the administrative professionals have been very positive about their ergonomically designed chairs and modular workspace furniture. No complaints about fatigue or musculoskeletal problems have arisen since the new furniture was delivered. Mueller reported this back to purchasing for their records on the supplier selected to fulfill the order.*

Evaluation feedback to the supplier is also important. While most organizations recognize the importance of notifying suppliers when a problem exists, there is little consensus about the frequency for conducting routine supplier evaluations. For many firms an evaluation is done only once a year. Regardless of the frequency of performance evaluations, evaluation and management of suppliers is very important to maintaining a quality procurement cycle.

Check Point—Section C

Directions: For each question, circle the correct answer.

C–1. What process has been popular since the 1960s for assigning purchasing, inventory control, receiving, and storage to one division to achieve total system integration?

A) Central supplier

B) Electronic data interchange (EDI)

C) Global procurement

D) Materials management

C–2. With all the technology changes over the past decade, a mid-size organization implemented a three-year replacement cycle for microcomputers and peripherals. This year the budget was approved to order 15 microcomputers, printers, and a server for the finance areas. These items come under what purchasing category?

A) Capital asset
B) Information system
C) Maintenance, repair, and operating items (MRO)
D) Services

C–3. To ensure that the organization continues to purchase only from firms who have high-quality products and services, what type of reference should the organization maintain?

A) Potential supplier list
B) Preferred supplier list
C) Request for proposal (RFP)
D) Trade database

D. Inventory and Storage

Office supplies are critical to the effective and efficient operation of the organization. However, management of these supplies often is overlooked. With the costs of storage space increasing, management of inventory is important. Depending on the size of the organization, there are alternative approaches to inventory management.

1. *Inventory Management.* Management of inventories is important to the successful operation of an office. Organizations rely on a variety of techniques to control the investment made in inventories. The more common **inventory management** approaches include: supplier-buyer partnership, electronic data interchange (EDI), inventory reviews, cross-functional teams, and an inventory record system.

   a. *Supplier-buyer partnership:* A supplier-buyer partnership supports developing a close working relationship in order to lower inventory costs and improve control. Successful partnerships are a "win-win" situation for the buyer and seller. A trusting supplier-buyer partnership is common for MRO procurements.

   b. *Electronic data interchange (EDI):* EDI provides computer-to-computer exchange of standard documents (purchase orders, invoices, payments) between two businesses. These structured documents are transmitted from one information system to another through secure networks eliminating document printing and mailing for the buyer and data input for the seller. EDI lowers transaction costs and improves the purchase-cycle time.

   c. *Inventory reviews:* Often inventory is checked on a regular basis, weekly or semimonthly. Inventory reviews force organizations to define inventory requirements. The administrative professional responsible for inventory reviews in the division should also attempt to identify causes of excess and obsolete inventory. Inventory levels that match office needs improve space utilization and can lower inventory costs for the organization. Basic considerations when conducting an inventory review include:

   • Review current inventory investment
   • Identify excess inventory items
   • Identify obsolete inventory items
   • Define possible causes for inventory problems

- Identify possible solutions to correct problems
- Work with employees to correct causes of inventory problems

d. *Cross-functional teams:* Many organizations establish cross-functional teams to control costs and standardize processes. Interorganizational procurement improves inventory control and space utilization. Lower costs are the result of buying in bulk (larger quantities) and lead to lower office supply costs. The team often maintains a preferred supplier list for the organization that allows positive supplier-buyer relationships to develop. Quality suppliers and a collaborative supplier-buyer relationship can impact the quality of products purchased and services received. Another responsibility of the cross-functional procurement team is to review and recommend new approaches and techniques for inventory management.

e. *Inventory record system:* Computerizing the inventory record system allows the organization to track actual inventory levels more closely and eliminate emergency ordering. An administrative professional could computerize the organization's inventory tracking system by developing an application using an electronic spreadsheet or a data management program.

Figure 10–1 lists the various inventory management approaches along with key benefits of each approach.

2. **Inventory Costs:** Inventory costs include the price of the item, storage costs, and costs of obsolescence. Revenue committed for these costs must be managed and controlled. The physical storing of inventory includes costs for storage space, insurance costs, and costs of maintaining the inventory.

a. *Risk:* Inventory risk includes theft, damage, spoilage, and obsolescence. Certain office items may be insured to cover loss of inventory (e.g., computer supplies).

FIGURE 10–1 Inventory Management

Approach	Key Benefits
Partnership	Supplier-buyer partnership supports working close together for greater control
Electronic data interchange (EDI)	Error-free transmission with reduction in purchase-cycle time Lower transaction costs
Inventory reviews	Forces organization to define inventory requirements Supports identification of causes of excess and obsolete inventory
Cross-functional teams for inventory reduction	Develops interorganizational support for inventory control New approaches and techniques generated
Computerized inventory record system	Closer tracking of actual inventory levels Eliminates emergency ordering

b. *Control:* When the supply storage area is located at the department level, administrative professionals need to establish a system of control. For **inventory control**, some organizations find that the honor system works. Other organizations have resorted to a locked storage area with only authorized access. The administrative professional with authorized access is responsible for keeping records of office supply distribution to individuals within the department.

c. *Full-service suppliers:* Many large organizations have consolidated the purchase of maintenance, repair, and operating supplies (MRO) with full-service suppliers. A **full-service supplier** is a single supplier for MRO items. Because of the size of the contract, the single supplier offers lower prices. Another advantage is management of just-in-time inventory by the supplier. Full-service suppliers meet the organization's office supply needs with next-day delivery, thus eliminating the need for storage space at the organization's location.

EXAMPLE: *A firm with 2,800 different MRO suppliers now deals with only four full-service suppliers. In exchange for a major contract, each selected supplier offered price reductions, 24-hour delivery on regular orders, and no paperwork (electronic data interchange (EDI) is used). When the administrative professional needs office supplies, the order form is submitted electronically to the supplier for next-day delivery.*

As organizations are dealing with the dynamics of electronic commerce, collaborative networks, and global markets and economies, the administrative professional becomes a key member of the organization's team by being knowledgeable about physical resource procurement and management.

Check Point—Section D

Directions: For each question, circle the correct answer.

D–1. In order to lower inventory costs and improve control, a supplier-buyer partnership is common for what type of purchase?

A) Capital equipment
B) Maintenance, repair, and operations
C) Office furniture
D) Services

D–2. Lower transaction costs and improvement in the purchase cycle time is achieved through

A) computerized inventory record systems

B) cross-functional teams
C) electronic data interchange (EDI)
D) inventory reviews

D–3. Lower prices, just-in-time delivery of office supplies, and reduced storage space costs are benefits an organization can achieve through a

A) computerized inventory record system
B) cross-functional team
C) full-service supplier
D) preferred supplier

For Your Review

Directions: For each question, circle the correct answer.

1. What design model uses flexible walls and furniture and open aisles to accommodate communication flow throughout the division?

    A) Bull-pen
    B) Modern office
    C) Private office
    D) Traditional

2. Strategic plans, job functions, computer requirements, and ergonomics are factors to consider when

    A) allocating workspace
    B) designing office layouts
    C) developing long-range plans for work areas
    D) procuring furniture and equipment

3. Business processes and the links between processes for a computer-based information system are graphically illustrated in a/an

    A) data flow diagram
    B) information chart
    C) layout chart
    D) process chart

4. For document routing (electronic or manual), total quality management advocates that process steps (operation) should be

    A) in the middle of the document routing process for verification and audit purposes (cross-checking)
    B) included only if the step adds value to the final document
    C) integrated with other operations to improve the overall quality of the document
    D) minimal; no more than 10 processes for each document

5. An office layout chart is used to illustrate

    A) assigned work areas for administrative professionals
    B) existing office procedures
    C) information flow resulting from a communication system
    D) the movement of a document in order to develop a workflow pattern

6. The recommended workspace allocation for an administrative professional is

    A) 70 to 100 square feet
    B) 100 to 150 square feet
    C) 150 to 200 square feet
    D) 200 to 250 square feet

7. Rutter needs to verify required workplace accommodations for employees with special needs. The best resource for obtaining this information is the

    A) Americans with Disabilities Web site
    B) Occupational Safety and Health Administration (OSHA)
    C) Quickboner Study
    D) Society of Human Resource Management

8. A survey conducted by the Society of Human Resource Management found that, in the United States, flex schedules, job sharing, and telecommuting are

    A) attractive employment options for new college graduates
    B) decreased when the economy is poor and unemployment is high
    C) encouraged by the networked enterprise
    D) typical family-friendly programs provided to working couples with children

9. To make efficient use of workspace, some organizations become partners and provide workspace, microcomputer, and support services to traveling professionals who pre-book the workspace for a specific time. This arrangement is called

A) hotelling
B) modern office design
C) modular space
D) motelling

10. When arranging the workspace, it is recommended that the display monitor be placed

A) at a left or right angle, whichever is more comfortable
B) behind sliding doors so the monitor is hidden when not in use
C) near a conversation module so the computer can be used during small-group meetings
D) on a raised platform meeting ergonomics height recommendations

11. What transcription equipment must organizations provide administrative professionals who transcribe material that has been stored on the enterprise network? A microcomputer and

A) dictation-transcription receiver
B) dictation-transcription unit
C) earphones and foot pedal
D) telephone headset and software

12. Peripheral office equipment (e.g., postage meter, folding machine) used within the division should be

A) centralized in an organization work area
B) dispersed to employees in the division who use the equipment the most
C) located in a work area central to the division
D) provided to each administrative professional who requires the use of the equipment on a regular basis.

13. Sagen needs to mail a package that weighs two pounds. Using the postage meter for stamps, the most efficient way to ensure sufficient postage is to

A) approximate the amount and increase it by one dollar
B) call the post office for the postage amount
C) go to the post office to mail the package
D) use the postal service Web site to obtain the postage amount

14. Which approach is best for ensuring that administrative professionals are satisfied with their work environment?

A) Allow the administrative professional to help design his/her workspace
B) Buy ergonomically designed furniture
C) Paint the office
D) Provide classical background music

15. McArthey takes a short break from her computer tasks and walks to the lounge. An effective way to ensure that anyone passing by her modular office cannot view the information on her monitor is to

A) have a screen saver on her microcomputer
B) place a filter over the monitor
C) shut down the computer system
D) turn the monitor so the screen faces a wall

16. For purchasing options, the Internet, extranets, and e-commerce have opened the doors for

A) cross-functional teams
B) global procurement
C) materials management
D) computerized inventory record systems

17. To control office supply costs, many organizations

A) centralize capital assets
B) centralize maintenance, repair, and operating items (MRO)
C) decentralize capital assets
D) decentralize services

18. A computerized inventory record system automatically indicates when an item needs to be purchased. What triggers this action?

    A) Inventory review
    B) Purchase requisition
    C) Reorder point
    D) Requisition number

19. The administrative professional responsible for maintaining the Marketing Department office supplies sends a supply request to a full-service supplier. What document is eliminated in this approach?

    A) Inventory record system
    B) Invoice
    C) Purchase order
    D) Purchase requisition

20. Mueller & Associates is considering new modular furniture for all offices. To identify quality sources for obtaining the type of furniture they want at the best price, Mueller & Associates should develop a

    A) potential supplier list
    B) preferred supplier list
    C) request for proposal (RFP)
    D) trade database

21. When specifications about new technology are vague, what is the best way to select the supplier to receive the purchase order?

    A) Preferred supplier list
    B) Face-to-face negotiations
    C) References from industry leaders
    D) Request for proposal (RFP)

22. The Roundhouse Dinner Theater has a control mechanism that links purchasing approval for general supplies to the appropriate section manager. The control mechanism is a

    A) computerized inventory record system
    B) purchase order number
    C) request for proposal (RFP)
    D) requisition number

23. What inventory management approach is being used when the administrative professional checks office supplies for the accounting and finance departments on a semi-monthly basis to determine if an order needs to be placed?

    A) Computerized inventory record system
    B) Cross-functional team
    C) Inventory review
    D) Partnership

24. The inventory management approach that should generate new management techniques is the

    A) computerized inventory record system
    B) cross-functional team
    C) inventory review
    D) supplier-buyer partnership

25. By offering an exclusive contract to one office supplier, Marquip Interiors received a 10 percent reduction in price and 24-hour delivery on orders. The office supplier is referred to as a

    A) continuous supplier
    B) full-service supplier
    C) partner
    D) preferred supplier

Solutions

Solutions to Check Point—Section A

Answer	Refer to:
A–1. (B)	[Overview, A and A-3-b (3)]
A–2. (D)	[A-2-a (1)]
A–3. (A)	[A-3-b (4)]

Solutions to Check Point—Section B

Answer	Refer to:
B–1. (B)	[B-1-c]
B–2. (C)	[B-2-a (1) (b), Chapter 3 B-5-g and Chapter 11 A-2-b (2)]
B–3. (B)	[B-3-b]

Solutions to Check Point—Section C

Answer	Refer to:
C–1. (D)	[C-1]
C–2. (A)	[C-3-a]
C–3. (B)	[C-4-b (2)]

Solutions to Check Point—Section D

Answer	*Refer to:*
D–1. (B)	[D-1-a]
D–2. (C)	[D-1-b]
D–3. (C)	[D-2-c]

Solutions to For Your Review

Answer	*Refer to:*
1. (B)	[A and A-3-b (2)]
2. (C)	[A-1]
3. (A)	[A-2-a (1) (a)]
4. (B)	[A-2-a (1) (a)]
5. (D)	[A-2-a (1) (b)]
6. (A)	[A-2-a (2)]
7. (A)	[A-2-a (4)]
8. (B)	[A-3]
9. (A)	[A-3-b (4) (a)]
10. (D)	[B-2-a (1) (a) and B-2-b (4)]
11. (C)	[B-2-a (1) (c)]
12. (C)	[B-2-a (1) (d)]
13. (D)	[B-2-a (4)]
14. (A)	[B-2-b (2)]
15. (A)	[B-2-c (3)]
16. (B)	[C-2]
17. (B)	[C-3-c (1)]
18. (C)	[C-4-a (1)]
19. (D)	[C-4-a (2)]
20. (A)	[C-4-b (1)]

21. (B)   [C-4-c (2)]

22. (D)   [C-4-d]

23. (C)   [D-1-c]

24. (B)   [D-1-d]

25. (B)   [D-2-c]

Chapter 11

Ergonomics

OVERVIEW

With the proliferation of computer usage by all business professionals, designing office environments for comfort, efficiency, and convenience is very important. Since the greatest cost of the work environment is the employee's salary, that person's comfort and productivity are important to the organization's success. **Ergonomics** is the scientific study of the relationship of employees to their physical environment, including the workspace and the tools that enhance the workspace. One of the basic goals of computer-based information systems is increased productivity. An ergonomic environment is an essential element in promoting and enhancing office productivity. The psychological, physiological, sociological, and interpersonal communication bases for ergonomics are presented to give administrative professionals a more thorough understanding of the basic theory of ergonomics in the workplace.

While working with technology, administrative professionals can experience repetitive-strain, visual, musculoskeletal, emotional, and psychosocial problems. For a number of years, researchers and medical experts have been concerned about the presence of possible health and work hazards in the office. Environmental and space designs enable administrators to address these concerns and provide working conditions that lead to increased productivity while possible hazardous conditions are diminished.

As the result of consideration for specific ergonomics factors, designers of office furniture and equipment are applying new approaches to workspace design and layout. Office personnel respond to the technological environment in the office both positively and negatively, depending on management's willingness to create an environment that takes ergonomics factors into consideration.

KEY TERMS

Absorption, 276	Biomechanics, 267	Early adapter, 265
Ambient lighting, 275	Carpal tunnel syndrome, 271	Emotional disturbance, 272
Anthropometry, 267	Decibel, 276	Ergonomics, 263

A. Rationale for Ergonomic Environments

The scientific study of the relationship of workers to their physical environment, including workspace and the technology being used, is *ergonomics*. Special attention to the worker-technology interface is important so that work and working conditions are adapted to give administrative professionals the best possible environment for performing their jobs. The administrative professional's level of productivity and morale are extremely important in being able to perform specific job tasks. Any element—whether psychological, physiological, sociological, or analytical in nature—that affects individual attitudes and performance is a part of ergonomics.

1. *Psychological Basis for Ergonomics:* Business professionals react more favorably toward their work when they realize that changes made in the physical environment will contribute to their own personal comfort and benefit. Psychological factors, in turn, affect the employees' behaviors and attitudes.

    a. *Rationale for technology:* Business professionals need to understand the reasons for automating specific office processes. It is very important that open lines of communication flow in all directions—from the top down, from the bottom up, and laterally.

    b. *Functionality for users:* The methods used to implement office systems in a useful, functional manner will affect administrative professionals' feelings about technology. They must perceive that work areas and individual workspace are designed for the effective performance of office tasks. However, the social needs of individuals must also be met and the causes of stress minimized.

    c. *Personnel development:* There continues to be an increasing requirement for information systems training and/or retraining addressing general purpose application software, groupware, the enterprise network, the Internet, and other emerging hardware and software technologies. Business professionals must be informed about the availability of technical or systems training/retraining applicable to their daily tasks and responsibilities.

    d. *Challenge:* In a computer-based information environment, the administrative professional who enjoys trying innovative systems and procedures will indeed face the challenge of adapting technology to tasks formerly completed through manual means.

        EXAMPLE: *Using a word processing program can be a new learning experience every day. Initially, most administrative professionals learn enough about the program to perform routine applications. As familiarity with the word processing program increases, most administrative professionals learn new and advanced features of this productivity tool applicable to their office tasks. Using the program help menu, seeking advice from support groups, and attending training seminars assist them in learning new word processing functions and applications.*

e. *Morale booster:* Improvement of office morale occurs when administrative professionals have some voice in establishing new processes, revising procedures, or selecting new office equipment. Change within the organization can be viewed in a positive way and as a morale booster.

f. *Employee attitude toward environment:* Sometimes employees openly express positive or negative attitudes toward their work and their workplace to co-workers or others around them. These attitudes may also be a reflection of the individual's work ethics or ability to deal with change.

g. *Employee reaction to change:* Business professionals typically exhibit different reactions to change. Employees may be willing to change, wait for others to change first, or resist change.

   (1) *Early adapter:* A person who is quick to change, study a new system, and try to implement it is an **early adapter.** Such a person is seen as a pioneer, one of the first to become familiar with the new system and to demonstrate to others its usefulness. This person is frequently seen as a trainer or technical support group leader—someone who keeps up to date with the technology and is anxious to show and help others.

   (2) *Late adapter:* A person who waits for others to implement a new system, then tries to "catch up" with the technology, is referred to as a **late adapter.** This person wants to be shown the success of the system before trying it but does see value to change. The late adapter has a difficult time keeping up to date with technology and is often considered "behind the times." Administrative professionals need to recognize late adapters and make sure they receive appropriate support.

   (3) *Nonadapter:* The person who prefers the status quo and does not typically accept change easily may resist and also encourage others to resist change. Typically, **nonadapters** begin to feel job-related stress that is negative.

h. *Motivation:* Administrators need to create a positive environment—one that will motivate business professionals to perform assigned functions. Some people find changes in office systems and procedures to be challenging experiences; the challenge becomes a motivator for these individuals. Others are more secure when processes are maintained and remain the same. Office leaders need to communicate with late adapters and nonadapters the benefits of any changes and guide and motivate these employees to make positive use of new technologies and opportunities. The motivated person is better able to face change than one who hesitates or is unwilling to try anything new or different.

2. ***Physiological Basis for Ergonomics:*** The physical structures within the office must be geared to the physical needs of the human anatomy.

a. *Environmental factors:* Factors such as furniture, lighting, atmospheric conditions, sound, and work area design constitute primary environmental factors.

   (1) *Workspace furniture and accessories:* Workspace with surfaces and a chair sized and shaped to accommodate the employee is very important in minimizing

fatigue and maximizing functionality and comfort. The basic premise is that business professionals who use ergonomically designed furniture personalized for their use will be able to produce higher quality work than those who use more traditionally designed office furniture.

EXAMPLES:

Posture chairs (with adjustments for backrest, armrests, and seat pan) are contoured to the human anatomy to provide better support for the body.

Work surfaces that provide a work arc permit the administrative professional to work easily from the left to the right or in the center of the workstation.

Proper positioning and adjusting display monitors and input materials for comfortable viewing can lessen possible eyestrain, repetitive strain injury (RSI), or musculoskeletal problems.

(2) *Lighting:* Types of lighting as well as placement of lighting contribute to employee comfort (see Section C-1).

EXAMPLE: *A medical office professional transcribing from recorded dictation may require task lighting that will permit easy viewing of soft copy as it is being produced. Ceiling fixtures may not provide adequate task lighting.*

(3) *Atmospheric conditions:* Controlled temperature, ventilation, and a regulated humidity level make the office pleasant and comfortable for employees. Enforcement of nonsmoking regulations has become essential in the business environment.

EXAMPLE: *Smoking at one's workspace is typically not permitted because of irritation to other office personnel and air pollution. Designated smoking areas are usually provided in employee lounges, eating areas, or outside. Office personnel who eat or smoke while working with magnetic media (disks and cartridges) may cause damage to the media.*

(4) *Office noise:* People react to noise or sound favorably or unfavorably, depending on the intensity of the sound (see Section C-3-c).

EXAMPLES:

Piped-in music may be relaxing and soothing, whereas noise caused by talking may be extremely distracting to someone who is concentrating on writing a detailed report.

Some firms have created quiet work areas, sometimes called "think tanks," where employees have uninterrupted time for creating and developing their ideas into special projects.

Many firms permit employees to work at home to ensure uninterrupted, productive time while working on special projects. Telecommuters work from their home the majority of the time.

(5) *Workspace preferred by employees:* Business professionals are affected by the amount and type of workspace provided for them.

EXAMPLES:

For claustrophobic reasons, some office personnel require a larger workspace.

Some administrative professionals prefer the open office, whereas others continue to prefer private offices that help eliminate distractions.

b. *Physiology of the worker:* Physiological factors are also important to meet the comfort needs of the worker.

(1) *The worker's body structure:* Physical dimensions, such as height or weight, must be considered in selecting appropriate furniture and technology components for work areas. **Anthropometry** is the study of human body measurements in order to design furniture (sizes, heights, and shapes) accurately scaled to the dimensions of workers' bodies. See *Workspace Design* (B-2-b) for recommendations regarding furniture and microcomputer adjustments for physical fit and comfort.

EXAMPLE: *Desks can be designed so an administrative professional can easily adjust the work surface to various positions. Most modular work surfaces have continuous adjustments for tilting, raising, and lowering work surfaces.*

(2) *Physical movement demanded of workers:* Work areas are being designed to minimize the strain of performing physical work, reduce human error, and increase efficiency. The study of the musculoskeletal effort of human beings is known as **biomechanics.**

EXAMPLES:

Placement of the telephone in the workspace within easy reach to the left or right ensures functionality. If the telephone and computer are frequently used at the same time, the administrative professional should consider using a telephone headset. Cradling the telephone between the head and shoulder causes muscle strain.

Keyboards can have palm or wrist rests at the front of the keyboard so users are able to position hands near the keyboard but not anchor the hand or wrist directly on the keyboard.

Display monitors have swivel bases so the monitor can be rotated easily to different positions. Slight changes during the day reduce fatigue and strain.

3. *Sociological Basis for Ergonomics:* Sociology is the study of human cultures, social relationships, and underlying principles of humans functioning in society. In the office environment, teams are becoming extremely important to the smooth functioning of the office. As people work, they become part of a social group. Workgroup clusters, teamwork, the facilitation of social communication, and the need for worker specialization are affected by the ergonomic nature of the office environment.

a. *Establishment of workgroup clusters:* Office systems require "clusters" of people to function cooperatively and effectively.

EXAMPLES:

The Technology Center requires the joint efforts of the administrator and all technical personnel. In addition, systems analysts have the responsibility of working with the functional areas and communicating information back to the Technology Center regarding functional requirements and needs.

The Information Processing Center in a large medical facility faces similar requirements. To prepare documents and reports for doctors, the information processing "cluster" must be designed to provide prompt and accurate service in order to meet deadlines.

b. *Emphasis on teamwork:* The success of group activities depends on a team effort, with each member of the team willing to take the lead in certain phases of a project and to assist with other tasks as needed. Groupware includes all software for information sharing, e-meetings, e-scheduling, and electronic project development and management.

   EXAMPLE: *The BIG Corporation is using groupware to facilitate new product development by a "Think Tank Team." Smythe, the Think Tank leader, recognizes that groupware is an important tool in enhancing internal as well as external communication to the team and project management. The online tools are available to team members 24/7 allowing them to easily communicate innovative ideas, check deadlines, and schedule face-to-face sessions when required. Smythe encourages and rewards team members who effectively use the groupware tools that support the team's efforts.*

c. *Worker specialization:* New computer technologies may require some business personnel to become specialized in applications such as document processing, financial analysis, or microcomputer productivity applications while other personnel may function in a more general capacity.

d. *Individual need for territoriality:* In the office environment, an administrative professional typically functions within boundaries established as personal workspace. An administrative professional may choose either privacy (closed design) or involvement (open design) with other business professionals, depending on the confidential nature of the work to be performed. To perform effectively on the job, an administrative professional needs "ownership" of a particular workspace.

e. *Qualified applicants:* Men and women who apply for office positions must possess specific entry-level skills to function effectively in these positions.

   EXAMPLE: *Keyboarding and other digital input skills, language, human relations, and computer capabilities are competencies considered essential information processing skills for administrative professional positions. Firms use tests as well as interviews to measure these skills prior to employment. Training programs have been established in many organizations to allow employees with potential to further develop essential skills for their present or future positions.*

f. *Career development:* People need to know that there are opportunities for advancement through promotion or lateral transfer. The clustering (or leveling) of work groups gives the impression of a hierarchy of positions to which workers may aspire.

4. ***Communication Theory as a Basis for Ergonomics:*** The office environment must be conducive to the type of communication required (written, oral, nonverbal, face-to-face, or electronic) to perform office tasks quickly, accurately, and efficiently. The physical structure of the office will either facilitate or hinder communication.

   a. *Types of communications:* Many office procedures still depend on written and face-to-face communication. More sophisticated telephone communication systems emphasize the importance of effective interpersonal communication. Information is also processed and transmitted electronically through networks using electronic mail, intranets, extranets, and the Internet. The type of communication system utilized depends on availability, speed of transmission, the procedures used, and the value placed on the information.

b. *Use of computer-based information systems:* Communication processes utilizing a variety of electronic storage and networks for transmission are essential components of today's office environment. People around the world receive and transmit information with one another through global networks. Electronic transmission of information internally within the firm or externally to other organizations improves the decision-making process within an organization.

EXAMPLE:

Instead of requiring the sales director to travel to the four branch offices four times a year, Painters & Associates had an Internet Relay Chat room created through their service provider. The chat room supports private electronic conferencing for two or more people. With proper enhancements (cameras and speakers at each site), conference participants can hear and see one another.

Another electronic alternative for the visual conference between the four branch offices is teleconferencing. To conduct a teleconference, Painters & Associates would have to design or rent an electronic meeting room equipped with conferencing technology.

Because it is important for branch personnel to interface with corporate personnel, Painters & Associates requires one of the quarterly meetings to be scheduled in the corporate headquarters conference room.

5. ***Other Ergonomic Concerns:*** Specific work functions and workflow processes are affected by the ergonomics of the workplace.

a. *Work functions:* An analysis of the steps and procedures in each office task, as well as clusters of related tasks, will reveal the people-technology interface required during the work process.

(1) *Individual office tasks:* Ergonomically, a specific office task must be analyzed to see whether there are ways to better relate the task to the technology used so that the individual employee will be able to work more comfortably and effectively. Ergonomics focuses on the comfort and convenience of the physical arrangement of the office and the appropriateness of hardware, software, and other technology used to perform a particular task.

EXAMPLE: *Answering every incoming telephone call is very important for The Rug Place, and performance reports indicate a large number of potential customers call every day for information. The difficulty McCoy, the owner, had was making sure every call was answered promptly and courteously by the Customer Service Center. A voice-mail system solved the problem. Any call not answered by the third ring transfers the caller to a menu allowing the caller to record a detailed message for a callback, stay on the line for the next available customer assistant, or be transferred to another department.*

(2) *Clusters of related office tasks:* Sometimes groups of related tasks need to be analyzed to determine the best ergonomics arrangement of office space and to ensure proper utilization of office furniture and electronic systems to enhance work performance. Within many organizations, information processing, reproduction, and communications centers have been established for the performance of specific clusters of related tasks.

EXAMPLE: *Rybak, a communications specialist, supervises the telecommunications division for Satellite Systems, Inc. For Rybak and the three communications staff members to function more effectively, a Communications Center was established for the communications team. In addition, the local area network for shared data/information and communication (e-mail) was enhanced with an intranet where discussion boards, procedures, and upcoming activities are communicated throughout the firm. The enhanced local area network replaces four separate LANs that were in operation for several years. Less physical space was required for the new equipment.*

(3) *Work logs:* Logging actual time spent in performing office tasks can provide insight into time requirements (in hours and minutes) as well as work allocation each day.

EXAMPLE: *If Harrison keeps a log for one week of the time required to update the financial records for the transaction processing system each day, he should be able to give his supervisor a more accurate estimate of the continuous time periods that he must sit at the computer for this task. Personal comfort at the workstation may necessitate a short rest period every two to three hours, or the firm may decide to go to source data automation and retrain Harrison for new responsibilities. Harrison should be involved in the analysis of the financial input system focusing on the use of electronic equipment for any of the tasks and for better acceptance of any changes.*

b.   *Workflow:* Following the path of a business document through the office helps ensure that there is no delay in transmitting the document or the information it contains from one location to another. Accurate preparation and speedy distribution of documents are vital. In addition, the physical effort exerted by people in moving documents to different work areas is an important consideration. Electronic transmission of documents improves transaction accuracy and processing/distribution time. An enterprise system addresses compatibility issues of hardware and software throughout the organization.

Check Point—Section A

Directions: For each question, circle the correct answer.

A–1.   As training on the new computer-based information system began, one administrative professional remarked, "This appears to be an easy system to learn; I can see benefits to office efficiency already." Which term best characterizes the administrative professional?

A)   Decision maker
B)   Early adapter
C)   Late adapter
D)   Nonadapter

A–2.   Work-group clusters, teamwork, and the facilitation of communication are prevalent in the office environment. These factors are addressed by the

A)   physiological basis of ergonomics
B)   psychological basis of ergonomics
C)   sociological basis of ergonomics
D)   technical basis of ergonomics

A–3.   The office must be conducive to the type of communication required. In a computer-based information environment

A)   chat rooms provide a central location where administrative professionals take breaks and meet informally

B) face-to-face interaction between office professionals is not required

C) information can be transmitted to other locations very quickly

D) nonverbal communication is very important

B. Understanding Health Hazards

More than 175 million Americans are estimated to work at least part of the day using a computer keyboard, pointing device, and monitor as part of their daily routine. The almost constant use of monitors, keyboards, and pointing devices by executives, managers, and administrative professionals is a concern to manufacturers, vendors, professional associations, and even government agencies conducting research to validate employee concerns and complaints. Employees have been concerned about the possibility of health problems as well as personal discomfort from prolonged user interface with a keyboard, pointing devices, a display monitor, and input (source) material.

1. ***Employee Health Concerns and Complaints:*** Employee health complaints tend to focus on repetitive-strain injuries, visual dysfunction, musculoskeletal problems, emotional disturbances, and psychosocial disturbances. Research efforts have centered on possible causes of employee complaints and discomfort and whether the display monitor may be a cause or an influential factor.

   a. *Repetitive-strain (repetitive-motion) injury or illness (RSI):* The U.S. Department of Labor reports that repetitive-strain or repetitive-motion injuries or illnesses can be a health danger in the workplace and perhaps the greatest single cause of occupational illness. **Repetitive-strain injuries** result from tasks that require continuous repetitive motion. Symptoms include stiff or sore wrists, numbness, loss of strength in arms or hands, or finger cramps while working. Administrative professionals should be attentive to early signs and seek medical advice.

   b. *Visual dysfunction:* Employees who have experienced computer vision syndrome or temporary visual distress (eye irritation, visual fatigue, blurred vision, headaches, and chronic disorders) raise the question as to whether the use of the display monitor is causing the **visual dysfunction** to occur. Discomfort resulting from visual distress appears to be caused by the following:

      • Poor design of computer monitors

      • Poor design of the physical environment of the office

      • Long intensive work intervals without adequate rest periods

      Research indicates that the use of the display monitor does not in and of itself cause chronic visual disorders or cause the vision of computer users to deteriorate faster than the vision of workers in other jobs. A German study found that users of display monitors perform up to 33,000 head or eye movements a day.

   c. *Musculoskeletal problems:* Some employees complain about pain or discomfort occurring in various body parts (neck, back, shoulders, arms, and fingers) as they work. Positioning of a keyboard at an appropriate height and distance is essential to avoid carpal tunnel syndrome and tendinitis. **Carpal tunnel syndrome** is the compression of a nerve leading into the wrist that results in debilitating pain and muscle weakness. **Tendinitis** is the inflammation of muscles at the points where they insert into the bones of the shoulders, arms, and wrists. Ergonomically designed display monitors, keyboards, pointing devices, furniture, and other work area components enable the administrative professional to assume proper posture while entering information at the computer. Such features as a specially designed keyboard and pointing devices, an adjustable display monitor, a variable-height work surface, and an adjustable posture chair seem to relieve most **musculoskeletal problems** that users may experience.

d. *Emotional disturbances:* Two types of **emotional disturbances,** mood disturbances and psychosomatic disorders, may affect employees' abilities to adequately perform tasks.

   (1) *Mood disturbances:* Anger, frustration, irritability, anxiety, and depression are some of the typical **mood disturbances** that employees experience. Executives and administrative professionals should be cognizant to minimize these disturbances so they do not disrupt others in the workplace.

   (2) *Psychosomatic disorders:* Some computer users have been afflicted with gastrointestinal disturbances, muscle tension, psychic tension, heart palpitations, and frequent perspiration. These ailments may be the result of **psychosomatic disorders.**

e. *Psychosocial disturbances:* Another area of employee concern focuses on specific problems related to the work environment. Stress related to the job, workload, pace of work, and poor or inadequate supervision have been linked to some chronic ailments. These work environment concerns are referred to as **psychosocial disturbances.** Although job-related psychosocial stress has been linked to some chronic ailments, these problems also arise from organizational, social, and job design changes related to new technologies in the workplace. Such disturbances can be minimized through training prior to implementation of new office systems.

2. ***Environmental and Workspace Design:*** Research into environmental and workspace design is influencing ergonomic office systems.

a. *Environmental design:* Screen glare, possible radiation emission from CRT monitors, temperature, and humidity are environmental factors that are continually being researched.

   (1) *Screen glare:* The question of glare on the screen is under constant surveillance by systems manufacturers. Vision complaints appear to be well founded if glare and contrast problems are not controlled. Some research indicates that there is a correlation between the measured intensity of glare reflections and annoyance experienced by computer users that can possibly result in visual problems. However, research has not as yet established definite relationships between the luminance of reflections and visual impairment.

   EXAMPLE:

   Some modifications can be made to a screen if glare is a problem. One of the most effective ways to deal with glare is to install a filter over the screen to absorb incoming light rays and reduce the amount of reflection from the screen's surface.

   Other alternatives for glare control include:

   • *Install a hood over the screen to block the screen from reflections*

- *Incorporate task lighting into the workspace*
- *Install window blinds that can be adjusted*

(2) *Radiation emission:* The National Institute for Occupational Safety and Health (NIOSH) research has been on potential radiation emission hazards. These studies, as well as those of the Food and Drug Administration (FDA), investigated the amount of radiation emitting from CRT display monitors. Researchers report that the CRT monitors emitted little or no harmful radiation under normal operating conditions. The emissions that were detected were well below any national and international standards. However, there remain questions of linkage with cancer and other illnesses. Doctors have cautioned pregnant office employees to avoid extensive use of CRT monitors because of the possibility of a miscarriage or harm to a fetus.

b. *Workspace design:* The type and nature of workspace adjustments will enable proper physical positioning of the person in relation to the keyboard, pointing device, display monitor, and input (source) materials. Figure 11–1 shows the primary factors and distances to be considered in designing workspace to meet physical comfort requirements. Distances in the display monitor triangle (eyes to screen to source materials) should be as short as possible.

By taking three measurements [(1) (a), (b), and (c)], administrative professionals can determine the correct chair height, keyboard height, and monitor position.

(1) *Three measurements:* The administrative professional should ask a colleague to assist in taking the following three measurements.

(a) *Knee height:* Wearing shoes regularly worn to the office, sit on the work surface so the edge of the surface touches the backs of the knees. Form a 90-degree angle with the legs. Have a colleague measure from the crease behind the knee to the bottom of the heel.

FIGURE 11–1   Ergonomic Workspace Layout

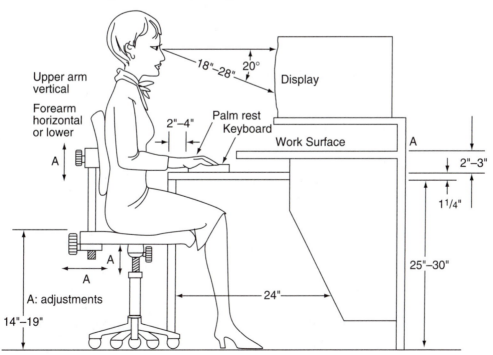

(b) *Elbow height:* While sitting on the work surface, have a colleague measure from the work surface to the tip of the elbow.

(c) *Eye height:* While sitting on the work surface, have a colleague measure from the work surface to eye height.

2. *Adjustment of chair, keyboard, and monitor:* Using the three measurements, the administrative professional's chair, keyboard, and monitor can be adjusted for a more ergonomically desirable position.

(a) *Chair:* Set the height of the seat pan to knee height [measurement B-2-b (1) (a)]. If the seat pan drops when the administrative professional sits down, raise the seat pan to compensate for the height change. If the seat pan is adjusted for a more comfortable angle and the tilt changes the height, adjust the height to the correct measurement [B-2-b (1) (a)].

(b) *Keyboard:* The keyboard home row height is the knee height *plus* elbow height [(B-2-b (1) (a) *plus* B-2-b (1) (b)]. If the keyboard is not adjustable, raise or lower the seat pan so that the difference in height between the seat pan and the keyboard is equal to elbow height [B-2-b (1) (b)]. A footrest should be added if the seat pan adjustment is too great.

(c) *Monitor:* Raise or lower the monitor so the top of the screen is at or slightly below eye level. This height should be approximately equal to knee height *plus* eye height [B-2-b (1) (a) *plus* B-2-b (1) (c)]. Position the monitor 18 inches to 28 inches away from the eyes.

3. ***Business Research into Productivity:*** National surveys sponsored by Steelcase, Inc., indicate that employee comfort in the office directly affects office productivity. Proper humidity and temperature, comfortable chairs, adequate lighting, and worker privacy were identified as having the most impact. Office productivity also increases when training is provided for using new technology (hardware and software).

Check Point—Section B

Directions: For each question, circle the correct answer.

B–1. Jacobs uses a desktop PC three to four hours a day. For the past two weeks, she has been experiencing frequent headaches and blurred vision. During an eye examination, Jacobs remarked, "I've never had this before. The display monitor I'm using must be causing the trouble." The doctor who examines Jacobs' eyes is aware of the research on the use of display monitors. An appropriate response from the doctor would be

A) "Besides looking at the terminal design, we need to also evaluate other physical factors."

B) "I recommend you limit using the display monitor to no more than two hours during the day to eliminate your problem."

C) "You're right. You really should ask for a transfer to a job that doesn't require you to use a display monitor."

D) "You are suffering from psychosocial problems from overuse of a display monitor."

B–2. One of the administrators whom Corirossi works for is in the habit of presenting "crisis work." Today it was an agenda to be sent to 25 committee members in the afternoon mail. The usual comment is "With your computer system, this job shouldn't take long." Corirossi experiences stress along with frequent headaches and nervousness. Typically, these are symptoms of

A) emotional disturbances
B) musculoskeletal problems
C) psychosocial disturbances
D) psychosomatic disorders

B–3. The administrative professional needs to ensure that an ergonomically designed workspace include a

A) display monitor at a left- or right-side angle to avoid glare
B) fixed position for the display monitor so it is secure
C) palm rest keyboard that is detachable so it can be positioned at the proper distance
D) work surface level with the keyboard for ease in working with task materials

C. Environmental Factors

Office design involves lighting, color, sound, air, surfaces, static electricity, power, security, and energy conservation as some of the external environmental factors that affect the administrative professional physically and psychologically.

1. *Lighting:* Primary considerations in analyzing lighting systems include the quantity of light present (foot-candles), brightness (footlamberts), contrast light reflectance, absence of glare, and uniformity. A **foot-candle** is the amount of light produced by a standard candle at a distance of 1 foot. A **footlambert** is a measure of brightness; it is a unit of measure approximating 1 footcandle of light transmitted or reflected.

   a. *Task lighting:* **Task lighting** is direct light that illuminates the work surface.

   b. *Ambient lighting:* Indirect light that illuminates the area surrounding the work surface is called **ambient lighting.**

   c. *Natural daylight:* Even though natural daylight is an efficient lighting source, alternative lighting systems must still be available.

   d. *Fluorescent lighting:* The most commonly used light source in office buildings is **fluorescent lighting;** its illumination resembles natural light.

   e. *Incandescent lighting:* Although **incandescent lighting** with filament bulbs tends to be less expensive, this type of lighting can produce more glare and shadowing on work surfaces.

      Many organizations are installing automatic light control systems as part of their energy conservation programs. These systems turn lights on in areas when in use and turn lights off when the areas are no longer in use.

2. *Color Conditioning:* The effect of color on the performance of people has been studied extensively. Specific colors cause people to react emotionally to the physical office environment.

EXAMPLES:

Color	*Observed Effect*
Red	*Heat, action, excitement*
Orange and yellow	*Warmth, cheerfulness*

Blue, green, and violet   Coolness, calmness
Purple   Dignity

Color and light are used together to produce varying effects. Dark colors used for wall coverings absorb most of the light falling on them, making the room appear to be dimly lit. Walls or panels of a dark or bright color can make a room or work area seem smaller than it really is. Pale colors on walls or panels will reflect light, making the work area appear brighter and larger than it really is. Employees tend to feel more relaxed in rooms that have some variation in color and light.

3. **Sound Control:** Another environmental consideration is the noise level in an office. Concern for sound control influences administrators to make use of materials that will absorb, reflect, or isolate sounds.

   a. *Absorption:* The engulfing of sound waves by environmental materials is called **absorption.**

   b. *Reflection:* The bouncing of sound waves off a material and back into space is known as **reflection.**

   c. *Isolation:* The prevention of sound waves from passing through environmental materials is referred to as **isolation.**

   The **decibel** is the unit measure of the intensity of sound. One decibel is the faintest sound that can be detected by the human ear.

   EXAMPLE: *Office noises range in intensity from 20 to 90 decibels, with 50 decibels being average for an office.* **Masking,** *also called white noise or white sound, refers to the use of a low-level, nondisturbing background noise to blend in with regular office noise, eliminating the "silent" sound (or total lack of sound) or covering distracting noise. Low-level background music is commonly used for masking.*

4. **Condition of Air:** The physical atmosphere of the office directly affects an administrative professional's productivity. Air temperature, air conditioning, humidity control, heating, and ventilation all affect the employees' comfort in the office. Among possible office hazards, indoor air pollution may be the most disturbing.

   a. *Sick buildings:* Although employees may not be able to see, smell, or feel the molecules of polluted air, sick buildings harbor dangerous pathogens. A **sick building** is infected with microorganisms (molds, bacteria, and viruses) elevated to levels that can make employees sick. Buildings with poor ventilation or ones that are airtight run the greatest risk of becoming a sick building.

   b. *Symptoms:* Sick building syndrome is recognized as a serious health risk. Symptoms include:

   - Irritation to the eyes, nose, and throat
   - Dizziness, nausea
   - Headaches
   - Chronic fatigue
   - Coughing, sneezing
   - Sinus congestion
   - Dry skin, skin rashes
   - Wellness when away from the building

It is important to realize that each of these symptoms may also be caused by other environmental or psychosocial factors.

c. *Corrective actions:* Air contaminants are living organisms (or reproductive parts of organisms) and can only be stopped by eliminating the conditions that enable them to grow. Corrective actions include the following:

- Clean contaminated areas
- Remove contaminants (e.g., moldy carpets, water-damaged ceiling tiles)
- Enhance or replace air filters on heating and cooling systems
- Provide room air cleaners for contaminated workspaces
- Remove furniture that emits formaldehyde fumes
- Enhance work areas and workspaces with plants that do not aggravate allergic conditions

5. **Surface Textures, Shapes, and Arrangements:** The versatility of office arrangements depends on the use of modular walls and furniture systems with textures, shapes, and arrangements that enable work areas to be comfortable and versatile.

a. *Movable partitions:* Available in a variety of shapes and sizes, movable partitions can be matched to suit a variety of needs. These panels can be assembled, disassembled, and rearranged easily with a minimum of effort and cost. Additional partitions can be added to existing arrangements. Acoustical control (sound control) provided by the panels depends on the degree to which the panel's material substance is able to absorb sound.

b. *Work surfaces:* Shapes and arrangements of work surfaces affect the ability of the administrative professional to produce high-quality work. Rather than seeing a desk surface of only one level (e.g., 30 by 60 inches), modular adjustable work surfaces are common in workspace design. The work surface may contain one level for keyboard and mouse, another for display monitor, and a third level for copy. It is important that sufficient copy space for materials and a document holder be incorporated into the design. Some document holders affix to the wall or computer so copy material can be held higher than desk level providing a better viewing angle for the administrative professional.

c. *Seating:* Comfort seating, with adjustments for raising or lowering the seat pan and raising, lowering, or tilting the backrest and armrests, satisfies employee needs. Figure 11–1 shows the various dimensions that affect seating in the office workspace. As a result of the efforts of the Business and Institutional Furniture Manufacturers' Association (BIFMA), the American National Standards Institute (ANSI) has established a standard for evaluating the safety, durability, and structural adequacy of general office chairs.

6. **Control of Static Electricity:** Electronically stored data can be erased if someone walks by and transmits static electricity. When two materials that have been in physical contact are separated, static electricity occurs. The amount of static charge generated depends on the surface of the materials, the amount of contact, the amount of rubbing, and the humidity.

EXAMPLE: *Carpeting, clothing, or furniture are common sources of static electricity. Contact between shoes and a floor covering creates static electricity.*

a. *Static on a person's body:* Static can be dissipated by touching a static dissipative table mat or printer cushion before touching the equipment.

b. *Static created from walking across a floor:* Several alternatives for dissipating static from the floor surface include the following:

- A floor covering of antistatic material limits the amount of floor-generated static

- A film treatment applied to carpet or tile floors generates only a very low static charge

- Antistatic mats (carpet or plastic) in areas immediately surrounding the sensitive equipment prevents the creation of static

7. *Power Sources:* An extremely important environmental factor is the power source(s) available for the electronic work to be performed in a given work area. Of course, it is essential that there be adequate power for whatever electronic operations are to be carried on in the work area so circuits will not be overloaded. Electrical power outages or electrical spikes can be a problem to the electronic workspace. Surge protectors help diminish the damage that electrical spikes can cause. In mission-critical areas, organizations install backup generators to ensure continuous electrical power to the area.

During a power outage, if the data have already been stored on a secondary storage medium (hard disk, disk, or disc), there is no problem; data already stored are not lost. However, if a power outage occurs as data are being entered, the data will be lost from the primary memory (RAM) of a computer-based information system. Administrative professionals need to use the *Save command* frequently while creating or revising documents.

8. *Security Control:* The employment of security personnel, the use of magnetic access cards and biometric controls, and television monitoring devices are security control measures used to secure the physical office environment. Although these new technologies are available, the password continues to be the most common security measure for authorized access to information on a computer-based system.

9. *Energy Conservation:* Many offices are establishing energy conservation programs monitored by computers and technicians in an attempt to conserve the amount of energy available for electricity, air conditioning, humidity control, and heating needed in specific areas of the entire office structure.

EXAMPLE: *Smart Systems was sponsoring a seminar in the auditorium at 10 A.M. To ensure comfort, the air conditioning automatically turned on at 9 A.M. and the lights at 9:45 A.M. After the room was cleared at the conclusion of the seminar, the lights were automatically turned off and the air conditioning lowered to a maintenance level. Smart Systems has decreased energy costs because of the automatic energy conservation system.*

10. *Employee Response to Environment:* Employees may exhibit positive or negative feelings toward the physical office environment as specific ergonomics factors affect their comfort and efficiency. The U.S. National Institute of Occupational Safety and Health and the Labour Canada Task Force on Micro-Electronics and Employment recommend that business policies and procedures be modified in the following ways to accommodate the needs of business professionals who work for extended periods of time at display monitors.

a. *Daily time limit for display monitor operation:* The maximum amount of time for a person to use the display monitor should not exceed five hours per day. To give the eyes a break, look away from the screen every 15 minutes.

b. *Rest periods:* At least once every hour, business professionals should get out of their desk chair and move around. Every two hours, a 15-minute break should be taken. Incorporate hand, arm, and body stretching exercises during breaks. Also, walks should be taken whenever possible.

EXAMPLES:

One Chicago firm separates information processing work into two types: productive work (work requiring use of a computer for business applications) and nonproductive work (proofreading and other tasks not requiring the immediate use of a computer). The administrative professional's daily routine typically includes both types of work to avoid discomfort resulting from computer operations for long periods of time.

Several state legislatures have enacted labor laws that mandate frequent rest periods for employees with prolonged periods at the display monitor.

c. *Reassignment to other positions:* Pregnant women should have the option to be reassigned to other positions because of potential radiation exposure or physical considerations. Research has not proved thus far that radiation from CRT display monitors does in fact cause miscarriage or birth defects, but pregnant women are being cautious about decreasing time spent using CRT display monitors. Temporary reassignments should occur without loss of pay, seniority, or benefits.

Check Point—Section C

Directions: For each question, circle the correct answer.

C–1. Low-level, nondisturbing background noise is called

A) absorption
B) isolation
C) masking
D) reflection

C–2. An electrical power outage is a potential problem at the computer-based work area because

A) information stored in secondary storage will be lost
B) information that is being entered when the power outage occurs will be lost
C) the administrative professional may not be able to reset the system
D) static electricity is created that can damage the computer system

C–3. Administrative professionals can react negatively if ergonomic factors affecting their work environment are not addressed. Health recommendations for employees who work extended time periods at the display monitor should stipulate that

A) administrative professionals who experience some discomfort working at the display monitor should be reassigned to another position
B) administrative professionals who work more than five hours per day at the display monitor should take rest periods every half hour
C) at least once an hour the administrative professional should get out of the desk chair and move around
D) two 10-minute rest periods need to be scheduled each morning and each afternoon

D. Ergonomics Standards and the Office Environment

At the outset of planning, consideration of several ergonomics standards and factors should result in well-designed offices that will enhance office productivity. Ergonomics standards, workspace, technology (hardware and software), and human physiology envelop many of the factors that should be considered.

1. ***Ergonomics Standards:*** Developed as a result of research by ergonomics specialists, **ergonomics standards** are being used in the design of office products for use throughout the world. These standards serve as guides for organizations contemplating the application of ergonomics factors to increase office productivity.

   a. *German Institute for Standardization and the Trade Cooperative Association:* The 30 standards developed by the German Institute for Standardization and the Trade Cooperative Association include the following types of items:

      - Keyboards should be detachable and ergonomically designed.
      - Display monitors need to be adjustable.
      - The keyboard slope should be no more than 15 degrees.
      - Display monitors should display dark characters on a light background.
      - Work areas and display monitors should meet specific height, depth, and viewing angle specifications.

   b. *Occupational Safety and Health Administration (OSHA):* With a large number of workspace designers and manufacturers expected to introduce new ergonomics products, the Occupational Safety and Health Administration (OSHA) initiated a proposal in the early 1990s to issue a set of ergonomics standards for work areas that would have required employers to reengineer the work process to limit the amount of time employees could spend at five repetitive tasks considered RSI risk factors (e.g., doing the same motion or motion pattern, using vibrating or impact tools, forcing hand exertions, unassisted frequent or heavy lifting, and working in fixed or awkward postures).

      In 1991, California was the first state to enact standards that required all workers to have chairs adjustable for height, support, and backward angle and backrests to provide lumbar support. Other standards pertain to monitors; keyboards; and arm, wrist, and foot rests. A few other states have followed suit and enacted similar standards, especially in terms of allowing workers who constantly work at display monitors to have frequent rest periods.

      In 2003, OSHA's first ergonomics guidelines were released covering the nursing home industry, retail grocery stores, and poultry industry. A Memorandum of Understanding with the United States Small Business Administration, Office of Advocacy, was signed by OSHA to distribute ergonomics information to small businesses. OSHA and the United States Chamber of Commerce have jointly developed a webcast on the willingness and ability of businesses to adopt and implement ergonomics policies. OSHA is in the final stages of reviewing several ergonomics tools, including work areas designed with computer technology. As evidenced by the progress over the past decade, ergonomics standards take a long time to develop and approve.

   c. *International Standards:* The British Standards Institution (BSI) is an independent national body responsible for preparing standards at the international level. The International Organization for Standardization (IOS) specifies that well-designed tasks should safeguard the worker's health and safety, promote the individual's well-being, and facilitate task performance. To meet these objectives, characteristics of well-designed tasks include:

- A variety in the activities and skills used
- A degree of individual control over the work pace
- Cohesion so the task forms an understandable part of the work of the organization
- Opportunities for employees to use skills and experiences to gain new skills
- Sufficient feedback on quality and quantity of task performance

IOS ergonomics standards also cover display monitors, keyboards, workspace, work environment, and software. Basic IOS ergonomic considerations for these office features are listed in Figure 11–2.

The IOS ergonomics standards have been developed with office-type tasks and environments in mind. Therefore, specialized environments may need an acceptable deviation from the standards. Also, a problem with standards is that technology develops faster than standards are adopted or changed. The standards, however, provide administrators and administrative professionals with accepted guidelines as a basis for ergonomic considerations.

2. ***Ergonomic Workspaces:*** A well-designed workspace enables an administrative professional to be both productive and efficient. Professional designers focus on providing a simple, responsive, cost-effective workspace environment. Of utmost concern are the types of activities to be performed at a particular work area.

   a. *Private work tasks:* Private work requires the administrative professional to think, read, analyze, or evaluate in a quiet atmosphere. The workspace design can provide protection from many outside distractions.

      EXAMPLE: *Work surfaces attached to five-foot panels to form a U-shaped work area can provide a much more private workspace than more traditional arrangements (see Figure 11–3).*

   b. *Public work tasks:* Some work necessitates face-to-face interaction in a more social setting. Even in this environment, the workspace design should maintain an atmosphere that is free from annoying distractions.

      EXAMPLE: *Within the modular work area, a round, freestanding table provides an adequate work area for two- or three-person conferences. The round table is indicative of open communication.*

   c. *Electronic work tasks:* Most business professionals—whether executives, managers, or administrative professionals—use electronic office systems (computers, telephones, and fax machines) in their work. An appropriate interface between people and the systems is essential. Networking with other departments is enhanced by an enterprise system.

      EXAMPLE: *Stevenson uses a computer located within her workspace. The equipment is placed so that she need only swivel her chair to the left to use it. The printer is located to the immediate left of the computer, providing her with quick access. Not only is she near the equipment, but she can readily communicate with other people who visit her because her workspace includes a U-shaped surface.*

FIGURE 11–2 International Organization for Standardization (IOS) Ergonomics Standards[1]

Ergonomics Standards	
Display monitor	• Character width-to-height: .5:1 and 1:1 required .7:1 and .9:1 recommended • Character size: uniform; no more than 5 percent variance • Between-character spacing: minimum 1 pixel width • Between-word spacing: minimum space equivalent to capital N • Between-line spacing: minimum of 1 clear pixel • Luminance balance: average 10:1 for frequently viewed areas • Glare: avoid without jeopardizing luminance or contrast; provide tilt and swivel features
Keyboard	• Alphanumeric layout: QWERTY • Slope: between 0 and 25 degrees; adjustable (tiltable) • Placement: Independent of display monitor and stable • Surface: matte finish, diffuse reflection factor between .15 and .75 using diffuse reflection chart • Keytop shape: moulded concave • Keying feedback: tactile preferred; audible with on/off switch and volume adjustable
Workspace	• Should facilitate efficient operation of display monitor and encourage comfortable and healthy posture • Easy reach to frequently used equipment controls, displays, and work surfaces • Opportunity to change position frequently • Avoid excessive, frequent repetitive movements with extreme extension of rotation of limbs or trunk • Support the back with a 90–110 degree angle between back and thighs • Work surface: minimum 4 feet by 2 inches; 4 feet by 2 feet 8 inches preferred • Knee room: at least 1 foot 10 inches wide and 2 feet high • Surface: matte (low reflectance) and free from sharp edges • Chair: five star and swivel; stable with easy movement. Adjustable: backrest height and tilt; seat height • Footrest: available • Document holder: provide if required • Cables: secure and protected
Work environment**	• Glare control: blinds and curtains, room layout, shielded fittings, equipment location, display monitor tilt and swivel, anti-glare window treatments • Noise level: less than 55 decibel if concentration is required less than 60 decibel for other tasks Reduce noise with acoustic materials and location of equipment • Ambient temperature: between 68 and 75 degrees • Relative humidity: between 40 and 60 percent • Lights: Adjustable secondary lights (task lights) should be available
Software++	• Natural, familiar, consistent style of working • Documentation, manuals, training • Relationship to the overall system • Backwards compatibility • Interface that matches the user tasks

**The work environment influences efficient operation and comfort for all office personnel. Individuals differ in their opinions of acceptable glare, noise, heat, and light, partly because different tasks may require different environments. For example, users who sit at their workspace for the majority of the time may have different environmental needs than users who move around the office. The environment should be adjusted for the comfort of the majority of office professionals, providing space in separate areas for unique differences that need to be accommodated.

++Software standards are still under review. There is some evidence that graphical user interfaces (GUI) allow office personnel to use the more holistic, creative left side of the brain rather than the analytical right side. This may partially explain why the GUI is easy to learn and appeals to a wide range of users.

[1]Adopted from British Standards Institution (BSI).

FIGURE 11–3 Work Area Arrangements

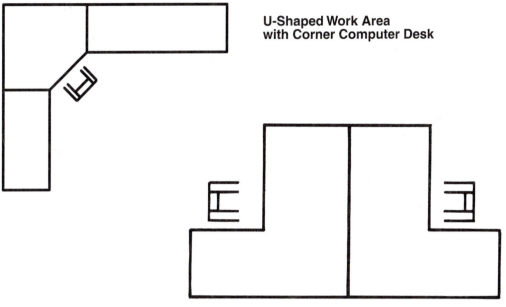

**U-Shaped Work Area
with Corner Computer Desk**

Traditional L-Shaped Desk Arrangement

Workspace design must provide an area conducive to the integration of people and the information with which they are working.

3. ***Selection of User-Friendly Hardware and Software:*** Keyboard arrangement, pointing devices, function keys, printer location, and type of display monitor must be considered in the ergonomics arrangement of the hardware at work areas and individual workspaces. Most software (system and application) uses a graphical user interface (GUI) that most administrative professionals consider user-friendly.

4. ***Human Physiology:*** Perhaps the most important factor is the human element—the worker—and the physical anatomy of the worker. How that individual adapts to the physical office environment is of prime importance.

Until standards are specified in terms of the performance to be achieved, suppliers must be identified who can demonstrate that their products are equivalent or superior to current ergonomics recommendations. There are many areas where the use of a standards-based ergonomics checklist can help with proper choices in establishing an office that meets ergonomics specifications.

Check Point—Section D

Directions: For each question, circle the correct answer.

D–1. Based on research by ergonomics specialists, ergonomics standards are used in the design of office products throughout the world. One standard of importance to the administrative professional is

A) incandescent lighting should illuminate the area surrounding the work surface

B) information technicians should computerize all office tasks

C) keyboard slope should be no more than 15 degrees

D) office walls should be painted deep red for a warm, relaxing environment

D–2. Ergonomics standards for office tasks and the environment are

A) difficult to develop because of individual differences

B) enforced by the United States Supreme Court

C) from the International Organization for Standardization (IOS), and the British Standards Institution (BSI)

D) policies the Occupational Safety and Health Administration (OSHA) enforce for businesses with more than 150 employees

D–3. Which one of the following is the most important factor in designing the office environment?

A) Ergonomic work areas

B) Human element—office professionals need their workspace designed for their physical anatomy and specific tasks

C) Selection of user-friendly hardware and software

D) Work processes

For Your Review

Directions: For each question, circle the correct answer.

1. A psychological basis for ergonomics, the personal development of administrative professionals, should be addressed through
   A) controlled temperature, ventilation, and humidity level
   B) establishing workgroup clusters
   C) open lines of communication informing administrative professionals about technology changes
   D) technology training or retraining applicable to office operations

2. Wilke was very interested in the new computer-based information system and began demonstrating to other administrative professionals the usefulness of the system. Wilke demonstrates the characteristics of a/an
   A) early adapter
   B) facilitator
   C) team leader
   D) technology specialist

3. Research and recommendations for the size, heights, and shapes of furniture and office equipment addressing physical fit and employee comfort are made through what field of study?
   A) Anthropometry
   B) Biomechanics
   C) Musculoskeletal
   D) Psychology

4. The Tahquamenon Hospital Medical Transcription Center operates 24/7 and is designed so documents and reports are completed within eight hours even though employee work shifts occur. The smooth transition between workgroups is addressed by
   A) biomechanics
   B) physiological ergonomics
   C) sociological ergonomics
   D) workspace designers

5. The success of collaborative activities depends on a team effort. The networked enterprise supports collaborative team activities by
   A) allowing employees to specialize
   B) eliminating the need for face-to-face communication
   C) providing groupware for project development and management
   D) supporting a 24/7 help desk

6. To efficiently and effectively transmit accurate documents to the right individuals, organizations should take into account
   A) communication theories
   B) physiological studies
   C) psychological theories
   D) sociological studies

7. Sore wrists, numbness, and finger cramps are typical symptoms of
   A) muscular dysfunction
   B) psychosocial problems
   C) psychosomatic disorders
   D) repetitive-strain illness (RSI)

8. What should an administrative professional do if she has early signs of carpal tunnel syndrome?

A) Investigate ergonomically designed office equipment and furniture

B) Join a physical fitness club and exercise at least three times a week

C) Make sure she looks away from the display monitor every 15 minutes

D) Request a modular office design

9. A monitor filter, task lighting, and window blinds are all recommendations for

A) controlling screen glare

B) improving workspace design

C) lowering energy costs

D) minimizing eye fatigue

10. Radiation emission continues to be a health concern with regards to

A) cathode ray tube (CRT) screens

B) flat-panel monitors

C) notebook computers

D) USB flash drives

11. What is the recommended placement for the display monitor triangle (eyes to screen to source material)?

A) As close to the user as possible within an 18- to 28-inch range

B) At a left or right angle

C) With the bottom of the screen at the end of the user's arm length extension

D) With the top of the screen slightly above eye level

12. Ambient lighting

A) directly illuminates the work surface

B) illuminates the entire workspace

C) is an efficient lighting source but requires alternative lighting systems

D) resembles natural light in its illumination

13. Which light source is the least expensive but produces glare and shadowing on work surfaces?

A) Ambient

B) Fluorescent

C) Incandescent

D) Task

14. While remodeling a modular office for a more cheerful environment and to make the work area appear larger than it really is, the workspace designer should recommend

A) dark-red fabric-covered panels

B) ecru material with blue fleck padded panels

C) panels painted a royal blue trimmed in a complementary light blue

D) wooden panels stained mahogany

15. Using fabric-covered furniture, walls, and décor to engulf sound waves is called

A) absorption

B) isolation

C) masking

D) reflection

16. Buildings that run the greatest risk of becoming a sick building have

A) furniture and office equipment that do not meet ergonomics standards

B) drafty windows and poor heating systems

C) insufficient lighting and narrow hallways

D) poor ventilation or are airtight

17. Removing moldy carpets, replacing air filters on heating and cooling systems, and discarding furniture that emits formaldehyde fumes are all actions to correct

A) environmental design problems

B) psychosocial problems

C) psychosomatic disorders

D) sick buildings

18. One way to dissipate static in a work area is to

A) adjust the humidity controls for the current seasonal conditions

B) install carpeting throughout the office

C) provide surge protectors for all electrical connections

D) remove furniture treated with formaldehyde

19. What is the best recommendation for business professionals who work for extended periods of time at a task?

A) Additional task lighting to improve illumination in the work area

B) Incorporate hand, arm, and body stretching exercises into their breaks

C) Make the task part of a work group cluster so projects can be rotated

D) Reassignment to another position to avoid the potential risk for carpal tunnel syndrome

20. Ergonomics standards are

A) difficult to enforce because of individual requirements

B) enforced by the International Organization for Standardization (IOS)

C) guidelines for organizations

D) policies businesses must follow or the employee can prosecute

21. In 2003 the Occupational Safety and Health Administration (OSHA) released ergonomics standards for

A) businesses with more than 1,500 employees

B) construction workers

C) nursing homes

D) truckers

22. To meet the objectives of the International Organization for Standardization (IOS), a characteristic of a well-designed task includes

A) a variety of activities and skills

B) freedom to complete the task without input from others

C) shared activities so employees can concentrate on specialized skills

D) supervision of activities so project deadlines are met

23. What specification does the International Organization for Standardization (IOS) recommend for an office chair?

A) Five star base and swivel

B) Footrest

C) Surface that absorbs sound waves

D) Web seat pan and back for ventilation

24. The noise level for administrative professionals who require concentration for the majority of their tasks should be

A) greater than 65 percent absorption

B) less than 55 decibel

C) less than 60 pixels

D) within a 20–30 reflection range

25. When using ergonomics standards, it is important to realize that existing standards

A) affect health issues but have little impact on productivity

B) may have to be adjusted for specialized environments

C) change frequently because of new technologies

D) need to be researched before there is acceptance by the business community

Solutions

Solutions to Check Point—Section A

Answer	Refer to:
A–1. (B)	[A-1-g (1)]
A–2. (C)	[A-3]
A–3. (C)	[A-4-a, A-4-b and A-5-b]

Solutions to Check Point—Section B

Answer	Refer to:
B–1. (A)	[B-1-b]
B–2. (C)	[B-1-e]
B–3. (C)	[B-2-b and Figure 11–1]

Solutions to Check Point—Section C

Answer	Refer to:
C–1. (C)	[C-3]
C–2. (B)	[C-7 and Chapter 2 A-2-a (2)]
C–3. (C)	[C-10-b]

Solutions to Check Point—Section D _____

	Answer	Refer to:
1.	(C)	[D-1-a]
2.	(C)	[D-1-b and D-1-c]
3.	(B)	[D-4]

Solutions to For Your Review

	Answer	Refer to:
1.	(D)	[A-1-c]
2.	(A)	[A-1-g (1)]
3.	(A)	[A-2-b (1)]
4.	(C)	[A-3-a]
5.	(C)	[A-3-b]
6.	(A)	[A-4]
7.	(D)	[B-1-a]
8.	(A)	[B-1]
9.	(A)	[B-2-a (1)]
10.	(B)	[B-2-a (2)]
11.	(A)	[B-2-b and B-2-b (2) (c)]
12.	(A)	[C-1-b]
13.	(C)	[C-1-e]
14.	(B)	[C-2]
15.	(A)	[C-3-a]
16.	(D)	[C-4-a]
17.	(D)	[C-4-c]
18.	(A)	[C-6]
19.	(B)	[C-10-b]

20.   (C)   [D-1, D-1-c]

21.   (C)   [D-1-b]

22.   (A)   [D-1-c]

23.   (A)   [Figure 11–2]

24.   (B)   [Figure 11–2]

25.   (B)   [D-1-c]

Practice Exam

Directions: For each question, circle the correct answer.

1. To increase productivity throughout the organization, all business professionals should have access to the
   A) executive support system (ESS)
   B) knowledge work system (KWS)
   ✓ C) office system (OS)
   D) transaction processing system (TPS)

2. Source data automation is used to input the marketing department's survey responses. The survey instrument is designed for
   A) digitized tablet and pen input
   B) magnetic-ink character recognition (MICR)
   ✓ C) optical mark recognition (OMR)
   ✗ D) pattern recognition

3. To address mission-critical concerns of data storage for the networked organization, many businesses utilize online data storage that includes assessment, design, and backup management through
   A) redundant arrays of independent disks (RAID)
   B) server farms
   C) storage area networks (SANs)
   ✓ D) storage service providers (SSPs)

4. For high transmission rates and greater security as well as low data transmission error (interference), an organization's network backbone should be
   A) coaxial cable
   ✓ B) fiber optic cable
   C) infrared channels
   D) celestial satellite

5. While making an important telephone call, Nicholas hears a soft beep on the telephone. Nicholas decides not to interrupt his call and lets the new incoming call go to voice mail. This is an example of
   A) call forwarding
   ✓ B) call waiting
   C) caller ID
   D) person-to-person calling

6. To enhance the success of an audio conference, an important guideline is to
   ✓ A) assign a moderator to ensure participation by everyone and that objectives are accomplished
   B) limit the number to four participants
   C) tape the conference and send a copy to all participants and executives
   D) use a laissez faire approach so participants feel free to express opinions

7. Listservs automatically send information (broadcast) to their subscribers. This method of disseminating information uses
   A) file transfer protocol (FTP)
   B) pull technology
   ✓ C) push technology
   D) telephony

8. Typical information on an intranet (Inside) includes
   A) advertising and search engines
   ✓ B) budgets, corporate policies, and upcoming events

C) product information and shopping baskets

D) purchase orders, distribution track-ing, and electronic payments

9. What security measure is an organiza-tion using when sent messages are coded and the recipient must have an authorized key to read the message?

A) Access control
B) Digital certificate
C) Encryption
D) Secure electronic transaction (SET)

10. An audit that uses quality test data for testing the input, process, and output of applications and security is

A) conducted during systems design
B) designed for fault-tolerant systems
C) one that should be conducted on a regular basis throughout the life-time of a system
D) used for data cleansing

11. When designing a document, rough sketches are refined into sketches that address how the document will be folded, where images will be placed, and how the document will be format-ted through type specifications. These refined sketches are called

A) comps
B) grayscale
C) greeking
D) thumbnails

12. The number of signatures for a four-panel fold is

A) two
B) four
C) six
D) eight

13. The credit box on a periodical listing the editor, writers, illustrators, and other contributors is called the

A) banner
B) masthead
C) printer spread
D) typography

14. What two design principles tie together the visual units in a document?

A) Alignment and contrast
B) Alignment and repetition
C) Contrast and proximity
D) Proximity and repetition

15. A small decorative stroke added to the end of the letter's main stroke is called a/an

A) em dash
B) font
C) sans serif
D) serif

16. The layout and design for Web publish-ing adhere to World Wide Web stan-dards through the use of

A) ascenders
B) hypertext markup language (HTML)
C) portable network group (PNG)
D) server farms

17. Yusov quoted from a current novel and included the text in his literary review. Reproducing the material from the novel in a literary review

A) falls under the public domain cat-egory
B) must also include the phrase "Re-printed with Permission" along with the name of the copyright holder
C) is covered by the copyright law fair-use clause
D) requires written permission from the publisher of the novel

18. A low-volume copier is also called a/an

A) convenience copier
B) digital copier
C) information distributor
D) page printer

19. Umlas has been asked to create a de-partment brochure. For the composi-tion process, Umlas needs his desktop PC and

A) groupware
B) knowledge work system (KWS)

C)   presentation graphics software

D)   word processing software

20.   A duplicating master can be prepared without having to rekey or redraw the document by using the

A)   diazo process
B)   electronic scanner
C)   information distributor
D)   photocomposer

21.   What imaging process can interface with microcomputers to produce high-quality, high-speed multiple copies?

A)   Diazo
B)   Fiber optics
C)   Laser
D)   Xerographic

22.   McDougald provides all sales representatives with monthly updates for their marketing handbook. What is the best finishing process for the marketing handbook?

A)   Ring binding
B)   Saddle-stitch binding
C)   Spiral-comb binding
D)   Velo binding

23.   The concurrent execution of more than one task of a single application is called

A)   multiprocessing
B)   multiprogramming
C)   multitasking
D)   multithreading

24.   A renamed version of Windows NT 5.0, a powerful operating system for high-end microcomputers and servers, is

A)   Blackcomb
B)   Windows 2000
C)   Windows CE
D)   Windows XP

25.   When working in a graphical user interface (GUI) environment, what does the computer monitor display when the system is ready to be used?

A)   Desktop
B)   Menu bar
C)   Open window
D)   Title bar

26.   When working in a graphical user interface (GUI) environment, frequently used software functions (system and application) can be activated by pointing and clicking the icons and buttons on the

A)   control panel
B)   menu bar
C)   taskbar
D)   toolbar

27.   If the response time for opening a file is slow, it may be that the file has been saved over many different sectors on the disk. What can be done to increase the speed of access and retrieval?

A)   Increase primary memory capacity
B)   Reboot the system
C)   Run the defragmentation utility
D)   Use the system edit utilities and resave the file

28.   The Windows operating system stores the location of the disk data clusters and data use information in a

A)   computer directory
B)   docking station
C)   utility menu
D)   Virtual File Allocation Table (VFAT)

29.   In order to remove all the files stored on the disk, identify bad sectors, and make sure the disk tracks and sectors are compatible with a specific operating system, execute a/an

A)   defragmentation utility
B)   format utility
C)   interpreter
D)   quick format utility

30.   C++ is a programming language where the modules (source code) must be translated into machine code (object code) by a

A)   compiler
B)   interpreter
C)   manipulation language
D)   system programmer

31. End users can check the microcomputer system diagnostics (performance) by using the

    A) computer directory
    B) control panel system utilities
    C) manipulation language functions
    D) security monitor program

32. Which type of database is common for a client/server network?

    A) Centralized database
    B) Hierarchical database
    C) Network database
    D) Object-oriented database

33. A database for storing Web site pages containing text, sound, video, and graphics is called a

    A) hypermedia database
    B) network database
    C) object-oriented database
    D) warehouse

34. Software that addresses generic business functions (accounting, marketing, finance, and operations) is called

    A) application specific software
    B) general purpose application software
    C) industry-specific software
    D) productivity software

35. What software has automated production operations?

    A) Computer-aided design (CAD)
    B) Computer-aided manufacturing (CAM)
    C) Distribution tracking
    D) Materials requirement planning (MRP)

36. Computerized inventory systems that record every addition or deletion from stock and update the quantity on hand regularly is called a/an

    A) general inventory system
    B) just-in-time inventory system
    C) perpetual inventory system
    D) real-time inventory system

37. Every time a new order is received at CCC, production is notified, the just-in-time inventory system is activated, a shipment date is scheduled, and accounting processes (accounts payable and receivable, product costing, and accounting reports) are automatically updated throughout the process with accurate and timely data. This is an example of a/an

    A) decision support system
    B) enterprise system
    C) management information system
    D) transaction processing system

38. Business organizations provide non-technical end users with powerful word processing, spreadsheet, database management, and presentation graphics software that is typically procured as a/an

    A) application specific program
    B) cross-functional program
    C) integrated package
    D) software suite

39. Hosto developed a spreadsheet application with data from the human resource division documents. The vice president expressed a concern that Hosto's application may inaccurately represent the organization's enterprise system transactions for personnel. The vice president is concerned about

    A) cross-functional integration
    B) data integrity
    C) industry-specific applications
    D) information access

40. What does it mean when a pull-down menu command is followed by an ellipsis (e.g., Replace . . .)?

    A) A macro virus has infected the program
    B) Subcommands are required to complete the process
    C) The function has not been installed
    D) The function is open and in use

41. While creating an itinerary for his boss, Zimmerman needs to open another document to copy some information. When using a graphical user interface (GUI), the quickest way to open the second document is to use the

    A) menu bar
    B) taskbar
    C) title bar
    • D) toolbar

42. In the Windows environment, end users and the computer system conduct interactive communication through a/an

    A) command-driven interface
    B) control panel
    • C) dialog box
    D) open window

43. When using a word processing program, preset default values include

    A) headers
    B) page numbers
    • C) page orientation
    D) justification

44. Fuller was keying "technology" in a word processing document and it extended beyond the right margin. The text was automatically placed on the next line. This is known as

    A) fetching
    B) kerning
    C) widow/orphan function
    • D) word wrap

45. Clip art inserted into a word processing document can be formatted so the image is to the left or right of the text, in with the text, behind the text, or in front of the text. To format the image layout for the desired text wrapping style, the administrative professional needs to

    A) first key the text, then insert the clip art
    B) format the clip art before inserting it into the word processing document

    C) left click to select the clip art, then use the format menu bar options
    • D) right click on the clip art and follow the context-sensitive menu

46. While editing a word processing document, Teagardin decided that the two lines in Section B at the bottom of the fourth page should be on the fifth page along with the text heading. To move the section heading and text to the top of page 5, Teagardin needs to insert a

    • A) hard page break
    B) section break
    C) soft page break
    D) widow/orphan command

47. When using productivity programs, tasks that are performed repeatedly can be automated through the creation of a/an

    A) control key
    B) domain function
    • C) macro
    D) Trojan horse

48. Letters running horizontally across the top of a worksheet (e.g., A, B, . . . IV) are used to identify the worksheet

    A) cells
    • B) columns
    C) rows
    D) workbook

49. An example of a worksheet formula is SUM(B29:M29). B29 is the

    A) active cell
    • B) cell reference
    C) row reference
    D) workbook reference

50. An example of a common worksheet business function is

    A) =B32/A5
    B) (C6*P3+C6)
    , C) =PMT(B2/12,B3,−B1)
    D) ('Total Sold'!C8)

51. In a worksheet, what is needed in order to find information in a list?

 - A) Formatted labels
 - B) Formula operators
 - C) Numeric data
 - D) Relative reference

52. A quick-and-easy way to work with a subset of data in a worksheet list without having to sort the data first is to use a/an

 - A) absolute reference
 - B) filter
 - C) logical operator
 - D) lookup function

53. Which numeric format aligns the dollar sign and decimal in the worksheet column?

 - A) Accounting
 - B) Currency
 - C) Euro convert
 - D) Numeric

54. In a database management program, what must be created so the database fields can be specified?

 - A) Data view
 - B) Record
 - C) Relation
 - D) Table structure

55. Predefined data formats for a database management application are set in the

 - A) data view
 - B) data query
 - C) database table
 - D) design view

56. What is the most effective way to present database output in a formal business format?

 - A) Forms
 - B) Macros
 - C) Queries
 - D) Reports

57. When using a doughnut graph, what section(s) can be exploded (pulled out for emphasis)?

 - A) Corresponding sections in both the outer and inner rings
 - B) One section from either the outer ring or the inner ring
 - C) Sections in the outer ring
 - D) Sections in the inner ring

58. Which presentation graphics view will duplicate on the microcomputer monitor how the slide transitions, effects, timings, and animations will appear during an oral presentation or on an information kiosk?

 - A) Normal
 - B) Outline
 - C) Slide show
 - D) Slide

59. An electronic presentation slide can be introduced from the top or bottom of the screen, the left or right side of the screen, and with or without sound. This feature is called the slide

 - A) animation
 - B) layout
 - C) template
 - D) transition

60. The primary interface for accessing the Internet is a/an

 - A) graphical user interface (GUI)
 - B) Internet service provider (ISP)
 - C) menu-driven interface
 - D) Web browser

61. The functional requirements for a business professional's desktop computer configuration is determined through

 - A) analysis
 - B) internal audits
 - C) systems design
 - D) troubleshooting

62. An organizational concern regarding end-user developed applications includes

 - A) inadequate interface with other organization and department systems
 - B) IT Division overload for application tests
 - C) software costs
 - D) time requirements for developing applications

63. After the final testing of a new course scheduling application, the business division replaced the manual scheduling system with the computerized

application. During the first year the business school used and tweaked the system. The college required all divisions to use the course scheduling application beginning with the second year. What cut-over method did the college use to computerize the course scheduling system?

A) Direct
B) Parallel
C) Phased
D) Pilot

64. A process chart is used to illustrate

A) distances and delays involved in an office procedure from start to finish
B) information flow resulting from a communication system
C) responsibilities assigned to each administrative professional within a division
D) the movement of a document in order to develop a workflow pattern

65. When an administrative professional's tasks require a high level of concentration and the information is very confidential, the best office design is the

A) modern office design
B) modular approach
C) open office design
D) private office

66. Electronic information flow among tasks, departments, and external partners is supported through the

A) enterprise network
B) intranet
C) knowledge work system
D) office system

67. Sabia needs to make a telephone call to a colleague in the information technology division and has forgotten her telephone number. What is the most efficient way to obtain the number?

A) Ask a support staff employee
B) e-Mail the colleague
C) Use the intranet directory
D) Use the Web White Pages

68. The purchasing category for outsourcing equipment upkeep is

A) capital
B) information system
C) maintenance, repair, and operating items (MRO)
D) services

69. A control mechanism for the buying organization that links purchasing approval to an authorized individual is the

A) computerized inventory record system
B) purchase order number
C) request for proposal (RFP)
D) requisition number

70. The inventory management approach that should identify causes for excess office supply stock is the

A) computerized inventory record system
B) electronic data interchange (EDI)
C) inventory review
D) supplier-buyer partnership

71. Business professionals who prefer the status quo and encourage other colleagues to also resist change often experience job-related stress. These individuals are referred to as

A) late adapters
B) nonadapters
C) skeptics
D) troublemakers

72. Studies on the musculoskeletal effort of human beings is known as

A) anthropometry
B) biomechanics
C) ergonomics
D) psychological

73. The amount of acoustical control provided by modular partitions depends upon the

A) absorption factor of the material used on the partitions
B) masking effect provided
C) reflection ability of the partitions
D) shape of the partitions

74. Low-level, nondisturbing background noise that blends with regular office noise is called

    A) absorption
    B) isolation
    C) reflection
    • D) white sound

75. The standard noise level for general office tasks should be

    A) between 40–50 decibels
    • B) less than 60 decibels
    C) masked 50 percent of the time
    D) within a 15–25 percent absorption range

Solutions to Practice Exam

Note: The reference includes the chapter number first, followed by the appropriate outline section in the chapter.

Answer	Refer to:	Answer	Refer to:
1. (C)	[1-C-1-c]	23. (D)	[8-A-3-b]
2. (C)	[2-C-2-c (1)]	24. (B)	[8-A-4-a]
3. (D)	[2-E-2]	25. (A)	[8-A-5-a and 8-B-1-a]
4. (B)	[3-A-3-a (3)]	26. (D)	[8-A-5-d (3), 8-B-1-b and 9-B-3-b]
5. (B)	[3-B-3-a]		
6. (A)	[4-A-2-a (1)]	27. (C)	[8-B-1-c]
7. (C)	[4-B-1-b (4)]	28. (D)	[8-B-1-c (1)]
8. (B)	[4-C-1-b]	29. (B)	[8-B-1-d]
9. (C)	[5-B-2-d (1)]	30. (A)	[8-B-2-a]
10. (C)	[5-C-3-b (2)]	31. (B)	[8-C-1]
11. (A)	[6-A-1-c (4)]	32. (A)	[8-C-3-c (4)]
12. (A)	[6-A-3-a (1)]	33. (A)	[8-C-3-c (8)]
13. (B)	[6-A-7-c]	34. (A)	[9-A-1]
14. (B)	[6-B-4]	35. (B)	[9-A-1-d]
15. (D)	[6-B-5-b]	36. (C)	[9-A-1-d (2)]
16. (B)	[6-B-7]	37. (B)	[9-A-2-a]
17. (C)	[6-C-2]	38. (D)	[9-B-1-a]
18. (A)	[7-A-1-a (1)]	39. (B)	[9-B-2]
19. (D)	[7-B-3-b (2)]	40. (B)	[8-A-5-a (1) (a) and 9-B-3-a]
20. (B)	[7-C-1-b (2)]		
21. (C)	[7-C-3-c]	41. (D)	[8-A-5-d (3), 8-B-1-b and 9-B-3-b]
22. (A)	[7-D-3 and 7-D-3-a]	42. (C)	[9-B-3-c]

Answer	*Refer to:*	*Answer*	*Refer to:*
43. (C)	[9-B-4-a and 9-B-4-k]	60. (D)	[9-B-8-b]
44. (D)	[9-B-4-c (2)]	61. (A)	[9-C-1]
45. (D)	[9-B-4-c (7)]	62. (A)	[9-C-1-b]
46. (A)	[9-B-4-e (4) (a)]	63. (D)	[5-B-2-a (3) (b) and 9-C-2-a (2)]
47. (C)	[9-B-4-i, 9-B-5-c, 9-B-6-h and 9-B-7-b (12)]	64. (A)	[10-A-2-a (1) (a)]
48. (B)	[9-B-5-a (2) (a)]	65. (D)	[10-A-3-a (1) and 10-A-3-a (2)]
49. (B)	[9-B-5-a (2) (c)]	66. (A)	[3-C-2-b (1) and 10-B-1-c]
50. (C)	[9-B-5-a (3) (e)]		
51. (A)	[9-B-5-a (6)]	67. (C)	[10-B-2-a (4)]
52. (B)	[9-B-5-a (6) (b)]	68. (D)	[10-C-3-b]
53. (A)	[9-B-5-b (1)]	69. (D)	[10-C-4-d]
54. (D)	[9-B-6-a (2), 9-B-6-a (2) (d)]	70. (C)	[10-D-1-c]
55. (D)	[9-B-6-b]	71. (B)	[11-A-1-g (3)]
56. (D)	[9-B-6-d]	72. (B)	[11-A-2-b (2)]
57. (C)	[9-B-7-a (3)]	73. (A)	[11-C-3-a]
58. (C)	[9-B-7-b (3) (f)]	74. (D)	[11-C-3-c]
59. (D)	[9-B-7-b (7) (a)]	75. (B)	[11-Figure 11–2]

Glossary

Absolute reference   Process of inserting a spreadsheet code into a cell formula to hold the row and/or column references constant (absolute) when the formula is copied to another cell in the worksheet; the row or column reference does not change when copied. (9)[1]

Absorption   The engulfing of sound waves by environmental materials. (11)

Acceptance test   The final systems test where users evaluate the entire system and indicate how well it meets the standards established at the beginning of the design or purchase of the system. (5)

Active cell   A highlighted (outlined in dark) area where data is entered into a spreadsheet program worksheet. (9)

Alignment   The design principle that ensures visual units on the page are horizontally and vertically connected; alignment and repetition tie together the visual units. (6)

Ambient lighting   Indirect light that illuminates the area surrounding the work surface. (11)

Animation   Special sound or visual effects that can be added to slides in an electronic presentation; this is not to be overused. (9)

Anthropometry   The study of human body measurements in order to design furniture (sizes, heights, and shapes) accurately scaled to the dimensions of a worker's body. (11)

Antivirus program   A software program on the organization's network, as well as desktop PCs, notebooks, and workstations, to detect and delete computer viruses. (5)

Application service provider (ASP)   A company that leases software as well as hardware to organizations through the Internet or a private network in an attempt to provide lower technology costs to the organization; an ASP manages all applications and computing services including updates and maintenance. (9)

Application software   Software that provides the instructions for processing general purpose applications for end users as well as applications specific to the organization's functional areas. (8)

Application specific software   Software developed by in-house application programmers, purchased from vendors, or custom developed by software vendors to process daily business operations according to the needs of each department's function; vendor software can be cross-industry application software (e.g., payroll, accounts receivable, or inventory) or industry-specific application software (e.g., credit loan programs, legal programs, or insurance programs). (9)

Ascender   The portion of a lowercase letter that is above the main body of a letter; in the English alphabet there are eight letters with ascenders: b, d, f, h, i, k, l, and t. (6)

Audio conference   A telephone call for three or more people to talk with one another; the conference call was the first form of audio conference. (3)

Batch processing   For efficiency, processing business transactions in a group at a future time. (1)

Binding   A method for holding all pages of a final document together; binding methods include case, fastback, lay-flat, plastic comb, saddle-stitch, sewn-and-glued, spiral, staple, stitching, three-ring, Velo, and Wir-O. (7)

Biomechanics   The study of the musculoskeletal effort of human beings. (11)

Biometric control   A security control that identifies an individual based on physiological or behavioral characteristics; (i.e., iris, fingerprints, signature, and keystrokes). (5)

Bit   A two-state (binary) electrical impulse in a digital computer system represented by the 1 digit for *on* and the 0 digit for *off;* an acronym for **bi**nary dig**it**. (2)

Boot   Method of turning the computer-based information system on. (8)

Bridge   A communication processor that provides connection between two similar networks. (3)

---

[1]The number in parentheses after each entry indicates the chapter location in the text.

Byte A string of bits (0s and 1s) representing a number or a character (alphanumeric character or symbol—including a blank space) in all digital computer systems; eight bits equals one byte. (2)

Camera phone A cell phone enhanced to capture photographic images that can be immediately sent to other camera phone users along with a message, downloaded to computers, or posted on the Internet. (3)

Capital equipment A nonrecurring asset intended for use over a period of years; includes office furniture, computers, printers, copiers, and other office equipment. (10)

Carpal tunnel syndrome The compression of a nerve leading into the wrist that results in debilitating pain and muscle weakness. (11)

Cell The intersection of a row and column on a spreadsheet program worksheet; end users input text, numbers, and formulas into the active cell. (9)

Cell reference A unique address for a spreadsheet program worksheet cell that consists of the column letter and row number. (9)

Central exchange system (CENTREX) A telephone system where each extension is assigned a seven-digit number for direct outward and direct inward dialing; leased from the regional telephone company. (3)

Central processing unit (CPU) Computer system component that manipulates raw data, moves information, and performs required arithmetic or logic operations in a digital computer system; consists of a control unit and the arithmetic/logic unit. (1) (2)

Centralized computing Processing data in a mainframe or supercomputer with users entering data from local input devices; used by organizations along with one of the other computing models (distributed or collaborative). (3)

Channel The communication link for transmitting data between the computer system and secondary storage or other computer peripherals external to the system. (2)

Client/server computing Widely used form of distributed computing where a microcomputer, mid-range computer, or a mainframe is a server to its clients (end user with a desktop PC, notebook, or workstation); data storage and management, processing logic, and an interface are shared between the server and client. (3)

Collaborative commerce Through shared digital systems, businesses collaborate with suppliers, engineers, manufacturers, and sales representatives to improve planning, production, and distribution of goods and services. (4)

Collaborative computing Networks are networked to accomplish integrated operations and link common processing tasks; the network infrastructure along with collaborative software tools support data, information, and process sharing. (3)

Collating The process of sorting each page into a set of pages using a stand-alone collator or a collator attached to a copier or a duplicator. (7)

Column (in)

Database management software The data fields in a relational database management system (DBMS) table (relation); each column in a database table must be uniquely named with one field as the primary key. (9)

Spreadsheet software Typically identified by a letter (A, B, . . . , IV) horizontally across the top of a worksheet; data in columns are read vertically. (9)

Word processing software Entering text, illustrations, graphs [charts], and pictures into a format resembling a newspaper format; the size and number of columns can be specified. (9)

Command-driven interface Interface that requires the user to enter brief user commands to the operating system for decoding and execution (i.e., MS-DOS). (8)

Compact disc (CD) An optical disc that includes compact disc-random access memory (CD-ROM), compact disc-recordable (CD-R), compact disc-rewritable (CD-RW), and digital video discs (DVD). (2)

Comprehensive sketches Sketches (often called comps) that provide colors to be used, number of pages and/or folds, trim size of the final document, image placement, number of columns (if applicable), and type specifications; a refinement of hardcopy thumbnails. (6)

Computer conference Participants designated to be part of the discussion transmit information to others either simultaneously or on a delayed basis anytime, anywhere; also referred to as a discussion forum. (4)

Computerized branch exchange (CBX) A computer-based telephone communication system for automated telephone switching and management. (3)

Context-sensitive menu An on-screen menu that provides a shortcut to functions related to the window or object the pointer is on at the time of a right click with an input device. (8)

Contrast The design principle that occurs when two elements are *noticeably* different; bold, italics, a thin line with a thick line (rules), a warm color with a cool color, a small graphic with a large graphic, or a horizontal element with a vertical element. Contrast and proximity emphasize important information. (6)

Control panel Module that allows the microcomputer user to change the appearance and functionality of the operating system; in a networked environment, the end user may be locked out from changing the functionality of their desktop PC, notebook, or workstation operating system requiring the assistance from an information technology specialist. (8)

Conversion The process of changing from the old system to a new one; methods include direct, parallel, phased, and pilot. (5)

Cracker A malicious hacker with the intent of disabling the computer system or cracking the system for a profit. (5)

Cropping Trimming the unwanted edges of an image. (6)

Custom-designed software Software developed by an in-house programmer or purchased or leased from a software vendor who provides installation, maintenance, and training services. (9)

Cybernetics The information flow resulting from the communications systems being used. (10)

Data conference Participants on a computer network with data conferencing software to view, revise, and save changes to text, graphics, drawings, images, and other material displayed on a shared whiteboard; the conference is simultaneous, in real time. (4)

Data flow diagram Diagram that graphically illustrates the computer-based information system's component processes and the flow of data between the processes. (10)

Data mart A small data warehouse containing only a portion of the organization's data for a specialized function or work group. (8)

Data tampering Intentionally or unintentionally entering incorrect or fabricated data or changing or deleting existing data stored in the organization's files and databases; typically done by organization insiders. (5)

Data warehouse System that integrates current and historical transaction data from the organization's multiple databases and/or storage area networks (SAN) so end users can use report and query tools to extract data for analysis and better decision making (datamining); operational TPS data are copied to a data warehouse as often as required—monthly, weekly, daily, or even hourly. (8)

Database administrator The information technology person responsible for the logical database design, development of the data dictionary, security of the data, and monitoring how others (both users and technical personnel) use data. (5)

Database management systems (DBMS) A system and an application software program that control the development, use, and maintenance of data stored in databases; for enterprise-wide data management, a mainframe or mid-range computer system is required. (8)

Datamining The analysis of data stored in a data warehouse to identify patterns and relationships for predicting future trends and consumer behaviors as well as making better decisions. (8)

Decibel The unit measurement of the intensity of sound; one decibel is the faintest sound that can be detected by the human ear. (11)

Decision support systems (DSS) An information system that uses transaction processing system (TPS) and management information system (MIS) data as well as external sources in sophisticated analytical models to support semi-structured decisions; an interactive environment where management can change assumptions, ask new questions, and change the variables in the DSS model. (1)

Defragmentation The process of rewriting parts of a file to contiguous sectors on a disk to increase the speed of access and retrieval. (8)

Denial of service Attacks where crackers flood a network or Web server with information requests in an attempt to crash the network. (5)

Descender The portion of a lowercase letter that falls below the baseline of a letter; in the English alphabet there are five letters with descenders: g, j, p, q, and y. (6)

Desktop Place where the operating system displays a taskbar and program or file icons once the computer system has completely booted; default icons include computer directory, documents, network places, recycle bin, and network browser. (8)

Dialog box Area where the end user and the computer system communicate; displays whenever the application or operating system software provides information to the end user or the software needs the end user to enter information or make a selection. (8)

Diazo A process for making engineering and architectural drawing copies where the original document is in a translucent state with printing only on one side of the page; accepts ink or pencil additions and special correction devices for deletions or erasures on the original. (7)

Digital certificate An attachment to an electronic document that verifies the sender to be whom he or she claims. (5)

Digital copier Copier that uses technology that allows data to be transferred in a series of bits from a computer-based information system, thus providing faster, clearer, and higher-quality output; also called an information distributor. (7)

Digital duplicating   Process that combines convenience copying with the economy of offset printing. (7)

Digital signature   A digital code attached to a document to identify the sender and message contents; to be legally binding, someone must verify that the digital signature belongs to the person who sent the data and that the data were not altered. (5)

Digital subscriber line (DSL)   A high-capacity digital transmission over existing twisted copper telephone lines from the office or home to the telephone switching station. (3)

Digital wallet   Software that stores credit card and owner identification to be used for e-commerce purchases. (5)

Digitizing   Converting data into digital information called bits. (3)

Direct-image master   A smooth paper material that is prepared by keying or writing directly on it with special writing implements (reproducing pens or pencils); one paper offset master can produce up to 2,500 copies. (7)

Document mode   An application software screen ready to accept keyed text for input; in a graphical user interface environment, the document mode is referred to as an active window. (9)

Domain function   Element required in a Web address and an e-mail address; six of the original domain functions are com, edu, gov, mil, net, and org. A Web site must be registered in a domain function. The e-mail address top-level domain is either a domain function or country reference with the domain function at the immediate left. (4)

Domain name   Name that identifies the host or network that services the e-mail account and contains subdomains separated by a period. (4)

Downtime   When the computer-based information system is not in operation. (1)

Dropped capital (drop cap)   Stylistic device used to emphasize the beginning of a section by setting the first letter with a larger and sometimes stylized font; drop caps are either inset within the paragraph or offset into the margin to the left of the paragraph. (6)

Early adapter   A person who is quick to change, study a new system, and try to implement it. (11)

e-Business   The internal integration within an organization to enhance and support communication and business operations electronically; internal networks, intranet, and the enterprise system support e-business operations. (4)

e-Commerce   Conducting business online, primarily over the Internet; Internet business models include business-to-consumer (B2C), business-to-business (B2B), consumer-to-consumer (C2C), and mobile-commerce (m-commerce). (4)

Eight-panel fold   Holding the paper in portrait orientation, fold it horizontally in half, then fold it vertically in half to create eight pages (panels—count both sides of the paper but use only four panels for printing); also called a French fold and often used for formal invitations. (6)

Electronic data interchange (EDI)   Provides computer-to-computer exchange of standard documents (purchase orders, invoices, payments) between two businesses (business-to-business commerce [B2B]) using private networks (value-added network [VAN]) or the Internet (virtual private network [VPN]) for transmission. (4)

Electrostatic imaging   The process of making an offset master or overhead transparency from an original using a copy machine. (7)

Electrostatic master   Copying original material (printed hard copy or copy drawn [usually with black ink] onto a sheet of bond paper) onto a sensitized offset master; electrostatic masters can be used to duplicate as many as 5,000 copies. (7)

Emotional disturbance   Disturbance that affects an employee's ability to adequately perform tasks; includes mood disturbances and psychosomatic disorders. (11)

Encryption   Coded messages requiring the receiver to have an authorized decryption key to read the message. There are one-key encryption systems, two-key encryption systems, and a hybrid of these two systems. (5)

Enterprise network   Network that connects an organization's distributed networks into one single network; differing technologies are addressed and also can connect to external networks. (3)

Enterprise system   An organization-wide information system that integrates key business processes so information flows freely between different divisions (manufacturing, accounting, finance, sales and marketing, and human resources). (4)

Ergonomics   The scientific study of the relationship of employees to their physical environment, including the workspace and the tools that enhance the workspace. (11)

Ergonomics standards   Guidelines for the application of ergonomics factors in office/furniture design; based on research by ergonomics specialists and used in the design of office products throughout the world. (11)

Euthenics   The science of bettering employee conditions by improving the work environment. (10)

Executive support systems (ESS)   An information system for senior management queries on external and internal data; projections about the future are provided for strategic decisions. (1)

Extranet   Provides authorized users outside the company limited access to the organization's private intranets in order to coordinate and communicate with business partners and customers. (4)

Facsimile (Fax)   Technology that is used in two ways in the electronic office: (1) sending a document from one location to another (facsimile transmission—fax) and (2) digitizing text from a printed page and transferring it to a computer disk/disc or to a master for printing (electronic scanning). (7)

Fault-tolerant system   An information system designed with duplicate hardware, software, and power supply so processing will continue during a system failure; important for mission critical operations. (5)

Fiber optic imaging   An electrographic process where tiny glass strands transmit information in the form of pulsating laser light from the original document to an electrically charged drum; toner is used to fuse the copy paper with an image of the original document. (7)

Field   Area that contains descriptive characteristics about a person, place, or thing in a database management system (DBMS) with each data field assigned a unique name; also referred to as a *data element*. (9)

File transfer protocol (FTP)   A communications standard for downloading and uploading files at remote locations. (4)

Filter   A quick and easy way to work with a subset of data in a spreadsheet program list without having to sort (ascending or descending) the data list first; only the rows that meet the criteria (filter) specified for a column are displayed and the data can be edited, formatted, printed, and used to create graphs (charts). (9)

Firewall   System that consists of software and hardware placed between the organization's internal network(s) and an external, unsecured network (Internet) to ensure that only authorized personnel have access to the organization's private network; also recommended for a traveling professional's notebook. (5)

Fluorescent lighting   Illumination that resembles natural light; common light source in office buildings. (11)

Foot-candle   The amount of light produced by a standard candle at a distance of 1 foot. (11)

Footer   A group of words or a short phrase that appears within the bottom margin of a page as an identification of the document; a footer can appear on every page, on every odd-numbered page, on every even-numbered page, or be deleted from selected pages in electronic documents. (9)

Footlambert   A measure of brightness; a unit of measure approximating 1 foot-candle of light transmitted or reflected. (11)

Foreign exchange   A special telephone service that provides customers a local number when calling a business located in another city; the toll charge for the call is billed to the listed number. (3)

Four-panel fold   Folding a piece of paper in half so the vertical fold is either a landscape orientation (holding the paper so it is wider than it is tall) or a portrait orientation (holding the paper so it is taller than it is wide); there are two signatures on a four-panel fold. (6)

Front-end processor   A small, specialized computer that communicates with the main computer system and manages all routine telecommunications tasks. (3)

Full-service supplier   A single supplier for MRO items offering just-in-time inventory management and lower costs. (10)

Gateway   A communication processor that connects two dissimilar networks and translates the differences between the systems so the computers can communicate with one another. (3)

General purpose application software   Software (word processing, spreadsheet, database management, electronic presentation, and graphs [charts]) used directly by the non-technical end users to develop common business applications; often referred to as productivity packages or fourth-generation languages (4GL). (9)

Global network   System that includes the networks of several organizations internationally; the Internet is the world's largest computer network. (3)

Global procurement   Making purchases world wide; impacted by Pacific Rim and Europe procurement options emphasizing quality at a lower cost, a shorter product life cycle due to technology innovations around the world, and the ability to coordinate purchasing activities through world wide networks (Internet, extranets, and e-commerce). (10)

Graph   Bar, line, pie, or doughnut graphs used to enhance the presentation of factual data; also called *chart*. (9)

Graphical user interface (GUI)   A combination of hardware and software that makes it easy for the end user to respond to computer messages, control the computer, and request information from the computer through the use of icons, bars, buttons, boxes, images, and pull-down menus; the end user points and clicks on the appropriate graphic with an input device (mouse, trackball, or touchpad). (2) (8)

Grayscale   An 8-bit mode with 254 different shades of gray producing what individuals call black-and-white images. (6)

Greeking   Nonsense type showing appropriate type size, line spacing, and text placement but does not include the final text; often used when keying the comprehensive sketch. (6)

Groupware   System that includes all software for information sharing, electronic meetings, electronic scheduling, team writing, and project management, as professionals work in an anytime-anywhere networked environment; supported by IT infrastructure, the Internet, and the World Wide Web (WWW). (4)

Gutter   The space between two sides of adjacent pages in a bound document; includes left-bound gutters and top-bound gutters. (6)

Hacker   A person who gains unauthorized access to a computer network for mischief. (5)

Halftone   Using a dithering process where dots are either on or off to reproduce on paper a continuous-tone image (i.e., a photograph that has been converted into a black-and-white image). (6)

Hard copy   A paper copy of a document. (1)

Hard disk   A nonremovable magnetic disk outside the processor unit for the computer's internal secondary storage; also referred to as a *fixed disk*. (2)

Header   A group of words or a short phrase that appears within the top margin of a page as an identification of the document; a header can appear on every page, on every odd-numbered page, on every even-numbered page, or be deleted from selected pages in electronic documents. (9)

Help desk   A support station staffed by an information technology specialist where end users can call, e-mail, or drop in to receive both hardware and software assistance; sometimes technology assistance is available 24/7 (24 hours a day, 7 days a week). (5)

Help manual   Documentation for each application (word processing, spreadsheet, database management, presentation graphics, and operating system) from the vendor to support end users with software and troubleshoot issues; a soft-copy manual (help menu) provides system and application assistance online and is typically accessed from the menu bar. (8)

Hot desking   Sharing space by two or more employees to efficiently occupy offices that are in use only 10 to 20 percent of the time; two approaches include hotelling and motelling. (10)

Hot site   An external location that contains a fully configured backup data center; includes all required hardware and software for a computer-based information system. (5)

Hypertext markup language (HTML)   Web standard that formats documents and utilizes hypertext links to other documents stored on computers in a network (LAN or WAN). (4)

Idea folder   A collection of sample documents in a folder as a helpful resource when brainstorming designs for future projects (flyer, brochure, post card, multi-page document, or other types of business documents). (6)

Incandescent lighting   Filament bulb that produces glare and shadowing on work surfaces. (11)

Information   Processed data that is timely, meaningful, and useful to the recipient. (1)

Information architecture   The conceptual design of how an organization achieves business processes (applications) and goals. (1)

Information center   A unit staffed with technology specialists responsible for supporting end users in using hardware and software, maintaining hardware and software, providing technology workshops and seminars, and recommending new purchases for the user's area of specialty. (5)

Information policy   Guidelines often posted on the organization's intranet for easy access and updates regarding the use, distribution, and security of information for the entire organization; formulating the policy is typically the responsibility of the Chief Information Officer with input from all organizational levels. (5)

Information technology (IT) infrastructure   A foundation that includes all the technical resources shared within the organization—computer hardware, software, storage, data management, and networks. (1)

Instant messaging   Feature that lets an online user know when a colleague is online so e-mail messages can be communicated back and forth in real time; requires client software. (4)

Interactive mode   *Frequent interchange* between the user at the data entry terminal and the processor unit during execution of a program; a two-way communication flow as the user responds to computer system prompts. (1)

Interface   A combination of hardware and software that makes data input, response to computer messages, computer control, and information requests easy through the use of function keys, screen prompts, menus, and/or icons; includes command-driven interface, menu-driven interface, graphical user interface (GUI), and social interface. (2)

International direct-distance dialing (IDDD)   Direct dialing an overseas call by using the international access code, the code for the country called, the city or area code, and the local telephone number. (3)

Internet   A global network that provides communication (e-mail, newsgroups, listserv, Internet Relay Chat, search, and e-commerce) anytime, anywhere; often referred to as the information superhighway. (4)

Internet phone   Microcomputers at both the sending and receiving location with a microphone, speakers, and software for audio conversations over the Internet; a video camera allows projection of the individual's image or objects being discussed. (4)

Internet Relay Chat (IRC)   With appropriate hardware and software, interactive, real-time text chatting over the Internet; some services provide audio and visual components to IRC. (4)

Internet service provider (ISP)   A commercial organization with permanent connection to the Internet selling temporary connections to subscribers (individuals, educational institutions, businesses, and governmental agencies). (4)

Intranet   A closed, private version of the Internet available only to approved employees who use the Web browser to create a rich, responsive collaborative environment for e-business; includes company news, forms, updates, corporate policies, databases, or any other information the organization determines important to business operations and employee communication. (4)

Inventory control   Securing inventory items through locked storage areas with authorized access or the honor system. (10)

Inventory management   A method to control the investment made in inventories; methods include cross-functional teams, electronic data interchange (EDI), inventory reviews, inventory record system (computerized), and supplier-buyer partnership. (10)

Inward wide area telephone service (INWATS)   A toll-free call for the caller by dialing a toll-free area code (800, 888, 877, 866, and 855) and telephone number; the party with the toll-free number pays for the call. (3)

Isolation   The prevention of sound waves from passing through environmental materials. (11)

Job recovery   When an operator is interrupted while making copies, the copier "remembers" the point where the original job was stopped and can continue the process from that point. (7)

Kerning   The spacing of words and characters on a line by intentionally decreasing the default spacing to improve the appearance of letter combinations. (6)

Knowledge work systems (KWS)   An information system used by knowledge workers to create new information and knowledge. (1)

Laminating   A process that protects and preserves documents and other frequently used items from wear and tear by permanently bonding the original document (both sides of a page) in a plastic film. (7)

Language translators   A system program that changes system and application software instructions (code), written in a programming language (C++, Visual Basic, HTML, COBOL), into a machine language (binary bits / 1s and 0s) understood by the computer; two ways to translate the system and application software instructions are with a compiler or an interpreter. (8)

Laser imaging   A process that utilizes a beam of light that reflects off a series of mirrors with the final mirror diverting the image to a drum that transfers the image to paper. (7)

Late adapter   A person who waits for others to implement a new system, then tries to catch up with the technology; such a person has difficulty keeping up to date with technology and is often considered "behind the times." (11)

Leading   The vertical space between lines in the text; if two different leading values are specified in a line of print, the larger value applies to the entire line. (6)

Listserv   An electronic public forum for registered subscribers to receive information on predefined topics; uses push technology. (4)

Local area network (LAN)   A private network that supports communication within an office, building, or firm at lower computer costs for the company by linking electronic devices so data can be shared easily and at greater speeds than otherwise provided. (3)

Magnetic disk   A common secondary storage peripheral for microcomputers where the disk can be removed from the disk drive and the data transported with the user to other computing environments. (2)

Mainframe computer   Computer that supports online services for several thousand users and provides processing for extensive computing applications with processing speeds greater than 1 trillion instructions per second (picoseconds) and primary storage ranging from hundreds of megabytes (1 million bytes) to gigabytes (1 billion bytes); also used as superservers for very large client/server networks. (2)

Maintenance, repair, and operating supplies (MRO)   Technical maintenance and repairs to the computer network and peripherals, general facility maintenance and repair, and office supplies (operating supplies). Specialized departments handle maintenance and repair (the IT Division and the Maintenance and Service Department), and office supplies are typically the responsibility of the Purchasing Department. (10)

Management information systems (MIS) An information system that uses transaction processing system (TPS) data to provide management with online access for structured summary and exception reports that address management functions (planning, controlling, and making decisions); reports are available on demand (when needed). (1)

Manipulation language Language that contains commands that permit end users to interactively extract data from a database management system (DBMS) for specific information needs (also called query); the most prominent manipulation language is structured query language (SQL). (8)

Masking The use of a low-level, non-disturbing background noise (background music) to blend in with regular office noise, eliminating the "silent" sound (total lack of sound) or covering distracting noises; also called *white noise* or *white sound*. (11)

Materials management Management of the combined related functions of purchasing, inventory control, receiving, and storage from an overall organizational concept (total system) handled by one division for potential cost savings. (10)

Menu bar Bar located just below the title bar that typically includes file, edit, view, insert, format, tools, and help functions; clicking or pointing on a menu option results in a pull-down menu for various functions specific to the application or operating system software. (8)

Menu-driven interface System that presents a menu of options on the monitor where the user selects the correct option by pointing and clicking with an input device (mouse, trackball, or touching a touch-sensitive screen); many automatic-teller machines (ATM) and information kiosks have menu-driven interfaces. (8)

Metal plates A camera captures the original material which is transferred to a metal master for offset duplicating of documents that are rerun; plates are saved and reused, producing as many as 50,000 copies per plate. (7)

Metropolitan area network (MAN) Connecting local area networks (LANs) with fiber optic cable for high-speed data transmission within a small geographic area. (3)

Microcomputer A digital computer that uses a microprocessor, an internal storage chip, an input/output chip, and any additional chips required by the system; includes desktop PC, workstation, notebook (laptop), and are often called *personal computers* or *PCs*. (2)

Microprocessor Computer component that includes the control unit and the arithmetic logic unit mounted on a single silicon chip; it is the main technology of microcomputers. (2)

Middleware An interface that translates different operating system (computing platform) protocols and manages the exchange of information among different computing platforms and hardware devices. (8)

Mid-range computer Computer that supports computing requirements for small to medium-size organizations as well as e-commerce and networking environments; two types of mid-range computers include minicomputers and servers. (2)

Modem A device that converts (**mo**dulates) digital data codes from the computer system into analog signals for transmission on telephone lines and **dem**odulates received analog signals into digital data codes for the computer system; required at both the receiving and sending locations. (3)

Monitor A common output device that allows the user to view soft copy by using either cathode-ray tube (CRT) technology, liquid crystal display (LCD) technology, or plasma technology. (2)

Multiplexer Allows one communication channel to carry data from multiple sources at the same time; required at both the receiving and sending locations. (3)

Multiprocessing The simultaneous (at the same time) execution of two or more application software programs in a computer system that serves multiple users; requires the computer system to have two or more central processing units (CPUs) as well as operating system software that supports multiprocessing. (1)

Multiprogramming The concurrent (switching back and forth) execution of two or more application software programs in a computer system that serves multiple users; requires the computer system to have multiprogramming operating system software. (1)

Multitasking Multiprogramming on a single user operating system (e.g., Windows 2000 and Windows XP on a home microcomputer or a notebook). (1)

Multithreading A form of multitasking that concurrently executes more than one task of a single application. (8)

Musculoskeletal problems Pain or discomfort occurring in various body parts (neck, back, shoulders, arms, and fingers). (11)

Natural language processing (NLP) Communicating with a computer in English or the natural language of the user. (1)

Negotiations A "win-win," face-to-face session with suppliers that is effective for purchases with vague specifications; the session should clearly discuss specifications, terms and conditions of the purchase, quality expectations, purchase procedures, delivery schedules, and continuous performance improvement objectives. (10)

Network engineer   An information technology position typically staffed by an electrical engineer with a specialization (certification) in networks who can address the information technology infrastructure—hardware, software, data storage, and networks. (5)

Network interface card (NIC)   An expansion card that connects the microcomputer to a network enabling the exchange of data between computers; the cables or wireless transceivers of the microcomputer must be connected to an NIC. (3)

Network topology   A network configuration used in local area and wide area telecommunications networks; three basic configurations are bus, star, and ring. (3)

Newsgroup   Independent forums where individuals can join the bulletin board discussion of their choice to share information and ideas; pull technology by using newsreader client software available on most Internet browsers. (4)

Nonadapter   The person who prefers the status quo, does not accept change easily, and may resist and also encourage others to resist change; typically feels negative job-related stress. (11)

Off-the-shelf software   Easy-to-use general purpose application software purchased from software vendors with supporting manuals and help services. (9)

Office layout chart   Charts the movement of a document using the actual floor plan of the office to develop the resulting workflow pattern; important for identifying personnel or departments that frequently work together. (10)

Office systems (OS)   An information system used by all organizational levels to manipulate and disseminate information electronically; designed to increase productivity by supporting the coordination and communication activities of the office. (1)

Offset cylinders   Three cylinders (master, blanket, and impression) that work together to produce the duplicated offset copy. (7)

Offset duplicating   Based on the principle that grease and water do not mix, the image area is receptive to ink (grease), and the non-image area is receptive to water; the material to be reproduced is prepared on a master—direct-image master, electrostatic master, or metal plates. (7)

Online processing   A processing method where a user enters transactions through an input device that is directly connected to the computer system; processing is in real time if the user receives immediate results. (1)

Open-office design   A large open area of work space with only a minimum of permanent walls, modular furniture systems, clustering of workspaces, the use of accent colors to enhance the work area décor, and aisle space to accommodate the communication flows throughout the division that is common for the business environment and for the home office; two popular approaches are office landscaping and the modular design. Also referred to as the *modern office.* (10)

Operating system   Software that manages the operations of the central processing unit (CPU); controls the input, output, and storage resources and computer system tasks. (8)

Optical disc   Laser technology that stores data by burning microscopic pits onto disc tracks. (2)

Pattern recognition system   A visual system that requires a camera to be the computer's eyes; visual systems are highly structured. (2)

Peer-to-peer computing   A form of distributed computing where all computers on the network can access organizational data, application software, public files, and peripherals connected to the network; through transparent access, unused disk space and processing power can be utilized for large computing tasks. (3)

Performance monitor   A tool that watches and adjusts the usage and performance of the computer-based information system; information technicians check output from the networked enterprise performance monitors to address system maintenance and issues; end users can check the microcomputer system diagnostics (performance) through the control panel system utilities. (8)

Personal digital assistant (PDA)   A popular mobile device in the handheld computer category with a touch screen and pen-based handwriting recognition for sending and receiving e-mail; accessing the Web; and exchanging information such as appointments, sales contracts, to-do lists, and client address books with a desktop PC or Web servers. (2)

Photocomposition   The process whereby the composer automatically sets the type as the text is being keyed from the keyboard; often referred to as direct entry composition. (7)

Pica   The measurement used for the width and length of a line; 6 picas equal an inch. (7)

Point-and-click device   An input device that allows end users to point and click (or drag) on graphical user interface icons, buttons, and symbols to activate operating system software and application software functions. (2)

Points   The measurement of a character size ranging from 6 points to 96 points, with 10 or 12 points being the most common point sizes; a 72-point character equals one inch. (7)

Port The connection point on a computer where the peripheral communication line is connected. (2)

Potential supplier list A list of perspective suppliers generated from marketing representatives, information databases, and trade journals. (10)

Preferred supplier list List that contains the names of suppliers whose past performance demonstrated quality products or services at a fair price; provides a means for the organization to deal with suppliers of known performance capabilities. (10)

Primary key A data field (column), also called a key field or a control field, that uniquely identifies a record in a relational database management system (DBMS); all records in the database table must contain unique data in the primary key field. (9)

Primary storage Storage made of semiconductor memory chips and divided into read only memory (ROM), random access memory (RAM), and cache memory; also called *main memory* or *internal storage.* (2)

Print run The number of finished pieces required when placing an order with a reproduction center or commercial print shop. (6)

Printer A common output device for hard copy; two types include impact and nonimpact. (2)

Printer spreads Arranging the pages in the order required for printing. (6)

Private branch exchange (PBX) A special purpose computer that accepts and transmits voice and data using regular telephone lines; no special wiring is required. (3)

Private-office design Offices separated from general office areas because of the confidential and private nature of the work, the high level of concentration that requires a quiet work environment, or the prestige and higher status for the business professional; also referred to as the bull-pen design, traditional design, or closed office. (10)

Process chart Chart that illustrates existing distances and delays involved in an entire process or procedure from start to finish. (10)

Programmer Technical specialists who write and maintain software instructions (code) for the computer; systems programmers specialize in system software. (5)

Proximity The design principle that groups related information together through the logical connection of the information (visual units), what information should be emphasized, and effective use of white space; proximity and contrast emphasize important information. (6)

Psychosocial disturbance Stress related to the job, workload, pace of work, and poor or inadequate supervision that can lead to ailments. (11)

Pull quote A small amount of text that is enlarged within an article to catch the reader's attention. (6)

Pull technology The user pulls information he or she wants off the Web. (4)

Purchase order A business document submitted to a supplier for an approved purchase. (10)

Purchase requisition An internal document submitted to the division in charge of purchases to activate the order process; often available on the organization's intranet. (10)

Push technology When requested information is automatically sent to a recipient; the recipient has asked for the information. (4)

Random access memory (RAM) Primary storage internal to the computer system temporarily available for processing business data; RAM is volatile memory. (2)

Read only memory (ROM) Nonvolatile primary storage, also called firmware, where critical system instructions available only to the central processing unit (CPU) for starting the computer are permanently stored by the computer manufacturer; variations of ROM include programmable read-only memory (PROM) chips and erasable PROM (EPROM) chips. (2)

Record A row in a relational database management system (DBMS) table that contains related data fields (columns); one field must be coded as the primary key to uniquely identify the record. (9)

Recycle bin Area that stores deleted items until emptied; if not emptied, any deleted item can be retrieved/restored. (8)

Reduced instruction set computing (RISC) Technology that enhances the speed of workstation microprocessors by embedding the most frequently used instructions on a chip. (2)

Redundant arrays of independent disks (RAID) Ten to more than 100 small hard disk drives combined into a single unit providing large storage capacities and high access speeds; RAID units are used to provide a fault-tolerant environment. (2)

Reflection The bouncing of sound waves off material and back into space. (11)

Relation A two-dimensional table in a relational database management system (DBMS) where data about a specific topic are collected; a separate table for each topic is created (i.e., products, suppliers, or prices). (9)

Relative reference When copying a spreadsheet program worksheet cell formula, the formula cell references change relative to the cell where it is copied. (9)

Reorder point A way to recognize the need to purchase an item. (10)

Repetition The design principle that repeats some aspect of the design throughout one-page and multiple-page documents for consistency and tying the visual units together; repetition and alignment unite the visual units together. (6)

Repetitive-strain injury (RSI) A workplace health danger that can result from tasks that require continuous repetitive motion; symptoms include stiff or sore wrists, numbness, loss of strength in arms or hands, or finger cramps while working. (11)

Reproduction The preparation of multiple copies or images. (7)

Request for proposal (RFP) Suppliers are asked to submit a bid on a prospective purchase; this is an effective method for items with straightforward specifications. (10)

Requisition number A control number from the buying organization that links purchase approval to an authorized individual. (10)

Rotating Pivoting an image around the image's center point; images can rotate 360 degrees at increments of .01 degrees. (6)

Row (in)

> **Database management software** A record in a relational database table that must have a primary key (control field). (9)

> **Spreadsheet software** Typically identified by a number (1, 2, . . . , 65,536) vertically down the side of the worksheet; data in rows are read horizontally. (9)

Saddle-stitch binding A process that uses two or more staples at the fold of the paper. (7)

Sans serif A typeface where no decorative stroke is added to the end of a letter's main stroke; often used for footnotes, endnotes, or headings. Sans means *without* in French. (6)

Scanning A process that digitizes text from a printed page and transfers it to a computer disk/disc or to an electronic master for printing. (7)

Search engine Tool to help users find information or services on Web pages (pull technology); most search engines offer advanced search features. (4)

Secondary storage Where data, information, application software, and system software are saved in files with unique names for future use; also called auxiliary storage. Common secondary storage media are magnetic disk, optical disc, DVD disc, USB flash drive, and magnetic tape. (2)

Security monitors Technology that controls the use of hardware, software, and data resources by maintaining statistics on system use and unauthorized access; the statistics provide IT technicians/managers with important security information. (8)

Security protocol Standards for providing a secure information technology environment; two protocols include secure hypertext transport protocol (S-HTTP) and secure electronic transaction (SET). (5)

Serif A typeface with a small decorative stroke (slab, wedge, or hair) added to the end of a letter's main strokes. (6)

Server farms Multiple servers maintained by the organization or a commercial vendor who then sells the services to an organization. (2)

Services Equipment repair (copy machines and telephones), maintenance not performed by staff, and grounds and facilities upkeep often contracted through outside sources at the organizational level; can be complex to manage. (10)

Shortcut A link to any item accessible on the microcomputer or the organization's network; displayed on the desktop as an icon, added to the operating system start button menu, or placed in specific folders. (8)

Sick building Buildings infected with microorganisms (molds, bacteria, and viruses) at levels that make employees sick; buildings with poor ventilation or that are airtight run the greatest risk of becoming a sick building. (11)

Signature A group of panels (pages) that are printed on one side of a sheet of paper for a document. (6)

Six-panel fold Holding the paper in landscape orientation and folding it in thirds to create six panels (pages); six-panel fold includes accordion, brochure, C, letter, spiral, tri, and zig-zag. (6)

Soft copy The electronic output viewed on a computer screen (monitor). (1)

Source data automation Eliminating the need for manually recording data on a source document and keying data input by using online terminals and input devices to enter data directly into the computer system at the time the business transaction originates. (1)

Source document An original record (hard copy) of a business transaction (i.e., time card, purchase order). (1)

Spam Unsolicited junk e-mail that interferes with work and can slow down the network to the point where efficient business communication and operations are affected by consuming valuable network bandwidth. (5)

Steering committee A committee that focuses on policies for the use of the information system, priorities for system development, budgets for information technology, system security, system maintenance, and system issues; usually chaired by the Chief Information Officer or an assistant with member representation from the information technology division and each functional division within the organization. (5)

Stitching A process that uses a roll of wire from which staples are automatically cut to the size needed. (7)

Storage Data, information, systems software, and application software are electronically held for future use in secondary storage; storage media include hard disk, magnetic disk, optical disc, DVD disc, USB flash drive, and magnetic tape. (1) (2)

Storage area network (SAN)   An enterprise-wide infrastructure dedicated to data storage by providing a high-speed fiber-channel network that interconnects different storage devices (e.g., database servers, RAID, and tape libraries). (2)

Storage service provider (SSP)   A professional service that assists with storage assessment, design, management, operations, and 24/7 online data storage and backup either on-site or off-site. (2)

Supercomputer   The largest, fastest, most powerful, and most expensive computer system; used by government agencies and large organizations involved in research-and-development activities that are mathematically intensive (i.e., aerospace industry, chemical industries, and weather forecasting). (2)

System software   Software that provides instructions to control computer operations, network management, database management, and system security for the organization's information system. (8)

Systems analyst   The liaison between information technicians and business users who translates business requirements and problems into information technology requirements; often considered change agents within the organization. (5)

Systems audits   Comprehensive audits on the computer-based information system to determine the effectiveness of all the security controls; includes external audits, internal audits, and data audits. (5)

Systems life cycle   A dynamic process that requires interaction with personnel at all levels within the organization for analysis, design, development, implementation, and operation and maintenance of the organization's computer-based information system. (5)

Table (in)

> **Database management software**   The organization for a relational database that looks like a spreadsheet program worksheet with intersecting rows and columns. (9)

> **Word processing software**   Module that consists of rows and columns where the end user can set the desired width of each column, set tabulations, view the table with or without ruled lines, include mathematical computations, and easily move to the desired input cell with the tab key. (9)

Table structure   Structure that contains a design view where each field within the relational database management system (DBMS) table (relation) is

identified; the following information is provided—field name, type of data for the field (e.g., text, numeric, currency, date/time, and autonumber), which field is the primary key, field size, and a description of each data field. (9)

Task lighting   Direct light that illuminates the work surface. (11)

Taskbar   Bar that contains a start button and icons for all application or operating system software that are running; the default location can be moved to the sides or top of the desktop, hidden, or customized. (8)

Technology support group   Individuals proficient with productivity software and technology who are identified to provide assistance to other end users within the organization. (5)

Telecommunications   The exchange of voice, data, text, graphics, or audio and video information over computer-based networks. (3)

Telecommuter   An employee who works at home and is connected to the office data through a communication channel (telephone line, cable, satellite). (1)

Telephony   The technology of translating sound into digital signals, transmitting the signals, and converting the signals back to sound at the receiving end. (4)

Tendinitis   The inflammation of muscles at the points where they insert into the bones of the shoulders, arms, and wrists. (11)

Tethered line   Line channels that are continuous; the three line channels are twisted wire, coaxial cable, and fiber optic cable. (3)

Text telephone (TT)   Telephones designed to accommodate individuals with disabilities (deaf, hard-of-hearing, or speech impaired). (3)

Thumbnails   Initial rough sketches on paper (brainstorming) to help establish basic ideas for the layout and design of a document. (6)

Tie line   A leased, private telephone connection linking business telephones in two locations; tie lines include T-1 line and T-3 line (dedicated service lines, DS1 and DS3). (3)

Time-sharing   Operating system software that provides a fixed amount of time to a user for processing. (1)

Title bar   Bar that displays horizontally across the top of the application or operating system software open window and includes the name of the software on the left side of the bar with minimize, maximize/restore down, and close buttons on the right side; the window name changes to coincide with the software window that is currently active. (8)

Toolbar   Bar located just below the menu bar that displays application or operating system software icons (tools) for frequently used menu options or commands that can be executed by simply pointing and clicking on the appropriate icon; can be customized to include only those functions the user frequently needs. (8)

Track spacing Spacing that adjusts the number of words on a line by squeezing or expanding text and adding or removing space from character combinations on a line. (6)

Transaction processing systems (TPS) An information system basic to business operations that captures daily business transactions as records, has highly structured processing, and produces automatic output on a daily, weekly, monthly, or quarterly basis for supervisors and operations personnel of the functional areas; output includes detailed reports, lists, and summaries. TPS data are used by other information systems (DSS, MIS, and ESS). (1)

Transitions Special effects to introduce a slide in an electronic presentation—introduction of a slide from the top or bottom of the screen, left or right of the screen, with or without sound, and with different speeds—to bring attention to a new section in the presentation or emphasize a key slide. (9)

Trapping Typesetting method that minimizes the gap of uninked paper between adjacent colors by expanding the ink so small amounts of color overlap and print on top of each other. (6)

Trojan horse A destructive program that masquerades as a benign application; does not replicate. (5)

Turnaround time The time it takes between submission of data to a computer-based information system and receipt of output information. (1)

Type font A group of letters, numbers, and symbols with a common typeface that consists of two elements—typeface and point size; font refers to the style of the characters. (7)

Typeface A specific type—sans serif (without serif), serif (old style, modern, slab), script, decorative, and Pi; each typeface comes in different type fonts. (6) (7)

Typesetting A process that electronically produces a master copy (camera-ready copy) in the professional type style and type size desired; also called cold type. (7)

Typography The overall arrangement and appearance of printed matter on a page that establishes a visual hierarchy by providing text and graphic accents that assist the reader in understanding the message and relationships between headings and subordinate blocks of text. (6)

Uniform resource locator (URL) A unique address required in order to place a Web site on the Internet; the URL must be registered in a domain function. (4)

USB flash drive An external Universal Serial Bus standard that supports data transfer rates of 12 Mbps (million bits per second); the portable storage drive holds 250 MB (megabytes) of data and plugs into the microcomputer USB port. (2)

Utility programs Operating system software programs for routine, repetitive tasks including creating directories, creating new folders, restoring deleted files, editing, security, disk defragmentation, and formatting disks. (8)

Value-added network (VAN) A private multimedia, multipath, third-party managed, medium-speed wide area network (WAN) shared by multiple organizations; services provided include network management, e-mail, electronic data interchange, and security. (3)

Video conference A conference usually in a room equipped with appropriate electronic media where participants' actions can be seen as well as heard for collaborative efforts; the two video conferences include one-way or two-way full-motion. (4)

Virtual memory Simulates more primary memory (RAM) space by dividing a software program into fixed pages whereby the system places into RAM only those modules (pages) currently in use and brings other "pages" from secondary storage when needed; allows users to work with application or system software that are more complex (larger) than what primary memory can handle at one time. (8)

Virtual private network (VPN) Used by many organizations for intranet and extranet security when the Internet is the network backbone. (3)

Virtual team Members of a group or different groups within the organization as well as from widely dispersed locations who work over the network (little or no face-to-face contact) with compatible groupware (software for writing and communicating [word processing and e-mail]), information sharing [chat (IRC) and data conference], electronic meetings [computer conference and video conference], scheduling [e-calendars], and electronic project management [timelines and tracking]. (9)

Virus A rogue software program that spreads throughout the network disrupting processing and memory operations and possibly destroying data; thousands exist, and approximately 150 new viruses are created each month. (5)

Visual dysfunction Temporary visual distress (eye irritation, visual fatigue, blurred vision, headaches, and chronic disorders) possibly caused by long intensive work intervals without adequate rest periods, or poor design of computer monitors or the physical environment. (11)

Visual unit Grouping like information together and separated from other units by white space. (6)

Washout   A potential folding problem that occurs when printed matter is trimmed off on the inside panels of a signature; also called creep. (6)

Web browser   A program coded in hypertext markup language (HTML) that translates other HTML documents into a Web page; users navigate the Web with a browser to visit Web sites as well as retrieve, view, and print Internet-posted information. (4)

Web designer   One who possesses the technical and aesthetic skills for developing Web sites. (5)

Web publishing   An efficient and convenient way to share information with others over the Internet and intranet; hyperlinked documents display text, animation, multimedia, and interactive environments for individual and team activities. (4)

Web site   All the Web pages maintained by one organization or individual; a Web site consisting of more than one page sets up a home page as an introduction to the site with interactive buttons for navigation. (4)

Webmaster   Information technology employee who monitors and maintains Web servers. (5)

White space   The area on a page that is blank—no text or graphics; professional designers make effective use of white space. (6)

Wide area telephone service (WATS)   A fixed monthly subscription (full business-day package or a measured-time package) for national, regional, or state area calls. (3)

Widow/orphan function   When on, the word processing software makes automatic decisions about page breaks by eliminating a single line of a paragraph on the bottom (widow) or top (orphan) of a page; the automatic page break ensures that two or more lines of a paragraph are on a page. (9)

Window   An overlay on the desktop for the specific operating system or application software in use; includes a title bar, menu bar, and toolbar. (8)

Wireless channel   Low-power radio frequencies or infrared technologies to transmit digital communications between communication devices; wireless channels include terrestrial microwave, celestial satellites, wireless networks, Bluetooth, and cellular (telephones and mobile devices). (3)

Word wrap   When a word extends beyond the right margin in a word processing application, the entire word is automatically placed on the next line. (9)

Work log   Logging actual time spent in performing office tasks to provide insight into time requirements (in hours and minutes) as well as work allocation each day. (11)

Workbook   The document mode where multiple worksheets are available through the active window in a spreadsheet program; the end user clicks on the appropriate worksheet tab to have the correct worksheet in the active window. (9)

Workflow   The transmission of information, as related to a specific process, through either face-to-face or electronic communication. (10)

Worksheet   A single spreadsheet organized into intersecting rows and columns that make up a grid (cells) for data input. (9)

World Wide Web (WWW)   A system of universally accepted standards (hypertext markup language [HTML]) for storing, retrieving, formatting, and displaying information over networks (local area network [intranet and extranet] and wide area network [Internet]); typically referred to as the *Web*. (4)

Xerographic imaging   A plain-paper copier process that uses a camera to project the original image onto a positively charged drum with the image adhering to the negatively charged plain sheet of copy paper; the image is permanently fixed with a powder or liquid toner and heat. (7)

Index